CBT for Chronic Illness and Palliative Care

CBT for Chronic Illness and Palliative Care

A Workbook and Toolkit

Nigel Sage

Michelle Sowden

Elizabeth Chorlton

Andrea Edeleanu

John Wiley & Sons, Ltd

Other Wiley Editorial Offices

John Wiley & Sons Inc., 111 River Street, Hoboken, NJ 07030, USA

Jossey-Bass, 989 Market Street, San Francisco, CA 94103-1741, USA

Wiley-VCH Verlag GmbH, Boschstr. 12, D-69469 Weinheim, Germany

John Wiley & Sons Australia Ltd, 42 McDougall Street, Milton, Queensland 4064, Australia

John Wiley & Sons (Asia) Pte Ltd, 2 Clementi Loop #02-01, Jin Xing Distripark, Singapore 129809

John Wily & Sons Canada Ltd, 6045 Freemont Blvd, Mississauga, ONT, L5R 4J3, Canada

Wiley also publishes its books in a variety of electronic formats. Some content that appears in print may not be available
in electronic books.

Anniversary Logo Design: Richard J. Pacifico

Library of Congress Cataloging-in-Publication Data

CBT for chronic illness and palliative care : a workbook and toolkit / Nigel Sage ... [et al.].
    p. cm.
  Includes bibliographical references and index.
  ISBN 978-0-470-51707-9 (pbk. : alk. paper)
  1. Chronic diseases–Psychological aspects. 2. Palliative treatment–Psychological aspects.
  3. Chronically ill–Rehabilitation. 4. Cognitive therapy. I. Sage, Nigel.
    RC108.C38 2008
    616'.044–dc22

                                                                                    2007044558

British Library Cataloguing in Publication Data

A catalogue record for this book is available from the British Library
ISBN 978-0-470-051707-9

Typeset in 11/13pt Times by Thomson Digital, New Delhi, India

Contents

Part II: The Issues: Some Psychological Problems

Section 2:   Information Sheets

Contents

Section 3: Record Forms

About the Authors

Nigel Sage is Consultant Clinical Psychologist in Cancer and Palliative Care at The Beacon Community Specialist Centre for Cancer and Palliative Care in Guildford, Surrey. He is an Accredited Cognitive Behaviour Therapist and also works in primary care mental health in Hampshire.

Michelle Sowden is Consultant Clinical Psychologist at Frimley Park Hospital where she has provided and developed a service to patients with physical health problems across the Clinical Directorates. She has a special interest in the application of cognitive behavioural and systemic therapies to the management of chronic medical conditions.

Elizabeth Chorlton is a Chartered Clinical Psychologist working at Frimley Park Hospital, in the Department of Psychological Medicine, with patients who are experiencing psychological difficulties as a result of physical health problems. In addition to her clinical psychology training, she has an MSc in the field of health psychology.

Andrea Edeleanu is Director of Specialist Therapies and Service User Involvement for Surrey and Borders Partnership NHS Trust. She works clinically in Community Health Psychology and provides consultancy and clinical supervision to colleagues in health, mental health and community services. She is a Consultant Clinical Psychologist, Chartered Health Psychologist and an Accredited Cognitive Behaviour Therapist.

Acknowledgements

This book grew from material prepared originally for a training project for staff working in either palliative care or with cancer patients in other settings. The authors gratefully acknowledge the vital contribution of Surrey, West Sussex and Hampshire (SWSH) Cancer Network, in sponsoring that training project.

We would also like to acknowledge the enormous influence on the content and structure of this book of Drs Stirling Moorey and Kathryn Mannix. Stirling has done so much to establish the role of Cognitive Behaviour Therapy (CBT) in the fields of oncology and palliative care that it is rapidly becoming a service requirement and many health professionals are now seeking some training. For us, his work at St Christopher's Hospice has been especially important because, along with the training project in Newcastle led by Kathryn Mannix, it has shown that staff with no background in mental health work can acquire and use cognitive behavioural skills. This has provided the inspiration for our own training programme and ultimately this book. Kathryn has also offered us encouragement and practical guidance with our training project for which we are very appreciative.

Grateful thanks are extended to Joanne Coombs for her help in preparing the chapter on the effectiveness of CBT to Ann Hatch, whose experience and skills as a physiotherapist have influenced numerous items included and to Maralyn Sage for her tireless work and patience with both the book and the training project that preceded it. A special thank you is also due to all the participants from our training courses who have taken the trouble to provide constructive feedback and persuaded us to publish. Their suggestions have enabled us to revise our course materials and make this a better book. In this regard a particular mention must be made of Maureen Adam and Susan Kobler who in dual roles as participants and seminar supervisors regularly provided ideas for improvements.

Finally, we wish to express our debt of gratitude to all the patients who, by sharing their experiences with us, have spurred us on to write this. We hope that the resulting book contributes to more people getting more help sooner.

Introduction

CBT in Chronic Illness and Palliative Care: A Workbook and Toolkit is divided into three parts and is intended to give the reader grounding in the principles and techniques of Cognitive Behavioural Therapy (CBT). Ideally, it should be used in junction with a taught course on the use of CBT with people who have life-changing illness or are terminally ill. The course will offer the opportunity to discuss working with these patients and the people close to them. It will give the student the chance to practice the skills they are learning through role-plays and small group exercises; and it will provide time for going back over material that has been difficult to understand or has been misunderstood.

However, such courses are rare, so the book has been written with the expectation that many readers will be learning these skills without the benefit of a supportive course. With this in mind, there are a number of exercises included that have been adapted from the courses we have run and we would ask you to follow these through very carefully if you intend to apply CBT skills in your clinical practice.

Part 1: The Workbook examines important issues and themes that need to be understood and considered by clinical practitioners as well as the basic principles of the cognitive behavioural approach. These range from wider aspects of behaviour change through to the specifics of assessing psychological needs. This material, together with key reference books and supplemented by the exercises at the end of each chapter represent the knowledge base for these core skills when applied to people with life-changing illness.

In **Part 2: The Issues** some psychological problems, obstacles and needs are referred to as "Problems". Relevant techniques and sample tactics are identified, providing an idea of how these CBT methods are applied in practice with each problem. Issues about implementing these procedures are covered in "Notes". Although not written in chapter format, close familiarity with the contents of this part of the book is extremely important.

Inevitably the selection of sample problems is far from comprehensive but the range is sufficiently wide to illustrate the scope of CBT usage. Consequently, when considering applying CBT methods, this part of the book should be consulted first. The intention is to give enough material for you to be able to:

- assess the problem or need
- indicate the typical cognitive-behavioural approach to coping
- where relevant include educational material that can be copied and passed to patients, carers or others
- assess improvement and need reduction.

Part 3: The Toolkit provides information on CBT methods in practice that may be of practical assistance when you are seeking to offer some help. There are plenty of different ideas for managing challenging psychological situations in the CBT literature and so, like the list of problems and needs, the suggestions for methods of helping included in this book could not claim to be exhaustive.

Part 3 is divided into three sections.

A fuller description of how to implement each CBT technique is provided in **Section 1: Techniques.**

Section 2: Information sheets includes further detailed guidance and information sheets which may be copied and used to assist in the CBT.

Section 3: Record forms provides methods for recording events, thoughts and plans in conjunction with the CBT techniques. These forms may also be photocopied.

A4 versions of all information sheets and record forms can be downloaded from the website free of charge and without copyright restrictions by owners of this book, for their own clinical use only.

PowerPoint slides for personal training are also available to view at the website.

PART I

The Workbook: The Cognitive Behavioural Approach

Chapter 1

What is the Cognitive Behavioural Approach?

Cognitive Behaviour Therapy (CBT) has been described by the pioneer of this therapy as:

> An active, directive, time-limited, structured approach.
>
> (Beck et al., 1979)

The therapy works by helping patients to:

> Recognise patterns of distorted thinking and dysfunctional behaviour. Systematic discussion and carefully structured behavioural assignments are then used to help patients evaluate and modify both their distorted thoughts and their dysfunctional behaviours.
>
> (Hawton et al., 1989)

With the cognitive behavioural approach there is recognition of the way in which all our responses are part of a complicated interplay of actions and reactions. In physics we accept the general law that every action produces a reaction. What is not always so well appreciated is that this applies in psychology too.

We are generally aware that our actions have effects on those around us as theirs do on us. The simple act of smiling at someone when they look at you will produce a reaction in that person. Perhaps they will smile back, treating it as a simple greeting; alternatively, they may interpret it as an invitation to come over and chat; under other circumstances their reaction may be one of anxiety or hostility, if they think you are laughing at them. What ever it is your action will produce a reaction, and that reaction, in turn will have an effect on you. Even a "non-reaction" (such as no glimmer of acknowledgement that you smiled) will carry *meaning* and provoke a specific reaction in you.

So our social environment affects our behaviour and our behaviour affects our social environment. To a greater or lesser extent the same is true for our physical and economic environments. We can influence (if not control) our comfort, wellbeing, affluence and future prospects. Our comfort, wellbeing, affluence and future prospects similarly can and do influence how we think, feel and behave.

From the cognitive behavioural perspective, however, it is the loops of cause and effect *within* ourselves that are of special interest. When I put my hand too close to the fire, the outside world (*external* environment) of intense heat sends signals of pain to my body's sensory receptors. From that point forward there are a series of reactions and interactions relating to my *internal* environment. The physical sensation of painful heat triggers emotional responses of intense dislike and thoughts of dangers to be avoided. But the most important and immediate reaction is a behavioural response of withdrawing my hand from the heat. Once this behaviour has happened, I experience a relief of the pain, my thoughts turn to labelling the hot object as something to be avoided or treated warily and it has acquired a negative emotional association.

So, in this example physical sensation has evoked a specific behaviour, reappraising thoughts, and an unpleasant emotional reaction. But these four elements (**physical sensation**, **behaviour**, **thoughts** and **emotions**) can interact in different sequences.

Let us take another example:

Jenny plans a picnic and is looking forward to it; then, on the day, it rains. If this event leads her to **think** "my day is ruined", then the **emotional reaction** will be as downcast as the weather, **physically** she is likely to experience a loss of energetic enthusiasm and her **behaviour** is likely to become restless and aimless. On the other hand, if the rain leads Jenny to **think** " I'll need a new plan for today", then any **emotional reaction** of disappointment will be tempered by **thoughts** about what else she can do with the day; this will produce a **physical response** of increased energy for planning and a series of **behavioural actions** around sorting out an alternative arrangement.

The *meaning* Jenny attaches to the event (that is, the way she thinks about the rain) determines her emotional, behavioural and physical responses and ultimately, therefore, the outcome for her of this damp day.

When it is a one-off event of only minor consequence, like Jenny's rainy day, then the effect of the way the event is interpreted is of no particular significance. However, when various events are lumped together in a single category and the same meaning is attached to all of the events in that category, then a pattern is emerging which is of greater influence in the person's life. It can be very helpful to us at times to have categories to put things into and sets of beliefs or attitudes to which we regularly refer. But sometimes the categories and attitudes can prove problematic.

Once again an example may help illustrate the point:

John **thinks** he makes a fool of himself whenever he introduces himself to other people. Because of this his **behaviour** is to hang back and try to avoid having to do it. The **emotion** that this produces is one of acute anxiety and feelings of awkwardness or even fear. He therefore experiences **physical sensations** of nervous stomach, heart pounding, sweating and blushing.

To make matters worse these **physical sensations** make John **think** that everyone can see he is very anxious and will consider him to be making a fool of himself as he predicted. This makes his **emotion** of anxiety more intense so that when he does introduce himself his **behaviour** displays nervousness in his speech, inappropriate or incomplete remarks, a rather unfriendly manner and a very abrupt departure.

By introducing the **behaviour** of leaving the situation, John's **emotion** is one of relief and this makes him **think** that he really is incapable of dealing with these social situations and should avoid them in future. This point of view is further supported by the **physical sensations** of exhaustion he feels afterwards which, to him, shows that he's just not up to doing these things because they take too much out of him.

John has identified a category of events about which he has formed some firm beliefs which pre-determine his responses to future events that he associates with this category. He has acquired a pattern which will cause him problems in the future unless he can recognise it and find ways to change it.

The example of John illustrates the back and forth interplays between the internal elements and also the interaction between the internal world of the person and the external environment around him or her.

In Figure 1.1.1 there is a diagrammatic representation of these interactions. In Cognitive Behaviour Therapy we nickname this commonly used diagram the "Hot Cross Bun" and it was originally devised by Padesky and Mooney (1990). We will refer to it often during this book. It illustrates very clearly that despite its name, cognitive behaviour therapy does not focus on cognitions (or thoughts) and behaviour to the exclusion of feelings. However, for the examples above and in the Hot Cross Bun diagram the word "feelings" has not been used: a distinction is drawn between physical sensations and emotions. In daily life people do not always make these distinctions and will use the word **"feelings"** to describe both.

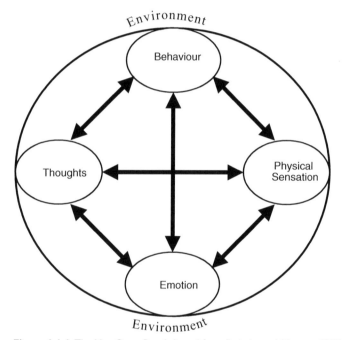

Figure 1.1.1 The Hot Cross Bun (adapted from Padesky and Mooney, 1990)

There are times when in cognitive behaviour therapy it is not important to separate the one from the other, but in work with people experiencing symptoms of physical ill health this distinction is often especially relevant; so explaining, understanding and emphasising this distinction can be very important.

Before leaving this introduction to the concepts of CBT, there are two more that cognitive behaviour therapists frequently use. One of these, like the "hot cross bun", is another image: the **"vicious circle"** (originally referred to as the "exacerbation cycle" by Beck, 1976). This can be illustrated by returning to John for a moment: he had decided that he could not cope with introducing himself to new people; and this caused him to be anxious; in turn his anxiety caused him to fluff his lines; because he fluffed his lines he believed he was confirmed in his opinion that he could not cope with introducing himself to new people. In this way he completed a "vicious circle" back to his start point.

Self-fulfilling prophesies of this kind are an important feature of what maintains the "distorted thinking and dysfunctional behaviour" referred to by Hawton et al. above. Identifying and breaking these unhelpful circles is an extremely important feature of cognitive behavioural interventions that will be discussed further in this book.

Finally, a quick tour around the cognitive behavioural approach would not be complete without some reference to **automatic thoughts**. Beck (1976) identified these particular thoughts as an important component in recurrent emotional distress. So what are they?

First, recall the example of the hand near the fire. Once I've pulled my hand back from the hot object and decided it is hazardous to me, I do not repeatedly have these thoughts every time I encounter the hot object again. I behave in a way that avoids me hurting myself and I am emotionally wary of being too close to the fire. My reactions seem to be independent of further thinking. Clearly, if I was actually "thoughtless", I would blunder into it and hurt myself; so I have seen it, recognised it as belonging to a certain category (of hot and harmful objects) and then responded according to that judgement. But this thinking process is very quick and I am hardly aware of doing it. We refer to these thoughts as "automatic". They are the immediate interpretive and decision-making thoughts that are triggered when certain events occur in our environment. They are so fleeting and we are so little aware of them that we never think them through. This makes them very powerful and influential because we make decisions based on them and yet, because they are hardly noticed and remain unexamined, they are rarely changed by experience or new knowledge.

A realistic reappraisal of the "hot and harmful, therefore stand back" thought about the fire is unlikely to lead to a change in either my perception of the fire or the decision regarding appropriate behaviour. But John, on the other hand, in our last example, experiences recurrent emotional distress because of his automatic thought that he is "incapable of dealing with these social situations and should avoid them in future". Like the perception of fire, this is also a self-protective strategy that alleviates immediate distress; but it leaves John at a major disadvantage in coping with a category of situations with which he will be faced time after time. Therefore, his episodes of distress will persist until he has had an opportunity to reappraise and change this thought process and the behaviour it directs him towards in favour of a strategy which he finds more effective in both alleviating immediate distress *and* managing the situations satisfactorily.

"Not coping" may often be considered to be the consequence of reducing emotional discomfort at the expense of satisfactorily dealing with situational demands *or* responding to demands at a high personal cost to emotional comfort. "Not coping" experiences are enough of a stimulus to begin an application of the cognitive behavioural model including identification of the automatic thoughts that are at work.

In the next chapter we will examine the relevance of this cognitive behavioural approach to people coping with life-changing physical health illnesses and disabilities, including those who expect their lives to be shortened by terminal illness. However, the cognitive behavioural approach is relevant to the experiences of all of us. We all have situations which we perceive as personal triumphs and disasters; we repeatedly fail to cope effectively with some challenges; we take for granted our abilities and skills that others lack.

Sometimes people very close to us are puzzled as to why we are so unsure of ourselves in circumstances which they consider to be less difficult, and so confident when we face others they consider more difficult. We surprise ourselves at times by taking a strong dislike to something (or someone) for no logical reason.

Recognising the thinking patterns (cognitions), including the automatic thoughts, which underpin these personal behaviours and emotional reactions, can provide all of us with valuable insights into how we cope day-to-day. If that is good enough for our patients then it should be good enough for us. Learning and understanding the cognitive behavioural approach will be greatly enhanced by applying it to oneself. At the end of every chapter there will be exercises you are asked to complete before moving on through this training workbook. Please stick firmly to that way of working unless you are using this book as part of a training course which is covering the same points in different ways.

Whether you are using this book on a course or training yourself, these first exercises in applying the cognitive behavioural approach to oneself are an important place to start the learning process.

Exercises

Before you proceed to the next chapter ensure that you take the time to do the exercises included at the end of this chapter. To use this book properly you need to complete all the recommended exercises.

Exercise 1

1. Think about a good friend who you have not seen in a long time. Remember the good times you have had with this person and the things you like talking to them about.
2. Now, imagine the phone rings; you pick it up; and there is your friend's voice at the other end, calling for a friendly chat. What are your immediate thoughts on hearing their voice? What emotion do you feel? How does your body react? What behaviour do you adopt?
3. Write these things down in the boxes below.

Thought	Emotion	Physical sensations	Behaviour

You may find it easier to fill in some boxes than others. Emotions and physical sensations can be hard to tease apart. Sometimes we do not really notice the thoughts that go with the emotions. The behaviours might be quite small (like a smile or a frown). If you find that one box is still empty, then write in something that is probably the sort of thing that would be the right response. Remember that the responses in the other boxes give you clear clues as to what is likely to be right for this box. For example, if you think "oh dear, what's wrong?" then the emotion is very likely to be worry or anxiety. If the emotion is annoyance then the thought may be something like "this is an inconvenient time to call" or some similar reason to trigger this emotional response.

Exercise 2

1. Imagine you are walking down the street in a local shopping area. It's a pleasant day and you are in no particular hurry, looking in shop windows casually as you walk along.
2. Further on down the street walking towards you but some way off you see a friend who you enjoy talking to and bump into quite often when you are out like this. You smile in this person's direction and feel quite sure that you have been spotted. Suddenly, this person disappears rapidly into the shop nearest to them without acknowledging you.
3. Imagine your reactions to this situation.
4. Now write them in the boxes below.

Thought	Emotion	Physical sensations	Behaviour

You may find you have quite a complicated set of reactions with more than one thought and emotion. Your behaviours may be a mixture too. In completing the boxes, try to ensure you have identified a specific thought for each emotion and vice versa.

Recommended further reading:

Greenberger D. and Padesky C. A. (1995) *Mind Over Mood: A Cognitive Therapy Treatment Manual for Clients,* New York: Guilford Press. A popular workbook for self-help from very influential cognitive behaviour therapists.

Padesky, C. A. and Mooney, K .A. (1990) Clinical tip: Presenting the cognitive model to clients. *International Cognitive Therapy Newsletter, 6,* 13–14 also available at www.padesky.com

Sanders, D. and Wills, F. (2005) *Cognitive Therapy: An Introduction.* London: Sage Publications.

Williams, C. (2003) *Overcoming Anxiety: A Five Areas Approach,* London: Hodder Headline Group. Along with *Overcoming Depression* in this same series, this is a British style of CBT self-help workbook and is backed up with a self-help website at www.livinglifetothefull.com

Chapter 2

The Relevance of a Cognitive Behavioural Approach for People with a Life-changing Illness

Receiving a diagnosis of multiple sclerosis is not an event that will be received unemotionally by Janet, a 33-year-old happily married mother of two. Her reaction to this news is one of intense distress, as it is to her husband and parents. This is not abnormal; it is not the wrong way to react and there is no reason to suppose that because she reacts in this way that she is doing herself lasting harm. In fact, quite the opposite may be true: that to react quietly and calmly with no show of distress could be storing up an emotional dam-burst for later.

At the point of hearing bad news such as this, it is unlikely that CBT has a useful role to play for most people (whether the patient or a close family member). A cognitive behavioural *approach* may, however, have an important role in influencing the thoughts and behaviour of those of us who have to break that bad news or provide professional follow-up since our own thoughts of having "failed" or feeling "hopeless about the future" for this patient may affect our communication and the help we offer.

So, the cognitive behavioural approach is relevant to the way in which health care professionals manage their everyday work with people going through the sorts of adverse life experiences that nobody wants and most people dread.

But just because the distress experienced by patients and their families under these circumstances is "normal" and "understandable", does not mean that there is no place for CBT. People vary greatly in their ability to accept, adapt and cope with the challenges of major health problems, especially life-threatening ones. The methods used in CBT focus on the practical here-and-now experiences in such a way as to be very relevant for those who are struggling to achieve these adjustments.

Early distress may be temporary, but for many people who are faced with life-changing ill health distress will be recurrent: life will become emotionally intense again at every point of change in health status or lifestyle. CBT techniques can be relevant in reducing the emotional intensity of these life events and encouraging a constructive response to new demands. For many people who are challenged in this way and for their families too, elements of CBT may be useful in assisting them to adjust to changed circumstances and also in becoming more resilient to further changes.

So a cognitive behavioural approach can help the health care professional to develop a more constructive attitude and the patient to develop better coping skills. There is, however, a third way in which it can be of relevance and use. The distress experienced by 25–33 per cent of these patients falls within the realms of clinical depression and clinical anxiety. CBT methods have been used to help with these mental health conditions for the past thirty years; they are just as effective when these conditions are reactions to physical health problems.

Early use of these methods reduces the risk of a downward spiral into a serious mental health problem requiring specialist mental health expertise.

In examining the relevance of a cognitive behavioural approach to people with life-changing ill health and their families, it is necessary to say something about what it is not. It is *not* "positive thinking". It does not involve trying to put a shiny gloss on things; stating positive affirmations in front of the mirror; pretending that things are better than they are; emphasising the good things and ignoring the bad; reassuring oneself that everything will get better; or deluding oneself into believing that this is an opportunity not a threat. These mental tricks may have their place in motivating a sales team, but they usually prove unsustainable in circumstances of intense emotional experiences and they do nothing to equip people for coping well with setbacks.

Returning to our theme of applying CBT to people with life-changing illness, let us look at how we might apply the Hot Cross Bun model to William's experience of a diagnosis of cancer. Figure 1.2.1 recaps the Hot Cross Bun in a way that will fit our example.

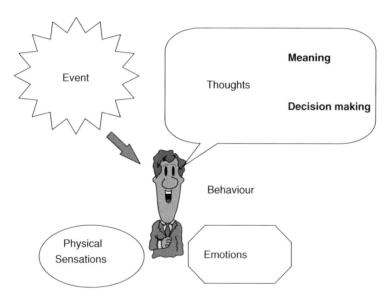

Figure 1.2.1 The cognitive behavioural model

Figure 1.2.2 illustrates a set of responses to this diagnosis of cancer. In this response set, the patient's **thoughts** express immediate defeat and self devaluation. Such strongly held beliefs will understandably lead him (we will call him William) to decide on **behaviours** that are passive and retiring, which (because he is doing nothing) will increase the **emotion** of hopelessness whilst his loss of drive leaves him with a **physical sensation** of being very tired all the time. Each of these four elements will feed back into each other and help to maintain or even escalate this depressive response set. We will refer to this as Response Set 1.

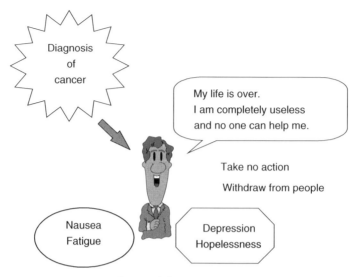

Figure 1.2.2 Response Set 1

An alternative response set is illustrated in Figure 1.2.3. This patient (William 2), facing an identical challenge, has a different (but *not* a "positive") perspective and the effects are different. The **thoughts** are acknowledging a difficult future, as in Response Set 1, but this time in a constructive way. These thoughts help him decide on **behaviours** which are intended to be useful in dealing with his situation. The **emotions** remain negative in nature but not overwhelming, instead adding some driving force which affects his **physical sensations**, making him feel energetic (perhaps even restless and tense). The restless energy will probably help him overcome reticence in telling people and getting on with his planning. As the plans develop, so he is able to focus on constructive things that he is doing, which in turn reduces sadness and encourages further helpful ideas.

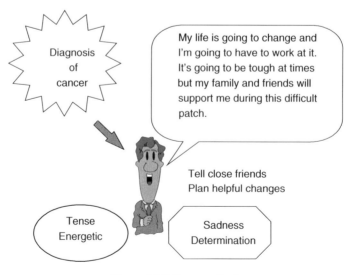

Figure 1.2.3 Response Set 2

In both these response sets, the interaction between the various elements serves to establish that particular response set. Response Set 1 is neither the *right* nor the *wrong* way to respond but, as can be seen in this example, there are consequences that appear to be less pleasant and less helpful than those associated with Response Set 2. As these examples illustrate, once established, the pattern of interaction between the elements and with the external environment maintains this response set through its own feedback loop. A loop can produce benefits (a "virtuous circle") as in Response Set 2 or disadvantages (a "vicious circle") as in Response Set 1.

CBT works by capitalising on the interaction between **thoughts**, **emotions**, **physical sensations and behaviour** to encourage a shift from unhelpful responses (such as that in Response Set 1) to others which have the potential for being more useful (such as that in-Response Set 2). By seeking to produce constructive changes in one element, the aim in CBT is to help produce changes in the others and so stop the maintenance of unhelpful response sets.

In breaking into these "vicious circles" and seeking to establish "virtuous" ones, the traditional focus in CBT has been on the **thoughts** (cognitions) and **behaviour** because the clinical work has been primarily with people with mental health problems. However, the role of medication in bringing about change in **emotions** has always been acknowledged and is often an integral part of the cognitive behavioural approach. The use of anti-depressants in particular can be helpful in reducing low moods.

Since his diagnosis with Crohn's disease, Dave has been feeling very down and fed up, he does not feel like seeing his friends and doing the sorts of things that his girlfriend, Caroline, knows would "bring him out of himself". Dave feels bad about disappointing Caroline but is sure that nothing is going to lift his mood and that by seeing his friends it would just get worse and bring them down too. He is locked into a vicious circle in which rejecting attempts at change has become part of the problem. Medication can help him change his pervasive emotional state, thus enabling him to think and behave differently. As long as the emotional change brought about by medication is used as an opportunity to bring about changes in thoughts and behaviours then it becomes possible to break the circle. If, on the other hand, the medication is used only to produce respite from the low mood but Dave continues to think and act in the same way as before, then he is very likely to quickly relapse into another low mood once the anti-depressant is withdrawn.

Similarly, it is important not to neglect the significance of the fourth "Hot Cross Bun" element: **physical sensations**. In addressing the needs of many chronic illness and palliative care patients, this element will be the most pronounced and will be profoundly influencing all the others. Physical sensations may be limiting what can be done, how much pleasure or satisfaction is derived; even how much attention is given to anything other than the physical experiences themselves. Nor do these sensations simply provide information about current bodily state for people with life-changing illness: certain physical sensations for these people may convey expectation about the future and trigger associations with the past: Helen sits by the open window and struggles with her breathing which seems to have become much more laboured since she started watering her pot plants. She suffers from chronic obstructive pulmonary disease (COPD) and does her best to put a brave face on this. However, looking out at her beloved garden and **thinking** about what she used to be able to do in it, has caused her to become **emotionally** quite upset and frightened about what the future may have in store. As she became more upset, she experienced changes in **physical sensations**: her breathing became more rapid and shallow, making her feel dizzy and more frightened. Her **behavioural response** has been to sit down and to gasp in fresh air. She is convinced that her COPD is getting worse. Anxiety naturally leads to change in the rhythm of breathing; because she suffers from COPD, Helen will be more sensitive to this change than most people. Unfortunately, she erroneously interprets this change as a worsening of her COPD and this, in turn maintains and perhaps heightens the anxiety (and thus the rapid shallow breathing).

It may be that other, non-CBT, interventions will play an important role in breaking into the vicious circles previously mentioned, by making changes in the experience of **physical sensations** (such as using analgesics for pain relief or oxygen for breathing difficulties). However, if cognitive, behavioural and emotional factors are playing a large part in why these physical sensations are occurring then reliance on physical intervention strategies may lead to inappropriate usage and psychological dependency on these methods of symptomatic relief. At its worst such dependency fuels the problem it is intended to help. For example, if Helen looked to an oxygen cylinder for help rather than an open window, then she could become anxious with breathing difficulties simply because her cylinder was running low or at the other end of the house.

It may be that the **physical sensations** are not amenable to very much change, in which case reducing their influence on **thoughts, behaviour and emotion** becomes the CBT challenge. Patricia's multiple sclerosis is quite severe and **physical experiences** include a host of unpleasant sensory disturbances as well as pain, fatigue and muscle control difficulties. Understandably, she has found coping with the relapsing-remitting nature of her disease extremely difficult. **Emotionally**, she goes to bed each night afraid to go to sleep because of **thoughts** that she might wake up with more problems the next day. She complains of feeling useless, of being left on the side-lines and of being cheated of the ability to enjoy family life. In terms of her **behaviour**, preoccupation with disease progression and her poor sleep pattern make it hard for Patricia to play any significant role in daily life with her family. If she is to achieve her ambition of becoming more useful and involved, she will need to be less influenced by symptoms and what the future might bring and more by how she can make a worthwhile contribution despite the current limitations of her physical condition. This will be a very difficult shift in focus of attention for Patricia to make and she will also need to re-evaluate her priorities in her roles within the family. In order to do this she will need to look at these roles from the perspective of the other family members as well as re-examining her own beliefs about what is important or not. A cognitive behavioural approach will enable her to do this effectively but, as well as her own motivation to achieve this goal, she will probably need the help of someone skilled in a cognitive behavioural approach.

Before looking at the various strategies that one might employ in helping Patricia to make these changes, it will be important to establish that this truly is a goal that she is motivated to achieve and that the problems that are stopping her from achieving it at the moment are fully understood. A truly cognitive behavioural approach requires that there is a careful *assessment* of the interplay between **environment, thoughts, behaviour, emotions** and **physical sensations**, so that a *formulation* can be developed that attempts to explain what causes and maintains the problems. Once this has been done, *goal setting* needs equally careful attention to ensure that goals address the identified needs and are shared and understood by the patient and the cognitive behavioural practitioner.

Each of these stages of the cognitive behavioural approach will be examined in closer detail in later chapters after having first reviewed the evidence base for using this approach and then considered the communication skills necessary to fulfil these stages.

Exercises

Before you proceed to the next chapter ensure that you take the time to do the exercises included at the end of this chapter. To use this book properly you need to complete all the recommended exercises.

Exercise 1

Think about what it would be like to be this man:

Geoffrey is a 45-year-old married man with two sons aged 12 and 8. He works as a health service physiotherapist.

A former rugby player and rower, he is now involved with youth teams in both sports. Recently he has been developing a keen interest in competitive sailing. He also enjoys hill-walking and some rock climbing.

His wife is a nurse and shares his enthusiasm for sports and outdoor recreational activities. However, the marriage has been under some strain in the past two years since he had a brief affair with another woman.

Both boys hero-worship their father and take a keen interest in sports to impress him.

His elderly parents who live five miles away are in poor health and depend on him and his wife for shopping and running around. They too rather hero-worship their son.

He was diagnosed with motor neurone disease two months ago following concerns about strange difficulties with speech and odd throat sensations. With each of the next series of exercises we can only know the answers by carefully exploring the experiences with Geoffrey himself. Each person makes individual interpretations of events, draws conclusions relevant to their own perception of themselves and the world and reacts in a way that is only fully understandable in that context. So, whilst we may have some fairly shrewd ideas about how this man might be responding, in therapy we cannot afford the luxury of making these assumptions. However, we can, for the purposes of these exercises, have a go at being in Geoffrey's shoes for a few minutes and guess at how we might respond if we were him.

Exercise 2

In his quiet moments what do you think are likely to be Geoffrey's most persistent recurrent thoughts?

1.	
2.	
3.	
4.	
5.	
6.	

Exercise 3

What thoughts will probably accompany each of these emotions?

Emotion	Thought
Guilt	
Frustration	
Despair	
Worthlessness	
Panic	

Exercise 4

Which emotions will probably accompany these physical sensations?

Physical Sensation	Emotion
Restlessness	
Breathlessness	
Exhaustion	
Cold sweat	
Tearfulness	

Exercise 5

What thoughts and emotions might account for these behaviours?

Behaviour	Emotion	Thought
Shouting at his sons		
Vigorous exercising		
Avoiding his parents		
Refusing to see friends		
Showing no affection to his wife		

In each of these exercises, it should have been possible to identify a thought or emotion that is natural companion to the other responses described. The thought should to some extent "explain" the emotion, and the emotion "explain" the behaviour. If your comments do not quite fit together in this way, look again to see if you can find a closer match. It is perhaps worth remembering whilst trying to find a suitable match that even at our most emotional and seemingly irrational, we are surprisingly logical (albeit that sometimes the logic is faulty).

Recommended further reading:

David, L. (2006) *Using CBT in General Practice: The 10 Minute Consultation,* Bloxham: Scion Publishing.

Moorey, S. (1996) When bad things happen to rational people: cognitive therapy in adverse life circumstances. Pages 450-469 in Salkovskis, P. M. (ed.) *Frontiers of Cognitive Therapy,* New York: Guilford Press.

Moorey, S. and Greer, S. (2002) *Cognitive Behaviour Therapy for People with Cancer,* New York: Oxford University Press.

White, C. (2001) *Cognitive Behaviour Therapy for Chronic Medical Problems. A Guide to Assessment and Treatment in Practice.* John Wiley & Sons, Ltd.

Williams, J. M. G. and Moorey (1989) The wider application of cognitive therapy: the end of the beginning. Pages 227–250 in Scott J., Williams J. M. G. and Beck A. T. (eds.) *Cognitive Therapy in Clinical Practice,* London: Routledge.

Chapter 3

Does Cognitive Behaviour Therapy Work? The Evidence Base

Introduction

The aim of this chapter is to provide an overview of the literature exploring the efficacy of cognitive behavioural approaches with life-changing illness. We shall see that the evidence base for CBT with a range of psychological difficulties in a mental health context is both substantial and impressive. We will then turn to the research within the specialist field and see that, rather encouragingly, whilst the evidence for applying cognitive behavioural approaches more specifically to life-changing illness is currently less substantial, it is still very promising.

Overall, there are studies that suggest that CBT can in some cases help people facing difficult and challenging illnesses to achieve a better quality of life and even increase their duration of survival. There is also evidence that CBT is cost effective, can reduce wastage of resources and, as in the case of pain, can play an important role in preventing patients from developing chronic and disabling conditions. The evidence base also suggests that CBT can be delivered successfully by therapists from different backgrounds.

As a note of caution, however, as with many areas of research, the literature exploring the efficacy of CBT with life-changing illness is fraught with methodological shortcomings and it is important that results are interpreted in this context. Additionally, where there is evidence in favour of a particular approach, there are often studies that contradict these findings so that studies often produce mixed results overall. Reviewers rightly critique studies rigorously, so that an accurate picture can emerge. For example, a common criticism of research is that where studies lack a comparison group it is not possible to attribute any changes observed to the CBT approach under investigation. It is equally possible that non specific therapeutic factors were the active ingredient in the process of change. However, whilst methodological shortcomings can lead to findings being overstated, the converse is also true. There are many ways in which study design can lead to the effectiveness of an intervention being underestimated.

Whilst reviewers tend to focus heavily on ways in which studies may have overestimated the effects of an intervention, it is important to balance this by considering ways in which in clinical practice an intervention may fare better. Ultimately our aim is to decipher what the evidence points to in the way of current best practice. It is therefore important to review the literature from this pragmatic standpoint. Where there are strong theoretical grounds underpinning the application of CBT to life-changing illness, a lack of positive findings may be due to the way in which the research has been conducted. Before reading the evidence base it is therefore helpful to be aware of some of the ways in which research may mask the effectiveness of an intervention.

1. *Research studies tend to employ a standardised approach* to intervention so that all patients receive the same treatment regardless of their individual needs, whereas in clinical practice we would tailor interventions to meet the needs of individual patients. Where there are individual differences in response to treatment, such studies may fail to produce statistically significant results. However, that is not to say that none of the patients benefited, or that if better matched to the needs of an individual the same intervention could not result in a more favourable outcome.

2. *Studies do not always involve patients with clinically significant levels of distress.* This means that the scope for change is limited. It may be that where patients are highly distressed an intervention would achieve a statistically significant level of improvement.

3. *Interventions may not be applied at a time in the care pathway when patients could benefit.* For example, participants may be recruited too early after diagnosis and this might limit the benefits they could reap at a later stage when the initial shock of diagnosis has been processed. In clinical practice, decisions about the timing of interventions would form part of the assessment process.

4. *Studies do not always include long term follow-up* and this might mean judgements are made about the effectiveness of an intervention before it has had adequate time to take effect. Where an illness and associated psychological difficulties have evolved over many years it seems reasonable to suppose that the full effects of interventions will take time to be fully realised. For example, when adopting pacing strategies patients with chronic pain may well cut levels of actively down to gain control over symptoms before gradually building up activity from a baseline. Premature measurement of physical activity levels might suggest the intervention has produced negative results when in fact the patient is progressing towards higher levels of activity with better symptom control in the longer term. In addition, where illnesses are characterised by a progressive deterioration, care must be taken to control for this when assessing long term outcomes, otherwise the benefits of interventions that have prevented any associated decline in psychological status or other outcome variables will not be realised.

5. *Studies sometimes use very small sample sizes* so that even if all patients benefited from an intervention, the study would lack the statistical power to produce statistically significant results. It would be falsely concluded that the intervention lacked efficacy.

6. *Outcome measures may not be sensitive to the changes being measured* or may not target what patients themselves deem to be important changes. Further some patients may change on some measures whilst others change on different measures so that taken as a group, even if all patients take away some benefits, statistically significant change is not achieved. For instance, some patients may find cardiac rehabilitation beneficial in enabling them to come to terms with a distressing cardiac event and this may substantially improve their quality of life. Others may use the process to develop an exercise programme that induces a greater sense of control over their future health. Both outcomes are important and helpful but taken as a whole may be masked by measuring change on a group basis.

When evaluating research, then, whilst it is important to be aware of ways in which research design could overestimate the effectiveness of an intervention, it is also important to consider whether there are grounds to suspect that in clinical practice a better outcome might be realised. This does not mean we should ignore the evidence base, but rather appreciate that it is only as good as the quality of the research being reviewed. When applying findings to practice there may be grounds for suspecting an intervention will be fruitful that has as yet little or no good evidence in its favour. At this juncture, your attention is drawn to the section on applying research findings to clinical practice, found towards the end of the chapter. This section expands on some of the points made above and discusses practical issues that arise in relation to applying the evidence base to clinical practice.

Students should persevere in reading this chapter thoroughly and carefully, even though it may be heavy going at times. A solid grounding in the evidence base is an essential component of applying a cognitive behavioural approach: good practice requires that interventions offered to the patient have proven efficacy and, quite rightly, an increasing number of patients want to know what evidence there is in favour of the different options presented to them.

A further reason for being familiar with the evidence base is that in financially limited health care systems, managers increasingly require proposals for new service developments, such as introducing cognitive behavioural approaches, to include data that backs up the assertions of the likely benefits of these developments. The material contained in this chapter may be helpful in negotiating the necessary resources to practice cognitive behavioural approaches, including protected time for supervision. It is also to be hoped that by reading through the evidence in support of CBT and its application to life-changing illness you may further increase your motivation to apply cognitive behavioural approaches to your own practice, perhaps even add to the evidence base.

In preparing the material for this chapter, the authors have drawn heavily on review articles that have explored the literature in detail. The key findings have been presented in summary format as a quick guide and reference for the interested practitioner seeking to apply evidence-based practice to their work. The chapter covers the areas of cancer and palliative care, cardiac problems, chronic pain, multiple sclerosis, diabetes, chronic obstructive pulmonary disease and Parkinson's disease. However, even if you practice in an area not covered by this chapter, there is much here that will be relevant. Reading the summaries will provide a flavour of what can be achieved with CBT, alert you to issues that are likely to arise with any life-changing illness and give you a feel for how to critique studies evaluating the effectiveness of CBT within your area of expertise.

Additionally, you are strongly encouraged to supplement the contents of this chapter with literature searches of your own to explore areas of interest in more detail, and ensure you remain informed of up-to-date work in the field. The limitations in research design listed above suggest that the effectiveness of CBT may have been underestimated in a number of studies. There is good reason to suppose, therefore, that in time, larger scale, better designed studies, will produce a more substantial evidence base that will further elucidate the effectiveness of applying CBT to life-changing illness. The exercise at the end of the chapter will help you to get started with making your own literature searches in this field.

The evidence base for CBT

Overall, as we shall see, there is an impressive evidence base for the effectiveness of CBT in a mental health context, strong theoretical grounds for applying CBT to address psychological issues associated with life-changing illness and a growing evidence base within the specialist field.

In 2001, the Department of Health (DoH) and the National Institute for Clinical Excellence (NICE) commissioned an extensive review of the literature so that "Treatment Choice in Psychological Therapies and Counselling" could be identified. A meta-review (a review of a collection of reviews) of the best available evidence was conducted and it was concluded that there is good evidence that CBT is effective with depression, panic disorder, social phobia, obsessive compulsive disorder, bulimia and generalised anxiety disorder.

This review found an impressive evidence base for the efficacy of CBT with a range of psychological difficulties in a mental health context. This is very relevant to our exploration of the evidence base for life-changing illness. There is a significant overlap between the issues that arise in a mental health context and those that arise in relation to ill health. For instance, life-changing illness may lead to difficulties in adjusting to losses and changes that result in clinical depression; and disfigurement caused by physical illness or its treatment may lead to body image issues that trigger social phobia. Providing care is taken to adapt interventions to take account of the effects of illness-related factors such as pain, fatigue or the side effects of medication, there is no reason to assume that the evidence base generated by work in a mental health context is not applicable to patients whose primary diagnosis is a physical health disorder. Consistent with this view, the meta-review also found good evidence for the efficacy of CBT with chronic pain and more limited but growing evidence for other somatic complaints including chronic fatigue, pelvic pain and pre menstrual syndrome. That is not to say the review would not have found evidence in favour of CBT for other physical health problems, however, the authors restricted the scope of their review to a small number of somatic complaints regarded as highly relevant to patients presenting in GP surgeries.

Bearing in mind that our patients with life-changing illnesses experience the same sources of psychological distress as the rest of the population, there is very good evidence here in favour of CBT for a range of psychological disorders relevant to working with people with life-changing illness.

In the following sections, the evidence bases for a range of life-changing illnesses are presented. Each section provides a brief introduction, highlights common psychological issues that arise in relation to that illness and provides a summary of some of the findings of evaluation studies in the area.

Cancer and palliative care

There are many different types and causes of cancer and it is beyond the scope of this chapter to go into details. Suffice it to say, however, that receiving a diagnosis of cancer is potentially a highly distressing experience. Cancer brings with it significant psychological challenges such as coping with uncertainty about the future and loss of control over one's health. It is not so much what the diagnosis actually means but what the individual perceives it to mean that will determine the level of distress experienced. In addition, medical and surgical treatment of cancer can be very demanding and present the patient with both temporary and permanent losses and changes. For instance, loss of energy and sense of wellbeing are common problems associated with chemotherapy and surgery may change the body and alter body image, as with mastectomy.

Given the likely losses and changes associated with having cancer, a period of psychological adjustment would be expected as the patient grapples to make sense of their experience. Perhaps not surprisingly, a significant number of individuals (studies suggest up to 20 per cent) will struggle to make this adjustment. They will present with clinically significant levels of anxiety and depression, body image issues and even symptoms of psychological trauma.

Difficulties in adjusting to and coping with cancer may be presented in clinic in a number of different ways. Patients and their relatives may report increasing social withdrawal, staying away from reminders of the illness, being preoccupied with what can go wrong or a fear of being alone. Patients experiencing adjustment difficulties may find it increasing difficult to adhere to long and complex treatments or to make decisions that they will be comfortable with in the longer term. It is important to note that adjusting well soon after diagnosis does not preclude difficulties arising at a later stage. Difficulties may, for example, emerge for the first time at the end of treatment or when a recurrence is detected.

It is important that psychological difficulties that extend beyond a period of adjustment in time and intensity are identified and managed. Whilst distress is inevitable, there is good evidence, as described above, that CBT is effective in treating depression and anxiety and no patient should be left to struggle with clinically significant symptoms that will impair quality of life and complicate the management of their illness. Reassurance that such symptoms are normal and understandable is not likely to be helpful and is usually inappropriate.

In their review of the literature, Moorey and Greer (2002) examine a number of issues. A brief summary of this literature is provided below. However, for a fuller exploration of the issues, the reader is encouraged to read the original text.

1. *Can CBT improve quality of life for people with cancer?*
Overall CBT appears to be effective in enhancing quality of life for people experiencing cancer. Some useful studies have enabled CBT to be compared to having no psychological intervention and to having supportive counselling, compared the effectiveness of applying it soon or later after diagnosis and assessed whether it can be effective in the later stages of the illness.

2. *Is CBT more effective than having no psychological intervention or receiving supportive counselling?*
Studies largely support that CBT is more effective in enhancing quality of life than having no psychological intervention or receiving supportive counselling. Greer et al. (1992) and Moorey et al. (1994), for example, compared the effectiveness of six sessions of adjuvant psychological therapy (APT) with treatment as usual in 156 patients with both newly diagnosed and recurring cancers. They found CBT to be more effective than treatment as usual. The benefits of receiving CBT, compared to having treatment as usual, were maintained at a one-year follow-up. In a further study (Moorey et al., 1998), an intervention comprising six sessions of CBT (Adjuvant Psychological Therapy) was found to be more effective than supportive counselling. Through comparing CBT with supportive counselling the results suggested that specific components of CBT are important ingredients in the process of change.

3. *Is CBT better applied early or late after diagnosis?*
Edgar et al. (1992) compared the effectiveness of five cognitive behavioural coping skills sessions administered early (11 weeks after diagnosis) or late (28 weeks after diagnosis). At four months (when the late intervention group has not yet received treatment), there were no differences between the groups. However, at eight months and one year follow-up, CBT applied late was more effective than CBT applied early.

One interpretation of these results is that the initial emotions experienced after diagnosis may impair the patient's ability to use CBT effectively.

4. *Can CBT be effective in the later stages of cancer?*

In order to evaluate whether CBT can be effective in the late stages of cancer, Linn et al. (1982) administered a form of counselling incorporating CBT strategies to 120 men, in an advanced stage of cancer, who had an average life expectancy of three to twelve months. The intervention focused on issues such as increasing meaningful activity, hope, self-esteem and reducing denial. The researchers found CBT to be more effective than having no psychological intervention. The results of this study provide some evidence for the efficacy of CBT in the later stages of cancer.

In summary, the research evidence suggests that CBT is more effective than having no psychological intervention or receiving supportive counselling. In addition, CBT appears to be more effective when applied later rather than earlier after diagnosis and CBT can be effective in the later stages of cancer.

If CBT is effective in enhancing quality of life for people with cancer, does the mode of delivery of the intervention affect outcome? Whilst psycho-educational groups and CBT groups cannot meet the specific needs of every individual, they are a means of delivering CBT to larger numbers of people and are potentially a relatively inexpensive mode of service delivery. But are they effective?

5. *Are psycho-educational groups effective?*
Psycho-educational groups typically follow a predetermined structure and may include the following elements:

- relaxation and stress management;
- communication and assertiveness;
- problem solving;
- helpful thinking;
- managing emotions;
- activity planning.

Useful research by Cunningham et al. (1989) compared the effects of two hours of psycho-educational therapy with supportive discussions across a period of six weeks. The authors found psycho-educational groups to be more effective than stand alone support. The authors concluded that improvements in mood were mediated by changes in perceived self-efficacy (Cunningham et al., 1991). They found that these improvements were applicable to various cancer types and stages of disease. Furthermore, the results of the study showed that psycho-educational interventions can be delivered successfully by therapists from different backgrounds (Cunningham et al., 1993).

6. *Is CBT delivered to groups effective?*
CBT groups are more individually tailored to personal needs in their application of techniques than psycho-educational groups. Research by Edelman et al. (1999a) compared the efficacy of twelve sessions of group CBT with supportive therapy for sixty patients with recently diagnosed breast cancer. Post-treatment CBT was found to be more effective than supportive therapy in improving quality of life and self-esteem. However, by four months follow-up, the effect of CBT was only equal to that of supportive therapy. This study did not find any long term benefits of group CBT over supportive therapy.

In contrast, Fawzy et al. (1990) compared the effectiveness of six sessions of group CBT with having no psychological intervention. They found that, after treatment, group CBT had a greater effect than having no intervention. In this study the benefits of CBT were maintained at six-month follow-up.

Overall, studies exploring the effectiveness of CBT groups have found it to be more effective than supportive therapy or having no psychological intervention. However, there is mixed evidence as to whether the benefits are sustained in the longer term.

7. *Should we select distressed patients for CBT or offer it to all?*

Having found that CBT is effective in enhancing quality of life in this patient group, it is tempting to offer it as routine to all patients. The advantage of this is that it can reduce stigma for those who are experiencing psychological distress. However, does the evidence base support this approach? In an interesting study, Moynihan et al. (1998) assessed whether CBT could help all patients with testicular cancer. They compared six sessions of CBT with treatment as usual. Interestingly, they found that many men with testicular cancer did not wish to receive therapy. Further, they also found that the men in the comparison group, who did not receive psychological intervention, improved to a greater extent than those who engaged in CBT. The authors concluded that offering CBT routinely is not indicated.

Summary of the above: Can CBT improve quality of life for people with cancer?

There is evidence that CBT is more effective than routine care in improving quality of life for patients with cancer. CBT is effective for selected patients who exhibit psychological distress. If it is not possible to screen patients for psychological distress, then, based on current evidence, the recommended treatment of choice is structured psycho-educational groups. The research literature indicates that intervening too early after a diagnosis of cancer may not be beneficial and may even be detrimental to the patient. Early intervention may interfere with existing coping resources and the heightened emotions experienced after initial diagnosis may hinder the patient's ability to use CBT. There is some evidence that psychologically distressed patients may benefit from CBT even in the late stages of the disease process.

1. *Can CBT affect duration of survival?*

Historically, a principle assumption held by the medical profession was that the course of cancer could not be affected by psychological intervention. However, Spiegel et al. (1989) provided evidence to the contrary which sparked a large debate within the field. Spiegel et al. (1989) found that women with metastatic breast cancer who received group therapy survived, on average, for 18.9 months longer than women who did not receive group therapy. Subsequent research by Richardson et al. (1990) and Fawzy et al. (1993) supported the finding that psychological intervention could indeed have an effect on the duration of survival.

However, the claim that psychological intervention could increase duration of survival was based on studies with small sample sizes with patients undergoing different psychological interventions for different types of cancer at a variety of stages in the disease process. Moreover, more recent work (Edelman, 1999b) produced contradictory findings. Edelman followed up a sample of 121 patients with metastatic breast cancer who had received CBT. The results showed that CBT had not increased duration of survival at two and five-year follow-up.

No randomised clinical trial designed with survival as a primary end point and in which psychotherapy was not confounded with medical care has yielded a positive effect (Coyne et al., 2007). On this basis we must conclude that there is no consistent evidence that CBT increases the duration of survival for patients with cancer.

2. *Is a fighting spirit helpful?*

It was initially claimed that a fighting spirit led to better adjustment and duration of survival (Moorey & Greer, 2002) and this work paved the way for CBT in the field of cancer and palliative care. However, earlier claims about the effects of fighting spirit have been refuted (Petticrew et al., 2002). Rather than thinking in terms of adjustment style per se, it is probably more useful to consider which strategies help individual patients to cope at different stages of different cancers. A fighting spirit may be helpful in coping with some aspects of the illness but if the individual is exhausted and emotionally depleted a more passive approach may be useful at least in the short term. Denial, for example, can help a person carry on with life in the face overwhelming bad news.

Conclusions

Whilst some very useful and interesting work has been done, methodological shortcomings limit the strength with which conclusions can be drawn. The effectiveness of CBT with cancer patients may be affected by a number of factors, including the type of cancer, the stage of disease process and patient characteristics. Care must be taken when generalising the results of these studies across different individuals with different cancers at different stages in the illness.

In conclusion, with the above qualifying remarks in mind, there is a good and growing body of evidence that CBT is beneficial for people with cancer, though the benefits are in terms of quality of life and not duration of survival. Current evidence indicates that CBT, as a formal intervention, should not be provided as part of routine care and patients should be screened for psychological distress before being offered intervention. Psycho-educational groups are likely to be cost effective but their efficacy relative to individual therapy is unknown. Current evidence advocates adopting an individual approach to gauging which coping strategies will help the individual master the challenges associated with the illness at any stage.

Cardiac problems

In a medical emergency the focus of care is on saving life, rather than preserving psychological wellbeing. Nevertheless, a heart attack is a very frightening event. Not surprisingly, such events are associated with high levels of psychological distress. It is common for anxiety and depression to persist for more than a year after a heart attack. Bearing in mind the perceived threat to life together with the loss of personal control, it is also not surprising that a small but significant number of individuals go on to develop symptoms of psychological trauma.

Surgical interventions for coronary heart disease (CHD) also have the potential to be very threatening and patients may feel uneasy not only about the risks of surgery to this vital organ but also about changes being made to an organ that we see as a central part of our emotional selves. How many of us have, for instance, used the phrase "In my heart I felt it was the right thing to do" or seen the phrase "Forever in my heart" engraved on a tombstone?

Hearts can easily be monitored through feeling our pulse or we may be aware of a thudding in our chest during periods of anxiety or when exerting ourselves. As such it is easy to see how perceived disturbances to normal heart rate and rhythm could trigger anxiety and panic; indeed high levels of anxiety and panic are associated with ventricular arrhythmia and its treatment with Implantable Cardiac Defibrillators (ICD) (White, 2001).

There is substantial scope for psychological disorders to complicate the management of patients with cardiac problems. Following myocardial infarction or coronary bypass graft surgery, depressive symptoms, such as lack of motivation and loss of energy, are likely to reduce activity levels, thereby acting as a barrier to effective rehabilitation.

This could have a significant impact on outcome. Inactivity also tends to lower the threshold for experiencing angina (Lewin, 1997) so that, over time, patients experience a greater level of symptoms at a lower level of activity. It is easy to see how this could develop into a self perpetuating cycle whereby lack of activity and reduced sense of control over the symptoms increase depression, which in turn, leads to a further reduction in activity level.

Whilst psychological symptoms act as a barrier to rehabilitation and lead to poorer outcomes overall, they may also have implications for effective use of resources. Psychologically mediated symptoms such as chest pain and palpitations may be hard to distinguish from symptoms arising from cardiac pathology. If patients' underlying psychological difficulties are not addressed, their continuing anxiety may lead to them seeking further reassurance. They may repeatedly seek referral to a cardiac specialist, leading to a waste of cardiology clinic time. There is good evidence that CBT is effective for patients with non-cardiac chest pain (Mayou et al., 1997) and that it may prove to be a cost effective solution from the point of view of both patient quality of life and health resource utilisation.

There are a number of ways in which CBT can contribute to the psychological well-being of people with cardiac problems. These include the amelioration of non-cardiac chest pain, cardiac rehabilitation following myocardial infarction and coronary artery bypass graft surgery, managing angina and management of the psychological impact of treatment such as Implantable Cardiac Defibrillators (White, 2001).

In the following section the literature pertaining to cardiac rehabilitation will be presented as there is a substantial body of literature addressing this area. For a more complete review of cardiac problems, the reader is referred to White (2001).

Cardiac rehabilitation

The aim of cardiac rehabilitation is to enable patients to make lifestyle changes that reduce their risk of further problems and enhance their quality of life, following heart attack and / or coronary artery bypass graft surgery. The process requires active participation on behalf of the patient to make and sustain changes in the long term. Typically cardiac rehabilitation programmes incorporate a number of elements such as exercise, dietary advice, drug regimens and psychosocial interventions. Within the literature, there are many studies assessing the effectiveness of cardiac rehabilitation programmes and, of greater import here, the added value of psychological interventions over and above other multidisciplinary components. Reviews of this evidence base have attempted to answer pertinent questions such as whether CBT can affect duration of survival and restore quality of life following a cardiac event, whether modifying psychological risk factors such as Type A Behaviour (TAB) and depression affects outcome, and whether cardiac rehabilitation programmes are cost effective. Below is a summary of some of the conclusions reviewers have drawn from the evidence base to date.

1. *Can CBT affect duration of survival?*
In a review of the literature, Bennett and Carroll (1994) concluded that programmes targeted at reducing Type A Behaviours, smoking cessation, increasing exercise and stress management strategies, were effective in reducing psychological distress and increasing effective coping in the short

term. They also found the programmes to be associated with positive behavioural change. However, whilst the programmes were found to enhance quality of life, the authors concluded that there was little consistent evidence that these changes had a positive impact on heart disease mortality and morbidity. They speculated that this latter finding could have resulted from shortcomings in the studies available at that time.

In a more recent review, Linden (2000) concluded that psychosocial interventions, when added to other active rehabilitation conditions, could improve the odds for mortality and for nonfatal MI recurrence. This is a significant finding and a persuasive argument for including psychosocial intervention in the rehabilitation process.

Whilst current evidence suggests that psychosocial interventions can affect duration of survival, and this is an exciting finding, the nature of psychosocial approaches varies so greatly across studies it is difficult to make recommendations for particular interventions. In fact in the absence of more carefully controlled studies, it is not possible to establish whether specific psychosocial components add benefit over and above non-specific factors such as emotional support derived from the group process. That is not to say that CBT is not effective. It is a common component of cardiac rehabilitation programmes and the evidence in favour of these approaches is good. However, it is not yet established whether CBT adds value over and above other psychotherapeutic ingredients.

Linden also points out that since his conclusions are drawn from data from meta-analyses, it is difficult to determine individual differences in response to treatment. As mentioned in the introduction, matching interventions to meet patients' individual needs may yield better results than standardised rehabilitation packages.

2. *Does modifying Type A Behaviour affect outcome?*

This appears to be a contentious issue in the literature. In earlier studies researchers explored the relationship between CHD and a global pattern of competitive, hard-driving behaviour and a tendency towards hostility, known as Type A Behaviour (TAB). Initially, TAB was considered to confer as high a risk for CHD as biological risk factors. However, later studies contradicted this finding, casting doubts on TAB as a risk factor for CHD. Given the theoretical links between TAB and risk of CHD, the lack of evidence in favour of a relationship between the two may be an artefact of study design. For example, the different components of TAB may confer different levels of risk. As such, studies into the risk presented by different components of TAB may prove more fruitful than those that have looked at TAB as a single construct (Sebregts, 2000). There is some evidence to suggest that hostility is more strongly associated with CHD than feeling angry or bearing an attitude of cynical mistrust, for instance.

In terms of the impact of modifying TAB on outcome, the Recurrent Coronary Prevention Project (Friedman et al., 1984) compared the effectiveness of group cardiac counselling with cardiac counselling combined with TAB modification in a large sample of people who had experienced an infarction six months previously. Cardiac counselling comprised discussions aimed at increasing adherence to prescribed dietary, exercise and drug regimens. TAB modification consisted of cognitive and behavioural techniques such as relaxation training, cognitive restructuring and graded behavioural assignments. The combined intervention was associated with significantly greater changes in global ratings of TAB and those components of TAB thought to be associated with CHD, including hostility, than cardiac counselling alone. At 4.5 year follow up the re-infarct rate was almost halved in the combined treatment group relative to the cardiac counselling group and death from MI was also significantly reduced in the combined treatment group. At first glance, the results of this study are impressive in terms of reducing risk and also suggest that specific CBT techniques are more effective at reducing TAB than cardiac counselling alone. However, in their review, Bennett and Carroll (1994) identify some issues that undermine the strength of the findings. For example, the reduction in risk of a further cardiac event cannot be attributed to the TAB modification because other psychological changes took place in participants. These changes could equally well have accounted for the reduced risk. Also it has been argued that the group receiving the TAB modification had a better prognosis from the outset, so finding that this group did better becomes less meaningful. It has been argued however, that it is unlikely that this alone could account for the substantial differences between the two groups (Johnston, 1992).

So what can we conclude? The above reviews suggest that there is conflicting evidence as to whether TAB confers a risk for CHD but that research into the relationship between specific components of TAB and CHD may prove more fruitful. There is some evidence that modifying TAB reduces risk of re-infarction, with evidence in favour of CBT in particular as an effective approach. However, shortcomings in research design mean that firm conclusions cannot be drawn.

3. *Does treating psychological disorders improve life expectancy?*
Depression (Frasure-Smith et al., 1995) and anxiety (Kubzansky et al., 2000) have been shown to have an adverse impact on prognosis suggesting that treating psychological disorders in post-MI patients is potentially very beneficial. Psychosocial treatment has been shown to reduce anxiety and depression in this patient group, with some evidence of reduction in the biological risk factors associated with clinical depression (Carney et al., 2000). However, there is as yet no evidence from randomised controlled trials that psychological treatment of depression and anxiety improves patients' prognosis, that is, no evidence that successful treatment of these conditions reduces the biological risk of a further cardiac event.

4. *Do psychosocial interventions improve quality of life?*
Following an extensive review of the literature, Linden (2000) concludes that cardiac rehabilitation programmes are effective in reducing anxiety and depression in addition to mortality and cardiac event recurrence so that overall quality of life is improved.

5. *Are cardiac rehabilitation programmes cost effective?*
In his paper, Linden (2000) argues that cardiac rehabilitation programmes are cost effective and that in general the more extensive the programme, the better the outcome, although he cautions that at some stage more treatment will not add more benefit.

6. *Should psychosocial interventions be offered as part of routine care?*
As with patients with cancer, Linden (2000) advocates screening patients for psychological distress before referring them on for psychological treatment in preference to giving all patients the same length and type of treatment.

Summary

Cardiac rehabilitation appears to be a cost-effective approach to improving quality of life and life expectancy in patients who have experienced myocardial infarction and/or bypass graft surgery. Current evidence suggests that rehabilitation programmes should focus on managing behavioural risk factors (such as smoking) and psychological risk factors (especially anxiety and depression). Linden recommends providing this in a group format incorporating standard instruction in stress management, emotion coping and adherence to lifestyle changes. He further recommends providing additional input, on a case-by-case basis, for patients experiencing severe anxiety or depression or those having difficulty with behavioural changes such as smoking cessation or adherence to exercise and nutrition guidelines.

Limitations of the research

Whilst there is a substantial and growing body of research addressing important questions about the role of psychosocial interventions in cardiac rehabilitation, methodological shortcomings such as small sample size and lack of comparison groups mean that conclusions about the effectiveness of CBT in this context must be regarded as tentative. As yet, beyond general recommendations, it is not possible to determine which interventions work for whom and whether certain specific CBT interventions are more effective than non-specific therapeutic factors such as group support. Scheidt (2000) points out that meta-analyses can lead to erroneous assumptions and asserts that more carefully constructed studies are needed to improve the number, size, generalisability and scientific rigour of trials in the area of cardiac rehabilitation.

Conclusions

There is a wealth of literature exploring the many ways in which psychological factors contribute to the experience of cardiac problems. Psychological factors are generally accepted as playing an important role in recovery from a major cardiac event and may even contribute to it in the first place. Cardiac events have the potential to be frightening and traumatic experiences and not surprisingly are associated with high levels of psychological morbidity. Likewise treatment of cardiac problems can itself be stressful. The literature suggests that psychosocial interventions have a substantial contribution to make in helping patients regain their quality of life following such cardiac events, and even improving life expectancy. However, further research is needed to clarify the precise role of CBT in this process.

Chronic pain

Chronic pain is pain that persists beyond three to six months after initial onset, by which point tissue healing associated with acute injury will have taken place. Contemporary models of chronic pain suggest that it results from changes in the central and peripheral nervous system and does not signal tissue damage. Chronic pain has implications for all areas of life, including family relationships, social functioning and work status. Not surprisingly, rates of psychological disorders in this patient group are high. Moreover, the scope for psychological factors to influence the development of acute injury into a chronic and disabling condition is enormous and indeed psychosocial factors are generally regarded as at least as important as biomedical variables in the development and elaboration of chronic pain.

Problems arise when individuals with chronic pain continue to believe that the pain signals ongoing tissue damage. Fear of harm results in avoidance of movements that trigger pain. The resulting reduction in activity levels leads to general deconditioning and ultimately more pain on movement. Increased pain on movement in turn triggers more fear and a reduced sense of control over the pain. As the patient becomes more inactive so depressive symptoms are likely to be triggered. Depression is likely to further reduce activity levels and so on in a downwards spiral.

Early models of chronic pain tended to dichotomise pain as either organic or psychogenic and an attempt was made to identify the pain prone personality. It is important to be aware that much of the psychosocial research into chronic pain has been correlational studies that show that chronic pain is associated with a range of psychological factors. However, this type of study may lead to erroneous conclusions being drawn regarding cause and effect. Whilst pre-existing psychological disorders are likely to lead to poorer outcomes, it is just as likely that living with chronic pain causes the changes in emotional wellbeing, perceptions of control over aspects of one's life, low self-efficacy and family dysfunction so commonly reported in these studies.

Nowadays whilst the role of psychosocial factors in the development of chronic pain and disability is undisputed, there is greater recognition that the attitudes and beliefs that play a central part in this process reflect widely, even culturally, held misconceptions of chronic pain. The role of iatrogenic factors has also been acknowledged. Since investigations are usually carried out to exclude sinister pathology, many patients will never receive a diagnosis that explains the cause of the pain. A lack of diagnosis and explanation can fuel difficulties in accepting pain and making appropriate lifestyle changes. Lack of diagnosis may also lead to patients repeatedly presenting for investigations. This will broaden the scope for conflicting expert opinions to further confuse the patient's understanding of the pain. Investigations may also reveal wear and tear changes that do not necessarily account for the pain but which sound frightening and feed the patients fears and avoidance behaviours ("Your back's knackered"). Moreover, pain is an invisible and private experience, which can be neither quantified nor measured. As a result, many patients report feeling disbelieved by the medical world and by their family and this can only add to the difficulties of living with pain. It is not uncommon for patients to report questioning the validity of their own pain as a result.

Whilst pain is an invisible and private experience, pain behaviours are overt signs of pain and probably most usefully viewed as a form of communication about pain. Whilst they can be observed and measured and have been subject to much research, it is important to remember that they tell us very little about the personal experience of pain. Earlier interventions employed operant behaviour therapy to modify what were perceived to be unhelpful pain behaviours such as grimacing or altered gait. Whilst these interventions generally met with success, the implications of modifying pain behaviours for improving the patients' quality of life remains less clear. More recently the emphasis has shifted towards cognitive behavioural models that emphasise the importance of understanding key cognitions that drive pain-related behaviours and the need to modify these to help patients regain control over their pain and resume a more active lifestyle. These cognitions and behaviours are known as Yellow Flags or psychosocial risk factors for the development of chronic pain and disability. These risk factors are barriers to effective rehabilitation and modifying these as early on in the care pathway as possible is now strongly recommended in order to optimise outcome.

In summary, contemporary approaches to the management of chronic pain emphasise the need for CBT interventions to target the psychosocial risk factors involved in the development and elaboration of chronic pain and disability following acute injury (Watson & Kendall, 2000; Linton & Hallden, 1998). These risk factors include fear of harm or re-injury, perceptions of having low control over the pain, low self-efficacy for managing pain and catastrophic thinking about the future together with associated behavioural responses such as avoidance of activity, cycling between under and then over-activity, and hypervigilance to bodily sensations. A further development in the field has been the recognition of the importance of helping patients adjust psychologically to their pain, such as enabling greater acceptance of the long term presence of pain in their life (McCracken, 2005). This in turn enables patients to face the consequences of their pain and begin making the necessary lifestyle adjustments.

The typical mode of delivery of CBT for people with chronic pain is multidisciplinary group work supplemented in some cases with individual work. The aim is to alter the patient's perception of and response to pain to reduce distress and enable them to enjoy a more productive and active lifestyle rather than attempting to eliminate pain *per se*. Pain management programmes are run in both in-patient and out-patient settings. A typical programme would include education about chronic pain and skills training in goal setting, pacing activities, managing unhelpful thinking, assertiveness techniques, ergonomic advice and developing a plan to manage relapses. Since family members can inadvertently exacerbate the difficulties of living with pain, programmes may also include a partner session.

A number of studies have explored the efficacy of CBT with chronic pain, including whether CBT adds value over other components of multidisciplinary pain management programmes, comparing the efficacy of CBT to other psychological approaches to managing pain and to unstructured group discussions and identifying individual differences in response to treatment. Whilst overall there is good evidence that CBT makes a substantial contribution to the management of chronic pain, within the literature a diverse range of CBT techniques has been applied to the management of pain and a single definition of cognitive behavioural intervention for chronic pain would be difficult to elucidate.

1. *Do CBT interventions add value over other multidisciplinary treatment approaches?*
A systematic review by Morley, Eccleston and Williams (1999), of twenty-five trials, compared the effectiveness of CBT to waiting list comparison and alternative treatment comparison conditions. The authors concluded that active psychological treatment based on the principles of CBT was effective in terms of changes in measures of pain experience, mood, cognitive coping and appraisal, activity level and social role functioning. When compared to other treatment approaches, CBT was found to be more effective on outcome measures of pain experience, cognitive coping and appraisal and social function. Overall, the authors concluded that active psychological treatments based on the principles of CBT are effective.

A further review by Ostelo et al. (2005) concluded that CBT interventions that combine treatment targeted at pain related cognitive factors such as the meaning of pain and expectations of control over pain with respondent treatment targeted at modifying the physiological response system such as progressive muscle relaxation, are effective relative to waiting list comparison conditions. There were insufficient data to draw conclusions as to whether the benefits were sustained in the longer-term. However, the authors also found that adding CBT to other treatment modalities such as physiotherapy and education does not change outcome either in the short or long term. In contrast to Morley et al. (1999), Ostelo et al. (2005) conclude that whilst CBT is effective, it is not more effective than other modalities of treating chronic pain.

There is good evidence that CBT is effective in improving outcome for people with chronic pain, but it is not clear if CBT is superior to other treatment modalities.

2. *Is CBT effective in modifying psychosocial risk factors (Yellow Flags) for chronic pain and disability?*

Historically, most pain management programmes have targeted a range of psychological and social factors that are now known as Yellow Flags and more clearly understood to play a role in the development and elaboration of chronic pain and disability. Whilst, they have not necessarily been referred to as Yellow Flags, the studies included in the Morley et al. (1999) and Ostelo et al. (2005) reviews would have been addressing a range of these risk factors. Sowden et al. (2006) describe how their CBT-based pain management programme has been modified to more specifically target four Yellow Flags that appear particularly salient in the literature. For example, the modified programme targets education and CBT techniques more fully at altering fear-avoidance beliefs and behaviours. The results of this uncontrolled pilot study suggested that the programme successfully modified three of the four risk factors and results were largely sustained at follow-up (Hatch et al., 2005). Contained within the (2006) paper is a description of how the standard programme has been modified and which techniques are considered to target specific risk factors. However, the link between specific interventions and changes in Yellow Flags reported by the authors is speculative. So, is there evidence that specific techniques target specific aspects of chronic pain to achieve a particular outcome? In more recent years there has been a refining of the cognitive behavioural model of chronic pain with greater recognition of the central role of fear-avoidance in the development and maintenance of pain and disability. It would be especially helpful to identify techniques that are most effective in addressing fear-avoidance issues.

In a review of psychological approaches to the management of pain, Roelofs et al. (2002) conclude that exposure *in-vivo* embedded in a cognitive behavioural treatment is more effective than graded activity in targeting important cognitive and behavioural risk factors. Compared to graded activity, graded exposure substantially decreases levels of pain-related fear, pain catastrophising, pain disability, pain vigilance and increases physical activity.

We should note in this context that pain management programmes typically include some form of graded activity, involving pacing up of activity from a baseline. This is not the same as graded exposure. Graded exposure involves the patient systematically engaging in increasingly fear provoking situations so that the threat value of the feared situation is reduced and cognitions modified through gaining new evidence. Ultimately both interventions aim to increase activity but graded exposure more explicitly targets the fears that are maintaining inactivity.

In an interesting study that compared CBT with operant behavioural therapy (OBT), Thieme et al. (2006) concluded that different modes of psychological therapy target different aspects of the syndrome to produce different outcomes. In their study, CBT was found to be superior in treating affective distress whilst OBT produced greater improvements in functional limitations. The authors recommend that CBT might be especially beneficial for patients with high levels of cognitive maladaptation to the pain and high affective distress, whereas OBT might be especially efficacious in patients with high levels of pain behaviours and low physical functioning (Thieme et al., 2006).

Whilst structured group work appears to have been the favoured method of delivery of CBT to patients with chronic pain, and there has been a tendency for all patients to receive a standard package, recent work has begun to tease apart those factors that predict outcome. Following a review of the literature, McCracken and Turk (2002) conclude that highly distressed patients who see their pain as both an uncontrollable and highly negative life event derive less benefit than others patients. They conclude that "every patient's pain, suffering and disability are kept in place by a different set of influences". They advocate the need to identify and address the important and changeable influences maintaining these problems for the individual.

Finally, there has been growing recognition that whilst pain management programmes are effective, the real challenge to services is to provide a long term model of care that supports patients to manage their pain across the life span. One cost effective means of providing long term input is via support groups. Whilst the literature pertaining to support groups was not reviewed in relation to preparing this chapter, one study the authors came across might have implications for their effectiveness. By including an attention-placebo group in their study, Thieme et al. (2006) were able to evaluate the effectiveness of unstructured group discussions. CBT led to a reduction in pain intensity and improvements in cognitive and affective variables, but patients in the attention-placebo group showed deterioration on the outcome measures. The authors concluded that unstructured discussions of pain-related problems (in this case fibromyalgia) may actually be detrimental (Thieme et al., 2006).

Conclusions

Chronic pain is an excellent example of where psychological factors significantly influence outcome following acute injury. Indeed psychosocial factors are generally regarded as at least as important as biomedical variables in the development of chronic pain and disability.

There is a growing body of evidence that CBT is effective in the management of chronic pain and should be applied early in the care pathway to optimise outcome. More specifically, the need to target those factors that act as barriers to successful management of pain in any given individual is gaining recognition. Whilst CBT has been shown to successfully modify these risk factors, there is only preliminary evidence indicating which specific techniques most effectively target any one particular risk factor to produce the best outcome.

Multiple sclerosis

MS is a chronic autoimmune disease of the central nervous system, resulting in demyelination. Damage to myelin, the protective sheath surrounding nerve fibres, interferes with messages within the brain and between the brain and other parts of the body. The illness can lead to a wide range of difficulties, including problems with sight, sensation, mobility, bladder and bowel control, co-ordination, cognitive functioning, sexual functioning and mood variability.

For some patients MS is characterised by periods of relapse and remission, while for others it has a progressive course. In all cases, a diagnosis of MS present patients with a variable condition, that has an unpredictable progression such that patients have to face the possibility of sudden increases in symptoms and disability at any time. Being diagnosed with MS presents patients with significant psychological challenges, requiring a huge emotional adjustment. As with all life-changing illnesses, living with MS has implications not just for the individual but also their families and wider social network.

Given the demands of the illness, it is of no surprise that patients with MS are more likely to experience psychological disorders than the general population. In fact, the prevalence of depression is high even when compared with other groups with physical illness. MS is also associated with higher rates of suicide (Siegert & Abernethy, 2005).

Depression in people with MS may be associated with specific brain lesions, although the relationship between the two is not strong and is poorly understood. However, it is important to be aware that the high rates of depression found in this patient group may not be entirely accounted for by psychosocial factors. Moreover, management of psychological disorders in people with MS will need to take account of individual cognitive and memory difficulties associated with the condition. These may play a role in the development of psychological difficulties and have implications for the effectiveness of CBT interventions. With this in mind, standard interventions may need to be adapted to meet the needs of individual patients. It is worth noting that, whilst this appears to be a contentious issue in the literature, studies have shown that moderate to severe depression may impair specific aspects of cognitive function in people with MS (for example, speed of information processing and working memory). It follows that some aspects of cognitive impairment may be modified by appropriate management of depression, although this is not yet substantiated through research studies.

Given that psychological disorders can impair quality of life for people with MS and exacerbate symptoms, there appears to be considerable scope for psychological intervention. Whilst a review of the literature reveals a paucity of research into the benefits of CBT with people with MS, a limited number of studies have explored a range of important issues.

1. Can CBT enhance quality of life?

Group psychological therapy including CBT strategies and physical exercise has been found to improve "depressive coping style", together with short-term improvement in "vitality and body dynamics" in patients with MS (Tesar et al., 2003). However, because the group therapy comprised a number of components it is not possible to ascertain the effects of CBT specifically in improving outcome in this study.

Schwartz (1999) found that a coping skills group promoted significant gains over time in psychosocial role performance, coping behaviour and numerous other aspects of wellbeing compared to peer telephone support. This intervention enabled participants to improve the quality of their lives despite the continued progression of the illness.

These two studies provide some evidence that CBT is associated with improvement in quality of life in people with MS, although further studies are required to determine the active ingredients in the process of change.

2. Is CBT effective in treating depression and anxiety in patients with MS?

Based on the results of a meta-analysis, Mohr and Goodkin (1999) conclude that patients with MS and depression respond well to treatment with either psychotherapy or antidepressant medication. They note that psychotherapy with an emphasis on coping skills is more likely to be effective than insight oriented therapy and that CBT is more effective than supportive-expressive group therapy (Mohr et al., 2001). This suggests that CBT interventions are likely to be most effective overall in treating depression in people with MS.

Consistent with the above, Bruggimann and Annoni (2004) conclude that CBT, including identification and modification of unhelpful thoughts and beliefs, activity scheduling and graded task assignment is an appropriate treatment for some anxious or depressed patients with MS. CBT has been shown to improve mood, anxiety, adherence to medication, and appraisal of self-control (Bruggimann & Annoni, 2004).

In addition, the benefits of treating depression also appear to generalise to improvements in subjective ratings of fatigue in patients with MS (Mohr et al., 2003) and improvements in the use of and satisfaction with social support (Mohr et al., 2004).

Conclusions

There is some evidence that CBT is effective in enabling people with MS to improve their quality of life. There is good evidence in particular that CBT is effective in treating depression and anxiety and in helping people adjust to, and cope with, having MS (Thomas et al., 2006). The benefits of treating psychological disorders in this group appear potentially to be far reaching. Further research may be able to clarify which components of CBT are most effective in treating psychological disorders in this patient group.

Diabetes

Diabetes is a condition in which the amount of glucose in the blood is elevated because the body cannot use it properly. In the short term, poor glycaemic control can be an immediate threat to life and in the long term it is associated with a range of unpleasant and potentially life threatening complications such as problems with the eyes, kidneys and nervous system.

There are two types of diabetes. In Type1 diabetes the body is unable to produce any insulin. This type of diabetes is associated with an early onset. In Type 2 diabetes the body can still make some insulin, but not enough, or insulin is produced that does not work properly. Type 2 diabetes is associated with a later onset, unhealthy lifestyles and obesity.

Whilst large-scale studies have demonstrated that strict glucose control can delay the onset and progression of long term complications (DCCT, UKPDS), given the consistently high level of self-management required to achieve this, the scope for psychosocial factors to influence outcome is substantial. Snoek and Skinner (2002) identify five main psychological problems that complicate the management of diabetes. These are depression, stress and anxiety, eating disorders, self-destructive behaviours and interpersonal/family conflicts.

Depression has been found to be more prevalent (Anderson et al., 2001), chronic and severe among people with diabetes than in the general population. Symptoms of depression such as loss of motivation are likely to present significant barriers to self-management and require early detection and management. Being diagnosed with diabetes is likely to be distressing, especially as the life long implications of the condition dawn on the patient. As well as being a trigger to depression, difficulties in adjusting to the diagnosis or being presented with complications may cause significant levels of stress and anxiety. Whilst no consistent relationship between stress levels and glucose control has yet been demonstrated, it is plausible that stress has the potential to disrupt glycaemic control both directly through the effects of stress hormones and indirectly via deterioration in self-care behaviours.

In addition to the role of stress in complicating the management of diabetes, more specific anxiety-related problems have also been identified. These include fear of hypoglycaemia and fear of long-term complications. Patients who are fearful of hypoglycaemia may be reluctant to maintain strict glycaemic control and this could become a barrier to self-management. Fear of future complications could become a trigger for obsessive self-management, including excessive self-monitoring. Whilst this could have positive implications for the patients' long term physical health, it is likely to undermine their quality of life at least in the short term and could lead to burn out with the condition. Conversely high levels of fear could result in cognitive and behavioural avoidance of diabetes-related issues leading to poor self-management.

Eating disorders are a further set of psychological difficulties that have serious implications for self-management of diabetes. Since good self-management is associated with weight gain, patients with eating disorders may manipulate their insulin in order to control their weight. There may also be issues connected with low self-esteem commonly found in people with eating disorders, including patients believing they deserve to be punished and withholding management to this end.

Self-destructive behaviours may also be associated with a range of other psychological issues and difficulties especially during adolescence. Rubin and Peyrot (1992) define self-destructive behaviours as chronic or periodic serious mismanagement of diabetes resulting in extremely high HbA_{1c} (an indicator of poor management), frequent episodes of diabetes ketoacidosis (DKAs) and recurrent severe hypoglycaemias. Poor self-management may be a form of help seeking behaviour, being used to elicit contact with health care professionals in patients with unmet psychological needs. Such patients often attract derision and contempt and a clear psychological formulation can go a long way to enabling a frustrated health care team to maintain a constructive approach.

Given the implications of diabetes for the patient's life both in the long and short term, living with diabetes is likely to affect other family members. They may for example have to take over management of the condition, including giving injections, when the patient becomes acutely unwell and unable to retain control. Witnessing "hypos" or living with the threat of future complications is likely to be very stressful. Family members may find it hard to balance the patient's need to enjoy life in the short term with the implications this may have for their health longer term. Management of the condition is highly likely to be subject not only to individual psychological issues but also to wider family dynamics.

In their review, Snoek and Skinner (2002) explore the extent to which psychological interventions improve outcome for people whose management of diabetes is affected by depression, stress and anxiety, eating disorders, self destructive behaviours and family dysfunction. They look at outcome both in terms of reduced distress and improved glycaemic control. A summary of key findings is presented below, supplemented with results from additional studies where applicable.

1. *Can CBT alleviate depression and improve glycaemic control?*
In a randomised controlled study, Lustman et al. (1998) showed that individual CBT was more effective in treating depression than antidepressant medication, in people with Type 2 diabetes, even controlling for the benefits of a diabetes education programme. The benefits of CBT remained greater than antidepressants at follow up. Whilst no differences in glycaemic control were seen between the groups post-treatment, by follow up the CBT group had lower levels of HbA_{1c}. This suggested that CBT not only reduced symptoms of depression, but was also more effective than antidepressant medication in improving the management of diabetes in this group.

In a more recent study, Piette (2005) explored CBT aimed at increasing activity levels in patients with diabetes and depression. Therapy was delivered individually by a CBT trained nurse-clinician in twelve weekly one-hour telephone sessions. Physical activity levels in these patients improved with an increase of 20 minutes walking at 3 miles per hour each day. Whilst this study had a small sample and was uncontrolled, it is a good example of an effective intervention to improve healthy living delivered by a nurse therapist who did not have face-to-face contact with the patients.

2. Can stress and anxiety management improve self-management?

As mentioned above, being diagnosed with diabetes and being faced with a lifetime of intensive self-management of the condition is potentially very stressful. In recognition of this, stress management has increasingly been incorporated into self-management programmes. A small number of studies have specifically explored the benefits of managing stress.

In a randomised controlled trial, Spiess et al. (1995) compared the effectiveness of an intensive programme to reduce distress at onset of diabetes with conventional education, in adults with Type 1 diabetes. The programme comprised two hospital visits plus group meetings starting one month following discharge. At three months follow-up, the treatment group were less depressed and less in denial than the comparison group. However, by longer term follow-up only the differences in denial were sustained and metabolic control did not differ between the two groups.

In a further study, Henry et al. (1997) compared the effectiveness of a combined cognitive behavioural stress management programme in improving anxiety and diabetic control in patients with Type 2 diabetes, with a waiting list control group. The treated group improved in terms of stress and anxiety but not glycaemic control.

The evidence suggests that cognitive behavioural stress management improves psychological symptoms, but no consistent evidence demonstrates that this leads to an improvement in glycaemic control.

3. Can CBT reduce fear of hypoglycaemia and fear of long-term complications?

In theory, traditional approaches to managing anxiety should be effective in addressing specific diabetes-related fears. However, whilst psycho-education has been shown to help patients lower their fear of hypoglycaemia (Gonder-Frederick et al., 2000) no studies applying CBT to fear of hypoglycaemia have been reported (Snoek & Skinner, 2002).

Group behaviour modification has been shown to reduce fear of long-term complications and increase acceptance of diabetes in patients with Type 1 diabetes, however, this did not lead to improvements in HbA_{1c} (Zettler et al., 1995).

CBT appears to be a useful approach for managing specific diabetes-related fears. It seems reasonable to suppose this would lead on to better self-management but this has not yet been established in research literature.

4. Can CBT enable patients to overcome needle phobias?

Needle phobias that result in avoidance of injecting insulin and self-monitoring through blood tests have serious implications for diabetes self-management. Whilst there is good evidence that CBT is effective with injection phobias (Ost et al., 1992), no controlled studies of needle phobias in diabetic patients have been reported (Snoek & Skinner, 2002). However, unless having diabetes presents special difficulties for treating needle phobias, it seems reasonable to assume that CBT will be effective with this population with implications for improving glycaemic control. Again, further research is needed to clarify this issue.

5. Is CBT effective in the management of eating disorders in patients with diabetes?

In their review, Snoek and Skinner (2002) found only two studies reporting the benefits of psychological treatment of eating disorders in diabetes. The first of these was a randomised controlled trial evaluating the effects of a psycho-educational programme in young women with Type 1 diabetes. The programme was successful in improving disordered eating attitudes but no improvement was found in terms of purging by insulin omission, or HbA_{1c} levels (Olmsted et al., 1997). The second study, also a randomised controlled trial, evaluated the effects of CBT group therapy on binge eating in women with Type 2 diabetes, compared to non-prescriptive therapy (NPT). Frequency of binge eating was found to predict HbA_{1c}. Binge eating decreased significantly in both groups by the end of treatment. However, the CBT group therapy was associated with fewer relapses at follow up (Kenardy et al., 2000).

The results are promising in terms of improving aspects of eating disorders in people with diabetes but studies to date have not found that this generalises to improvements in glycaemic control.

6. *Can CBT improve self-management of diabetes with patients exhibiting self-destructive behaviours?*

A range of psychotherapeutic approaches have been evaluated in relation to improving self-management of diabetes. In their review, Snoek and Skinner (2002) cite the following examples: hypnotherapy is superior to standard medical treatment in improving HbA_{1c} and fasting blood glucose in adolescents with Type 1 diabetes (Ratner, 1990); psychoanalytic treatment of children and adolescence with diabetes helps 'drive a wedge between their diabetes care and their neurotic difficulties resulting in improved glycaemic control (Fonargy & Moran, 1990); intensive patient education and treatment improves adult patients' mental coping ability but not glycaemic control (Viinameki et al., 1991); Relative to patient education from a nurse specialist, Cognitive Analytical Therapy (CAT) improves interpersonal functioning and more sustained, though not statistically significantly different changes in glycaemic control (Fosbury et al., 1997).

However, studies of the effectiveness of CBT more specifically in promoting self-management of diabetes in populations exhibiting self-destructive behaviours are more elusive with only one study being reported in Snoek and Skinner's review paper. This study, found that brief cognitive behavioural group training (CBGT) improved HbA_{1c} levels at long term follow up in patients with Type 1 diabetes (Snoek et al., 2001). The research findings suggest that in general psychological interventions are effective in improving self-management of diabetes, with evidence in favour of the benefits of hypnotherapy and psychoanalysis in particular. There is some evidence that CBT more specifically brings about positive change.

7. *Is family therapy incorporating elements of CBT effective in managing interpersonal conflicts associated with diabetes?*

As discussed earlier, diabetes is strongly associated with family stress and interpersonal conflicts. Research suggests that better family functioning is associated with less deterioration in glycaemic control and acute complications (Skinner et al., 2000) and a review of family function may be helpful when considering how to improve self-management in an individual.

In terms of outcome studies, Guthrie et al. (1990) found that progressive relaxation training in parents was effective in improving glycaemic control in children with diabetes in families described as highly distressed. Behavioural family therapy has been shown to be more effective than support groups or current therapy in improving family functioning and adherence to treatment. However, whilst the intervention led to improvements in glycaemic control, this deteriorated over time (Wysocki et al., 2000; Wysocki et al. 20001). It is concluded that behavioural family therapy appears to be more beneficial than support groups for targeting family conflicts (Wysocki et al., 1997).

Conclusions

The best available evidence suggests that CBT is effective in treating depression in patients with diabetes, leading to improved management of diabetes as measured by changes in HbA_{1c}. Preliminary data suggests that CBT addresses a range of other psychological factors known to complicate self-management of diabetes such as stress, anxiety, eating disorders and self-destructive behaviours but further work is required to determine whether this leads to an improvement in diabetes self-management and longer term outcomes. Family therapy containing behavioural elements appears to be effective in resolving family conflicts but not improving glycaemic control (Snoek & Skinner, 2002).

Chronic Obstructive Pulmonary Disease

Chronic Obstructive Pulmonary Disease (COPD) is a serious and largely irreversible illness characterised by a progressive reduction in functioning due to symptoms such as fatigue and breathlessness (dyspnoea). The term includes both emphysema, which results from destruction of the alveolar walls and obstructive bronchitis, which results from destruction of the small airways. Not only does it impair quality of life but it is also associated with high rates of re-admission to hospital and therefore has significant cost implications.

Anxiety, panic disorder and depression are common problems for people with COPD and compound the impact of the disease on quality of life. They may also increase admission rates to hospital, delay discharge and reduce uptake of therapeutic activities requiring physical exertion. Given the implications of psychological disorders for quality of life and health care resources, there are good reasons why psychological disorders associated with COPD deserve careful management. However, is CBT effective in addressing such difficulties in people with COPD?

A typical mode of service delivery for people with COPD is multidisciplinary rehabilitation programmes that incorporate exercise training, patient education and psychosocial interventions (for example, stress management). Such programmes are generally regarded as efficacious in improving health status and quality of life (American Thoracic Society, 1999). However, the role of psychosocial interventions, and more specifically, CBT, in producing change is less clear. In their paper exploring the role of anxiety and depression in COPD, Stanley et al. (2005) cite three studies that have shown that psychosocial interventions (for example, education, relaxation and cognitive techniques) reduce anxiety and depressive symptoms and increase functional status among patients with COPD (for example, Blake et al., 1990; de Godoy & de Godoy, 2003; Gift et al., 1992). However, other studies have reported that psychosocial interventions add no benefit over and above other traditional rehabilitation strategies (for example, Sassi-Dambron et al., 1995). Stanley et al. (2005) point out that none of the studies focused on patients with clinically significant levels of anxiety or depressive symptoms and as we noted earlier this may have limited the scope for change.

When considering CBT models of anxiety and panic, it becomes readily apparent that there is significant scope for anxiety, panic and respiratory symptoms to exacerbate one another. Dyspnoea is likely to be a trigger for anxiety and panic and, in turn, catastrophic misinterpretation of symptoms is likely to exacerbate respiratory problems. This would suggest that CBT interventions developed from CBT models of anxiety and panic should be applicable to the management of anxiety and panic associated with COPD. However, is this substantiated by the research literature?

A number of studies have explored the effectiveness of CBT in reducing anxiety in people with COPD. For example, Kunik, et al. (2001) assessed the effectiveness of CBT comprising a single two-hour group session including relaxation training, cognitive interventions and graduated practice, followed by homework and weekly telephone calls for six weeks, compared with an educational intervention. They found that CBT produced superior results in terms of reduction in anxiety and depressive symptoms, although this did not lead to changes in physical functioning.

Eiser et al. (1997) found that patients with COPD and co-existent anxiety treated with psychotherapy that combined education about the role of anxiety in breathlessness with coping skills (for example, relaxation training) aimed at anxiety reduction had increased exercise tolerance relative to a comparison group.

There is therefore some evidence that CBT interventions are effective in reducing anxiety associated with COPD.

Whilst these results are encouraging, a number of methodological shortcomings mean that conclusions about the efficacy of CBT in improving outcome for people with COPD must be drawn somewhat tentatively. Following a review of the literature, Rose et al. (2002) conclude that there is a lack of consistent evidence that psychologically based interventions reduced anxiety in COPD. They point out that whilst some studies did produce significant results, they had differences in baseline indices making assessment of change difficult. Further, a variety of measures were used across studies making it difficult to clearly define the patients in terms of disease severity, subjective experience of dyspnoea and the extent of anxiety. Consequently, they were unable to perform meta-analysis to produce a global indication of intervention effectiveness. However, Rose et al. (2002) point out that theoretical models suggest that CBT should be effective in treating anxiety and panic in this patient group with implications for enhancing quality of life and it may well be that further research will substantiate this claim, once more specific hypotheses are tested, teasing apart the ways in which CBT can address such difficulties.

Furthermore, many of the studies included in their review did not give sufficient follow up intervals to measure changes that might take place in the long term. Where symptoms have developed over many years, it seems reasonable to speculate that the full effects of interventions may take some time to be realised. Longer term follow up might therefore yield more promising results. Long term follow up may also be required to observe any generalisation of the benefits of reducing anxiety and depressive symptoms to enhancing other aspects of quality of life in populations with COPD.

Finally, in a useful report of preliminary data from a multi-component CBT treatment programme, Stanley et al. (2005) discuss individual differences in response to treatment and highlight how different patients can benefit from different treatment components. It may be that studies of individually tailored approaches to managing anxiety and panic in populations with COPD would also yield more effective results than studies comparing standardised group treatments.

Conclusions

There is some evidence that CBT-based interventions are a useful component of rehabilitation, leading to a reduction in psychological symptoms and improved physical functioning. There are strong theoretical grounds for applying CBT to the management of anxiety and panic in people with COPD although this is not yet substantiated by a clear and consistent body of evidence. Nonetheless some smaller scale studies have produced interesting findings, suggesting that the patient experience can be improved with relatively low cost implications. There are reasons to suppose that longer term follow up might yield better results.

Parkinson's Disease (PD)

Parkinson's disease (PD) is a progressive neurological condition with debilitating symptoms. The symptoms include slowness and difficulty in initiating and executing movements, resting tremor, rigidity, postural instability and cognitive impairment. There are broad reaching implications for all areas of daily life, including speech, gait, sleep, sexual functioning and self care. Perhaps not surprisingly, given its fluctuating and unpredictable course, many people with PD develop symptoms of anxiety and depression and rates of depression may be even higher than in groups with other long term illnesses. In turn, psychological distress is likely to result in an increase in PD-related symptoms such as trembling and immobility.

In addition to the scope for adjustment difficulties, PD also has features that are observable to the outside word, such as lack of facial expression and tremor. For some individuals this causes embarrassment and even a sense of shame and such emotions could precipitate social withdrawal. Problems with facial expression could also lead to others misinterpreting the patient or even making rude comments, both of which will compound social anxiety. The prospect of being dependent on family members may also induce feelings of guilt or of being a burden and maintaining a positive self image is a major challenge. Finally, a fear of falling, which is a real possibility, may also be an issue for some people with PD and there is scope here for a vicious cycle to arise whereby psychological symptoms increase the likelihood of falling and vice versa. There are therefore a number of ways in which CBT could be helpful in alleviating psychological distress in individuals with PD such as managing symptoms of depression, addressing issues around shame, guilt and social withdrawal and tackling anxiety associated with falling or with uncertainty about the future.

Whilst the high rates of depression in people with PD could reflect difficulties adjusting to the illness, depression in PD might be mediated by neurological changes associated with the disease itself, for example, as a result of changes in serotonergic pathways. Psychological issues may also result from the side effects of treatment. Levodopa can cause motor complications and feelings of doom, helplessness and hopelessness are associated with sudden inability to move (the "off" period of motor complications). It is not clear whether the changes in mood associated with motor freezing reflect a psychological reaction to these motor changes or whether changes in mood might be mediated by altered dopamine levels.

PD is more prevalent in older populations. This in itself is not a barrier to effective CBT and neither is a suspicion that the psychological symptoms have a biological cause/contribution. As with any individual, patients with PD benefit from a careful assessment of their individual needs. However, it is important to be alert to particular difficulties associated with the effects of phase and subtype of the illness, the decline in health, the severity of disability and any co-morbid illness. Cognitive impairments may also mean that CBT techniques have to be adapted to optimise outcome, for example, frontal lobe dysfunction could lead to impaired capacity for self-talk, an increased likelihood of making literal interpretations of situations, and difficulties processing and retaining new information (Crews & Harrison, 1995). Adaptations recommended by these authors include encouraging the patient to verbalise rational thoughts, having frequent discussions of abstract thinking, involving carers in sessions to support between session homework and providing written information.

Studies exploring the effectiveness of CBT for psychological disorders associated with PD are scarce but have produced some positive findings. Ellgring et al. (1993), for example, examined the usefulness of CBT techniques including stress management, cognitive restructuring, social skills training, modelling, role-play and relaxation training. Skills were taught to both patients and caregivers in a series of five two-hour seminars held over a course of two to three months. Seventy-four per cent of participants were found to use relaxation techniques and positive self-instruction in every day life. However, the effect of this on the management of depressive symptoms was not measured. Interestingly, the authors found that the size of the group patients attended affected outcome. Those who attended groups of five or six people used strategies more often than those attending larger groups.

Dreisig et al. (1999) compared the effectiveness of individually tailored CBT with a comparison group who received treatment as usual in patients with PD. The group who received CBT improved on a range of outcome measures relative to the comparison group. With only nine participants the sample size was small, however, the benefits of tailoring treatment seem to have been borne out by the results of this pilot study.

Feeney et al. (2005) found group CBT to be effective in treating depression and anxiety in people with PD and the benefits were sustained at one month follow-up. The sample size was very small (n = 4) and the study lacked a comparison group so it is not possible to deduce whether the CBT intervention was effective relative to other non-specific therapeutic factors.

In recognition of the implications of cognitive impairments such as executive dysfunction for the application of CBT, Dobkin et al. (2006) evaluated the effectiveness of a modified CBT intervention. The intervention included three to four separate caregiver psychoeducational sessions dispersed throughout the course of CBT for depression in PD. All three patients included in the study demonstrated clinically significant improvements in depression and a reduction in negative cognitions. There were minimal improvements in anxiety. Caregivers demonstrated a notable improvement in techniques for recognising and responding to patients' negative thoughts.

In a more recent study, incorporating a larger sample (n = 15), Dobkin et al. (2007) evaluated a modified CBT treatment that included a separate intervention for caregivers, focusing on strategies for offering social support, and ways to respond to patients' negative thoughts. As with the earlier study, patients experienced a significant reduction in depressive symptoms and negative cognitions. They also reported an increased perception of social support. Gains were maintained at one month follow-up. Whilst the results of such small scale and uncontrolled studies need replicating before any firm conclusions can be drawn, these preliminary results suggest that CBT can be beneficial to patients with PD who have cognitive impairments, through involving partners in treatment.

Conclusions

Very little research has explored the efficacy of CBT in addressing the multiple difficulties associated with PD and what has done has been compromised by small sample sizes and a lack of comparison groups. Whilst there is evidence that CBT is effective in reducing psychological symptoms, it is difficult to determine which components of CBT are effective in addressing different aspects of the experience of living with PD. Nonetheless, the interesting studies described above highlight the importance of tailoring interventions to meet the unique needs of individuals and suggest that, with appropriate modification, such as involving partners, CBT can be helpful to patients with cognitive impairments.

For an excellent review of the feasibility of using CBT for depression associated with Parkinson's disease, the reader is referred to a paper by Cole and Vaughan (2005). This describes eloquently the many ways in which PD affects people's lives, the issues that may arise in therapy and suggestions as to how to modify interventions to accommodate symptoms of the disease.

General conclusions

So what can we conclude from exploring the literature regarding the efficacy of applying CBT to a range of life changing illnesses? First, we learnt that there is an impressive evidence base for the effectiveness of CBT with a range of psychological difficulties arising in a mental health context. We then went on to explore the evidence more specifically in relation to various life changing illnesses. It was argued that there is no reason to assume that the evidence base for psychological difficulties in a mental health context does not apply to difficulties associated with life-changing illness, providing the implications of the illness are taken into account and the approach suitably modified. Given this, and the strong theoretical grounds for applying CBT to life-changing illnesses, it seemed reasonable to assume CBT would be effective in relation to life-changing illness.

However, the evidence, whilst being very promising is perhaps not as extensive as one would hope, largely due to a lack of research. There appears to be evidence that CBT can improve aspects of quality of life across a range of illnesses, including cancer, diabetes and MS, can improve life expectancy after myocardial infarction, can play a role in preventing the development of chronic pain and disability following acute injury and can be adapted to work effectively with people with cognitive impairments. There is some evidence that CBT can be a cost effective mode of intervention and that it can be administered successfully by therapists of different backgrounds. On the other hand, for some aspects of life-changing illness very little high quality research has been conducted so little is known about how the benefits of improving psychological wellbeing might generalise to improving outcome. For instance, in theory reducing psychological barriers to self-management of diabetes should lead to better diabetes control and therefore better health outcomes in the longer term; but there is a paucity of research addressing this issue. Evidence that CBT improves physical health would almost certainly help to attract funding and support to apply CBT within medical settings.

As discussed earlier, the research method used can lead to the effectiveness of an intervention being overestimated, such as when a lack of comparison groups makes it difficult to know whether the "effective" intervention was actually better than unstructured support or even simply time spent with the practitioner. In other studies the research method may have masked the effectiveness of the intervention, such as when data is collected before the intervention has had time to take full effect or when sample size means the study lacked statistical power.

It is important that studies are critiqued rigorously, to ensure that in due course, high quality evidence emerges. It is reasonable to assume that in time further research will expand the body of evidence supporting the effectiveness of cognitive behavioural approaches with life-changing illnesses, giving clearer pointers as to which specific interventions will be effective with specific presenting issues and the extent to which addressing psychosocial issues in life-changing illness will improve not only patients' emotional wellbeing but their physical health too. In the meantime, we can be confident that CBT is in general an effective form of psychological therapy with much to offer people with life-changing illness.

In the final section of this chapter we will consider some of the practical implication of applying research findings to clinical practice.

Applying research findings to clinical practice: some pointers

At the start of this chapter we briefly discussed the importance of evidence-based practice in a contemporary health service. In theory, we identify the nature of the patient's presenting problem and turn to the literature to determine the treatment of choice. Where we are dealing with clearly defined problems that can be closely mapped onto problem areas that have been thoroughly researched with clear findings and implications for treatment or management in the research literature, this is relatively straightforward. However, a number of difficulties arise when applying research findings to real life, especially in relation to psychosocial research.

1. If a particular issue has been explored, the research method is often flawed and findings inconsistent or down right contradictory.
2. Our patients often are not a good match for those who have been samples in research studies. They may be of a different age, gender, ethnic origin or marital status or they may have more than one problem that seems to complicate management of both problems. This makes it hard to determine the extent to which the research evidence is applicable.
3. Many studies either describe interventions in vague terms, for example, "psychosocial approach" or incorporate so many elements it becomes hard to determine which ingredients were the effective ones that could be used in a typical, brief clinic session.
4. A lack of comparison groups means we cannot assume that non-specific therapeutic factors, such as being nice to the patient, were not the active ingredients and perhaps the very thing we should be striving to provide.

5. Whilst some well designed and robust studies consistently point in favour of certain approaches for certain problems, we do well to remember that it would be a rare study indeed that found that all patients improved on all measures.

6. A particular intervention may have been shown to be effective when applied within a group context but not necessarily in individual work. This does not mean it is not effective in a one-to-one setting but careful consideration needs to be given as to whether the active ingredients of the group therapy have been identified and can be replicated in one to one work. We should not, for example, underestimate the potential benefits of non-specific factors such as group membership in effecting change.

7. We must be careful to present this evidence base clearly to patients. At best treatments have usually only been demonstrated to work for a certain percentage of individuals and we must be careful not to overstate findings.

All of the above (and you may well think of more issues) should not put us off striving to apply evidence based practice in our daily work. Rather we need to be aware of the picture presented overall within the literature, draw intelligent analogies in presenting problems to fill in the gaps, and take care not to overstate the evidence when discussing treatment options with patients.

In our clinical practice we need to develop a carefully individualised treatment approach based on a thorough assessment and carefully devised formulation. The evidence base will highlight areas to be explored with a particular patient, helping us focus in on pertinent issues but we must remain receptive to the patient's unique and individual experience. Treatment options should be elucidated by the formulation process described in a later chapter with due consideration being given to the evidence-base for different approaches. No approach should be discarded simply because there is a lack of research evidence in favour of it. However, we do need to be able to justify the approach we adopt and show a rationale for the intervention selected, especially if it goes against the current evidence-base. Progress with any patient should be carefully evaluated to gauge the effectiveness of the approach taken and interventions should be adjusted in the light of this information.

Exercises

Before you proceed to the next chapter it is important that you take time to do the exercises included at the end of this chapter. To use this book properly you need to complete all the recommended exercises.

Exercises

Conduct a literature search to identify articles that explore the efficacy of CBT with a long-term condition of your choice.

1. Consider which search terms you will use. Examples include: the name of the condition, CBT, psychosocial interventions, coping, quality of life and psychological disorders.

Remember broader terms widen the search and specific terms narrow the search. If you get few results, broaden the search and try a different spelling or substitute a different word with a very similar meaning, for example, depression, depressive symptoms, mood disorders, depressive disorders may yield different results.

2. Check out the use of terms such as "and /or" in broadening or narrowing the search, for example, "depression <u>and</u> CBT <u>and</u> psychotherapy" will yield different results from "depression <u>and</u> CBT <u>or</u> psychotherapy". Look at the differences in results that are produced by varying these terms.

3. Access a variety of data bases such as: Cochrane Database, MEDLINE, PsychINFO and CINAHL and again note the differences in results obtained.

4. Select a relevant research article to study in detail.

When reading the article, actively evaluate the quality of the research in terms of

1. Sample size.

2. Whether or not the research method includes appropriate comparison groups allowing you to determine which aspects of treatment were the effective ingredients of change.

3. Consider whether the results, even if statistically significant, are clinically significant findings justifying the resource input required to make the changes.

4. Ask yourself whether you would accept this treatment based on this particular study?

5. Do the findings fit current theory? Do they contradict earlier findings? Is there a consistent picture building within the literature?

6. Is the sample representative of the patients you plan to treat or are there reasons to suppose that CBT worked with the sample under study for specific reasons that may not be applicable to your patients?

Chapter 4

Communication Skills in Health Care

In order to make a positive contribution to the patient's psychological wellbeing it is essential that health care professionals can communicate well.

This may seem an obvious statement to make with regard to all aspects of health care work with patients. Research evidence supports the common sense view that people are more cooperative if they understand what is happening to them. It also indicates that fewer mistakes and misunderstandings occur when the communication between a health professional and a patient is rated as good. Often the other skills of health care professionals will be judged in large part on their perceived skills as communicators by members of the public.

However, it is not the layman's opinion that usually counts in professional career progression; it is the good regard of professional peers that is most important in this context. So it is possible to be highly skilled and well thought of despite having poor communication skills with patients and carers. Nevertheless whilst it is possible to get away with not improving these skills, an absence of criticism, good professional standing and long years of experience are not sufficient reason for assuming that one's personal communication skills are satisfactory.

Furthermore, health care professionals spend a lot of their time communicating with each other and often socialise together. They live in a special sub-culture of illness and death involved in and witnessing things that other people barely know about; they acquire a different and detailed understanding of how the body works and how it malfunctions; and they use technical language and procedures that are outside general understanding. Consequently, once immersed in this sub-culture, it can be hard to retain good communication skills and a clear perspective on what might be "normal" for people who are not part of that health care sub-culture.

In this chapter we will not attempt to replicate or summarise the abundant literature on how to be a good communicator although further recommended reading at the end of the chapter will offer some guidance. Key points are summarised under appropriate headings in the Techniques section of the book as referred to later in this chapter.

Instead, here we will attempt to examine some of the issues and themes that underpin the need for good communication skills and why well-intentioned and potentially good communicators do, at times, come unstuck.

Time constraints and the need for action

Our communication skills are the basic tools that offer access to the patient's problems and they also provide our primary method for assisting with them. This book can be viewed as being entirely about communication skills and putting them to work for the patient's benefit. However, it would also be possible to attempt to use material in this book as a set of problem-solving strategies to be applied in a standardised fashion as and when specified problems present.

Whilst the emphasis on communication may seem more personally attractive and politically correct, can we afford to neglect the more immediately action-orientated problem-solving approach? There is often a feeling that this "do-something" pressure comes directly from the patient and that we will fail in our role unless we respond to it straight away. Furthermore, as most health care professionals are working under considerable time constraints they are inclined to believe that the quicker they come up with a "solution" or coping technique the better for all concerned. This action-orientation feels like the professionally responsible thing to do and that the finer elements of good communication skills should be of lesser priority:

Pauline is 59 and has been sitting in her chair doing very little since she was told that she suffers from angina. She is lost in her thoughts, cries quite a lot and seems to be fearful of any form of exertion. This has been going on for several weeks now and her husband has become quite worried which is why they are visiting their GP who is very sympathetic, assures Pauline that lots of people are frightened by this diagnosis but that regular exercise is important. She suggests that Pauline gets back into her usual domestic routines and responsibilities as soon as possible. Pauline and her husband took five minutes to describe the situation and Pauline's GP took about five minutes to reassure and advise her. None of it felt rushed and the GP was very caring and concerned in her manner. So, if the problem for Pauline was one of misunderstanding the nature of angina and the hazardousness of activity, then this brief health education exercise and guidance will probably have been quite useful to her. But do we or the GP know enough to be sure that this was her problem and that this action plan was the right one? What were the thoughts that Pauline was so lost in? Why did they make her cry? What does she understand about angina? Does she have any other misconceptions about it? Why did Pauline's husband attend the appointment with her? Are there other things about her mood and behaviour that are worrying him?

It may have taken the whole ten minute interview and a bit more besides for Pauline's GP to get the answers to all of these questions. Then there would still have been more time required to discuss the information, offer advice and develop a suitable plan of action. It could have been simply a slower route to get to the same point and therefore seemingly a very inefficient use of time. However, this caring GP would have been appalled if she had discovered that Pauline had left that consultation believing that she had just been told to "stop dwelling, lots of people go through this and you've just got to get on with it".

For Pauline this harsh interpretation is the first of three potential problems regarding this consultation. The second is its narrow focus and very specific guidance. By being so precisely directive the GP has left little scope for Pauline to justify following up on this. Pauline believes she has been given instructions and that there is the expectation that she will go away, do it and it will work; if she does not do it then she thinks that will be seen as being unco-operative, she then gets what she deserves and there is no "legitimate" reason for going back to the GP. On the other hand, if she does comply with the advice and it fails to make much difference then it still remains the only specific advice offered for this situation, so there is not much point in troubling the GP with it again anyway as it simply confirms Pauline in her view that this is what she is now stuck with for life.

The third problem with this consultation for Pauline is that she remains detached from what she is being asked to do. Her husband is worried about her and her GP has a plan for helping, but what does Pauline want? If she follows this advice, is it to help stop her husband from worrying, or to please her GP? Or is she meant to follow it for some other reason? Whatever the reason might be, it is far from clear and yet Pauline is expected to co-operate in quite a demanding course of action. She is unlikely to find this easy, so her motivation needs to be quite high. She will find it hard to motivate herself unless she understands something of how this course of action might help and believes in it sufficiently to considering it "worth a try".

Our well-meaning GP may be lucky. Perhaps Pauline went home reassured and confident that with support, encouragement and a watchful eye from her husband she can now get back to normal. However, the GP has risked being misinterpreted because she did not take the time to check back with Pauline what Pauline had understood. She has also risked being kept in the dark about what happens next because her confidently directive style did not encourage Pauline to believe that different things help different people and so to be experimental, reporting back on what does and does not seem helpful. Finally, she has risked perpetuating a state of passive dependency in Pauline by setting out a plan and not encouraging Pauline to take responsibility and ownership of a plan of her own making which she (Pauline) considers worthy of an investment in time and effort.

Rooting out misunderstanding and erroneous assumptions, discovery through discussion and experimentation, and a collaborative effort to identify the patient's personal goals lie at the core of good communication skills in a cognitive behavioural approach whether the contact is a fifty minute in-depth interview or a ten minute surgery consultation.

Fundamental Principles

There are some fundamental principles of good communication in every day life that deserve specific mention because they can be surprisingly hard to adhere to in a health care setting.

1. *Preserving dignity* can be hard when someone is ill, especially when that person requires care and health checks that are intrusive and embarrassing. This may seem very clear when we are considering undressing for an examination or in the use of bedpans. Whilst less immediately obvious it also includes coping with personal questioning and opinions, and situations where emotions are laid bare. It is important to show sensitivity to the potential loss of dignity and make efforts to preserve it, even at the expense, momentarily, of persisting with necessary lines of enquiry. However, the temptation can be to avoid exploring these difficult areas altogether. Sensitivity helps, avoidance does not, whether we are talking about questions or bedpans!

2. *Compassion* needs to be shown with even the most difficult and demanding of patients. Loss of dignity, vulnerability, despair, fear, pain and even cognitive impairments may account for uncharacteristically unreasonable behaviour. Some are stronger and braver than others; the less resilient need to be understood and supported without feeling critically compared to others. Similarly, social and cultural norms may influence emotional responses, behaviour and expecta-

tions. Tolerance, sympathetic understanding and acceptance of differences are the hallmarks of a compassionate approach. But it is not a license for turning a "blind-eye" to problems. Sensitively setting boundaries of appropriate conduct and heightening awareness to the effects of certain responses on other people (including ourselves) also fit well within a compassionate approach.

3. *Privacy* is a prerequisite for any communication involving personal disclosure. It is quite normal for people to be reluctant to speak openly and frankly when they feel they may be overheard by others. The presence of other family members or friends will also influence what is said and how the person behaves. Poor sound-proofing and being observable will inhibit communication and generate distractions as well as denying the possibility of confidentiality. Despite being inappropriate, bedside and cubicle conversations when the patient can be seen and overheard are quite usual in hospital health care. This is undesirable with a cognitive behavioural approach and every effort should be made to avoid it if at all possible when working with these methods. Similarly, in community health care, it is common for other family members to be present or intruding on conversations with the patient. Health care professionals often feel that it is not appropriate to dictate what happens in someone else's home. Whilst this is of course true, it is also important to bear in mind that it is not appropriate to carry out treatment procedures (including a cognitive behavioural approach) in an unsafe manner or under unsuitable conditions which, without privacy, is now the case. Asserting clinical requirements as for a medical procedure is probably the best way of thinking about it at such a moment.

4. *Confidentiality* is frequently a concern when people begin to make personal disclosures. Lack of privacy, sharing of information, access to notes and disclosures to other family members are all issues which need to be constructively addressed before embarking on sensitive interviewing and conversation. When information is shared with colleagues there needs to be a similar understanding to ensure that they do not inadvertently breach the agreement with the patient. When using a cognitive behavioural approach, much of the information and discussion content is only of relevance to those directly involved in this activity; discretion should be exercised as to what information needs to be shared with the wider health care team and some information (such as notes, diaries and record forms) may most appropriately remain with the patient. Demands from close relatives for more information should be referred back to the patient. Also, confidential disclosures from these people that cannot be shared with the patient should be discouraged. These are problematic because they breach the trusting and honest relationship with the patient and often supply information that is ultimately unhelpful because it cannot be used without betraying the confidence.

5. *Honesty* is an important part of professional integrity and cannot be sacrificed without harming the therapeutic relationship. Colluding with others to mislead the patient (even in the patient's "best interests") undermines a cognitive behavioural approach and should lead to a termination of this type of psychological intervention. But is colluding with the patient's self-protective deceit or denial similarly incompatible with a cognitive behavioural approach? The collaborative approach has already been identified as being at the core of good cognitive behavioural communication, but that is by no means the same as collusion. A cognitive behavioural approach can probably be successfully maintained as long as there are constructive plans to be worked on in an open and honest way and the "collusion" is no more than passive acceptance of the deceit or denial by the health care professional. However, positive therapeutic value will be lost if the health care professional is expected to actively support the denial or deceit in order to maintain a collaborative approach. Under any circumstances where honesty has to be sacrificed to maintain contact (and in the rich mix of human experiences there are occasionally situations where this could be necessary for good health care reasons), it should be recognised that the particular

health care professional caught up in this role should not be the one to engage in the use of the cognitive behavioural approach.

6. *Setting boundaries* needs time and attention at the outset of new interactions with a patient because it may be hard for her or him to determine appropriate expectations. For a moment, put yourself in the place of someone who does not work in health care. Most people have the good fortune to have had very limited exposure to health care professionals: occasional visits to the GP surgery for a seven minute consultation, general chats with health visitors who came to the house when the children were babies and a very few but memorable dramas and seemingly interminable waits in A&E with nasty cuts and broken bones. But do any of these experiences provide a suitable reference point for what to expect of a visit to or from a health care professional who (whether you know it or not) intends to discuss the full implications of your life-changing illness and its psychological impact? Even for those whose health problems have caused them to have a lifetime of visits to one specialist service or another, there will be a set of expectations about this latest contact that will not necessarily be relevant to your role or the implementation of a cognitive behavioural approach. It can seem awkward to begin with if you have never done it before but it will be helpful to the patient in deciding how best to use the time or even to choose not to proceed at all if you identify what is going to happen during the interview (the agenda), how long it will last (including whether it is a one-off contact or part of a planned series) and what may be relevant issues to raise (in relation to your role and purpose for visiting).

The Communication Skills Sets

Bernie is 70 years old and has been married to Grace since they were both 20 and not long before he was diagnosed with a chronic heart condition. They have never really understood exactly what this condition is but have learnt to put up with it and adapt their lives accordingly. They decided not to have children in case he passed it on and to avoid making him worse. Life has been sad and rather hard but they have always remained close and stoical. In the past few years Bernie's condition has steadily worsened, severely limiting his activities and causing several medical emergencies requiring hospitalisation and blood transfusions. His breathing has become laboured and his voice is rather weak. He has lost a lot of weight and looks frail and elderly. Currently he is back in hospital and has had another blood transfusion but seems less resilient. The young doctor has told him that it is only what he should expect. The nurse, who calls him "Jim", sorted out his toilet needs and helped him get tidy and sat in his bedside chair for Grace's arrival. She pulls the curtain between Bernie's bed and the occupied one next to him as Grace arrives and she tells Grace to cheer him up because he's been fretting too much. She then leaves them to be alone together. But, the staff are also concerned that Grace is too "clingy" and is not being realistic about her own future after his death and that she ought to be doing more. There has been some discussion about giving them a break from each other by arranging some respite care and Bernie has been told about this prior to his wife's arrival. As Grace is chatting about the garden and what the dog has been up to the ward sister comes up and softly asks if "Gracie" can come and have a word with her. Grace looks frightened and Bernie begins to cry quietly.

Building the communication to the point of meaningful psychological involvement (therapeutic engagement) involves several communication skill sets: respectfulness skills, effective communication skills, listening skills and basic counselling skills. Figure 1.4.1 illustrates the model.

In order for effective communication to occur there needs to be a degree of mutual respect and trust. If either party finds it hard to respect the opinions of the other then communication between them is likely to become difficult. Feeling disrespected by the other will similarly produce barriers to good communication. See Technique: Respectfulness skills for further details on establishing a respectful and trusting relationship.

Developing and sustaining the respectful relationship will in part depend on effectively communicating the necessary information in a clear and understandable manner. However, in order to strengthen the respect, it is necessary to show a willingness to change or add to what is being communicated in response to the information coming from the other person. See Technique: Effective communication for further details.

In order for the two-way flow of information, ideas and opinions to become effective communication it is, of course, necessary to be good at listening to each other. Good listening skills therefore form the third vital component of the basic communications skills sets. Demonstrating that one is listening is also important feedback to the other person that the communication flow is functioning properly. See Technique: Listening skills for further information.

Rapport has been established when one has a trusting and respectful relationship in which it is easy to talk and feel listened to. Without rapport it will be hard to develop a proper understanding of the psychological issues. Once rapport has developed, it becomes possible to encroach further into areas of emotional sensitivity. The basic counselling enquiry skills are described in Technique: Basic counselling skills.

If we return to Bernie and Grace, how well are the ward team doing with their communication skills?

We can give them almost full marks for observing **the fundamental principles** we have already described. They are sensitive to Bernie's dignity and privacy needs, they are

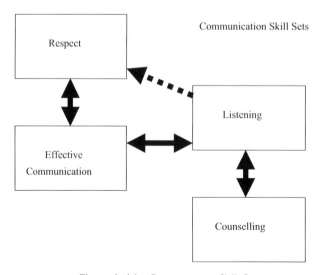

Figure 1.4.1 Communication Skill sSets

sympathetic and compassionate about the couple's present circumstances and eager to find some way of helping that extends beyond this present hospital stay. They are being honest about Bernie's changing situation and wish to discuss this privately with each partner and Grace is being invited somewhere quiet and confidential by the ward sister who has made time to have this discussion without interruption.

That is as good as it gets.

The ward team are confronted by some surprising emotional reactions from a couple who they have come to regard as quiet and undemanding "model patients". If we jump forward ten minutes in this scenario we see that despite the best efforts of the ward sister, the interview with Grace is not going well: she is meeting strong resistance to the plan, together with tears and some anger when she tries to confront Grace's stubborn determination not to face the reality of her situation. Bernie, too, has continued to be distressed and is trying to say that he wants to die in his own bed although the other nurse, who is comforting him and telling him not to upset himself because some respite care will be good for both of them, does not hear this clearly.

So where has it all gone wrong?

In terms of the **communication skill sets** identified above there are a lot of problems. We can examine each in turn:

1. *Respect*. Whilst Bernie and Grace have been known and well liked by ward staff, there is little evidence of them being respected at all. Their personal situation has been discussed and evaluated as "problematic" and Grace labelled as "clingy". Nobody has established whether or not the couple are happy with their present lifestyle arrangements and plans for the future. Because they have not asked, they will not know that this couple have long acknowledged that Bernie will probably die first and never really expected him to live as long as he has. Their great hope now is that he will live long enough for them to celebrate their golden wedding anniversary. There is a tacit understanding that Grace will go to live with her widowed sister when Bernie dies: the two couples were always close.

  They have been stereotyped as a sad and lonely but lovable old couple. Even Grace has been patronised as a "model patient" and no one has taken the trouble to discover that "James" is Bernie's first name but that he has never used it or its shortened form. He was too unwell to say anything the first time he was admitted and called "Jim" but he has now got used to it as his "hospital name", so he and Grace share a quiet joke about it. "Gracie" on the other hand is a private affectionate name that he uses with his wife at times of intimacy and seriousness. He was deeply upset when he heard the ward sister use it. She happened to hear him call his wife "Gracie" on one of his very bad days recently.

  The situation between the ward sister and Grace deteriorated in their interview when Grace got upset and accused the hospital of trying to take Bernie away from her and the sister had to raise her voice to tell Grace that she had got it all wrong and needed to calm down. Again this showed a lack of respect for Grace's point of view and distress. Talking over somebody is a device for dominating and is also very disrespectful.

  There are other features we could cite as evidence of poor respect but enough points have been made to identify that the ward team will have made errors of judgement because of their lack of respect for this couple. Similarly, the couple will have picked up enough information to know that staff friendliness does not extend to respect and that there are things best kept to themselves.

2. *Effective communication.* In this example the lack of respect has already led to stereotyping, judgemental attitudes and unfounded assumptions, so however carefully the ward sister proceeds

with her interview she is destined to fail as an effective communicator. She has not asked the right questions to be in command of her facts, so lacks the credibility to impart information, let alone offer advice. More fundamentally, she has not established what Grace and Bernie already know and what else they need to know if she is to proceed constructively with her own planned agenda for this meeting. At the same time the other nurse is failing to communicate her reassurance effectively because Bernie is talking about dying whilst she's saying "don't upset yourself". Previously the young doctor has made assumptions about what Bernie knows and understands; he has made vague comments about "what you should expect" but has not elaborated on this nor encouraged Bernie to ask questions. Everyone assumes that because Bernie has been ill with a chronic condition for 50 years then someone has already explained it all to him, forgetting that (as Bernie said it to a friend once) "in the old days people didn't used to ask those sorts of questions and you just did what the doctor told you. Ever since it has never seemed the right time to ask and besides, they are ever so busy".

Communication will have been impaired further by the lack of preparation. Although the team had discussed what they wanted to communicate and the ward sister had made a plan as to how she was going to approach this, there had been no preparation time for Grace. Bernie has been told the plan and left to think about it until Grace knows, but Grace is feeling put on the spot to make a decision and is quite shocked, having hoped to hear that he was about to be discharged home. Bernie's distress has been triggered by the unexpected removal of his wife to an interview room to be told something out of his hearing.

3. *Listening.* In descriptions of listening skills a lot of emphasis is rightly placed on the body language signals that indicate that the speaker has our interest and attention. However, the most important skill is the listening process itself: especially the active listening achieved by checking back on what has been said, making notes and summarising, and asking relevant follow up questions in order to more fully understand what has been said. Pauses and silences are often identified as useful techniques for encouraging the speaker to say more, but they can also be extremely valuable to us for assimilating and reconsidering what has been said. Regardless of the body language, Bernie and Grace know that they have not been listened to: they have been told many things but asked very little; there have been few silences into which they felt encouraged to volunteer ideas and opinions and even fewer pauses suggesting that their comments were being reflected on. Even now the nurse is so preoccupied with offering comfort that she fails to hear what Bernie is distressed about. The ward sister is not listening to the fact that Grace has a very realistic view of the future and some very precise plans; she only hears that Grace is blocking their own plans.

There has been no dialogue with this couple. Communication has been largely one way. It is quite possible, and indeed often the case in health care, that we offer good quality care and support to people without dialogue. But this is only true where the goals of that care are confined to the overt need tacitly agreed with the patient. In this case that tacit agreement is limited to something akin to "make me comfortable and get me well enough to go home". Anything beyond that care contract will need to be agreed through discussion.

4. *Counselling.* To give advice and guidance to people is a simple dictionary definition of counselling and it is one that frequently fits well with the role of health care professionals when describing a process of education and instruction in which the health care professional occupies a position of "expert". To counsel well in this role involves recognising and staying within the strict bounds of that expertise. However, we use the word "counselling" to describe an altogether different form of role relationship between health care professional and patient in which it is the patient who is identified as the "expert" and the skill of the counsellor is to assist the patient in

putting that expertise to good use. The ward sister and staff nurse have confused these two roles. The ward sister could quite appropriately counsel Grace on how to manage Bernie's poor appetite, adapt his medication to changing circumstances and so on; but to examine wider aspects of this couple's life together, she would need to change roles and ask the questions that recognise Grace to be the expert and encourage her to reflect on her expertise. Similarly, the staff nurse has the expertise to manage Bernie's symptoms, make him less distressed by them and help him be more comfortable; only Bernie can alleviate his emotional distress, although she can help him. She can do this by encouraging his inner "expert" to examine what he is getting upset about and assist him in correcting misunderstandings, developing alternative perspectives and similar changes to his thinking which he can then put to good use to calm himself down.

In our scenario, sadly, the ward sister and staff nurse would have their work cut out here. First, they would need to make a personal attitude shift towards respecting these two people as being experts about their own lives. Second, they would have to seek a dialogue by giving time and attention to asking questions that encourage lengthy answers in order to give them the information necessary to understand the issues and think about strategies for helping. Third, they would need to be able to demonstrate that they really listen and can be trusted with the information they gain. Only with those skill sets properly in place would they be credible in the counselling process.

There is no tragedy in our scenario, there are no demons, and there is no malpractice or negligence. Both members of staff have behaved very professionally and neither Bernie nor his wife are complainers or even likely to perceive reason to complain. This is a perfectly ordinary small upset which can be put to rights. But on a busy ward there is a risk that not enough time will be allowed for sorting out the problems: Bernie will continue to worry that he will not be allowed home, Grace will continue to view well-intentioned suggestions as interference and criticism and the sister and staff nurse will be satisfied with their own communications performance and more convinced than ever that this couple are failing to face up to the realities of their situation.

Although not high drama, it is this sort of gulf in mutual understanding that is a daily feature of many health care interactions with our patients and their families, it can colour our relationships with them and can influence the outcome of our interventions. As with our earlier scenario with Pauline's GP, we can prevent misunderstandings and bridge the gulf by retaining respect for each person's individuality, making no assumptions, asking lots of questions, listening to the answers and always working *with* them in a collaborative endeavour.

Longer sessions can make it is easier for us to communicate well and (perhaps) achieve some point of resolution or formulate a plan; in shorter sessions it is necessary to settle for smaller steps and that, in turn, requires a willingness to resist the (usually self-inflicted) pressure for action and problem-solving, settling instead for an agreement to discuss further.

In the next chapter we will examine in more detail some of the features of communication skills that are especially important in applying a cognitive behavioural approach. The exercises below should help you determine whether you are ready to proceed to this level of working or whether first there are aspects of your work environment or communication skills that require further attention.

Exercises

Before you proceed to the next chapter take time to do the exercises included at the end of this chapter. To use this book properly you need to complete all the recommended exercises.

Exercise 1

1. Identify a recent personal and sensitive discussion you had with someone for whom you provide professional care and support. Make a note of:
   a. The theme of the discussion
   b. Where it took place
   c. How long you allowed for it and how long it actually took
   d. Who else was present or in ear-shot
   e. At least one way in which you demonstrated each of the six fundamental principles
      fundamental principles
   f. At least one way in which you demonstrated each of the four communication skill sets
      communication skill sets
2. Make a note of at least three improvements you will try to make in items b.-f. for the next conversation that you have like that.

Exercise 2

1. Keep a record of personal events and your immediate reactions to them during the next week using the Record form: CBT diary in Part 3 of this book.
2. Include good and bad events, large or small. Try to include some that give pleasure, some that annoy, some that amuse and some that disappoint.
3. If you have difficulty filling in any of the columns refer back to Chapters 1 and 2 for further guidance.
4. Other ways to access missing information will be to:
   a. Imagine yourself back in that situation
   b. Ask yourself "What sort of thought would I have been having if my emotion was this?" or "What behaviour did this thought lead me to show?" etc.

Exercise 3

Identify three friends or colleagues who are going to be willing to be guinea-pigs whilst you are learning about the cognitive behavioural approach. Check with each of them that:

1. They are prepared to talk about some aspects of their personal reactions to things at home or at work.
2. They have no major personal or family problems at present since your skills learning would be quite inappropriate for helping under such circumstances.
3. They have no expertise in using a cognitive behavioural approach beyond the level that you have reached and are not receiving some form of psychological therapy.

4. They can think of a small personal goal that they have so far failed to get around to working on that may benefit from advice and encourage from someone else (that is, you).
5. They can each meet with you every week to ten days for at least half an hour.

You need three because

1. Learning is helped by being able to practice more than once.
2. Some exercises will be more appropriate with one person and others with another.
3. Different goals and circumstances require different approaches.
4. Sometimes opportunities to work together prove to be more limited than originally expected.
5. Personal circumstances change.

Recommended further reading:

Burnard, P. (1997) *Effective Communication Skills for Health Professionals. Second edition.* Cheltenham: Stanley Thornes Publishers.

Davis, H. and Fallowfield, L. (eds.) (1991) *Counselling and Communication in Health Care,* Chichester: John Wiley & Sons.

Faulkner, A. and Maguire, P. (1994) *Talking to Cancer Patients and their Relatives*, Oxford: Oxford University Press.

Nicholson Perry, K. and Burgess, M. (2002) *Communication in Cancer Care,* Oxford: British Psychological Society and Blackwell Publishing.

Other relevant books in the BPS and Blackwell "Communication and Counselling in Health Care" series can be found at www.bpsblackwell.co.uk

Chapter 5
Cognitive Behavioural Communication Style

The communication skills required for almost all forms of psychological intervention are essentially as described in the previous chapter. However, as we build further on those foundations the influence of the type of psychological intervention begins to affect the communication style.

The nature of a cognitive behavioural approach is for it to be directed towards determining and achieving specific goals, exploring and adapting specific techniques in the efforts to attain them. This influences both the style and content of cognitive behavioural communications; some of the distinguishing characteristics are discussed in this chapter. None are unique to a cognitive behavioural approach but some may seem surprising to those familiar with some other forms of psychological interventions.

In our examination of these features, we will view the experience from the perspective of a 22-year-old diabetic called Tania whose chaotic eating pattern is a serious threat to her wellbeing. Tania has had diabetes since she was 14 years old and seemed to have adjusted quite well to having to manage this condition until she went to university. Whilst at university she saw a counsellor for these chaotic eating problems and found it helpful. Since graduating these problems have intensified again and she is now attending her second session with a diabetic clinic counsellor who has explained to her that she intends to use a cognitive behavioural approach.Tania was quite surprised at how different the session had felt compared with her visits to the university counsellor. As before, she seemed to be the one who did all the talking but it had seemed more structured somehow and with less interest in what had happened in the past. She explained that in her previous counselling they had agreed that she was suffering with low self-esteem and had worked on ways to like herself more. The new counsellor agreed that this was important information and that identifying ways of enhancing self-esteem may again be a part of the work they needed to do together. However, the information this counsellor seemed especially interested in knowing was about the eating pattern itself, what she was thinking when she felt hungry and when she was eating at the "wrong" times or eating the "wrong" foods. She even asked Tania what she meant by "wrong", which seemed quite puzzling to Tania and had led her to think about it some more after the session. Unlike her previous counsellor, this one had made lots of notes during the session and at times (such as when they were discussing the meaning of "wrong") had wanted to write down Tania's comments word for word. She had also asked Tania to collect some more information about her eating routines for her to bring to this second session. That had seemed quite reasonable at the time but Tania had found it surprisingly hard to do. At this second session the counsellor has promised to explain more about the cognitive behavioural approach.

1. Note taking

Often in psychological interventions, note taking, like the desk, is seen to be a barrier between the interviewer and the patient. It formalises, even "medicalises" the relationship and interferes with the ability of the interviewer to observe the reactions of the patient. These are all very important points to consider. However, it is quite normal to make notes during a cognitive behavioural interview and in particular to make a precise record of some of what the patient says as he or she says it. This process is particularly important in early sessions where specific details will help in the understanding of the problems and the clarification of goals to be worked towards. Sharing and checking back this written record with the patient is quite appropriate and sets a tone of collaborative working. Sometimes making copies of particular notes or diagrams for the patient to take away can be useful. The notepad in full view becomes a regular feature of these sessions, setting a style of reflecting over ideas that also often fits in with record-keeping assignments carried out by the patient as part of the action plan. Most of these notes, whether written by the health care professional in session or by the patient between sessions, will record aspects of current mood, thoughts and behaviours.

By delaying the note-taking until after the session, the interviewer risks missing the particular turns of phrase used that may capture important and subtle aspects of the patient's attitudes and assumptions. There is also an increased risk that the interviewer's own beliefs and perceptions will interfere with delayed recall and the opportunity will have been lost for checking back with the patient for clarification. In summary, note-taking is a powerful tool for facilitating detached reflection on personal thought processes (cognitions) by the patient as part of a collaborative activity with the interviewer. It helps bond the relationship and set the tone for this style of psychological intervention.

2. Psycho-education

Explaining the rationale of the cognitive behavioural model and its relevance in this particular instance facilitates patient engagement with the approach. Relevant information about other aspects of psychological processes is also introduced where appropriate (for example autonomic arousal and anxiety). This involves a role shift for the health professional from asking questions, listening and taking notes, to one in which the patient is encouraged to do these things and the health care professional presents information, ideas, draws diagrams and supplies handouts with relevant information. Doing it properly involves ensuring that this is more discussion than lecture and care needs to taken not to use jargon or leave the patient confused or overwhelmed.

In this second session, Tania will be given an explanation of the cognitive behavioural approach that will be very similar to the one provided in Chapter 1 of this book. Its possible relevance to her situation will be illustrated by discussion of the emotional impact of the word "wrong" in her thoughts (sometimes it makes her feel very guilty and other times very resentful), the effect of these emotional responses on her behaviour, the physical consequences of her behaviour and her subsequent thoughts about herself. Done well, this explanation of the model and its relevance to her will help her understand herself a little better and begin to give her a sense of the possibility of gaining some control over this confusion. Further discussion of the long term consequences of poor diabetic control is done in a way that checks out her current understanding (which is very good) and clarifies points less fully understood; it avoids being a lecture or reprimand, concentrating instead on ascertaining and reinforcing Tania's own commitment to doing something about this.

3. Formulation and contract setting

The collaborative nature of the relationship between patient and health professional when using a cognitive behavioural approach is established through a clear agreement (sometimes written out and signed) as to the goals to be worked towards, the methods to be used, together with commitment by the patient to apply them, the role of the therapist and the timescale of the treatment plan.

With the basic treatment model and common understanding of the issues covered, Tania and her counsellor spend the remainder of the session discussing more fully the goals of their work together, what this might entail, the commitment this will require and any potential problems with this "contract". In the next session more work will need to be done using the cognitive behavioural model to help understand what sets off inappropriate eating and chaotic patterns, together with what keeps them going on even when Tania wants them to stop. The counsellor explains to Tania that as they work on this together they will be developing a "formulation" that may help them work out how best to bring about changes that will stop this happening. This "formulation" will be a diagram or written description of how one thing leads to another, setting off a chain reaction and causing Tania to get locked into repeating the same old pattern even though it is not what she wants.

4. Agenda setting

Each session is structured and usually follows this sequence:

   a. Agenda review
   b. Homework feedback
   c. Next topic from treatment plan
   d. Homework setting

Life events and information from homework feedback may cause topics to be repeated or changed. Sometimes developments and new information lead to a review of the formulation and goals. These variations can all be contained within the session structure of a cognitive behavioural approach.

Tania's second session has gone very much to plan. The counsellor told her that they would discuss the cognitive behavioural model and treatment goals at the end of the last session and in the discussion at the beginning of this session they both agreed these were still the right topics to focus on once they had reviewed the information about her eating pattern that Tania had brought along. Since Tania had found it hard to do this homework, they also agreed to discuss and try to understand why she had found it so difficult since this might be relevant to the problem itself and to how future between-session tasks are designed. By the end of the session Tania has agreed to a new assignment (a "CBT diary") which follows quite logically from their topic (the cognitive behavioural model) and she has some expectation as to what the theme of the next session will be (Formulation) and why her assignment (or "homework") may help with this even if she feels rather embarrassed about what she is writing down in this diary and may be getting it "wrong" (that word again).

5. Directing conversation

The constraints of session time and the therapy contract usually help to focus the attention of both patient and health professional. However, there will be times when it is necessary to remind the patient of this. If change is to be achieved then a systematic approach is needed and shifting from issue to issue (or problem to problem) will prevent any change being achieved. The patient who resists this direction either needs a chance to re-evaluate the contract priorities or requires a less goal-orientated therapy approach. This systematic and structured form of communication is not simply facilitating a cognitive behavioural approach, it is the beginning of the *application* of that approach for the patient's benefit.

Tania found the new counsellor's style quite a surprise at the beginning. In her previous counselling she had been encouraged to explore whichever ideas and feelings came into her mind, but this counsellor has directed her towards focusing on specific experiences in detail. When Tania raised other points this counsellor has made a note of them on the pad, agreed to discuss them more fully later and then encouraged her to focus again on the subject in hand. In summarising what Tania has been telling her the counsellor has then also returned to these other points to review whether they have now been covered or need further discussion? Whilst some do, Tania decides that most of the important material has actually been covered very effectively as they have worked through this interview in a way that seemed to begin to tie it all together.

At the end of the session she tells the counsellor that she did not have the sense of being all-over-the-place and "even more of a mess than I thought" which is how she had felt on occasions with the previous counselling. The counsellor thanks Tania for the feedback and explains that as most of the problems she has been experiencing are probably linked to one another then following the common thread may enable them to find they have fewer issues to deal with than Tania had previously supposed. The counsellor also warns Tania that she could not guarantee that every session will be like that since sometimes more issues come up than there is time for; she advises Tania that if she wants to avoid that sense of being overwhelmed and confused then it will be important for them to stick firmly to a few themes that fit within the time allowed in the session and schedule other themes for future sessions. The counsellor also points out that in order to achieve their agreed goals then there may be little opportunity to address other issues. For this reason she proposes to regularly review with Tania whether they are working on the right goals or whether other issues have become more important.

In Tania's case, the counsellor has decided that it is especially useful to highlight the fact that she intends to continue to be directing their conversations back to the agenda and the contract goals. This is because from the outset Tania has easily diverted into many different topics and has explained that she found it hard to comply with the homework assignment because of difficulties disciplining and organising herself. This behaviour is part of the problem for which Tania is seeking help, but it is also a problem that could undermine the help itself.

6. Intrusive questioning

Using the cognitive behavioural approach we seek to understand the thoughts that help to generate distressing emotions and non-coping behaviours. To identify these thoughts sometimes requires persistence with an enquiry that is evidently going to induce that same emotional distress in our sessions. Whilst respecting any wishes of the patient to go no further, it is important not to be deflected from the enquiry simply because it will provoke an unpleasant emotion or reveal more personally sensitive information. Some of the most powerful and influential thoughts that contribute to the patient's problems can be very effectively accessed in this way, including ones that the patient may find hard to identify at other times. The patient who routinely avoids accessing distressing thoughts and wishes to continue doing so may not be suitable for a cognitive behavioural approach.

Another difference that Tania has noticed between the counsellors has been that when she got upset and tearful during one of her university counselling sessions, the counsellor would sit quietly until she felt ready to go on and then perhaps ask her to reflect on why she had become upset. This cognitive behavioural counsellor responds rather differently: after a short pause she asks about the thoughts and images Tania is having even as she is sitting there crying; she is quite gentle with her questioning but she does not wait until Tania has recovered and, in fact, sometimes while exploring those thoughts and images even more emotions are stirred up.

7. Socratic questioning

Following the line of reasoning wherever it may lead (or "Socratic method") is a prominent feature of this communication style and a corner stone of the whole cognitive behavioural approach. Unlike "open questions" which are used to facilitate expansive responses that are not restricted by the questioner, Socratic questioning is a technique designed to discover personal assumptions and contradictions through a persistent specific line of questioning. However, for it to work beneficially, it needs to be done in a relaxed and light-hearted style, not like an aggressive interrogation.

Tania has been aware that this counsellor asks her lots of questions, gives little advice and offers few comments; yet they seem to be working on an agreed plan that is well-organised and feels like it came from Tania's own ideas and wishes.

This Socratic method, which is also referred to as *guided discovery* is such an important skill in the cognitive behavioural armoury that we will devote more time to examining it in detail in the next chapter.

8. Record keeping

Written records form an important part of most cognitive behavioural practice. As already described, notes, formulation diagrams and contracts are usually important documents in this work. The most commonly used records are those reporting on the homework assignments – such as thought records (see Record form: Thought record). Other documents can include information handouts given to the patient, the notes taken by the patient during sessions, specific homework instructions and particular thoughts or phrases to rehearse. These records form a central part of most cognitive behavioural sessions. Normally these records are kept by the patient and, together with the handouts, form a source of reference in case of future setbacks.

Now that Tania has been asked to keep a "CBT diary" and has received the handout about the cognitive behavioural model, she has decided to buy a folder to put them in. The counsellor has told her that there will probably be more handouts to follow in later sessions and she has asked her not throw away her eating pattern record or any of the record forms she keeps during these sessions because they will be useful as a future source of reference; so it seems like a good idea to have somewhere safe to store these things.

9. Homework assignments

Much of the work when using a cognitive behavioural approach is done *between* sessions. This work is determined during the session and aims to be specific, achievable and recordable. Following up on the outcome of homework assignments usually provides important information for the *in*-session work (such as identifying patterns of triggering events and the thoughts they generate). A lack of homework assignments can severely hinder cognitive behavioural progress. Patient non-compliance with homework indicates a need to re-assess the suitability of the homework assignment and why it proved problematic; this may lead to a reconsideration of the therapy contract. Reluctance to comply with any between-session assignments would indicate that the patient is probably not suitable for a cognitive behavioural approach.

Tania's counsellor identifies that one of the three goals they have agreed may need some more clarification but this can be explored further in their next session after she has done further record keeping, this time using a special "CBT diary" which is designed to help Tania practise viewing events from a cognitive behavioural perspective now that she has some understanding of the model. They discuss Tania's recurrent fears of getting it wrong and the value of learning through trial-and-error. They also discuss the problems of disorganisation from which Tania suffers and decide on a particular point in each day when she is most likely to be able to organise herself to complete this diary form. Once again the counsellor reminds Tania that she does not expect her to succeed 100%, but that 50% would be good.

Throughout this chapter we have followed the experience of Tania and the differences she has noticed between her previous counselling and the cognitive behavioural version she is now receiving. In the next chapter we will discuss the communication style feature that is probably going to have the greatest impact on her, but which, if it is done well, she will not really notice very much at all: Socratic questioning.

Exercises

Before you proceed to the next take time to do the exercises included at the end of this chapter. To use this book properly you need to complete all the recommended exercises.

Exercise 1

1. Interview each of your volunteers so as to
    a. Ascertain their idea for a goal and current problems in achieving it
    b. Explain the basics of the CBT model, ensure they understand it and its possible relevance to their goal attainment
    c. Set them the task of keeping a CBT diary of good and bad events (not necessarily related to their goal) between now and your next meeting.
    d. Ask them for honest feedback at the end of the session including constructive advice on how you might improve your skills.
2. Make notes as you proceed through the interview, seeking clarification of any points you do not fully understand.
3. Use diagrams and handouts from this book to explain the CBT model.
4. If possible, and with the permission of your volunteers, record your interviews in order to evaluate your use of good communication skills.

Exercise 2

1. Review your own CBT diary and check to see that you have managed to fill any gaps and that the entries for a particular event fit together and explain each other.
2. If you find that there is more than one emotion associated with the event then try to ensure you have identified a specific thought linked to each of those emotions.
3. If the CBT diary seems to have been confusing or muddled then try again over the next week now that you have had a chance to study it more carefully.
4. When you feel happy with the quality of the CBT diary record keeping then you can move on to the next exercise.

Exercise 3

1. Identify some fairly frequently occurring personal emotional responses such as irritability, feeling hurt, getting anxious or worried and using another CBT diary form record the events when these target emotions occur together with associated thoughts, and so on.
Or
    Identify a particular type of fairly frequently occurring situation which you find problematic and using the CBT diary record your responses whenever an event of this nature happens.
2. During the remainder of this Workbook course try to maintain this CBT diary alongside any other activities you are doing and irrespective of other exercises in this book.

Recommended further reading:

Beck, A. T.; Rush, A. J; Shaw, B. F. and Emery, G. (1979) *Cognitive Therapy of Depression.* New York: Guilford Press, especially Chapters 3–5.

Beck, A. T. and Emery, G. (1985) *Anxiety Disorders and Phobias*, HarperCollins Publishers, especially Chapter 10.

Padesky, C. A. (1997) *Collaborative Case Conceptualisation: A Client Session.* Center for Cognitive Therapy DVD available from www.padesky.com

There are also various audiotape interview materials available from www.padesky.com

Chapter 6

Guided Discovery: Using the Socratic Method

Our examination of the communication style used with a cognitive behavioural approach would not be complete without examining Socratic questioning.

Questions are the driving force of any interview. They set the tone and agenda of a meeting. They do much to determine what information is shared and which issues are explored. *Directive* questions will aim to keep the communication flow on a particular track whilst *non-directive* questions allow it to meander and deviate. *Closed* questions seek precise, often short, answers that usually lead to specific required pieces of information, whereas *open* questions invite longer answers encompassing a broader range of opinions and facts chosen by the interviewee. By viewing "directiveness" and "openness" as separate dimensions of questioning style we derive four different types of question. For more information about each type (examples and when they are useful) refer to Information sheet: Communication skills – four types of questions. Refer to the Recommended Reading for where to find more detailed discussion of these concepts.

The question and answer part of an interview will typically be at the beginning and will form a major part of the initial assessment and become less time consuming in subsequent sessions. This is not so typical when using a cognitive behavioural approach because the Socratic method is used extensively as an integral part of the treatment plan itself and not solely as part of assessment. The questions are intended to encourage some "re-thinking" about issues in order to bring about change. Generally, but by no means always, the questions have the characteristics of being "open" and "directive".

Before discussing its application more fully, we will examine why this method of using questions is attributed to Socrates.

Socrates and his method

Socrates and his dialogues are best known to us as recounted by Plato and Xenophon. Famously, Socrates never wrote anything down. Therefore, our knowledge of his opinions and methodology depend on the works of others, particularly these two writers, both of whom were once his students.

He was born in Athens in 470 BC and died by drinking hemlock when ordered to commit suicide by the state in 399 BC. He had offended the Athenian government by asking too many clever and awkward questions: perhaps demonstrating just how potent his techniques can be. But that apart, his fame and lasting reputation are a testimony to the power and effectiveness of the Socratic method. We will look a little closer at what he did and what we can learn from that.

Anyone reading Plato's Republic, in which Socrates is portrayed in a series of conversations about justice, civilised society, education, culture, marriage and governance, will quickly realise that he asks a great many questions. He offers propositions and sometimes a choice of alternative propositions for people to consider and accept or reject. He then encourages them to think through the implications of their chosen position and discover whether they still agree with it or now wish to examine another alternative. By use of this method, his partners in these dialogues identify inconsistencies in their beliefs, faulty logic and erroneous assumptions that they are making. With his help, they each arrive at a new and different perspective with which they can agree; typically, they then adopt this as their own new viewpoint. An example of Socrates in action is provided here in paraphrased form. It illustrates how he uses questions to encourage a process of thinking something through, but it also shows up some of the potential problems with this method if we want to adapt it for clinical use in addressing the personal problems people might have.

Socrates	You want us to add to our previous definition of justice by saying that it is just to do good to one's friend if he is good, and to harm one's enemy if he is evil.
Polemarchus	Yes, that puts it fairly.
Socrates	But is it really right to harm any man?
Polemarchus	It certainly is. We ought to harm bad men who are our enemies.
Socrates	If we harm a horse do we make it better or worse?
Polemarchus	Worse.
Socrates	Worse, that is, by the standards by which we judge horses?
Polemarchus	Yes.
Socrates	And a dog if harmed becomes a worse dog by the standards of canine excellence?
Polemarchus	Surely.
Socrates	But must we not then say of a man that if harmed he becomes worse by the standards of human excellence?
Polemarchus	Certainly.
Socrates	But is not justice the standard of human excellence?
Polemarchus	It surely must be.
Socrates	Well, musicians will hardly use their skill to make their pupils unmusical or riding masters to make their pupils bad horsemen.
Polemarchus	Hardly.
Socrates	Then will just men use their justice to make others unjust? Or, in short, will good men use their goodness to make others bad?
Polemarchus	That cannot be so.
Socrates	For it is not the function of heat to cool things, but of its opposite: nor the function of dryness to wet things, but of its opposite.

Polemarchus	No.
Socrates	Well then, it is not the function of the good man to do harm but of his opposite.
Polemarchus	Clearly.
Socrates	Then since the just man is good. Polemarchus, it is not the function of the just man to harm either his friends or anyone else, but of his opposite, the unjust man.
Polemarchus	What you say is perfectly true, Socrates.
Socrates	So it wasn't a wise man who said that justice is to give every man his due, if what he meant by it was that the Just man should harm his enemies and help his friends. This simply is not true: for as we have seen, it is never right to harm anyone at any time.
Polemarchus	I agree.

The problems for us in this example lie in its cleverness. Socrates has apparently got a clear idea as to the point he wishes to make and leads Polemarchus through a series of logical steps to the same conclusion. We, on the other hand, will alienate those we wish to help if we get too clever and make them think they are wrong to think the way they do, if we try to be ruthlessly logical to the exclusion of other perspectives, and if we seem to have a fixed plan as to where the discussion must lead. Furthermore, in this particular example, Socrates is coming up with all the ideas and for much of the time requires no more than agreement from Polemarchus (who could have switched off from the whole thing and begun to think about what he is having for dinner). Without Polemarchus having had to work on it for himself in order to get to this conclusion, his final concurrence by no means gives us confidence that he has taken any ownership of this point of view.

The Socratic method as part of a cognitive behavioural approach

Three attributed quotes from Socrates may help us focus on some important consideration when we are using his method.

1. *"To find yourself, think for yourself"*. In a cognitive behavioural approach Socratic questioning is heavily used for precisely this purpose not only during the initial interviewing and goal planning but throughout the whole process of offering help. Through the Socratic questioning, new personal perspective can be tested against personal standards and emotional considerations as well as logic and practical realities. By putting in a lot of hard work on the task, the patient is likely to arrive at conclusions that she/he can later properly recall as her/his own.
2. *"One thing only I know, and that is that I know nothing."* Rather than being clever and knowing all the answers, the cognitive behavioural questioner respects the fact that the patient has expertise about her/himself and can be helped to find suitable personal answers through the questions. This is often a very hard shift in attitude for health care professionals to make. The need to have the answers at their fingertips will often put them off from embarking on a series of questions to which they do not already have planned responses. Nevertheless, to do the task properly requires

getting used to adopting this attitude and becoming comfortable with asking questions from a standpoint of complete naivity and ignorance, trying to make as few assumptions as possible and offering no advice or opinions except in the form of options for consideration.

3. *"Wisdom begins in wonder"*. By using the Socratic method we are encouraging the patient to take a fresh look at things. We both, patient and questioner, start by looking at the situation almost as though it was completely new to us; neither of us can be sure where that process of re-examination will takes us. We struggle with it, we puzzle over it, we test out possibilities and we continue to work at it until we arrive at a useful perspective that seems to meet our needs. In this way it is a truly collaborative effort during a voyage of discovery.

In describing this process as a "voyage of discovery", remember that the title of this chapter refers to *"guided* discovery". Let us follow the analogy a little further. Great explorers such Magellan, de Gama, Columbus and Cabot took great risks in venturing into the unknown but they all set off with some idea as to where they were going. Each of them had charts and theories that influenced and guided them. Ultimately, all of them had to drastically alter their beliefs and expectations as they acquired new information. The same thing applies with our Socratic "voyages of discovery". We will often have some ideas as to where our line of questions may lead, especially if we have had experience of people with similar problems. Nevertheless, like these illustrious sailors, we need to be open minded to all possibilities, constantly seeking answers and receptive to information that may not fit our plans. Curiousity and puzzlement will serve us well in forging a close collaborative relationship. It may also send a reassuring message to the patient that this problem is a challenge worthy of attention and requiring serious consideration: it is not a silly and simple matter that any fool could solve.

Applying the Socratic method

Brenda is a 60-year-old lady who recently retired from her part-time job as a school secretary. With her husband, Roger, she has been planning to do a lot more travelling when he retires in three years time. They have two children (married sons) and three young grandchildren of whom Brenda has hoped to see more now she has retired. Sadly, four months ago Brenda had her worst fears confirmed. During her last year of working, she had noticed some difficulties with her typing and other things she did in the office. She had wondered whether she was showing signs of arthritis in the joints although she did not really have pain as such; anyway she was really worried about the shakiness she seemed to have developed in her hands and she could not see why that would be caused by arthritis. Now she and her husband know that she has Parkinson's disease and she has become very despondent and withdrawn, whilst, as she sees it, Roger seems to try to carry on with life as though nothing has happened. She finds his attempts to cheer her up very irritating and it has led to some upsetting arguments between them recently.

It is easy to empathise with Brenda. How would any one us feel if faced with a similar situation? She has lost her hope for a trouble-free and healthy retirement in which she and Roger can catch up on all those things that they had promised themselves for the future. She has images of herself becoming progressively more dependent and restricted to her home. She feels cheated out of the interesting travel and varied lifestyle she has worked towards; and she feels denied her opportunity to become the doting grandmother that she remembers from her own childhood and looked forward to re-enacting with her own grandchildren. She feels frustrated that Roger does not seem to have properly grasped the full implications of her situation as she has done and that he continues to live in "cloud-cuckoo-land". Because this has led them to argue like they have never done before, this makes her feel guilty for being the cause of bad feeling and fearful that it can only get worse as the disease progresses.

Brenda is upset by her own behaviour but cannot see a way out of her plight. So far as she can see, she is trapped and helpless. Whilst she believes there is no hope for things to be any different, she is turning to us for help. We feel the pressure to come up with some answers for her and can easily make the mistake of trying to provide them. However, this is one of those situations in which we are not the experts: Brenda is the expert on her emotions, her relationships with her husband and family, her memories, her expectations, her hopes and fears, her lifestyle, her standards and her values. We discussed this previously in Chapter 4 when the ward sister had attempted to "counsel" Grace without appreciating that Grace was actually the expert on her personal life situation. Here, with Brenda and under the pressure from her to come up with helpful ideas, we could fall into the same trap as the ward sister, again with all the very best of intentions and even, on this occasion, at the request of the patient. It did not work for Grace and it will not work for Brenda for just the same reasons.

In this situation, Brenda has all the pertinent information. She has spent a lot of time reflecting on her circumstances and probably attempting to sort herself out. We have experience of similar situations for other people; however they are *similar* not the same. So in approaching Brenda's plea for help we should remember the quote from Socrates *"One thing only I know, and that is that I know nothing"*. We are best advised to start from the position of "Brenda as expert" and this is precisely the sort of situation when we should apply the Socratic method.

The purpose of Socratic questioning in problem solving

Whilst basic fact-finding and assessment of problems may be predominantly located in the early communications, we are likely to continue it throughout involvement with our patients in order to do our work properly. Socratic questioning will be a useful tool in this process: exploring issues from the position of "patient as expert" in order to more fully understand them from the patient's perspective.

However, in the problem solving process this Socratic questioning serves a somewhat different purpose. As Socrates says *"To find yourself, think for yourself"*. In order to achieve this purpose the ideas need to come from and belong to the person answering the questions and not from the questioner. To this end the questions are directed towards two objectives:

1. *Reframing ("reconceptualising") the issues* in such a way as to be helpful for problem solving. This will involve more precisely defining what the problem is, what causes it to be a problem, why it is difficult to solve and what would be the benefits of solving it. These may seem basic

questions with answers that are blindingly obvious to both questioner and respondent; but making no assumptions and following the thinking through from these basic building blocks helps to tease out:

    a. False assumptions – such as believing that because I am in my mid forties, have led a healthy lifestyle and regularly exercise at the gym I should not have got this disease and there must be an explanation for why this has happened that the health professionals could give me if only they could be bothered to investigate it properly.

    b. Inconsistencies of beliefs – such as believing that I must be being punished for being bad to have developed such a nasty disease and at the same time admiring the good qualities of others similarly affected (including famous ones such as Pope John Paul II, Linda McCartney, Stephen Hawking).

    c. Contradictory views – such as the potential conflict that can arise from thinking that "I must be a good patient and look after myself or I will let everybody down" and also thinking "I will let everybody down unless I pull my weight in all my roles as a parent and partner".

    d. Double standards – such as considering myself to be "giving in" to illness because I need to rest, whilst at the same time advising others in a similar situation to avoid doing too much and making sure they rest.

    e. Faulty conclusions – such as attributing my partner's quiet mood to being because of feeling fed up with me and not wanting to be around this sick person any more when in fact there was reason at the time for feeling sadness and no evidence that I was being criticised or rejected.

2. *Developing a way forward* which, from the answers to the questions, seems to be the best or right option to pursue. Again, it is the person answering the questions who needs to believe this, having thought it through to this conclusion. In order to get to that point, the questioner facilitates by asking questions that seek to clarify:

    a. Alternative perspectives – including alternative explanations for a particular event and alternative ways of evaluating it (in terms of fairness, rightness, badness, and so on).

    b. Choices – including the desirability of alternative outcomes and the options for action that might influence those outcomes.

    c. Means by which to make choices – including the evaluation of costs and benefits (financially, emotionally, energy-wise, and so on) for each option, consideration of personal standards and values, and assessment of likelihood of achieving the intended outcome.

The questioner resists offering advice, solutions or opinions, restricting input to the questions that guide the thinking and the additional options or points for consideration that may have been otherwise overlooked. Through these inputs the questioner can and does, of course, gently influence the thinking but does not induce passive acquiescence or provoke active resistance to new ideas. The ideas given most attention are not imposed by an outside "expert" but generated and evaluated by the person who is answering the questions.

The clinical nurse specialist to whom Brenda has been explaining her issues is familiar with Socratic questioning and faced with the pressure from Brenda to come up with some answers, recognises that this is a situation in which she would be wise to apply this approach:

Brenda:	There is no point to life any more.
CNS:	Why do you say that?
Brenda:	Because I can't see any.

CNS:	Is that a change from before?
Brenda:	Yes, I used to have a future to look forward to.
CNS:	Do you have no future at all?
Brenda:	Not much of one because this Parkinson's disease will destroy my life.
CNS:	So what will you do with the future you do have?
Brenda:	I don't know.
CNS:	Have you got any plans?
Brenda:	Not really, and that's why life seems so pointless.
CNS:	Would making plans that fit with a changed future give life some more point?
Brenda:	Well, not really because I'm never going to be able to do the things that I had so wanted to do when I retired and if I can't do those things then there seems no point in anything else.
CNS:	Can you tell me what those really important things are?
Brenda:	I had so many plans and hopes. Now they all seem spoilt. I used to talk to my colleague in the school office about the things we would do once Roger retired and it just makes me want to cry when I think about what I used to tell her.
CNS:	Yes, plans like that are great for lifting our spirits, aren't they? That's why at a low point like now, it may be good to look at those plans again. Even though some of them might have to change, it is important for us not to jump to any conclusions, so, because they were a source of happiness before, I think it might be helpful for us to look at some that have been especially important to you. Can you think of two or three that were the biggest source of pleasure to you or the loss of which are perhaps causing you the most sadness now?
Brenda:	I used to picture us getting up on a bright sunny morning, deciding it was a nice day to go to the coast, phoning one of my daughters-in-law to see if any of the children wanted to come and then just taking off. I used to think about some of the lovely cities I would like to see abroad, that I've never got to yet. I had plans to make changes to the garden and to take up water-colour painting classes. That's never going to happen now!
CNS:	Which of the things you have mentioned there can't happen now?

The specialist nurse notes down the plans Brenda has and the difficulties she foresees. They continue this line of discussion by exploring in more detail each of the plans, its importance and value to Brenda, the obstacles mentioned, the degree to which they are actual or potential obstacles, possible strategies that Brenda can come up with for overcoming those obstacles and the benefits to her of doing so. For example:

CNS:	Now shall we turn our attention to the water-colour painting classes, you mentioned? Were they something you had wanted to do for some time?

Brenda:	Yes. I did several evening courses on art appreciation, drawing and painting over the last five or six years and had intended to do a proper daytime course and join a regular water-colours group once I retired.
CNS:	As with our discussion about the problems relating to day trips out with the grandchildren and visits to Vienna and Venice, I'll start by asking you "So what is stopping you from doing this?"
Brenda:	I think this one will prove much harder to sort out than those were.
CNS:	Oh, why's that?
Brenda:	Because the Parkinson's will directly affect what I am doing.
CNS:	Can you explain why?
Brenda:	Quite simply because my tremor will make it hard for me to paint properly.
CNS:	What do you mean by properly?
Brenda:	I can't produce the results I want.
CNS:	Is that what happens when you try to write?
Brenda:	My writing is not as neat as it was but it's still not too bad at present, but it is bound to become impossible in time.
CNS:	So, at present, you can achieve the results you want with writing well enough. Could that be true for painting as well?
Brenda:	Yes, possibly. But it won't last.
CNS:	Could you enjoy the results of your work, now, even if it won't last for always?
Brenda:	Perhaps, but it still won't be as good as before I had this tremor.
CNS:	So you could never paint as well as you did before?
Brenda:	Well that's not entirely true because I was pretty hopeless before so I could probably improve on that with more time and practice.
CNS:	So if you gave more time and practice to water-colour painting now, you could probably do better than before?
Brenda:	Yes.
CNS:	Would it please you to achieve that?
Brenda:	It certainly would. But supposing I find the tremor gets worse and I don't achieve it?
CNS:	Do you only attempt things you are certain of succeeding at?
Brenda:	No, of course not. I take your point. It's worth having a go, now, whilst I can. Who knows, maybe the tremor will make me even more creative! But, being serious for a moment here, I have been thinking, as we have been talking, about how important painting with water-colours really is. Maybe water-colours are too fiddly and I would do better with oils or something. What I could do is discuss it with the tutor I had before and who I see and chat to quite regularly. He'd be able to help me decide what would be the best.

They agree that this would be a good plan. The specialist nurse then recaps on their discussion and the courses of action (including this one) that Brenda has decided on, checking that she is still happy with each of them. The nurse finishes by saying:

CNS:	I know that this has been a demanding session for you and we have talked about some painful issues. I hope you feel nevertheless it has been useful because you have worked very hard and come up with some very helpful ideas. None of this is intended to make us pretend that some bad things are not happening in your life. But facing those things realistically does not mean that you have to give up all the good things in your life to make way for the bad. In fact, the more you can work to keep good things happening, the better you are likely to cope with the bad.
Brenda:	I know that the thoughts about what might happen in the future will keep coming back but I appreciate your help in getting me to remember to live life in the present and focus on what I can do to achieve what I want for myself in the immediate future. So, thank you for that.
CNS:	When we meet next time, we can see how well you have managed to do in fulfilling the tasks you have identified, what might help you move forward with those tasks and what could assist in keeping that focus on the here-and-now in the forefront of your thinking.

In terms of the aim of Socratic questioning, Brenda would almost certainly agree that she has done a lot of thinking in this session and that most of the ideas (including the one about consulting her ex-tutor) have come from her. So has the nurse achieved the two objectives of using this method of questioning mentioned earlier?

1. *Reframe the issues.* Brenda experiences feelings of hopelessness and despair based on what she considers to be a realistic appraisal of what the future holds for her. Through her discussion with the nurse she has begun to recognise that her own decisions and behaviour are fuelling the despondency and irritation that she is feeling and that whilst she may not be able to change the future, she can do much to change the here and now. And at the very least not make a bad situation worse than it already is.
2. *Develop a way forward.* Brenda has spent time in this session identifying some goals for herself. These goals are largely ones that she had previously had but in recent times they have been discounted as being impossible for various reasons. With the help of alternative perspectives and examination of options, she has determined how these old goals could be adapted to new circumstances and committed herself to some constructive actions towards achieving them.

This does not mean that the nurse has "fixed" Brenda's psychological problems. They have begun to work on her feelings of despondency but her anger and irritability including the untypical rows with Roger are a source of much distress to Brenda. It is their plan to make this a major focus of the next session and the Socratic Method will again be the main tool used in this work.

Features of Socratic questioning

The characteristics of this method of enquiry can be summarised as follows:

1. *Naïve approach* – Questions start from absolute basics and are asked in a simple and informal manner that is conversational in tone rather than inquisitorial. The questions focus on seeking to understand the respondent's personal perspective as though hearing of this set of circumstances for the very first time. The questions encourage the person to draw upon and consider experiences, opinions and assumptions that already influence thinking. Normally, the respondent will be able to answer the questions very easily because this personal perspective information is readily available to be brought to mind. Sometimes, however, there will be hesitancy because the questions identify gaps in the reasoning or even raise doubts in beliefs about which the person was previously quite certain.

2. *Assume nothing* – In trying to be as naïve as possible, the questioner tries to make no assumptions about what is meant or how the other person might feel. In discussing painting, the nurse even asks Brenda what she means by "properly". Resisting making any assumptions enables questioner and respondent to understand more fully what they are really talking about and also to identify what is not understood or has not been further examined.

3. *Non-judgemental attitude* – The questions enable both to examine inferences being drawn from specific events without taking up a particular stance in relation to those inferences. For example, the inference that taking up water-colour painting is a waste of time once one has started to develop Parkinson's disease is explored quite thoroughly without the specialist nurse in any way suggesting that Brenda is wrong to think like that. To have done so, could have caused Brenda to become defensive and resistant to alternative ideas. The questioning allowed Brenda to re-examine her views with an open mind to other possibilities.

4. *Advice-free discussion* – The questioning method enables the questioner to guide the conversation along potentially fruitful lines without telling the person what to do or how to think. The person is encouraged to distinguish between facts, personal beliefs and general opinion. The questioning focuses in more detail on those facts, beliefs and opinions that appear relevant to the problems and so steers the person's thinking to alternative perspectives. The specialist nurse never offers any advice or opinion about the feasibility or otherwise of water-colour painting for Brenda (and would be completely unqualified to do so) but through answering the questions Brenda offers herself some new advice. In fact, she goes even further with her own advice-giving than one might expect from simply answering the nurse's questions. In her head she seems to have asked some more questions, perhaps about how important it is that she paints in water-colours rather than oils, and her answers to these questions have led her to generate a plan of action with which she is pleased. So when we make use of the Socratic method we are often also training our patients to use it too.

5. *Curious-minded* – Even though we do not offer advice and opinion when we use the Socratic method, we do voice the possibility of alternative perspectives. The nurse is curious to know whether writing is the same sort of problem as painting for Brenda. In this way, the nurse has begun to encourage Brenda to explore alternative perspectives but without in any way suggesting that these two things are necessarily the same. With Socratic questioning we put forward options with a curiosity as to why one might be preferable to another. We express them as points to consider with no commitment "to buy". In this way, we remain guided by the person's response rather as the person is guided by us through our questions. This makes it a truly collaborative endeavour and one with which it is impossible to predict where you will end up. Both participants in the exercise find it a "voyage of discovery" when it is done well.

6. *Focused on constructive outcome* – The effort needs to feel productive to the patient. Brenda would not have felt happy with a session that seemed to be an endless stream of questions leading nowhere and finishing without some sense of conclusions. It is impossible to start with real confidence that the lines of questioning are going to arrive at solutions to the problems (especially if the problems need to be better understood first). However, it is possible to remain determined to ensure that the guided questioning will lead to some helpful end-points. The most striking of these will be action plans that may be problem-solving in nature or (more likely) investigative or experimental. In fact, at several points during the session, Brenda had definite results from the questioning as each of the abandoned plans was re-examined and ideas for refreshing those plans were generated. For the trips abroad she determines that she can go straight ahead and implement solutions. Regarding her painting, she intends to investigate possibilities further with someone whose opinion she values. Testing out her plans to visit the grandchildren more may involve experimenting with some new ideas ahead of her husband retiring and then reviewing whether other alternatives need to be considered. Brenda can leave the session with several follow-up actions. But, even during the session, there may be opportunities for the Socratic Method to feel helpful. This happens when the patient finds a new perspective more useful than the old one and especially when its usefulness extends across a range of situations. For Brenda this has involved recognition that recently she has fallen into the trap of expending all her mental energy on imagining the future and neglecting the present. She has recognised that this has led her to act as if this anticipated future is actually happening now. By telling herself "don't cross bridges before you get to them" she has found herself able to appreciate that she can still do almost all the same things she could do five months ago, prior to her diagnosis. Examining how the same new perspective may apply in other circumstances enables the patient to go from the specific situation and develop a more general principle. This is valuable in sustaining patient motivation within the session and by finding wider applicability we greatly increase the value the patient places on a new perspective in the longer term.

"Wisdom begins in wonder" said Socrates and this method of enquiry is intended to demonstrate just that. For many health care professionals steeped in the mission of finding solutions to problems this can be a very difficult and threatening change of interviewing style. However, when we are prepared to face the truly difficult issues that trouble our patients in this open and honest manner, wanting to understand, without ready-made answers and not protected by a shield of "expertise", then we embark on a genuinely collaborative mission of discovery for both of us with insight and wisdom as our planned destination.

In using a cognitive behavioural approach, this method is always a core skill and sometimes the only technique required to help bring about the changes our patients are seeking. Before moving on to look at how you might use it in assessment and problem solving try to ensure that you have thoroughly understood and practised Socratic questioning as described in this chapter, using the exercises at the end of the chapter and perhaps followed up with some of the recommended reading. Summary information about the method is to be found in Techniques: Socratic questioning and Information sheet: Socratic questioning examples.

Exercises

Before you proceed to the next chapter take time to do the exercises included at the end of this chapter. To use this book properly you need to complete all the recommended exercises.

Exercise 1

If possible, record these sessions with your volunteers.

1. Review the CBT diaries of each of your volunteers, discussing any difficulties they may have had in completing it and reviewing their understanding of the cognitive behavioural model on the basis of their entries.
2. Identify ways of overcoming record keeping problems and further clarify the Hot Cross Bun if necessary.
3. Go through each of the individual entries using some Socratic questioning to enhance your understanding of just why certain thoughts and emotions were evoked by certain events for that person.
   a. Try to resist making assumptions.
   b. Be "naïve" but not annoyingly so!
   c. Try to fill any gaps where thoughts or physical reactions, and so on, were hard to identify
   d. Identify one thought to match each emotion where there are multiple entries against a particular event.
4. If more work is needed to get to grips with the CBT diary then ask the volunteer to repeat the exercise for the next week. If more work is not needed then ask the volunteer to keep a CBT diary specifically related to issues related to the goal they have identified and the difficulties encountered at present.
5. At the end of the session ask the volunteer for constructive feedback on your communication skills and whether or not they see the relevance of this cognitive behavioural approach to the issues they have raised.

Exercise 2

1. Evaluate your use of the Socratic method in each of these interviews in terms of the two purposes (reframing and developing a way forward) and six features mentioned in the chapter.
2. Make a note of improvements you plan to make next time.

Recommended further reading:

Padesky, C.A. (1993) *Socratic questioning: changing minds or guided discovery?* Keynote address to European Congress of Behavioural and Cognitive Therapies - paper available from www. padesky.com

Padesky, C. A. (1996) *Guided discovery using Socratic Dialogue.* Center for Cognitive Therapy DVD available from www.padesky.com

De Botton, A. (2000) *The Consolations of Philosophy,* London: Penguin Books – for a light and humorous but informative read about Socrates and some other philosophers relevant to cognitive and other psychological approaches.

Chapter 7

Assessment

Introduction

The idea of problem assessment and formulation with reference to psychological issues can sound very mysterious and grand, conjuring up images of the patient on the couch revealing the inner workings of his or her mind and childhood experiences to a bearded man with an Austrian accent. The reality is reassuringly more ordinary and familiar than that.

Most clinical practitioners in any speciality will do something very similar with every new patient or presenting problem. For a health care professional faced with the challenge of assisting someone with the management of their pain there will be a need to first make an evaluation (or *assessment*) of the patient's subjective experience of this pain, together with its perceived location, associated activities, coping strategies and emotional impact. This information, in conjunction with knowledge of the disease, will lead to a likely explanation (or *formulation*) as to why this pain is experienced in this way, by this patient, at this time. Strategies for effectively addressing the pain, or identifying the need for further investigation, will follow based on this explanation.

The following chapters on assessment and formulation will proceed along this familiar path of clinical practice, whilst highlighting specific aspects that are particularly important when using a cognitive behavioural approach.

Cognitive behavioural assessment

Cognitive behavioural assessment is centred on the basic idea that our reaction to an event is determined by the complex interplay of thoughts, emotions, behaviour and physical sensations we have discussed earlier. As illustrated in Chapter 2, with the example of William's response to his diagnosis of cancer (Figures 1.2.2 and 1.2.3), a different pattern of interaction between these four elements can lead to a very different response to an event and determine whether or not the response is ultimately helpful or unhelpful to the individual. The example of William will be used throughout this chapter to illustrate the cognitive behavioural approach to assessment.

As with pain, the challenge for the health care professional who seeks to help in the management of psychological distress will be to assess the patient's experience of problems, factors influencing occurrence, coping strategies and repercussions. The aim of a cognitive behavioural assessment is to develop a shared understanding of the problem(s) in terms of specific interactions of thoughts, emotions, behaviours and physical sensations that relate to those problems.

Whatever the pressures on the health care professional to come up with methods for dealing with a problem, a proper assessment is a prerequisite for effective cognitive behavioural intervention. Without it, the treatment methods selected could prove inappropriate, ineffective, or even counterproductive. The focus of the assessment will be on the present situation but it is often valuable to ask about past episodes of similar problems and previous attempts to resolve these understanding circumstances of previous similar problems and knowledge of why past coping strategies have failed, can lead to identification of important aspects of the problem that have not been appreciated fully in the past.

However, an in-depth understanding of the patient's personal history is not usually required when employing a cognitive behavioural approach but when an assessment indicates that a fuller understanding of the past will be necessary then those with specialist psychological therapy training (including CBT therapists) become the most appropriate providers of this help. In the context of a professional role that is primarily focused on providing physical health care treatments, it is important for you to consider what you can realistically achieve in the time that you have available with the patient. The priority must be to understand why this problem is occurring here and now, and how you can help the patient to tackle it by addressing the thoughts, emotions, behaviours or physical sensations that contribute to, or maintain it. This is likely to be of greatest relevance on those occasions where the psychological problem is directly affecting how well you can help the patient whilst attempting to carry out your usual role. Very occasionally, this will not be the case: you happen to be the right person, in the right place at the right time and it would seem uncaring to fail to respond to the apparent need even though it is outside your usual area of work. Under such circumstances an initial assessment will almost certainly be appropriate for you to undertake even if your role extends no further than that. At such times the assessment will be in part about you as well as the patient. It will be necessary to make a realistic assessment of your own knowledge and skills in relation to the identified problem, the time commitment you will need to make, the support of your team and availability of other resources as and when required. We will return to this theme in the decision making chapter, "When to act".

Assessment process

In general, the main method of cognitive behavioural assessment is a one-to-one conversation with the patient, where the problem is discussed in detail and specific questions are asked to collect information that will inform your understanding of the problem. In conducting this conversation the Socratic questioning style and other communication skills discussed in the earlier chapters are relevant, as they encourage the patient to fully describe their experiences and beliefs using their own words (See Techniques: Socratic questioning).

The assessment is the first opportunity to introduce the patient to the cognitive behavioural approach. By asking questions about the thoughts, emotions, behaviours and physical sensations associated with the problem you are encouraging the patient to think about the importance of these factors, perhaps for the first time. For example, prior to assessment, William has probably not considered how his thoughts about his diagnosis of cancer might be directly influencing his mood and determining what action he takes. The assessment can help to extend his understanding of the presenting problem, introduce him to the cognitive-behavioural approach and help him see how the problem may be tackled.

During the assessment we are trying to collect information to answer several questions of particular value to the cognitive behavioural approach. For this reason, there will be some degree of structure and direction to the interview. However, it is important to think about how we ask those questions, how we guide the interview and how we create a safe and supportive atmosphere. As described in the Communication Skills chapter, a non-judgemental and empathic style is part of the cognitive behavioural approach and this is just as true during the assessment phase as it is at any other stage of contact with the patient. The way in which you ask the questions will influence the building of a therapeutic relationship with the patient. If that relationship is going to be good then, although you have a clear idea of the information that you need to collect during the assessment, the patient needs to feel listened to and given a chance to tell his or her story without sensing that the questions imply a particular judgement or betray a robot-like indifference to the answers.

Assessment questions

In the cognitive behavioural assessment we are especially interested in answering three particular core questions that influence and guide the content of the assessment interview.

1. *What is the problem that the person would like help with?*
2. *What are the situations, thoughts, emotions, behaviours and physical sensations associated with the problem?*
3. *What are the immediate and longer-term consequences of the problem?*

Whilst examining these questions we will return to the example of William and his responses, but first we will fill in a few more details about him. William is in his mid- 30s, single and lives alone. His relationship with his girlfriend of three months seems to be getting quite serious but he has always been wary of commitment and enjoys his independence. Six weeks ago he was diagnosed with testicular cancer but assured that with radiotherapy treatment for this seminoma the prognosis was really very good. With this information in mind, we will now return to our core questions.

1. *What is the problem that the person would like help with?*
What is the person doing, or not doing, that he or she would like to change? For example, is this person crying all the time and would like to be able to control this better? Is the person feeling useless because of not being able to work at the moment and wanting an improved sense of worth?

It is very easy for us to make assumptions about what we think the person should want to change, or to become caught up in what other professionals, or family members would like to change. This is especially true when the person who comes to us is caught up in a set of circumstances that we see as understandably distressing. However, in reality, what we and others see as "problems to work on" can be very different to those that the person is actually motivated to change. If we choose to focus on a problem that is not really a priority for the person, then the cognitive behavioural intervention is less likely to be effective or valued.

In the case of William, we need to discover the problem for which he is motivated to seek help. If he comes to us whilst he is experiencing Response Set 1, he might say that he would like to "feel better", which could refer to wanting to improve his physical symptoms of nausea and fatigue, but could also refer to his depressed mood, or to his thoughts about being "useless". In our William example we have characterised a shift to Response Set 2 as a largely successful adjustment to his circumstances. However, even with this response set, William might be wanting help such as making changes to his social life, so that he can manage his physical symptoms and cope with treatment whilst remaining as active as possible. He may be troubled by feelings of inadequacy as a man despite his apparently "positive" attitude. All of these scenarios would suggest a different focus for the intervention and it will be necessary for William and his interviewer to clarify this together during the assessment, bearing in mind that even William may not be clear about what the problem is for which he would like help at the beginning of this assessment process.

Once you have identified the problem (or problems) the next step is to find out whether this is very specific, relating to only one particular aspect of life, or if it is a more general problem affecting several areas. For example, is William being very irritable with his girlfriend (perhaps because of expectations that she should understand more than other people), whilst not being impatient with anyone else, or is he generally less patient with everyone (perhaps because he believes that other people feel sorry for him because they see him as having become pathetic)?

2. *What are the situations, thoughts, emotions, behaviours and physical sensations associated with the problem?*

In everyday life we blur the boundaries between thoughts, emotions, behaviour and physical sensations. At work we might say things like "I feel that I haven't achieved much today" or "I feel that this treatment approach is the best in this instance". The statement "I haven't achieved much today" is actually a thought or belief, rather than an emotion or physical sensation as suggested by the words "I feel...".

William, in Response Set 1, might say something like "I feel my life is over" and "I feel useless". The statements "my life is over" and "I am useless" are actually thoughts or beliefs and as illustrated in Response Set 1, the emotions that William experiences in response to thinking this way are depression and hopelessness.

Because in the cognitive behavioural approach we separate out the thoughts, emotions, behaviour and physical sensations that are associated with the problem, we ask specific questions about each of these components. In William's case, we would want to ask:

- "What thoughts go through your mind when you think about your diagnosis?"
- "What emotion do you experience when you have that thought?"
- "What physical sensations occur in your body when that happens?"
- "What do you do/how do you react/ how do you cope when you have that thought with that emotion?"

Thoughts

In terms of assessing the thoughts component of the "hot cross bun", we seek to identify the automatic thoughts that pass through the person's mind when the problem situation or event occurs. However, we might also want to ask about the meaning attached to a specific event in terms of what it says about the person, about their health, about their life in general, and about their future.

In the case of William it will be helpful to explore what he thinks a diagnosis of cancer means in terms of the likely physical impact of the disease and its treatment, the impact it will have on his identity as a man, his ability to live his daily life as before, the likelihood of achieving his personal goals and the implications he imagines it might have for his future.

Emotions

When asking about emotions it might be that there is more than one emotion associated with a problem and we then need to identify the specific thoughts, behaviour and physical sensations that might help us understand more fully why each of these emotional reactions have occurred. William might experience an increase in discomfort following an activity and feel anxious because he thinks that the discomfort means that he is causing damage to his body, but he might also feel depressed because he thinks that this is yet another activity that he can no longer dare do. In Response Set 2, William experiences both sadness and determination in association with his diagnosis. Looking at the thoughts identified in this response set, we might quite logically predict that his sadness is associated with his thought that "my life is going to change", and his determination with a thought such as "I can do this". However, it is also possible that his sadness might relate to the thought of not being able to have a family of his own or that he wished he was not the cause of worry and concern to his family and friends. Asking William what thoughts go through his mind when he is feeling sad, and what types of situations tend to trigger the sadness will help us understand the true nature of his sadness emotion and how we can best help him deal with it if we both consider this relevant to the identified problem.

Physical sensations

When we enquire about physical sensations we ask about noticeable bodily sensations experienced at the time of the events under consideration. As well as physical reactions to the events this will include symptoms of ill health and environmental influences. For patients with life-changing illnesses distinguishing between the physical symptoms of the condition and the symptoms and physical changes associated with emotional responses such as anxiety and depression can prove quite difficult for both the patient and the health care professional. There is often considerable overlap but distinguishing between them plays a major part in determining the most appropriate form of intervention. William experiences fatigue in Response Set 1 and whilst this might be associated with his cancer treatment, it might also be a symptom of his depression. A full assessment of his mood would therefore be helpful in this case, perhaps using the questionnaire measures discussed later in the chapter.

Behaviour

In assessing behaviour we want to know what the person is doing and what they are not doing in response to the problem; we also want to consider what purpose this behaviour is serving and whether it helps or hinders effective coping. Particular examples of behaviour might be: to seek social support and talk with other people about the problem; to use distraction as a means of taking attention away from the problem; or avoiding situations to try and prevent the problem from occurring. In the case of William, Response Sets 1 and 2 highlight two entirely different behaviours that he could choose. In Response Set 1, William withdraws from people, whereas in Response Set 2 he tells close friends about his diagnosis. By identifying these behaviours we can discuss with William how they will influence the events, thoughts, emotions and physical sensations that immediately follow.

3. *What are the immediate and longer-term consequences of the problem?*
As well as assessing the immediate thoughts, emotions, behaviour and physical sensations we also want to identify the consequences of the problem for other situations, including the responses of

other people. The repercussions of the person's response will influence how the problem develops or diminishes over time.

If William becomes tearful when talking to friends about his diagnosis and his girlfriend becomes embarrassed and recommends that they go home straight away, this is likely to reinforce any beliefs that he has about it being "wrong to cry in front of other people". This may lead him to avoid seeing his friends until he feels fully able to control his tearfulness. In the longer-term, the absence of supportive friends and social events may leave him feeling isolated and more depressed and overwhelmed by his illness and may have a negative impact on his ability to cope with his condition as described in Response Set 1.

On the other hand, if his partner encourages him to stay and the friends are also accepting and supportive, this would probably reduce his worry about what people think of him becoming upset and is likely to motivate him to continue socialising, despite some episodes of tearfulness. Over the longer-term this would probably help to improve his mood and leave him feeling supported throughout his illness and treatment.

If William chooses to withdraw from his friends, believing that he is an embarrassment and no one can help then, over time, his friends might equally withdraw, assuming that he prefers to be left alone or does not like them anymore. This will increase his social isolation, reduce opportunities for enjoyment and probably exacerbate his depression. If, on the other hand, he chooses to discuss his diagnosis with his friends, they are much more likely to maintain close contact with him and offer support on a practical and an emotional level.

Assessment tools

It is often useful to supplement the information collected during the one-to-one conversation by asking the patient to complete questionnaires, diaries or record forms.

1. Questionnaires and rating scales

Questionnaires can be useful in determining the presence and severity of symptom clusters, such as pain, fatigue, depression and anxiety, and also they can be useful in supporting or confirming a clinical judgement. However, their usefulness is probably greatest in measuring change over time, rather than as diagnostic tools, since asking the patient about their symptoms and experience of them often gives a reliable indication of their presence and severity.

A simple measure used in cancer studies and of more general applicability is the "Distress Thermometer" (NCCN and ACS, 2005). This is a 0 to 10 rating of how distressed the person feels (0 = no distress; 10 = extreme distress). Asked to make this rating at regular intervals during treatment will enable a simple assessment of current experience and change over time and treatment.

The Beck Depression Inventory II (BDI –II) (Beck, Steer & Brown, 1996) is a widely used, reliable and valid tool for the assessment of depression. However, it was originally designed for use in mental health settings. There is often considerable overlap between the symptoms of depression used in this questionnaire (that is, fatigue, loss of appetite, sleep disturbance, reduced concentration) and those associated with physical health conditions such as chronic pain, cancer and MS. Items relating to these overlapping symptoms can artificially raise the overall depression score, and fail to provide an accurate assessment of mood. The Hospital Anxiety & Depression Scale (HADS) (Zigmond & Snaith, 1983) provides a useful alternative and screens for both anxiety and depression. This tool has been developed for use with people with physical health problems and attempts to avoid this potential distortion by removing the majority of physical symptom questions. This would be a useful questionnaire to ask William to complete as part of the assessment of his mood.

A useful source for other relevant questionnaires and rating scales is White (2001). This book describes a range of questionnaires and measures that are available for use in the assessment of cognitive-behavioural aspects of specific medical conditions as well as illness in general.

When selecting which measures to use, consider what we are hoping to discover by using the tool; ensure that it will help understanding of the identified problem together with the factors related to it and also that the tool is reliable and valid for the purpose we are planning to use it.

2. Diaries and record forms

Diary sheets and record forms that can be completed by patients between sessions to record salient information about the presenting problem or the thoughts, emotions, behaviour and physical sensations that relate to it are of frequent clinical use. These records often serve to enhance the patient's understanding as well as our own. Although standard diary forms exist, it is often possible to devise a record form with the patient and decide together what information would be most helpful to collect (See the Record forms section).

If we decided that assessing William's symptoms of discomfort or fatigue might be helpful then we could ask him to keep a record of daily activity and to record how these symptoms fluctuate over the course of the day or week. This would help us highlight any relationships between particular activities and symptom levels (See Record forms: Activity diary). Such diaries are invaluable in identifying targets for intervention and directing the clinician to appropriate strategies such as pacing and activity planning. They also help patients understand more clearly how they can and do directly influence these experiences.

As an introduction to understanding connections between the four elements of the "hot cross bun" it is often useful to ask the patient to keep a diary of the thoughts, emotions, behaviour and physical sensations that arise in association with significant events generally (both good and bad) or more specifically with the identified problems (See Record forms: CBT diary). For example, you might ask William to record episodes of depression emotions that occur and ask him to record the events, thoughts, physical sensations and behaviour that accompany these episodes. By recording examples of the problem over a one to two-week period, William can provide a much clearer picture of the problem and of the factors that relate to it. Moreover, this diary can pave the way for the use of more detailed record forms later in therapy, such as the form for challenging unhelpful thoughts (See Record forms: Thought record) when making cognitive interventions.

Assessment as an ongoing process

Although a great deal of cognitive behavioural assessment takes place in the first session and the first homework task, the assessment process continues throughout treatment. Over time, new information comes to light: some of it indicates the process of change related to the application of the cognitive behavioural approach; some of it may offer new insights and lead us to suggest a slightly different explanation of what is happening and why (formulation). For example, William may have previously said that he was not going out socially because he was too tired but now admits that he is not going out because he is worried that he may burst into tears if someone asks him questions about his illness. This new information gives a different understanding of the source of the problem and suggests a different target for intervention. This role of assessment in helping us build a formulation, and sometimes rebuild or develop a new formulation, forms the subject matter of the next chapter.

Exercises

Before you proceed to the next chapter take time to do the exercises included at the end of this chapter. To use this book properly you need to complete all the recommended exercises.

Background to exercises

Derek is a 55-year-old married man. His wife is 50 years old and has not worked since their two children were born. The couple have a married son aged 30 years who lives locally, who has two young children. They also have a 25-year-old daughter who lives at home as she can't afford to buy a property of her own.

Derek was reasonably fit and well until five years ago when he experienced a sudden heart attack and required bypass surgery. The operation was successful and the doctors told Derek that he had made a good recovery.

In the past two months Derek has begun experiencing sleeping difficulties. He finds that he regularly wakes in the night with chest pain, palpitations and drenched in sweat. He describes feeling constantly on edge and irritable.

He has been to see his GP and has also attended A&E on two occasions following these episodes. Both his GP and doctors at the hospital have said that the chest pain is most likely due to indigestion, but Derek is not convinced. Four months ago a colleague at Derek's work died following a heart attack.

Exercise 1

Imagine that Derek has been referred to you for help in managing his symptoms. Think about the information that you would want to collect during your assessment in order to fully understand his problems and to know how best to tackle this. Consider all four aspects of the "Hot Cross Bun" model. Under each heading write down three questions you would want answered during your discussion with Derek that would help you determine whether there is a problem for which a cognitive behavioural approach could be relevant instead of or as well as a medical intervention.

Identified **Problem** for which help is sought
Associated **Events:**
Associated **Thoughts**
Associated **Emotions**
Associated **Physical sensations**
Associated **Behaviour**
Consequences of the problem: immediate and long-term

Exercise 2

Take some time to consider what thoughts might be going through Derek's mind in association with the physical sensations that he is experiencing. What might he think his symptoms mean for himself, his future and his family? Then consider what emotions each of these thoughts might trigger, and how they might influence his behaviour over time.

Event and Physical Sensations:

Wakes in the night with chest pain, palpitations and drenched in sweat.

Thoughts	Emotions	Behaviour Immediate and later actions
About himself		
About the future		
About his family		

Recommended Further Reading:

Powell, T. (2000) *The Mental Health Handbook 2nd edition* Brackley: Speechmark Publishing Ltd. A wealth of information (including assessment tools and handouts) is available in this book and all the materials can be photocopied by the owner of the book.

White, C. A. (2001) *Cognitive Behaviour Therapy for Chronic Medical Problems:* A Guide to Assessment and Treatment in Practice. Chichester: Wiley. This book is a very useful companion to this book and includes some helpful questionnaires.

Wright, S., Johnson, M. and Weinman, J. *Measures in Health Psychology Portfolio*. Swindon: nfer-Nelson. These tools will help establish an assessment resource and can be photocopied.

Chapter 8
Formulation

What is a formulation?

With our cognitive behavioural assessment we aim to come up with a formulation of the problem that will indicate the most appropriate target for intervention. The term *formulation* refers to an understanding or explanation of the patient's identified problem and of the factors that have contributed to, or are maintaining, this problem. When using a cognitive behavioural approach we achieve this understanding whilst working through the assessment information with the patient. By using this collaborative method we can achieve a formulation that makes sense to both patient and health care professional and belongs to both. If the formulation is presented to the patient as the product of the deliberations of the health care professional then it will be much more likely to be seen as the explanation provided by the "expert" and as such to be treated as a fixed model into which all the facts must be made to fit. Our cognitive behavioural collaborative approach aims to make the formulation a "work in progress" to be tinkered with and adapted by both the patient and the health care professional as and when new information or developments indicate some re-appraisal.

We can think of the assessment and formulation process in terms of a jigsaw, where the assessment involves collecting all the individual pieces and the formulation process involves fitting these pieces together in the best possible way in order to see the overall picture. Sometimes the pieces can fit together in more than one way, but what is important is finding an explanation that makes sense and that appears to be the best jigsaw "fit" based on the current information.

Sometimes there is a bit of confusion between the cognitive behavioural model, or "Hot Cross Bun", and the problem formulation. The Hot Cross Bun illustrates the general principle of how thoughts, emotions, physical sensations and behaviours exert influence on one another (see Figure 1.1.1). In contrast, a *formulation* attempts to describe a very specific *sequence* of thoughts, emotions, physical sensations or behaviours that follows a triggering event and leads to a particular outcome. In mapping that sequence in a diagram the formulation will not therefore look exactly like a "Hot Cross Bun".

We will discuss two types of formulation diagrams that are especially useful in the cognitive behavioural approach: the "vicious cycle" and the "downward spiral". A **vicious cycle** formulation demonstrates how an interplay between thoughts, emotions, physical sensations and behaviours loops back to perpetuate and reinforce the problem. A **downward spiral** formulation illustrates a "domino effect" whereby one thing leads to another, often following an initial unhelpful appraisal of the triggering event. The vicious cycle helps us to explain how a person can get stuck in a particular pattern, repeating it and reinforcing it. In this way it will explain why a problem will be maintained over a long period of time and perhaps across a range of situations. The downward spiral helps us to demonstrate how certain (sometimes small) trigger events can escalate and produce disproportionate consequences or lead to responses that are not recognisably related to the original trigger.

Vicious cycle formulation

In order to illustrate a vicious cycle formulation we will refer back to the case example of Derek which appeared in the exercises at the end of the chapter on assessment. Derek is having problems sleeping. After a heart attack five years ago he received bypass surgery, but he does not trust that this solved the problem and so remains worried about his health. Recently he has experienced sleeping difficulties and chest pains on and off. Despite GP and A&E staff reassurances about the problem most likely being indigestion, he remains concerned that something has been missed.

An example of the type of formulation that might be derived from an assessment interview with Derek is shown below in Figure 1.8.1. This illustrates how a vicious cycle can be set up whereby the more he thinks that his chest pain indicates an impending heart attack, the more anxious he feels. The more anxious he feels, the more the physical sensations of anxiety increase (including chest pain and heart racing), which in turn reinforce his fears. In order to help Derek, it will be necessary to break this vicious cycle that maintains his problem.

Learning to calm down might significantly reduce some of the physical symptoms that worry Derek so much. Calming down might prove even more effective if he can challenge the unhelpful thoughts and behaviours that feed his fear of having a heart attack.

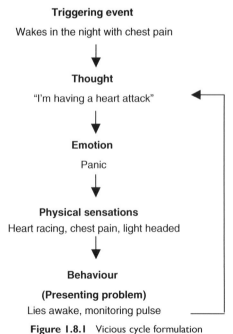

Figure 1.8.1 Vicious cycle formulation

Downward spiral formulation

The following case example illustrates a downward spiral formulation that might be developed from an assessment interview with Felicity, who is troubled by her behaviour towards her son. Felicity has conflict with her 19-year old son, Darren, who accuses her of trying to control him. Darren had his first epileptic-seizure when he was 17, just before he was due to take his driving test. He has been angry and resentful of his epilepsy and Felicity has frequently felt she needed to remind him of the possible consequences of neglecting his medication, of drinking too much and of doing things which could prove dangerous if he were to have a seizure. She feels very responsible for his wellbeing; she also understands how frustrating it must be for him and wants to be supportive. Despite this she feels she keeps doing the wrong thing and they end up arguing. As an example of what can go wrong Felicity describes one Thursday night when Darren was late home from the pub and, although very tired, she waited up. Whilst waiting she heard an ambulance go past and got very worried. However, when Darren came in an hour later instead of just being relieved and happy to see him she shouted at him. She now feels bad about this, but knows it is likely to happen again unless she can learn to stop it.

As can be seen from Figure 1.8.2, each thought in the chain leads on to associated emotions, physical sensations or behaviour, escalating to the point where Felicity has primed herself to shout at her son when he walks in the house. There are several points in this chain where intervention could bring about constructive change using a cognitive behavioural approach. Felicity might be helped by coming up with new thoughts that do not stir up worry and anger, she might benefit from techniques that calm the physical sensations and she might want to consider different ways of behaving that help her cope better with her "burden" of responsibility and her emotions. Changes at each of these points on the flow chart could help to interrupt the downward spiral. We will need to clarify how typical of the problem this incident is because that information will help us develop our formulation and decide what intervention is most appropriate. If Darren frequently stays out late, never phones and often does not come home at all this might lead us to consider interventions such as helping Felicity to re-appraise the boundaries that she sets with her son and how to problem solve issues that might arise whilst negotiating new boundaries.

Alternatively, Felicity might admit that her son usually tells her what time he will be home, is not typically late, but that this is just an example of the fact that she finds it difficult to relax while he is out or does not know what he is doing, for fear of what might happen to him. This formulation would suggest that Felicity's personal sense of responsibility and thoughts about her son's safety together with her inability to relax would be more appropriate targets for intervention.

Diagrammatic and written formulations

So far we have described formulations as flow charts but not everyone understands diagrams easily so some of our patients may prefer a written explanation. Either way the formulation will aim to be as simple as possible, highlighting the factors that contribute to and maintain the problem. It does not have to include or account for all the information

Triggering event
Hears an ambulance

↓

Thought
"He's had an accident or a seizure"

↓

Physical sensation
Heart pounding, dry mouth, clammy hands

↓

Emotion
Fear

↓

Behaviour
Jumps up and paces the floor

↓

Second thought
"I know it's probably not him but I can't help worrying.
He's so inconsiderate and irresponsible.
He has to learn to take more care of himself
and not put me through all this stress"

↓

Emotion
Anger

↓

Physical sensation
Tense stomach, knotted muscles, hot

↓

(2ⁿᵈ Trigger Event
Hear the front door open and close)

↓

Third thought
"Here he is. How dare he keep doing this to me?
This has got to stop right now"

↓

Presenting problem behaviour
Shouts at son as he walks in
"You are so bloody thoughtless!"

Figure 1.8.2 Downward spiral formulation

collected from the assessment process: an easy to remember formulation with the bare minimum of detail will be of greatest use to the patient when trying to put changes into practice. The following case description shows how both a written and flow chart style of formulation can be produced from the same assessment information.

Margaret was diagnosed with breast cancer eight months ago and underwent a lumpectomy and radiotherapy treatment. She is making a good physical recovery. Margaret is tired and tearful a lot of the time. She spends most of her days in the house alone. She gave up her voluntary work when she was first diagnosed, and has not gone back to it. Her husband is being very helpful and supportive, currently doing all the housework. Margaret complains of being bored and isolated and is seeking help because of this. Nevertheless, she has been making little effort to build a social life and her husband does not seem to encourage her to do so.

The assessment interviews and assignments reveal specific thoughts, emotions, physical sensations and behaviours that help explain her situation and this is drawn together with a history of her difficulties. Following diagnosis, Margaret gave up her voluntary work. She believed that it was impractical to continue with it whilst undergoing treatment, having been warned of the tiredness associated with radiotherapy. After treatment, she was worried that voluntary work would make her tiredness worse and that she would not cope, so she did not return. Her husband had similar worries about her overdoing things and so he took on most of the housework. Both of them share a belief that she should rest as much as possible until she has completely recovered and the tiredness has gone. Margaret has also felt unable to go out in public because of her tearfulness and stopped attending social activities for this same reason. As well as causing shame and embarrassment for herself and her husband, she believed that it would make other people feel awkward and uncomfortable to see her distressed; so she felt she should wait until she had recovered her composure more reliably before she started to see her friends again. Her husband's perspective was slightly different: contrary to Margaret's assumption, he did not find her tearfulness embarrassing, nor did he think that her friends felt like that either; but he recognised that visits from friends caused her to feel upset and uncomfortable so he considered it his responsibility to protect her from intrusions from other people until she finds them less difficult to handle.

In making sense of what is happening and why it keeps happening we can present a simple formulation in either a short written description or illustrated with a flow diagram. When we are writing up reports or putting the information in letters the written format may be preferred and sometimes the patient prefers it in this format too. Other times people find a visual representation in the format of a diagram easier to visualise and memorise; examples of both are included here regarding Margaret's situation (see Figure 1.8.3).

Using the formulation to plan an intervention

Once we have agreed a formulation with the patient the next step is to consider what type of intervention might help bring about constructive change. Often there may be more than one point in the formulation at which an intervention can be made, and the choice will depend on factors such as the patient's priority goal. Whenever possible it is a good idea

Flowchart formulation

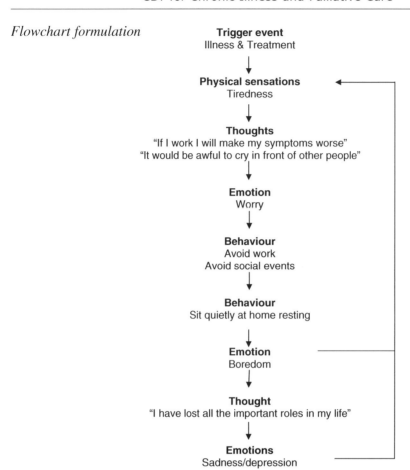

Figure 1.8.3 Margaret's problem formulation

Written formulation:

Fear of not coping with her symptoms has led directly to Margaret feeling bored and isolated. She has given up her work role to avoid tiredness, and her social contacts to avoid others seeing her cry. But in so doing she has been left without a sense of purpose and structure to her life, which has triggered symptoms of depression, including tiredness and tearfulness, which serve to maintain the problem.

to start with changes that are the easiest with which to achieve some success. On some occasions having completed this formulation and identified the types of intervention necessary, we will have completed our role with the patient. We might decide that we lack the skills, facilities or time to help the patient tackle these problems; the formulation will form the basis of a discussion with the patient about these issues and will usually help us identify referral on to another health care professional or to another agency that can better provide the appropriate assistance. These decisions will be discussed in more detail in the following chapter.

Formulation, learning and the collaborative effort

Time pressures and an enthusiasm for taking action to solve problems can make it hard for us to slow the process down and put effort into formulation development. However, learning how to create useful cognitive behavioural formulations is a skill worth struggling to master because it is so valuable in identifying effective interventions and avoiding putting effort and time into strategies that do not produce the sought after results. By working with the patient to produce the formulation together we may feel that the process is inefficient and that by doing it alone we could do it quicker. We may feel that the joint working shows up our own personal inadequacies in struggling to work out a usable formulation. However, it is a good investment of time and effort. The collaborative endeavour encourages the patient to fully participate in revising the formulation as further information is added and circumstances change. Working on it together helps the patient understand the thinking behind the choice of suggested interventions and why they might be effective. Even our struggling whilst trying to develop a meaningful formulation has its benefits since it reassures the patient that this process is individualised to meet personal needs and circumstances. Finally we should remember that the collaboratively achieved formulation facilitates learning: the patient learns how to understand and deal with the present problem in the course of developing this formulation. Armed with this knowledge the patient is better equipped to prevent relapsing back into the same problem at a later date and to avoid unwittingly creating new problems by stumbling into similar pitfalls in other situations.

Exercises

Before you proceed to the next chapter take time to do the exercises included at the end of this chapter. To use this book properly you need to complete all the recommended exercises.

With each of the exercises below we can only *know* whether the formulation that we have derived actually fits with the patient's experience by discussing it with them. However, for the purposes of these exercises, have a go at being in each person's shoes and trying to work out what a reasonable formulation of their difficulties might look like.

Exercise 1

Background information:
Norman is 57 and a Project Manager in the telecomms industry. He is married to **Linda** aged 50 and a housewife. They have three children (two daughters of 22 and 18 and a son of 13).

Key points from Norman's situation:
- Diagnosed with macular degeneration 18 months ago.
- Initially had very positive attitude towards medical profession and prompt action taken.
- Refused to "give in" to depression or doubt about effective treatment.
- Now feels let down and forgotten about by the medical profession.
- In the process of being medically retired and has stopped working.
- Difficult with the girls – lots of arguments.

- Tearful and irritable with wife.
- Distant with son.
- Impatient with his own elderly parents.
- Enjoys seeing the eye clinic nurse – the only person who understands – but doesn't believe it is of any real help.
- Feels he has become a nasty, grumpy old man but cannot help himself.

Based on these facts and the information in Norman's diary try and come up with a vicious cycle formulation that accounts for Norman's reaction to daily situations involving other members of his close family. Try to ensure that your formulation accounts for Norman's presenting psychological problem and that it covers all aspects of the "Hot Cross Bun", and demonstrates how the problem is maintained.

Norman's cognitive behavioural diary					
Date	Event	Thoughts	Emotions	Physical sensations	Behaviour
21/3	Daughter leaving washing up	She is just using us	Angry Frustrated	Tense	Shouted at her and told her to be more considerate
25/3	Asked son about his homework. Got sulky response	He doesn't respect me. I'm a useless father	Depressed	Tired	Sat and watched TV all evening
28/3	Phone call to my parents	They are so wrapped up in their own problems and don't care about me	Irritated and hurt	Fidgety and restless	Told them "I can't talk for long" and hung up
30/3	Tried to mow the lawn	I have to keep up my stand-ards and not let this beat me	Annoyed	Sick and aching	Had to stop after 15 minutes
30/3	Argument with wife for criticising me for tak-ing so long	She's sup-posed to understand but just makes her own demands	Irritated and sad	Tired and unwell	Lay on the bed all evening
31/3	Phone call from daugh-ter at univer-sity	She doesn't want to talk to me and isn't coming home at Easter to avoid me	Sad and hurt	Tired and feeling unwell	Told her I was all right and handed phone to wife

Exercise 2

For the next two exercises we are going to return to the case example of Geoffrey, which you were asked to consider in Chapter 2. As you will remember, Geoffrey is a 45-year-old physiotherapist, who was diagnosed with MND two months ago following concerns about strange difficulties with speech and odd throat sensations. He is married with two sons aged 12 and 8. Geoffrey has been an active sportsman.

His wife is a nurse and shares his enthusiasm for sports and outdoor recreational activities. However, the marriage has been under some strain in the past two years since he had a brief affair with another woman.

Both boys hero-worship their father and take a keen interest in sports to impress him.

His elderly parents who live five miles away are in poor health and depend on him and his wife for shopping and running around. They too rather hero-worship their son.

Geoffrey has presented saying that he should be coping better with his illness and can't understand why he is so anxious and tense all of the time.

Geoffrey's CBT Diary			
Thoughts	**Emotions**	**Physical sensations**	**Behaviour**
I'm going to die	Fear	Stomach churning, tense, sweaty palms	Couldn't sit still, paced about
It is going to be really horrible	Dread	Stomach churning	Sat with head in my hands
My wife won't be able to stick it. She will leave me	Loneliness	Weak and tired	Cried
I can't bear the thought of my sons seeing me like this	Self-loathing	Agitated, tense, sick to the stomach	Beat fists against head
My parents have always been so proud of me. This will devastate them	Anxious	Butterflies in stomach	Got up and paced around
Oh no, it is happening already, I feel really weak	Panic	Weird feeling in head	Checked my body to see what else was happening
Get a grip, you're a physio, you should be coping better than this	Shame	Tense and restless	Went out for a run (while I still can) to clear my head

Geoffrey has provided a thought diary that he completed whilst sitting alone on Saturday afternoon watching rugby on TV. He got up to make a cup of coffee and found that he felt weak in his arms and legs and unsteady on his feet.

Use the information in Geoffrey's diary to come up with a diagram formulation that you could share with him that explains his presenting problem of sudden panic attacks whilst at home.

Does your formulation of this situation appear to represent a vicious cycle or more of a domino effect?

Exercise 3

Imagine that you are writing to Geoffrey's GP and want to share your formulation with them, so that they can better understand Geoffrey's difficulties. Try and summarise the information from your diagram formulation into a simple written explanation, which covers the bare bones of the formulation.

Recommended further reading:

Nikcevic, A. V., Kuczmierczyk, A. R. and Bruch, M. eds. (2006) *Formulation and Treatment in Clinical Health Psychology*, London: Routledge.

Dudley, R. and Kuyken, W. (2006) Formulation in cognitive-behavioural therapy: there is nothing either good or bad, but thinking makes it so. In Johnstone, L. and Dallos, R. (eds.) *Formulation in Psychology and Psychotherapy*, London: Routledge.

Chapter 9
Deciding on a Course of Action: Part 1

There are special considerations that confront the health care professional who is using a cognitive behavioural approach to work with people with life-changing illnesses and these come to the fore during the assessment process and formulation development.

Those whose role primarily focuses almost entirely on the patient's psychological health (such as counsellors, psychologists and psychotherapists) may find it routinely appropriate to use cognitive behavioural methods to thoroughly assess and develop in-depth understanding of the psychological issues and carry this through into therapeutic action plans.

Other health care professionals with a wider remit for physical as well as psychological care (such as palliative care nurse specialists) or with a more specific role focused on particular interventions in patient care (such as physiotherapists, speech therapists, dieticians) need to be able to define and limit their use of a cognitive behavioural approach more precisely and will use it less routinely. For these health care professionals the cognitive behavioural approach is intended to facilitate the fulfilment of their normal work tasks, not hijack their time or sideline their skills in order to undertake a completely different role as a cognitive behaviour therapist.

The issues raised in this chapter are intended to help with the evaluation of the information gathered from the patient thus far in terms of when to act and also how to prioritise the attention given to certain problem areas and aspects of the cognitive behavioural methodology to fit within the scope of "doing my usual job even better".

Assessment

The start point in considering whether or not to use a cognitive behavioural assessment will be evidence of psychological distress together with either obstacles to your fulfilment of your usual role or failure to achieve expected outcomes that is not explained by other (non-psychological) factors. Under these circumstances both patient and health care professional are likely to experience a sense of insurmountable obstacles or of "going round in circles". The purpose of the assessment will be to seek evidence of poor acceptance, adaptation or compliance that in some way interferes so that the potential benefits to the patient of your help are lost or distress is not relieved as predicted. The cognitive behavioural approach is designed to assist people in developing more helpful and adaptive approaches (see Figure 1.9.1) which reduce or circumvent obstacles and break vicious circles and the assessment process needs to identify the unhelpful sticking points.

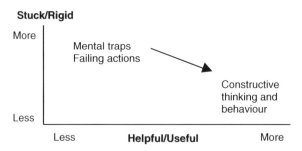

Figure 1.9.1 The adaptive shift

If an understanding of what those difficulties might be remains elusive then further assessment is required and it may be that additional expertise is required to complete this task. Consideration of referring on to mental health professionals will also be relevant when the psychological distress is itself the primary problem rather than contributory to the problems you are attempting to address. High distress scores on assessment tools such as the HADS and Distress Thermometer (see Assessment chapter) would be another reason for early consideration of referral to mental health services. Unfortunately, because services for people with mental health difficulties are often limited, there may still be a need for you to consider ways of continuing to offer help at least to the extent that it enables you to perform your own role properly.

The classification of the problem to be dealt with will be helped by the accumulation of information through the assessment process together with the statements made by the patient (and perhaps others) as to what the problem is. Formal diagnosis is often not appropriate since actual mental health pathology is not going to be present in many of the patients with life-changing illness and in any case it is not part of the role of health care professionals outside of the mental health specialty to make that type of diagnosis.

However, some way of categorising and labelling issues is very useful when trying to decide whether it is possible to offer help. A selection of relatively common psychological problems has been included in Part 2 of this book. Suitable methods of cognitive behavioural intervention for helping with these problems have been included in the "Toolkit", which is Part 3 of the book. Using the assessment information to determine the problem should also enable you to make an initial decision as to whether you can consider the possibility of offering help.

Put at its simplest, if the problem is not in the book then it is doubtful that you have the tools to help.

Unfortunately, however, that is slightly too simplistic a statement precisely because we are not using diagnostic labels. In our daily lives when referring to commonly occurring sources of psychological difficulty and distress we use all sorts of different phrases and place the emphasis on different aspects of the issues we face. So in assessing whether or not you can offer help using the scope of this book, it will be necessary to become familiar with the other terms that might be relevant when describing this problem. Also you will need to consider the possibility that, because different aspects might be emphasised in this book, the problem identified by you and the patient could be embedded under a problem labelled with an entirely different heading. A table is included with a glossary of possible alternatives but it is recommended that you become very familiar with the contents of Problem Descriptions in Part 2. The formulation may also assist with the problem labelling by making it possible to prioritise the salient features that need to be tackled.

Formulation

The role of the formulation in a cognitive behavioural approach is to enhance understanding by teasing out the cause-and-effect relationships that generate and sustain unhelpful attitudes, poor coping behaviours, persistent emotional distress and avoidable physical discomfort. Formulations are best understood and easiest to work with when they are relatively uncomplicated, so starting with a simple formulation that directly addresses the pertinent issues is probably going to be the most useful type. This formulation can then be improved and developed as and when this seems helpful. Once again, as with the assessment, the role of the health care professional figures prominently in the selection of relevant problems for which a formulation will be developed.

Both patient and health professional may find that awareness of how to bring about effective change is improved by devoting time and attention to developing and testing a formulation related to the identified problem. But there are likely to be occasions where this is not the case:

- If it is already obvious to health professional and patient what the repeating and perpetuating features are, then there is no need to elaborate the formulation further unless the seemingly appropriate interventions do not produce the expected results. The patient who already understands that fatigue is being made worse because of poor pacing does not need a diagram illustrating how the problem is generated. The health care professional can move quickly to strategies for improving pacing, returning to formulation only if implementing those strategies seems problematic.
- Formulation is only *useful* if it enhances understanding and influences the course of intervention. When changes in understanding are not required and options for action are limited or controlled by other circumstances, there may be little value in a formulation exercise. The patient who is aware that she is dying, is bed-bound and is hoping to go home to die, does not need a formulation to help her understand her anxiety and frustration, nor will it increase the range of cognitive behavioural interventions that ward staff can use to help her cope. However, a return to consideration of a formulation may prove necessary if, despite attempts to minimise her distress, she remains highly anxious and frustrated.
- The formulation may indicate that you are not the best person to offer help at this point. The formulation might reveal that you are getting stuck because the patient does not accept the problem exists for which you are offering help, or that others have done all they should have done before involving you. It might show that there is an entrenched attitude of helplessness that induces apathy and that applying a cognitive behavioural approach to this will require more time and attention than your role permits. The formulation could point to a mental health problem such as obsessive-compulsive disorder that is interfering with the patient's ability to co-operate with your care plan. Treatment for these more complex mental health issues will require the skills of a psychological therapist or psychiatrist. The formulation in these

circumstances will perform an important role because it helps identify and explain alternative courses of action that are appropriate, thus reducing the likelihood of the patient feeling rejected or a failure.

- There may be no agreed formulation. This could be because it has proved too difficult to determine or because there is no shared understanding between patient and health care professional. If we cannot work out what is happening and why, or if we cannot agree on it with the patient, then the collaborative endeavour is beginning to break down and the need for another opinion is indicated. This may be simply a matter of peer consultation in which case the health care professional takes the assessment information to a knowledgeable colleague with the agreement of the patient and returns with new ideas to share. On the other hand, the degree of disagreement or difficulty may be such that a thorough re-assessment is called for, and including the possibility that the difficulties actually lie in the relationship between the health care professional and patient. Under these circumstances it will be the patient who gets the consultation with the knowledgeable colleague.

Concluding remarks

The cognitive behavioural assessment and formulation process does much to enable us to determine appropriate courses of action. For the cognitive behaviour therapist this decision making includes an answer to the question: "Does this problem seem appropriately addressed by a cognitive behavioural approach?" For health care professionals working with people with life-changing illness there is a need to answer two additional question: "Does this work relate appropriately to the work I do within my role with this patient?" and "Does the problem(s) identified through this assessment and formulation process fit within the framework of the psychological problems described in Part 2 of this book?"

Even if the answer to all three of these questions is "Yes", there are yet further questions to ask as the collaborative endeavour proceeds. These questions relate to the nature of the agreed goals and therapeutic interventions required to achieve them. Once again the health care professional needs to ask questions about skills and capacity when deciding whether to take a course of action to help or to refer on. We will return to this decision making process after considering goal setting and methods of achieving change in the next few chapters.

Exercises

Before you proceed to the next chapter take time to do the exercises included at the end of this chapter. To use this book properly you need to complete all the recommended exercises.

Exercise 1

1. Turn to Part 2 of this book and study the table of problems and alternative terms used.
2. Think about problems you have identified with people for whom you provide care and the terms you and they have used to describe their problems.

a Do they exactly fit some of the terms used in this table?
b For any problems that do not fit the terms in the table, can you find a reasonable match between Problems Descriptions used in Part 2 and the way you and your patients described these problems?

3. Make a list of the most commonly occurring psychological problems (using your patients' phrases) for use with future exercises in the book.

Exercise 2

1. Review your own CBT diary and the pattern of negative emotions and problematic events. Find something from that record that you would like to change.
3. Develop a simple formulation including all the relevant information (and nothing more) that helps explain why this occurs

a What triggers it?
b What maintains it?
c Why it has been/will be difficult to change

Exercise 3

1. With each volunteer review the problem orientated CBT diary material.

a Clarify the information using Socratic questioning
b Ask about other relevant information not included in the diary (past experiences, external pressures etc.) that may be relevant.
c Do you have enough information to begin developing a formulation?
d If not then identify what further information needs to be collected and how to get it.

2. When you have enough information for you both to begin work on a formulation have a go at developing one together that explains what causes or maintains the problems that stop the volunteer achieving the goal they have identified.
3. Ask the volunteer to continue keeping the CBT diary and to study the formulation.

But,

If CBT diary information or the formulation indicate that there is a major psychological or other difficulty that will require specialist skills input, discuss how best this need can be met and how to access that help then end your involvement with this problem area and select something different to work on with your volunteer.

Chapter 10

Goal Setting and the Step-by-Step Process

Physical health problems can seem very 'real' in comparison to emotional difficulties. Physical symptoms can seem more pressing. Dealing with emotional problems may feel like a 'bit of a luxury': something to be dealt with later. This may be quite appropriate: when people are acutely ill their physical needs must be addressed first. Further, many health care staff, carers, partners and families find it easier to address and support people's physical needs and prefer to avoid intruding on the emotional issues. Health care professionals can also be inclined to dismiss emotional problems as perfectly reasonable and normal under the circumstances, thus encouraging complacency and fatalism that this is how it has to be. Lastly, many people fear that emotional difficulties, particularly prolonged ones, are a sign of weakness or personal failure.

Constructively addressing these problems and developing a shift of emphasis towards the possibility of change may be quite a surprise to our patients and some may resist the shift of focus away from problems, but goal setting is the stage in the therapy process where we agree with the patient what we are going to work on in the time we have together. In order to do this, we have to change the focus of our work. While we are assessing and formulating the problems, we have worked together collaboratively on understanding what is wrong, what the problems are, where they came from and how vicious circles in our thoughts, behaviours, emotions and physical sensations keep the problems going and keep the person stuck. If all has gone well so far then by means of the formulation we have helped the patient deduce some common threads running through a set of seemingly unconnected problem situations into a much smaller set of problem response patterns. The formulation shows that following the common thread in differing circumstances does much to explain the occurrence of the individual problem situations. Now, in agreeing goals we switch the focus from understanding these common threads to considering how to change them, identifying what the patient wants to achieve. We have to start considering what is hoped for and what is possible.

At its simplest the goal setting process involves identification of a suitable goal to work towards, clarification of how the situation is at present and the steps to be taken to get from how things are now to the identified goal, whilst taking into account the obstacles likely to be encountered along the way. With the right goal, the appropriate cognitive behavioural interventions begin to fall into place. Without that goal, the health care professional can appear to be working in a rather haphazard way, the patient may fail to appreciate that progress is being made or understand why it is being made, and the end point for this help may be quite difficult to determine.

The Step-by-Step Process

It may seem a banal point to emphasise, but knowing where we are going is usually something we want to determine before we set out on a journey. However, all too often in attempting to alleviate the distress of others we can be tempted into identifying a course of action that seems sensible and pursue it without having a clear idea as to where we are heading. Consequently an investment of time and effort into determining suitable goals is very worthwhile. The process of doing this well rightly dominates the contents of this and the next chapter but in order that the other aspects of the step-by-step process are not forgotten and to demonstrate the guiding role that the goal plays, we will start with an overview of the process.

If we continue our journey analogy a little longer, the more precisely we have identified our destination the more likely we are to arrive there by the most direct route and be clear as to what we need to prepare for the journey. We will also know when we have arrived and what we are likely to do when we get there. Incidentally, we also need to know from where we are setting out: if we have got our geography wrong about either start point or destination, we are going to get rather lost at some point.

In planning a cognitive behavioural intervention, we need to know very precisely both our destination (**goal**) and how things are at present (**start point**); we want to chart a route of change (**action plan**) that identifies all the tasks that need to be performed in order to achieve the change (**steps**) and take into consideration all the factors that may impede progress towards the goal (**obstacles**). In this book we refer to this as the **step-by-step process** and it is illustrated in Figure 1.10.1.

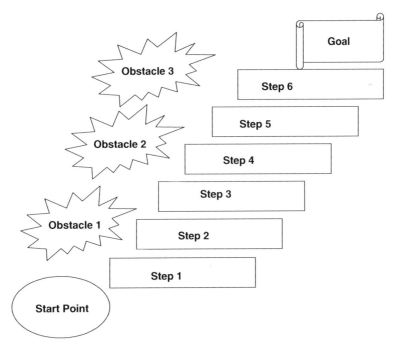

Figure 1.10.1 The step-by-step process action plan

At the start of structuring our cognitive behavioural intervention we will spend time with the patient considering all of the components of the step-by-step process (see Information sheets: Goal setting and the step-by-step process, Goal setting: examples; Record forms: Goal planning – step-by-step record) so we need to have a clear understanding of appropriate things to include in each of them.

The characteristics of suitable goals

The purpose of the goal setting activity is for health care professional and patient to collaboratively identify and agree positive goals. In examining this purpose we will return to the example of Felicity and her problems with her epileptic son, Darren (see page *** for background information). In transforming the identified problems into a course of constructive action, we need to agree with the patient what we aspire to achieve by the end of the process. To this end we need to determine goals that have certain characteristics.

1. *The goal addresses problems relevant to the patient's reasons for seeking help.* Felicity has a number of problems in her life which are important to her and relevant to her difficulties with Darren. She recently discovered that her husband has been having an affair and they have been discussing divorce in a reasonably amicable manner since the marriage has been in a poor state for several years. However, because of her worries about her own future as well as Darren's, Felicity has been sleeping badly. Waiting up for Darren when he gets home late has afforded an excuse for not going to bed and tossing and turning all night. In explaining the background to the problem in this way, Felicity has given the epilepsy clinic doctor who had agreed to see her lots of leads to follow and it would be very tempting to explore more of the marital or sleep disorder issues and focus on ways to deal with those effectively. Indeed, it may be easier to offer advice and action plans in relation to these issues than to come up with suggestions for managing a young adult determined to break all the rules. However, Felicity is seeking guidance about her angry outbursts towards her son and her goal will involve change from that current situation. Other issues may be of relevance along the way but she will need to be convinced that they contribute directly to attainment of her goal.
2. *The goal is relevant to your professional role with the patient and within your competencies.* The patient may pick a goal which is right for them but will require onward referral because the work that needs to be done is not within the scope of the service you provide or your competencies. The clinic doctor has an interest primarily in Darren's lifestyle and compliance with his management of the epilepsy. She is rightly focused on ensuring that Felicity does not inadvertently drive Darren in the wrong direction. The doctor also recognises that neither mother nor son seems to be displaying psychological pathology and referral to local mental health care services would be inappropriate.
3. *The goal can be worked on frequently enough* for new options to be tried, their impact assessed and further adaptations made within the time-scale of your involvement. Felicity admits to getting angry with Darren three or four times a week. Although their spats are not serious enough to warrant referral to a mental health specialist, the frequency makes them significant as a "corrosive" influence on the mother-son relationship at a delicate time in the hand-over of responsibility from mother to self-management. The doctor has decided that she can afford to give Felicity two or three more appointments to help with this problem using a cognitive behavioural approach and that there are likely to be enough opportunities during that time for Felicity to develop better strategies and achieving some goal that meets Felicity's needs.

4. *The nature of this goal is within the scope of what the patient can influence and change.* The person must have direct ownership of the problem and potential control of the attainment of the goal; our goal-setting will immediately run into major problems if the goal depends on someone else changing. For example: "I want to be more open with my partner about my feelings" is a goal that is personal and within my own control (even though the partner's response can only be guessed at). On the other hand, "I want my partner to be more open with me about his feelings" is personal but not within my control.

Fortunately for the clinic doctor, Felicity already recognises that it is her anger that needs to be worked on and not her son's behaviour. It would have been very easy for her to have come to this meeting and blamed her son for causing her to get upset and concluding that he is the problem that needs fixing. As he does not agree that he is a problem, he is not seeking to fix anything and changing his behaviour is proving to be beyond Felicity's influence. Therefore, she has rightly concluded that it is her own capacity to cope with his behaviour that she set her sights on changing with help.

5. *Achieving this goal will bring benefits the patient desires.* Frequently we find ourselves encouraged to help patients work on goals which others want on their behalf or which patients believe they ought to want for themselves but do not. These are not positive goals because the patients do not have positive attitudes towards them and do not own them as personal goals. Several of Felicity's friends have advised her that the best thing for Darren would be for him to move out and fend for himself and that she should confront him with a "shape up or ship out" ultimatum. Felicity knows that Darren will be moving out one day soon and can see the logic of the argument that if she does not know what he is up to then it is less likely that she will be worrying and getting upset. However, they do have a close relationship and she wants him to move out on a positive note when he feels ready. She also knows that whenever that is she will miss him when he has gone. This is made all the more poignant because her husband is now moving out and Darren is the youngest and will be the last of the children to leave. She dreads the idea of being in this house on her own and cannot make Darren's departure her goal.

6. *The goal will be achieved at acceptable personal cost and risk.* Where the patient believes that the personal costs or risks involved will be too high to justify the potential benefits then we have a goal that is the wrong goal for this person. For example legitimate questions that would need to be answered might be: "If I start to behave in this way will my husband still love me?" or "If I take the time I need for relaxation, will I be able to live with the consequences of what I do not get done?" The patient needs to be comfortable with the answers to questions like these before progressing towards making any change. Felicity has already rejected suggested goals from friends because she does not want Darren to leave home at this time.

7. *The goal is a SMART goal.* During the goal setting exercise, particular goals will be selected from a range of possible goals and checked to see that they have the other characteristics we have listed here but we also need to ensure that health care professional and patient both have the same clear understanding of what that goal is and what will have happened when it is attained. In other words, they seek to make each goal a SMART goal.

It is much harder to achieve that triumphant moment of scoring a goal when the goal posts keep getting moved. Unfortunately, in psychological and social concerns we are frequently the culprits who move our own goal posts. SMART is a strategy for helping us fix the goal posts and the net so they do not move whilst the game is in progress.

Sometimes it can be useful to explain to the patient about SMART goals, but whether or not the patient is aware of SMART it will always be important for the health care professional who is using a cognitive behavioural approach to ensure that agreed goals meet the SMART criteria. So what are they? In different books they are phrased slightly differently but in this book we use the acronym SMART to stand for Specific, Measurable, Achievable, Relevant and Timely. Let us look at each in a little more detail.

a) *Specific* refers to the need for sufficient detail to be able to determine whether or not the goal has been achieved. "Go for walks" tells us the activity but nothing else whereas "Go for a walk around Kew Gardens for two hours" gives a very precise description of the activity that would be considered a successful achievement of the goal.

b) *Measurable* means we want it to be a goal for which we can measure progress. Sometimes that progress can be measured in time or distance or similar normal measuring ways. The two hours at Kew is an example of this. Building stamina to do a two hour walk will be helped by knowing that prior to trying this goal the person has managed half an hour, then one hour, then two hours round a local park before visiting Kew. Sometimes the measuring will be more subjective and will involve tasks that are increasingly difficult psychologically for the patient or are necessary to be done prior to the goal task. Whichever type of measuring is done, it enables progress towards the goal to be charted. We will discuss this further in the section on Step-by-Step Approach later in this chapter.

c) *Achievable* requires that health care professional and patient believe that it is possible to reach this goal at some point if all the tasks that contribute to its attainment are completed. Miraculous and fantasy goals together with goals that are about changing other people are of no practical value in a cognitive behavioural approach because they offer no scope for the person to do something which is constructive and under personal control. But this is a little more complicated than that because sometimes people do achieve unrealistic goals and many others get satisfaction from at least trying to achieve them. Much will depend on the personal value attached to the tasks to be worked on along the way to the goal and the achievability of those tasks or sub-goals. We will look at this again in the section on hope and possibility in the next chapter.

d) *Relevant* may seem an odd criterion to include, since why would anyone choose an irrelevant goal. However, it can very easily happen that we set up a goal that is not quite addressing the problem that the patient originally described. Sometimes the idea of doing anything rather than nothing is very tempting but a watchful eye on the relevance of the goal to the patient's problem should prevent us falling into that trap.

e) *Timely* can be a harsh or frustrating criterion on occasions. A perfectly good goal that exactly meets the need can be ill-advised if this is the wrong moment to try to work on it. Sometimes patient's health or resources make it inappropriate for now to pursue this very good goal. Other times there are other changes taking place that may affect whether or not this goal is going to be appropriate and again it is not going to be right to proceed with it at the current time.

For Felicity to know that she has achieved her goal what will she have needed to demonstrate to herself? Her initial response to the doctor is "Always feeling close to her son and never getting cross so that he feels he can talk about his concerns to her". They both agree that this sounds like a highly desirable goal but "feeling close" seems rather vague and "always" and "never" make it difficult to measure. Consequently, with this statement it would be very difficult to know when the goal had been achieved. It is also perhaps a little idealistic to be expecting to be permanently feeling close when clearly there can be all sorts of situations arising in ordinary life that are quite likely to create some degree of tension and conflict between a parent and young adult offspring. So as a goal there is doubt about it being achievable. In fact, they realise this statement even fails the hurdle of relevance since "closeness" and "getting cross" were not the identified issues. The problem had been about Felicity failing to deal with her annoyance and concern without shouting at Darren. A relevant goal will specifically address the issue of shouting and, perhaps, losing her temper in other identifiable ways. Finally, Darren has already made it clear that he feels that his mother is trying to control his life, so, however desirable it may seem to work on strategies for "feeling close" this is very likely to be the wrong time to be trying to do it, since Darren may misinterpret this as further attempts at interference and control.

A SMART goal for Felicity is quite likely to involve managing to resist shouting at Darren or lecturing him even in situations when his behaviour causes her to feel annoyed or concerned. The goal that mother and doctor agree on will be an alternative, low key expression of her disapproval or some other behavioural strategy and attitude towards him that Felicity regards as constructive.

In addition to these characteristics, good goals have other features:

8. *The patient's belief that things can be different* is going to heavily influence commitment to a particular goal. Does the person believe a better state of affairs can be achieved? "I can't see the family agreeing to share more responsibility for household tasks" or "I have to keep working to pay the mortgage and bills" might keep someone stuck in old behaviour patterns or roles and reluctant to explore alternatives. Felicity finds it difficult to believe she can stop herself getting unreasonably angry when she is worried. The goal needs to take into account the reality of circumstances and the consequences of change if it is to be believable; and those circumstances and consequences need to be acceptable to the patient. So, in sharing out responsibilities among the family an acceptable goal might acknowledge that "The kids will make a fuss and complain; things won't get done and I will leave them not done but I will stick to my guns and work with this new rota". Reducing work hours might involve looking for ways of reducing the mortgage and bills and accepting lifestyle changes to achieve that. Felicity will not be able to learn not to care what happens to Darren or even to stop being frustrated with him, but she can perhaps learn to manage her anxiety and anger better so that she does not shout at her son or do other things that fuel his belief that she is trying to dominate and control him.

9. *The goal has the potential to be a "Quick Win"*. Success breeds success and the ability to achieve some valued goal quickly will tend to boost morale and encourage an air of hopefulness with regard to other, perhaps slower or more difficult to achieve goals. Finding such a goal as a first area of work can be a useful bonus but it is not normally essential. Felicity and the doctor discuss other aspects of Felicity's behaviour that may need to change to lessen the tensions between her and Darren and identify that her concerns about his health include secretly checking up on whether he has taken his medication every day. Resisting the temptation to do this would help Felicity accept less responsibility for Darren's welfare and demonstrate that she can control behaviour despite the urge to act it out. This is a goal she feels confident she can achieve straightaway with enough determination and so it is agreed as a useful goal to work on whilst beginning to plan how to manage the anger better.

10. *The goal offers the opportunity to learn something that may have wider relevance* for the patient: it establishes a new understanding which may be transferable to other areas of their life. Again, the "quick win" goal described above for Felicity may prove particularly useful not only because it boosts her morale but also because it challenges the general belief that "I can't help myself" which she has always used to justify her outbursts and her interference in his life. By demonstrating that she can resist the temptation to check his medication, she will challenge that belief. If she fails to achieve this goal then an understanding of what made it difficult to achieve will at least move her one step closer to being able to challenge the helplessness belief.

Characteristics of the Start Point

In order to determine the steps to be taken towards attainment of the goal, there is a need for SMART-like precision throughout the step-by-step process including the start point.

The start point will describe circumstances as they are now in terms that are similar to those used in the goal. A good start point will describe all the features of the goal as they are at the present time. With respect to our formulation this start point will fairly precisely reflect some or all of the problematic outcomes. If there is a mismatch between formulation and step-by-step start point then we need to redefine the start point or the goal from which it was derived. We can expect formulation, start point and goal to form a coherent whole; when they do not do so or if they cease to do so as the cognitive behavioural intervention proceeds, then there is a need to review the formulation and the step-by-step process.

With a clear start point we are assisted in the recognition of suitable early steps to be undertaken and the obstacles to be overcome or circumvented. Felicity will include reference to shouting at Darren three to four times a week and her attitude that he should appreciate the reasons for her concern.

The characteristics of "steps"

Moving through a process of change from how things are now to how the patient wishes them to be in the future is rarely achieved with a single action. Frequently the level of "stuckness" that brings us to considering a cognitive behavioural approach comes about because single steps have been tried and have failed or because the patient has felt too overwhelmed by the magnitude of the task.

1. *Chunking.* By using the step-by-step process we seek to break a large task into a series of smaller "chunks". Each chunk is in effect a mini-goal contributing to the move towards achieving the major goal. We refer to these mini-goals as the steps. Each step has characteristics similar to those we have described for goals: the need to be SMART, to produce benefits at an acceptable cost, to be relevant to the patient's goal, to be believed in by the patient etc. The practicalities of goal setting will be described in the next chapter, but it is worth noting here that largely the same practicalities apply to the process of determining suitable steps: identifying how it may be realistically undertaken and what options there are, determining the level of difficulty this presents to the patient and the level of commitment there is to its attainment etc.

    In the process of scrutinising and testing these steps it is not unusual to discover that what initially seemed to be a very manageable "chunk" now appears to be a greater challenge. This is especially true when we find the patient unwilling to take the next step or remaining uncomfortable with one that has been seemingly achieved. The step-by-step process should include a willingness to re-examine problematic chunks and perhaps further sub-divide them to create new steps that overcome the difficulties.

2. *Sequencing.* In the course of preparing a series of steps there is often a need to consider the order in which these steps are undertaken. We can characterise three different types of sequencing of these steps and it may be helpful at times to consider which type of steps sequence is going to be most appropriate to use. For our purposes we have given each of these sequences a name:

a) *Forward steps.* Having broken the task into a series of chunks in order to make it more manageable it does not particularly matter in which order the chunks are tackled. For example a task (weeding the garden) may be broken into smaller chunks of time (10 minutes) and each step (bit of garden that is to be weeded) is of equal importance and effort.

b) *Stepping stones.* There may be a logical sequence to the steps because one chunk depends on another, so we cannot move on to the second step until we have achieved the first. For example, in planning a holiday we will probably want to first examine whether we can afford one, follow this by considering where we would like to go, then study the options available and finally book it. Whilst other sequences of these steps would be possible they would be far less helpful.

c) *Step ladder.* Sometimes our chunks vary in difficulty or demand and there is a benefit to be gained from ordering them to reflect this so that the easiest, simplest or least demanding are at the beginning of the sequence and there is a progression through to the most difficult and demanding at the end. This type of hierarchy of steps is particularly useful when early completion of easier steps reduces the difficulty experienced with later ones. For example a child is taught to read by first concentrating on short, simple and very familiar words often associated with pictures of the object described by the word; later the words learnt become longer and more complicated (such as verbs, articles and prepositions) with fewer clues as to their meaning. The later reading challenges are made easier because the child has made sufficient progress with the earlier tasks.

3. *Dealing with roadblocks.* The step-by-step process will have identified the potential difficulties in progressing towards the goal in the form of the identified Obstacles. In designing suitable steps these obstacles and other practical considerations will need to be taken into account.

a) *Tackle the roadblock.* Sometimes the design will involve incorporation of specific steps that tackle the roadblock (such as spending time working on overcoming a fear of water if you want to learn to swim);

b) *Await developments.* Sometimes further progress on this action plan will await another goal having been achieved or events elsewhere occurring that remove this roadblock (such as awaiting news of contract completion before proceeding to detailed planning of renovations to the house you hope to buy).

c) *Circumvent the roadblock.* On yet other occasions the steps will be designed to get around the roadblock, leaving it in place but coping despite it being there (such as using a personal music system to block out the noise of a busy open plan office whilst completing a difficult task requiring lots of concentration).

As Felicity and the doctor discuss steps it becomes apparent that she is not going to require very many specifically related to managing her anger in front of Darren. A step ladder sequence of least to most annoying situations in which to try out calmer strategies will probably meet this need. However, before beginning to climb that ladder there are some logical stepping stones to cross which involve understanding more about her own reactions and learning a new set of responses for when he annoys her. She also has to deal with a potential roadblock: Darren's behaviour is unlikely to improve as a result of the changes she plans to make and he may even push the boundaries of her tolerance a little further, so her strategies for coping need to include steps that enable her to get around a roadblock she can neither remove or wait to be removed.

The characteristics of obstacles

The step-by-step process is a continuous balancing act between encouraging and inspiring the possibility of change and tempering this with consideration of the difficulties that beset the process. Sometimes the patient is quick to raise the matter of obstacles to progress, even to the point of using them as a justification as to why it cannot happen. At other times it will be the health care professional who having inspired the patient to constructive plans now has to remind the patient that sheer force of will may not be enough to attain the desired goal.

In the goal setting process, consideration of difficulties and limitations will have already influenced the specified goal(s). An obstacle that cannot be addressed by any of the three ways for *dealing with roadblocks* described in the previous section necessitates a reconsideration of the goal, because that goal has ceased to be *achievable* in its present form.

Therefore the obstacles that are included in the step-by-step process will be ones which can impede progress to our goal but are not expected to completely thwart that progress if they are dealt with effectively.

Many, if not all, of the obstacles will be immediately apparent because they are included in the formulation and explain why the problem occurs, why it is maintained and why progress to the desired goal has not been achieved before. There may be some others that lurk in the shadows either previously overlooked in the absence of a constructive plan or not apparent until progress is being made.

Some obstacles (such as a physical disability) may be insurmountable but that does not mean that we cannot find a way to get round them (again, as already discussed regarding *roadblocks* in the previous section). Some may be problems that require specific constructive goals of their own (such as a negative attitude that encourages the person to avoid challenges). Others may be practical considerations for which allowance needs to be made because they will restrict progress in some way (such as limited stamina or financial hardship). Whether they are physical, psychological or day-to-day in their nature, these obstacles should be included in the step-by-step process and constructively addressed in the action plan.

Felicity has recognised several obstacles that will impede progress towards her goal. First, Darren will continue to seek independence from her controlling influence and she will want to fight him on this because of his epilepsy. Second, his pursuit of the normal ("irresponsible") lifestyle of a young adult will be a source of anxiety for her, also exacerbated by his epilepsy. Her poor sleep pattern will increase her tendency to be rather intense and emotional in her reactions. For the first of these obstacles, Felicity will need to learn how to relinquish control, accept that she cannot prevent her son from having seizures (or coming to harm) and co-operate in a handover of responsibility for his wellbeing to Darren himself. Techniques for managing and reducing anxiety together with a constructive plan for improving sleep may help her cope better with the second and eliminate the last of these obstacles.

Concluding remarks

The step-by-step process action plan provides a contract between patient and health care professional that provides both with a clear understanding of the way in which the cognitive behavioural approach can help facilitate a process of change from a situation that both understand to be unsatisfactory and problematic towards an objective that both agree would represent a change for the better. Sometimes more than one action plan will be worked on simultaneously: this is particularly likely if an obstacle in one plan is identified as suitable for a similar step-by-step process. Some plans will look very similar to the step-by-step process action plan included in the record form section of this book, but others will require a different number of steps and obstacles (perhaps fewer or perhaps many more), and others again will require lengthier goal and start point statements than this form design permits. The collaborative endeavour between patient and health care professional determines the design of this contract. Use a form if it is helpful, but design your own if it is too restrictive. Either way the health care professional should ensure that the plan is written down and shared with the patient. In this way, as with the formulation, both have a shared understanding. With this plan it is possible to chart progress and goal attainment, identify difficulties in progress and, if necessary, re-think the formulation. Backed up by the formulation, the step-by-step process action plan(s) becomes the hub of the cognitive behavioural approach.

Having given an overview of the step-by-step process, we will turn our attention in the next chapter to the mechanics of actually obtaining this information and some of the difficulties that health care professionals face when patients feel too powerless or hopeless to consider taking constructive action.

Exercises

Before you proceed to the next chapter take time to do the exercises included at the end of this chapter. To use this book properly you need to complete all the recommended exercises.

Exercise 1

1. Look again at the exercises at the end of Chapter 8 and the formulation work you did concerning Geoffrey.
2. Imagine you are working with him and try to develop a goal for a cognitive behavioural approach. Use a copy of the Record form: Goal planning – step-by-step record and write out a goal that you think that the person you have chosen would find acceptable and check it against the SMART criteria, adapting it as necessary. (In clinical practice of course we would do this in consultation with the patient but for this exercise you are pretending to be the patient too.)

Remember

- If the goal does not affect the formulation then it is not relevant to the work you are doing with the patient.
- Your SMART goal if it is achieved will break into Geoffrey's downward spiral in the formulation and change the outcome.
3. From the information you have about this patient it should be possible to describe a clear start point relevant to the SMART goal. Include this on the record form.

4. Again from the information available it should be possible to identify the obstacles that currently prevent the goal from being achieved. Write these on the forms as well.

Remember

- Many of the relevant obstacles will be represented in some form or another within the formulation.
- If there are triggers or maintaining factors from the formulation that are not taken into account within the steps and obstacles then the plan is not yet complete.

5. Identify a few of the steps (especially early ones) that might be needed to be taken in order to move towards this goal. Once again, it is only through consulting and planning with the patient that you can really determine whether the steps are in the right sequence or broken into small enough "chunks", so you need to pretend to be both the patient and care professional.

Remember

- At this stage your work is focused on identifying tasks, not on ways of doing them.
- Look at the identified problem situation(s) and not the other issues you can imagine arising with MND.

Exercise 2

1. Review your own formulation and check it against the new CBT diary information. Is there anything in the formulation that needs to be changed?
2. Once you are happy with the formulation think about a positive goal that would be the desired outcome if you could change the process described by the formulation. Then identify a SMART goal that would represent the change you would like to see.
3. Use a copy of the Record form: Goal planning – step-by-step record to enter the goal and complete the rest of the sections attempting to identify all of the necessary steps and acknowledging all of the obstacles.
4. Select some form of record keeping that might help you monitor progress and flag up difficulties. Look through the forms in the record forms section of Part 3 of this book for some ideas.

Remember

- The first steps are often the hardest and so need to be very small.

Some notes for those who are struggling to find suitable personal material:

- Our patients *present* us with problems for which we seek to provide some help.
- In these learning exercises we are seeking to *find* problems of our own.
- If finding a problem has proved difficult then you may be helped by taking a slightly different tack for yourself (and maybe even for one of your volunteers if they are struggling too).
- If there is no problem emerging from diary material or reported issues, then identify a small challenge you would like to work on such as something you avoid doing or have never got round to dealing with and turn that into a SMART goal. It should also be possible for you to draw a simple formulation that explains why it is a challenge and why you've never got around to it before.

Chapter 11
The Practicalities of Setting Goals

Like formulation development, the goal setting and step-by-step process is often very untidy as we question old beliefs and develop new ideas, then go back and forth between new knowledge and former plans of what to do. Goals may be re-written several times and "simple" steps sub-divided into more realistic "even simpler" steps as these suggestions are considered against other relevant information or tested against practical reality. We will examine how order and structure emerges from this apparent chaos as we describe the mechanics of this process.

Phases in the goal setting process

The phases of the goal setting process are laid out in Figure 1.11.1. The health care professional helps the patient move through the cycle in a mainly clockwise direction while recognising that from time to time it may be necessary to back track to an earlier stage to check new ideas against the old and see how well adopting them may enhance progress.

Throughout the process the health care professional maintains a cognitive behavioural communication style which facilitates clarification of hopes and exploration of options whilst moving towards resolution of what the goals will be. As mentioned in the chapters on communication, this will include curiosity (how does x relate to y?, how do they know . . .?, what happened then?, and how did that feel?), warmth (clear positive regard for the person as they describe this difficult material), collaborative endeavour (sharing professional knowledge without taking the expert position and treating the patient's experience and self-knowledge as comparable expertise), compassion (understanding that people do what they do for the best, to the best of their ability, empathising with but dispelling shame and guilt) and possibly humour (not ignoring irony and the funny side of the situation when the patient sees it that way).

1. *Agenda setting phase*
At the start of the process it is important to agree that the next block of time will be devoted to setting goals for the work you are going to do together. The goal(s) may follow very specifically from the problems identified in your current work together or from the material you have assembled in the assessment and formulation work you have done previously. In shifting from problem identification to goal setting it can be useful at this point to explain why goals are important (for giving focus and structure to the work, helping in monitoring progress and determining when the cognitive behavioural work is completed).

How does the person want to be? How can he or she manage the problems in a way that feels satisfying to them? We need a clear sense of how they would be if they were managing really well. We need to consider all the possibilities. Together we have to create a sense of hope and purpose

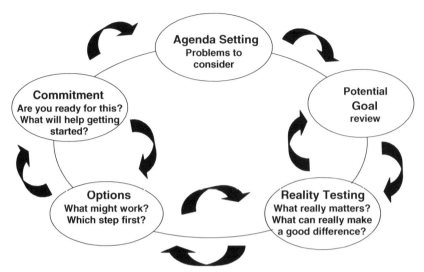

Figure 1.11.1   Phases of the goal setting process

and stimulate enthusiasm. This hope must be firmly grounded in reality. It is not helpful to hope for a magic cure or winning the lottery to take care of financial problems, since that is outside the person's control and hard to believe in. Helpful hope is about being in touch with the reality and seriousness of the difficulties, accepting that they are not going to go away and may even get worse. When we take a cognitive behavioural approach, we focus on the power we have to choose and change what we do, think and through that, feel. We set our work with the person in the context of what they value and what other goals and plans they have both within the health care setting and in other areas of their lives.

You will recall Norman, from the chapter on formulation. He is a man recently medically retired from work with rapidly developing blindness, who is feeling very low and anxious. He feels that the doctors have given up on him due to the progression of his sight loss. He is angry that his employer has "put him on the scrap heap" after years of loyal service. On top of this he is beginning to feel useless at home because he can no longer do the practical chores and he is worried about the burden this is placing on his wife. He believes his children take advantage of his wife's good nature and should help her more. He feels hurt that they only seem to have time for him when he can do something for them and feels they respect him less now he does not have a job and does less at home.

Norman has kept a week's diary of events in his life. He has recorded several incidents of trying to do chores when he ended up so overwhelmed by the experiences of frustrating failure and depression that he went to bed for several hours. He has recorded several rows with his wife, mostly over the children not helping her more with household chores. He has also noted that he got cross with the children about providing assistance, both with his son who declined his father's help with maths homework and with his daughter when she sought Norman's help with a car problem.

Norman's diary information is represented in the Hot Cross Bun diagram format in Figure 1.11.2, his problems and their impact on him are summarised in Table 1.11.1.

As we can see, Norman is aware he has a lot of tough problems. His mood is low and he is feeling very bad about himself. He knows he should not speak to his family in the way he does. He

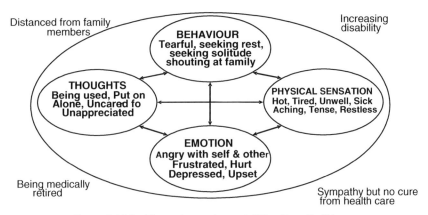

Figure 1.11.2 Norman's experiences in "Hot Cross Bun" format

Table 1.11.1 Norman's problems and their impact on him

Problem	Impact
Life is becoming limited	– Anxiety – Depression
Reduced ability to do tasks and prospect of further reductions in ability to come	– Lowered self esteem – Anxiety that others are rejecting him – "They have only ever valued me for what I did, not who I am"
Need a lot of rest	– Unwilling to rest – Constant need to test if can do more
Pain, stress and fatigue are almost continuous problems	– Reduce ability to hide anxiety and frustration ('on a short fuse') – Increase tendency to shout, be verbally aggressive
Feeling cut off from wife	– Desperate to do something to help her – Enraged when efforts to help her fail – Lonely – Useless

knows he wants to feel close to his wife but has no clear sense of any power he has which could make this happen.

Now we know what the problems are, we need to help Norman switch from a problem focus (passively describing what is wrong) to a possibility focus (actively processing his experience and formulating a personally meaningful and clearly articulated, desired goal). We need to help him develop a clear vision of how he would like to be in this situation and raise his expectations that if he makes a few changes to how he thinks or behaves, this can make a difference to what he experiences.

Table 1.11.2 Questions for helping generate goals

- What would you like to achieve?
- What would need to have happened for you to walk away feeling this time was well spent?
- What would you like to be different when we finish this work?
- What would you like to happen that is not happening now?
- What would you like not to happen that's happening now?
- How realistic is that outcome?
- Can we do that in the time we have available with these sessions?
- Will that be of real value to you?

2. Potential goal review phase

Starting from the identified problem list you are now seeking to generate a possibilities list. Select one problem from the list that you both agree would be a good place to start and begin to identify possible goals. Good questions to use to help people develop ideas about goals include those listed in Table 1.11.2. These questions and the others mentioned in this chapter can also be found on Information sheet: Goal setting questions.

In this second phase, the task is to help the patient see not just the problem, but also the alternative ways of how things might be and where change is possible. Using Socratic questioning in particular we can encourage the patient to be more flexible in thinking about the problem, its causes and the options for what can be done about it.

When the goal remains unclear, the health care professional can help the patient identify an inspiring vision of how things could be and use this to form the basis of the goal. The change task facing the patient can at times be a very hard one and when that is the case the goal must really stimulate enthusiasm in order to create the momentum to start the change process. In a later section we will examine ways of helping patients find inspiring visions and enthusiasm.

Returning to Norman, once he began to see the list of problems as one of possibilities, he spotted a theme which he recognised from other areas of his life. He realised that he based most of his sense of what he was worth on the value of the work he did. He realised he assumed others only wanted him for what he could do for them also. All had been well until he became ill and lost the ability to do all the things he had once done. He was under pressure from his doctors to adapt to his disability in a more realistic manner. He was concerned about how much this left his wife having to do.

From discussion of the options (see Table 1.11.3) it became clear that Norman's priority was to improve his relationship with his wife. It was easy to see that he was inspired by the possibility of making progress with this issue: his expression and his posture changed and he became much more animated. He recalled how he approached problems in project management and with his counsellor

Table 1.11.3 Norman's possibility list

- *Enjoy relationship with my wife*
- *Feel good about myself*
- *Make a contribution to family life*

began to generate ideas to refine into a SMART goal. He used his homework sheets to study how often the rows with his wife happened and noted that they were often linked with him trying and failing to do things as normal and that this too was often linked with when he was tired. He also noticed that feeling tired nearly always meant he got low and made his thoughts of being useless and forgotten more compelling. He began to have some ideas about how he could schedule time with his wife to be more likely to be enjoyable for them both.

Norman expressed a strong preference for focusing on the relationship with his wife as being the most important thing at this time.

3. *Reality testing phase*

In this stage the health care professional is checking the information gathered about the identified problem in the formulation to see that this goal is relevant and also that it is a goal that can be progressed within the limited opportunities available for working together with the patient. Examples of appropriate questions are included in Table 1.11.4.

Norman was having almost daily arguments with his wife which ended with him shouting. This was a new and very upsetting thing in their relationship for Norman and he believed his wife felt the same. It was having an impact on their intimacy and making it difficult to resolve everyday problems well. For example, he has noticed that many shouting matches happen at lunchtime on Sunday. Sunday morning has always been his time for cutting the lawn. Now he is finding the mental effort and fiddly aspects of getting the mower out of the shed and starting the motor frustrates and exhausts him before he has even cut a blade of grass. However, he does not allow himself to be beaten and perseveres; he finishes cutting the lawn and puts the mower away which is another fiddly task that winds him up. When he has finished he goes through the kitchen to wash his hands. These days, because he takes longer with this task, his wife has usually almost completed the cooking of Sunday lunch by the time he has finished and often makes comments that he should start earlier or wait until after lunch to do this; other times because she is now in a rush to get things served, she asks him to quickly lay the table or to pass something she needs. Norman feels criticised and that his struggle to be normal has gone unappreciated (even though he has gone to great lengths to cover up the fact that he is struggling). He becomes overwhelmed with rage and responds angrily.

Table 1.11.4 Questions for reality testing goals

- What changes have you tried so far?
- What happened when you tried them?
- What would happen differently if you made this change?
- Do you know of any situations when that has happened?
- How do you feel when you imagine making this change?
- What obstacles to progress do we need to consider?
- What else do we need to consider?
- Who else will be affected if you make this change?
- How do they see the present situation?
- How are they likely to react to the change?
- What other consequences (good and bad) might follow from this change?

By seeking to bring about change that focuses on the possibility of enjoying his relationship with his wife, Norman will need to review his whole approach to this Sunday morning ritual and the current goal that underpins it which has been to carry on as normal, making no allowances for changed circumstances and not admitting to the hardships this causes.

Once satisfied that a good positive and helpful goal has been identified the patient and health care professional are ready to consider what changes might make it possible to progress towards its attainment.

4. *Options phase*

Here the focus is on what the patient can do differently to start to get different results. This is an opportunity to think laterally and creatively together, generating lots of ideas and sometimes considering quite radical options; some options may not fall within the role of the health care professional with the patient including some which require skills and action that have nothing to do with a cognitive behavioural approach. When the best options seem to include actions that fall outside the scope of the cognitive behavioural approach then within the step-by-step process action plan the patient and health care professional attempt to identify how and when to include these options. Examples of some questions to ask are included in Table 1.11.5.

Norman has noticed that he is more likely to end up having a row with his wife if he has tried to do something useful without other people seeing how hard it has been for him. This suggests two potential options for action. One is to review his schedule and reduce the things that he finds particularly difficult and frustrating. Norman could see this could work but really was not keen to significantly reduce what he tried to contribute because that would make him feel more useless. The other was to be more open about how tiring and frustrating some tasks have become and also to begin to factor his slower work rate into his decisions about when to start a task. If he allowed more

Table 1.11.5   Questions for exploring options for steps

- What could you do to change the situation?
- What alternatives are there to that approach?
- What possibilities for action do you see?
- What have you tried in similar situations in the past?
- What have you seen others do in similar situations?
- Who might be of help to you in this situation?
- Who else should you involve or consult before you act?
- Would you like suggestions from me?
- Which options do you like/value most?
- What are the benefits and pitfalls of these options?
- Rate from 1-10 your interest level / practicality of these options
- Would you like to choose an option to act on?
- How difficult would it be for you to do this?
- Which would be the easiest step for you to take first?
- Is it easy enough, or do you think you would like to make it a little easier to be sure of doing it?

time for each task and made more allowance for his eyesight problems then he might be able to stay calm with the task itself or at least avoid taking out his frustrations on his unsuspecting wife.

This phase of the process should allow the development of one or two preferred avenues of exploration which include one or two possible goals and initial steps related to each of them. Yet more options may be held in mind for later. The intention is to ensure that there are goal and step options as consideration turns to the next phase and the level of commitment the patient has for working on these options at this time.

5. *Commitment phase*

In the commitment phase of the goal setting and step-by-step process the patient and health care professional consider what steps to take first, how to do them and what challenges or obstacles may present themselves. In the process earlier options remain open because this is in its way yet another reality test. So we need to establish whether the patient is still convinced this is a good goal. Is the patient committed to the course of action(s) that pursuing this goal will require? Examples of good questions to test commitment are included in Table 1.11.6.

Norman's ambivalence about aiming to do less became very evident at this stage in the session. He was prepared to consider changes such as pacing which might help him keep his contribution up at less cost to himself, but not committing to do less even if that did reduce the rows. However, he liked the idea of becoming more aware of how he was feeling and picking better times for difficult conversations. This approach fitted well with his sense of how he should be and how he used to be before he was ill – and he felt hopeful that it would make a difference.

As it became clearer that the positive goal and focus for work was to do with being open about fears and frustrations with his wife and solving problems that disrupted their time together, Norman needed little prompting to put aside certain issues. After all, Norman the project manager was used to solving complicated problems. Some patients will need more coaching and encouragement to deal with things one step at a time at this stage. Norman was able to break down the steps between where he was now, his starting point – at odds with and unable to problem solve important issues with wife – and where he wanted to be. He was able to contribute his sense of what things he would need to be able to know or do differently and together with his counsellor constructed a step-by-step

---

Table 1.11.6 Questions to check on commitment

- Will the achievement of this goal really make a difference to you?
- Will the achievement of this step really help towards achieving your goal?
- What are you feeling ready to tackle at the present time?
- Which of the next few steps seem frightening or impossible?
- Does the thought of them put you off making a start?
- What do we need to change to make these do-able?
- When will you take this next step?
- What might get in the way?
- What support do you need?
- Will you enlist that support?
- Will it be better to fail to make this step at all or to do it and for it to go wrong?

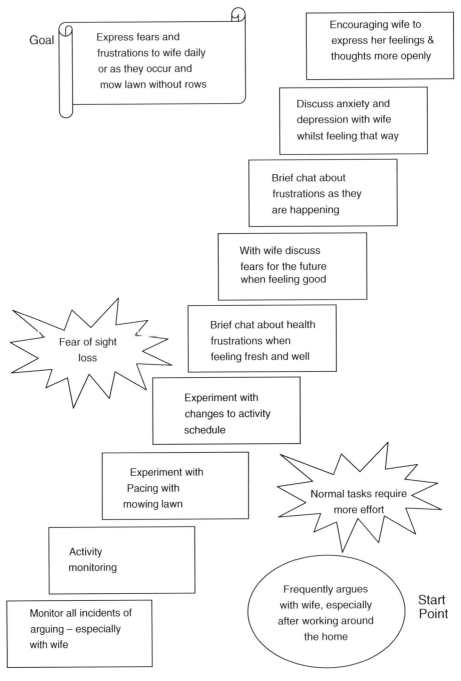

Figure 1.11.3 Norman's step-by-step process action plan

process action plan (see Figure 1.11.3) which would serve as a guide to the work they would do together and help them monitor progress.

Problems with goal setting

Finally, in this section we will briefly examine three problems that can emerge during the goal setting and step-by-step process.

1. *Lack of motivation*

At times the patients who we see are so overwhelmed by their problems that it is not possible to agree small specific goals that can be appropriately worked on within the context of the work we are meant to be doing with them or in the time frame we have to offer. This may become apparent to us:

a) Directly, with the patient clearly indicating that it is too much to cope with at the moment.
b) Indirectly when over a number of sessions we find the patient is

i) Changing focus and goal repeatedly
ii) "Forgetting" to do homework assignments
iii) "Forgetting" appointments

If, despite our best efforts, the goal setting and step-by-step process does not seem to be progressing to effective action then we should discuss this with the patient in order determine whether this is really work to be done now or if this is perhaps the wrong time for doing these things. It is better to ensure the patient knows what help is available and how to access it later than to try to persuade her or him to persist when motivation is poor.

2. *Problem complexity*

Some patients have had experiences in their lives that make it harder for them to cope with their illness. Some have personalities that make coping more challenging. In either of these circumstances there is an increased likelihood that the assessment and formulation process will reveal needs that appear to exceed the skills or resources available outside specialist mental health services. However, this is by no means always the case and we should remember that mental health specialists are just as intimidated by the challenges of physical health conditions (especially life-changing ones) as other health care professionals are by the problems of psychological distress. Consequently, we should not assume that the psychological needs of the very distressed patient with a life-changing illness will be met more effectively or skilfully by a mental health professional. We should use the assessment and formulation rather than just the personal history and past psychiatric diagnoses to determine whether there is a role for a cognitive behavioural approach provided by health care professionals who are not mental health specialists, even at times alongside those specialists.

Sometimes through the goal setting and step-by-step process it becomes apparent that the formulation was a bit too simplistic and that the problems really are more complicated than we had at first realised. Adapting the formulation to fit the new information reveals that, whilst providing assistance is possible, it is beyond the scope of what can be done in this setting. Referral on to another specialist, perhaps a psychological therapy colleague, can be something the patient finds a more acceptable option once the adapted formulation demonstrates why this might prove helpful. This will be a constructive outcome of the assessment, formulation and goal setting exercises undertaken and both patient and health care professional need to beware falling into the trap of interpreting this as "failure".

3. *Absence of hope and purpose*

Sometimes the patient needs to find some sense of inspiration and hopefulness before any other work can be undertaken. Knowing the health care challenges faced by some of our patients with life-changing illnesses and disabilities, we can ourselves fall victim to feelings of overwhelming hopelessness at times. However, we can usually think of patients who have managed to find sources of hope and purpose despite the most challenging of adversities. Thinking of these individuals can encourage us to persist in helping others with similar adversity find their own sources of hope and purpose.

If examples like this can help us as health care professionals shift out of our feelings of overwhelming hopelessness then we can be fairly confident that this will be an invaluable technique for helping our patients as well. Finding hope and possible goals through inspiring examples involves two stages:

a) Discovering what encourages, stimulates or inspires the patient?

   i) We can encourage the patient to recall past roles he or she performed well, to remember past experiences of success or other good feelings that stimulate a positive emotional reaction. We can ask "Do you ever feel like that these days" or "Would you want to recapture some of those feelings?"

   ii) We can ask the patient to think about themes from films, songs, stories or news items that stir positive thoughts and images.

   iii) Sometimes the patient can think of a heroic figure, a friend or a neighbour whose qualities the patient admires.

b) Converting fantasy to reality

   i) Having identified the invigorating idea the next task is to study the qualities that are especially important in making that memory, image or person a source of positive emotional responses.

   ii) With these qualities identified it then becomes possible to examine how goals might be developed that contain those qualities or enough of them to produce a goal which is stimulating and valuable to the patient.

This is a challenging task with patients who are usually very challenging themselves. Health care professionals often find it hard to balance their sense of not wanting to raise false hopes or encourage patients into unrealistic dreams and they are, of course, right to be concerned not to do this. However, whilst it is easy to avoid undertaking this difficult work, we should not overlook the fact that probably nobody else within the healthcare system will do it and these patients, who are so lacking in hope, are very needy.

To make it feel a safer exercise it can be broken into two separate tasks.

   a) The discovery of inspiring and positive images and memories is largely an enjoyable exercise for the patient when embarked upon in a light manner. The questioning in this stage of the process can often feel part of a relaxed conversation rather than an assessment process even though important information is being gleaned.

   b) Examining the information for clues as to how one might develop inspiring goals can be undertaken by the health care professional away from the patient initially if this feels safer and less pressurising for the practitioner. If it seems that there are possibilities for achieving a clear pathway to success then exploring these options more fully with the patient may prove highly rewarding.

A dream of marrying a beautiful film star and living happily ever after is not going to help the young man with muscular dystrophy except in that it starts him on the path to realising that his goal is an intimate relationship with someone about whom he can feel special. That in turn will lend itself to thinking through all the intermediate goals that may get him to that point, such as going to places where he can meet a few new people, being a bit more open about his thoughts and feelings, and so on.

Concluding remarks

With the goal setting and step-by-step process completed both the purpose and the nature of the cognitive behavioural interventions will be clear. There may be further adaptations as more information comes to light; however, it should now be possible to identify which techniques will most effectively bring about the desired changes and the next four chapters will provide an overview and introduction to the techniques you are most likely to need.

Exercises

Before you proceed to the next chapter take time to do the exercises included at the end of this chapter. To use this book properly you need to complete all the recommended exercises.

Exercise 1

1. Review the CBT diaries of your volunteers and the goals agreed at your last meeting with each of them.

    a. Does the information on the diary fit with this being a suitable goal?
    b. Does the goal fit with the problem and problem formulation on which you are working?
    c. If not, how should it be changed?
    d. Now explain about SMART and turn the goal into a SMART goal.

2. Use a goal planning – step-by-step record to specify start point, obstacles and steps ensuring the relevant formulation information is taken into account in the plan.
3. Decide on a relevant method for monitoring progress (mood chart, activity schedule etc). Ask the volunteer to start using the new record form, take home the plan and think about changes or additional steps that should be included.

Exercise 2

1. Find the list you prepared for the exercises in Chapter 9 of the most commonly occurring psychological issues with which you have to try to assist. For each answer the following questions:

    a. Is this a problem that is naturally part of the work you do with the patient?
    b. Is this a problem that interferes with your work with the patient?
    c. Do you usually have to deal with this problem yourself?
    d. Can you get help from elsewhere to deal with this problem?

2. If the answers to a, b and c are <u>all</u> "No" then exclude this problem from your list. If the answer to d is "Yes" then you can also exclude this problem from your list. If the answer to d is "No" or the answer to <u>any</u> of the others is "Yes" then this is a problem to think about in these exercises some more.

3. Identify up to five such problems that have come through the questions as appropriate for you to be dealing with as part of your job. For each one:

   a. Imagine a patient who has presented with this problem.
   b. Think of a possible SMART goal you could have agreed with this patient if you were seeing them now.
   c. Write this SMART goal down together with an idea of what the patient could have described as the start point. It doesn't matter that you don't know or can't recall the actual facts. These imaginary patients and their plans will be useful in later exercises, so keep your notes.

Recommended further reading:

Padesky, C. A. and Greenberger, D. (1995) *Clinician's Guide to "Mind over Mood"*, New York: Guilford Press, especially Chapters 1–3.

Chapter 12
Bringing About Change

The intention in applying a cognitive behavioural approach is to bring about change that is considered to be useful to the patient and to those who support her or him. This may seem a statement of the obvious but it is well worth reminding ourselves of it nonetheless. Not all forms of psychological care have this purpose. *Psychological support* is often intended to be just that: support through understanding, empathy and physical presence without attempting to facilitate change in the situation or the experience of it. If *psychological support* is what is being sought or is deemed to be what is needed then a cognitive behavioural approach is not appropriate because it is designed to encourage change in one form or another.

Recall our example of William and his alternative responses to a diagnosis of cancer (see Figure 1.12.1). William with Response Set 1 was overwhelmed by his diagnosis and languishing in a state of depression whilst our alternative William armed with Response Set 2 was showing determination not to become crushed by this news.

It would appear that some people quite naturally veer towards one or other of these responses. Temperament or experience has perhaps influenced William's choice; maybe his mood or physical discomfort at the time of hearing the news will have coloured his appraisal of the situation. William may have a strong religious belief or personal philosophy that shapes his attitude to adversity. It could even be the attitudes of other people or the manner in which the news is delivered to him that determines which response set he selects.

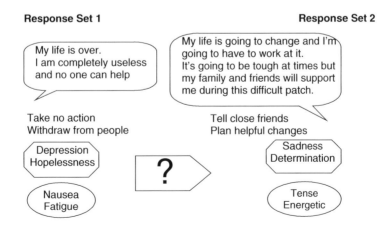

Figure 1.12.1   Moving William from Response Set 1 to Response Set 2

Whatever the reasons for William adopting Response Set 1, the challenge for the cognitive behavioural approach is not simply to explain why this is unhelpful and bad for him psychologically but to provide strategies to assist William in shifting towards Response Set 2.

For those of us familiar with working with people like William, there are three points that strike us immediately. First, most patients presented with a diagnosis of a potentially life-threatening illness initially respond with intensely negative attitudes and emotions: usually it is a mixture of panic and despair. Most people seem to modify their attitudes and emotions over the following few days and weeks. There are a few who have a constructive and business-like attitude from the outset, betraying little or no emotional perturbation; some others show acute distress throughout their illness. However, the majority seem to have strategies of their own that they apply to bring about change from Response Set 1-type to Response Set 2-type reactions without calling on professional expertise or outside advice to assist in this process. So a cognitive-behavioural shift is not only possible but actually very common and occurs quite naturally.

The second point that immediately comes to mind when thinking of the William-like people we have met is that they are rarely as consistent as this. One response set may be more frequently displayed, but for many people there will be significant variations in mood, behaviour and attitude. This changeability may, at its most intense, occur from situation to situation, not just from one day to the next.

The final point that we must never lose sight of is that William may prefer things the way they are even though we think he would benefit from change. For his own very personal reasons he may decide that this outlook and behaviour is right and appropriate, so we should not assume he would want the same things that we would want in his position. All of us at some time or another will have wasted many frustrating sessions trying to help someone who, ultimately we conclude, does not want to be helped. William may not be convinced that it is a good use of his time or that he has the stamina for this, he may think that it is morally wrong to diminish emotional suffering or that his credibility with others will suffer by receiving this help, or it may be that he just does not believe that this can work. His unwillingness to change may be quite general, but it could be quite specific to a particular situation or to the use of particular methods. In understanding William's resistance or reluctance these factors warrant careful examination.

So the messages for us from these three observations are:

1. *People can often achieve change very effectively for themselves and do not necessarily need us to interfere with their coping strategies.* In working to bring about change using a cognitive behavioural approach it will be necessary to avoid "de-skilling" William by jumping in too quickly with our own ideas and techniques, causing him to lose confidence in methods that have worked perfectly well for him over many years when trying to adjust to new circumstances.
2. *Just because today is a bad day does not mean that our help in changing that will be useful.* By trying to introduce change every time William experiences negative emotions and attitudes, we risk creating dependency and sending a message that it is "wrong" to have such thoughts and feelings.

3. *Even when we assist in bringing about helpful change there is no guarantee that it will persist.* William needs to know that he should expect setbacks and have some confidence that we have helped him prepare for them in the change strategies that we have worked on together.

4. *People will only make changes that they want.* William will commit to changes only when he believes in them and considers the cost (social and emotional, as well as financial) is acceptable. In offering our help, we are well advised to address these issues of desire and motivation quite early on.

   a. The *desire* for change is linked to dissatisfaction with things as they are and the belief that they could be different at an acceptable cost (in money, emotion, energy, friendship etc.). See Information sheet: Desire for change for further illustration.

   b. Desiring change and actually doing something about it are not the same however. *Motivation* for change requires that there is a belief that the change can be achieved and is personally relevant and beneficial. For example: many people with the desire to lose weight lack motivation to stick to a diet because they do not believe in their ability to achieve change or in the effectiveness of the diet programme. See Information sheet: Bringing about change for further illustration.

Similarly, in preparing a plan of action towards achieving goals, we need to keep *desire* and *motivation* firmly in mind whilst designing a series of steps: the benefits of tackling the step must be seen to be greater than the costs. If the patient believes that next step is too big to be achievable then motivation will wane. When tasks are avoided or no time is made for them then there is a need to review why motivation has dropped and what will need to be adapted in order to restore it.

Change and the "Hot Cross Bun" and Formulation

In the cognitive behavioural approach the interaction between all four elements of the "Hot Cross Bun" and with the environment makes it inevitable that there is significant overlap in when to use certain change methods and blurring of the distinctions between those that target **behaviour**, **thought**, **emotion** and **physical sensation**. A useful formulation will enable the practitioner who is applying a cognitive behavioural approach to identify points at which change will directly assist in overcoming obstacles and enabling the patient to move closer to achieving an agreed goal. However, identifying any point at which helpful change can be made that fits with the formulation does tend to have beneficial effects elsewhere in the "Hot Cross Bun" elements interaction and may facilitate goal attainment.

Peter is in his mid-40s and, despite his ankylosing spondylitis, has until recently coped well with the pressures of a demanding job as a senior production supervisor and enjoyed a lively home life with his wife (a part time teaching assistant) and three sons (aged 5, 8 and 11). He is now becoming concerned that he is not coping so well and losing his enthusiasm for things. He has become rather moody and feels tired most of the time. He has discussed the situation with his physiotherapist who uses his cognitive behavioural skills to help Peter understand a little more clearly what is happening. Between them they draw up the formulation shown in Figure 1.12.2. The formulation does not attempt to explain everything that is happening in Peter's life but it provides a reasonable explanation of what

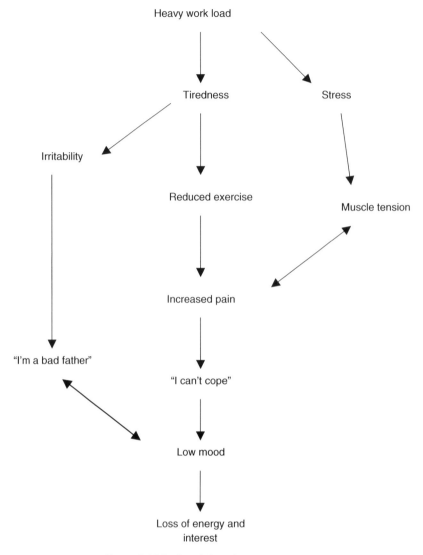

Heavy work load

Tiredness

Stress

Irritability

Reduced exercise

Muscle tension

Increased pain

"I'm a bad father"

"I can't cope"

Low mood

Loss of energy and
interest

Figure 1.12.2   Peter's formulation

is particularly troubling to him at the moment. More importantly, it identifies some of the links between things and where change might make a difference.

Physical interventions directed towards changing **physical sensation** will include surgery, physical therapies, exercise regimes and medication. As an example, the relief of Peter's pain by any of the above methods is likely to produce a lightening of his mood, increase his drive and enhance his interest in other events. Whilst surgery is not likely to be relevant, he and his physiotherapist both know that his neglect of his exercise plan ("because I haven't got the time and I come home feeling so tired") has a direct bearing on his present experience of pain. Increasing his use of analgesics has not proved a satisfactory option for Peter because of side-effects and the fact that he interprets this as a sign of not coping.

Environment and social change, together with other forms of exercise and medication may be used to directly affect **emotion**. As the mood lifts, so thoughts become more constructive which encourages purposeful activity and an improved feeling of well-being. Peter believes he has responsibility to his family and his employers that severely limits his ability to change anything in either his situation or how he manages it. He is, however, prepared to use relaxation exercises and other techniques suggested by his physiotherapist to alleviate some of the muscle tension and he has agreed to go to the doctor and discuss whether or not he would benefit from anti-depressants.

Whilst physical interventions, social-environmental changes and medication all fall outside the scope of this book, there are a number of cognitive behavioural change methods relating directly to physical sensation and emotion (such as relaxation exercises) that are covered in chapters to follow.

Most of the personal changes that are under our direct control can be identified as falling under the broad headings of **behaviours** and **thoughts**. Cognitive behavioural interventions are aimed predominantly at producing beneficial change in **behaviour** and **thought**. There are likely to be "hot cross bun effect" benefits to emotions and physical sensations derived from these changes, but, if we have developed a good formulation, the strongest and quickest of these benefits will be felt where there is a close link between the thought or behaviour and the emotion or physical sensation. If the formulation is correct, Peter will need to shift his beliefs so that he satisfies himself that he is OK as a father and that he does in general cope with things. Irritability and pain may have fuelled his thoughts of inadequacy, but it is the thoughts that must change if the low mood is to be lifted. Similarly, tiredness may have caused Peter to neglect his exercise regime and work stress may have encouraged increased muscle tension; however, it will be better muscle relaxation and exercising that alleviate the pain. These changes will not happen automatically simply because work stress and tiredness are reduced. Peter, without irritability, could still consider himself a "bad father" and despite having more time and energy, he could neglect to get back into doing his exercises regularly.

Consequently, in helping Peter achieve effective beneficial change, the physiotherapist needs to ensure that whilst working on "the bigger picture" of workload and parenting skill changes, he does not lose sight of the specific details of particular thoughts and behaviours that will have a direct impact on the immediate difficulties. Unfortunately, he also has to carefully avoid falling into the opposite trap of losing sight of "the bigger picture" issues that fuel the problems, whilst focusing on the specifics of "direct impact" thoughts and behaviours. If Peter is doing nothing to reduce the time pressures he is under, then he is unlikely to achieve a sustainable return to regular exercising. He will do no better with his view of himself as a father if, despite pep talks to himself and "good father" deeds, he continues to shout at his children and make them cry over trivial misdemeanours.

The formulation serves an invaluable function in enabling both Peter and the physiotherapist to keep "the bigger picture" and "the direct impact" thoughts and behaviours in continuous view during this process of bringing about beneficial change.

The general principles of psychological change methods are examined in the next three chapters. In the first, methods for achieving behaviour change are discussed and in the second, methods of cognitive change examined. The third describes other methods under personal control that can help change emotions and physical sensations. Specific techniques applying all these principles are described in greater detail in Part 3 of this book.

Exercises

Before you proceed to the next chapter take time to do the exercises included at the end of this chapter. To use this book properly you need to complete all the recommended exercises.

Exercise 1

1. Even without formulations it should be possible to develop step-by-step plans for your imaginary patients in order to practise mapping out a series of tasks from start point to SMART goal. You may find a colleague who knows the same patients helpful in identifying how the patient might react if you were doing this planning collaboratively.
2. Pay particular attention to finding acceptable first and second steps with which the imaginary patient would probably co-operate and succeed.
3. Identify the obstacles that you predict to be most likely to hamper progress and at what point in the progress these obstacles might become particularly obstructive.

Remember

- In real life we are likely to want to have the obstacle cleared from our path before we reach that point in order to avoid delaying progress.
- Overcoming obstacles may be something for which we develop a plan that proceeds or runs alongside the goal focused plan.

Exercise 2

1. Using the plan from Exercise 1 try to identify

   a. which steps and which obstacles can be left for the patient to resolve without further assistance from you
   b. which will raise issues of motivation that will need to be constructively addressed
   c. which will particularly require changes in behaviour
   d. which will especially require changes in thinking

2. For those steps and obstacles where social-environmental circumstances, emotional responses or physical sensation may seem in need of change, for the moment assign them to the behaviour or thinking change categories in accordance to which is most likely to be of benefit.

Exercise 3

1. With your own goal planning step-by-step record together with your personal formulation information repeat items 4. and 5. from Exercise 2.
2. Refer to the material from these two exercises whilst reading the next two chapters.

Recommended further reading:

Butler, G. and Hope, T. (1995) *Manage Your Mind*. Oxford: Oxford University Press, a host of practical ideas for personal change and improvement.

Chapter 13
Methods of Behaviour Change

When health care professionals start to learn about using a cognitive behavioural approach one of the first observations they usually make is that much of this is "common sense" and that they have often used these techniques but never known how to label them or seen them so systematically applied before. This is particularly relevant when we consider behavioural change techniques. We will have applied almost all of them to ourselves as well as to our patients. What we do in this chapter is distinguish them one from another and give them labels. Details on when and how to apply these behavioural methods are described in Parts 2 and 3 of this book.

Deciding to change

It may not sound very grand or sophisticated but it's certainly true that the most common way in which people bring about personal change is by deciding to stop doing things one way and start doing them another. As discussed in the previous chapter, the *desire* for change and the *motivation* to make it happen are critical factors in making that decision. In the absence of other difficulties, making the decision may be the only necessary step.

As health care professionals, if we have a role at all in this process, it will probably be through discussion and education to raise awareness of the desirability and possibility of achieving change. In many instances that advice and encouragement will prove sufficient for those we seek to help: they can manage the rest for themselves. (See Technique: Psycho-education). Sometimes we also need to assist in identifying the options available to decide between and perhaps the advantages and disadvantages, or costs and benefits, of those choices (see Technique: Weighing the pros and cons).

Returning to the example of Peter from the last chapter, it may be that once his physiotherapist has reminded him of the benefits of his exercise regime for maintaining fitness and reducing pain, he will resolve to make time daily to carry this out and proceed to do so routinely. But if, despite the exhortations of the physiotherapist, Peter is not convinced that the exercises make that much difference then the *motivation* to do them will be poor, and if the amount of pain he has been experiencing was easily tolerated then his *desire* to do something about it will be low. In Peter's case, we know that the pain has been getting him down, so the desire to do something about it is quite high; his past experience of the exercises has been that they are very effective, so again, we might expect that his motivation is also good. But his belief in his own ability to stick to the exercise programme and make it be effective will also influence his motivation. On this score there has to be some serious doubts because Peter has concerns about fulfilling his work and family commitments. For Peter, the decision to change will be important, but it will not be enough on its own.

Breaking old habits – stopping

Of course, sometimes it's not as simple as just making a decision. "Old habits die hard" and people easily slip back into them either because the habits are so deeply ingrained that they forget not to do them, or because the habits are so powerfully attractive that people find them hard to resist. The tussle to break old habits by simply *stopping* may involve:

1) *Consciousness-raising* – methods that make the person very aware of what he or she is doing so that they do not slip back through forgetting. These methods may involve writing things down when doing them or getting other people to comment whenever the undesired habit occurs.
2) *"Cold turkey"* – the sheer willpower technique of sweating it out and refusing to give in to the undesired habit despite strong urges. Encouragement and comfort from others and a firm vision of the future benefits once the habit is broken can be very helpful.
3) *Interference strategies* – these are methods that people devise to get in the way of triggering or carrying out the old habit – refusing to buy the favourite fattening foods if dieting (even for a partner), sitting in no-smoking rooms, wearing gloves so nails can't be bitten, not having alcohol in the house, and so on…
4) *Reward schemes* – creating personal incentive schemes, finding ways of giving oneself a personal pat on the back, can be very effective at keeping someone on track when the temptations to give up are strong. Sometimes the only reward needed is the approval of friends and family.

Peter would like to stop shouting at his children. He does not like this way of behaving and considers it wrong for a parent to be so unpredictable and scary. He has found it very difficult to stop behaving in this way. With the help of the physiotherapist, he devises a record form on which he will record every incident of his children being irritating and whether or not he shouted. They hope that if he can be systematic in recording these incidents, he will become more aware of his own behaviour and thus more able to bring it under conscious control. His wife is in on the plan and will give him comfort and praise as he struggles to achieve his objective.

But if we are going to be fair to Peter and encourage him to be fair to himself, then it is important to recognise that three boisterous boys are going to be irritating at times (his wife gets irritated too, after all). So, if he is not going to shout at them, how is he going to react? In this instance, it is not going to be simply a matter of stopping what we do not want to do, but of replacing it with something else.

Making new habits – committing

There are times when it seems that giving up an unwanted pattern of behaviour is the only objective of the change process, such as when someone gives up smoking. But often this leaves a "hole" in the person's set of behaviours. What does the ex-smoker do when he or she wants to relax for five minutes now that stopping for a cigarette is not part of that behavioural set? In the absence of a better plan, the ex-smoker may start to eat lots of biscuits or use more alcohol to help unwind. The old habit will have fulfilled certain functions in the person's life and will be missed; so it is often advisable to consider how best to compensate for its absence or at least fill the gap that is created.

Sometimes, we are adding a new habit to our set of behaviours because we have become convinced of its potential benefits, but remembering to do it or giving time and attention to it may still be problematic. Your dentist may spend a lot of time trying to educate you into the benefits of daily use of dental floss and you might completely agree that this is the right thing to do, but if your daily routines of dental hygiene have never included flossing before, then it might be a while before it becomes part of the fixed pattern. Some of our patients have a great deal of difficulty getting into good habits with taking medication, others with remembering to lift and carry heavier items correctly.

Like *stopping* an old habit, *committing* to a new pattern of behaviour can be quite a struggle of awareness (or memory) and willpower. In terms of *routine*, the more long-standing and frequent the old pattern, the harder it will be to substitute or insert the new one; regarding *desire,* the higher the "cost" the greater the doubt about really wanting to do it; and for motivation once again the more and greater the obstacles the more self-belief and energy are challenged. Some of the methods that can maintain awareness, boost desire for change and increase movement from intention to action are those mentioned above. *Consciousness-raising* would also include aides-mémoire such as Post-It notes and placing items such as tablets in conspicuous places. Also, *reward schemes* are again helpful in boosting morale and motivation: this may be as simple as telling someone what you intend to do and then telling them when you have done it.

Other methods are:

1) *Positive self talk* - "Practice makes perfect" is a good motto along with reminders that "it gets easier the more you do it" and "the sooner you start the sooner you'll finish". "I can do it" and "I'm not going to be beaten by this" are good fighting talk messages that can help. These are especially useful where self-belief is challenged.

2) *Thinking about the benefits* (including improved self-esteem) is always useful: "I'm going to feel so much better when this is done", "Life will be so much easier for me when I've made these changes". These thoughts can boost the desire when it sags.

3) *"Chunking"* – breaking large tasks into smaller units can often be a good way of establishing a new behaviour pattern or working towards a specific goal. This is a very valuable strategy for maintaining motivation and building confidence. The sense of being overwhelmed before one starts is a major cause of problems in establishing new behaviour patterns. We have already encountered this issue when considering goal setting and it applies equally here whilst considering specific behavioural changes. Rather than trying to do it all at once, our ability to cope is helped by introducing the changes one bit at a time.

   i) break the task into a series of smaller, more manageable tasks
   ii) set tasks that can be successfully achieved
   iii) ensure tasks will not be overwhelming
   iv) sort out priorities from among the smaller tasks

Peter, faced with the challenge of not shouting at his children even when they are being quite badly behaved, needs to consider the functions his previous behaviour fulfilled and how he intends to fill the gap. First, shouting was effective in subduing the children's unruly behaviour and he is not going to feel good about himself if he lets them get away with it completely. Second, shouting relieved most of his pent up tension and frustration;

does he have to keep it bottled up inside of him instead? A constructive alternative behavioural pattern needs to tackle these issues, not ignore them.

Even when a suitable plan has been devised, Peter still has the difficulty of trying to put it into action: remembering what to do and resisting the tempting "knee-jerk" response. Self-prompts and reminders will help him remain aware of what he is trying to achieve, whilst recall of the benefits of not shouting may help inhibit the urge to do so. Setting realistic limits to what he can achieve and using positive self-talk to reinforce the idea that "Rome wasn't built in a day" may help avoid an overly defeatist attitude developing as a result of slip-ups and setbacks.

Learning new skills

Changing behaviour often involves improving skills or even learning completely new skills. Sometimes it will be practical skills like learning to drive, learning to use the computer or learning/improving foreign language skills. Sometimes the skills will be coping techniques to help adapt and manage changing situations. Sometimes the skills are psychological in nature: looking at things from a new perspective, interacting with other people in a different way, approaching situations with a more helpful attitude, expressing emotions more openly.

Difficult and demanding health situations may require any of a number of new or better skills, particularly those useful for:

1. Reducing worry (see Techniques: Mindfulness exercises)
2. Calming nervousness (see Techniques: Mental and muscle relaxation exercises)
3. Gaining more sense of personal control in social situations (see Technique: Assertiveness)
4. Overcoming embarrassment and loss of confidence (see Technique: Graded activity)
5. Containing fatigue to reduce exhaustion (see Technique: Pacing)

Peter already knows that he wants to learn better ways of conducting himself when he is feeling angry and that he would like to be able to stay calm and not get angry at all. Through discussion with the physiotherapist about his difficulties in making sufficient time for his exercises, he is beginning to understand that he is not very good at pleasantly asserting his personal needs and saying "No" to extra demands at work and with the family. He can have lots of good intentions to do his exercises but he fails to turn these good intentions into actions unless he is prepared to disappoint the expectations of others. He needs to learn the skills of how to be more assertive in order to manage both his pain and his children.

Changing the environment

Many of the circumstances that cause dissatisfaction are linked to our surroundings and things with which we are involved. Our choice is to put up with things as they are or attempt to change them. Let us take an ordinary day-to-day example. When we sit in a hot and stuffy room we can:

- suffer in silence
- complain but do nothing about it
- open a window
- take off layers of clothing

The first two choices are the *passive* responses whilst the latter two are *active* responses. There may be very good reasons why a *passive* response is chosen (e.g. this hot and stuffy room is the office of our very scary and unsympathetic boss) but generally the *active* response is the better option.

You will recall the example of Margaret whose fear of tiredness and showing distress following her treatment for breast cancer was the subject of one of the formulation examples. As she was very concerned to avoid exhaustion sitting around, doing very little except watching TV and doing jigsaw puzzles, seemed "logical" especially as her husband was encouraging her to do this and he seemed so willing to look after her needs. But the benefits of being pampered quickly wore off and she started to feel lazy and useless. When this happens maybe the "caring environment" has outlived its usefulness and needs to be abandoned in favour of one which is perhaps less logical and convenient but more stimulating and rewarding. This would be the *active* response. Unfortunately, until now Margaret has continued to pick the *passive* response because it does seem "logical" and she does not want to seem ungrateful to her husband.

The *passive* option produces feelings of being "not in control", helplessness and resentment. The *active* option enhances feelings of personal control and well-being even when it is "illogical" and inconvenient. A strong sense of personal control is important to our self-esteem and "self-efficacy". Margaret may risk increasing fatigue by making changes to her day and situation, but even if she makes small mistakes she is likely to feel better than she does whilst she continues to play safe in her claustrophobic cocoon.

Before leaving the subject of changing the environment there is another evaluation of the situation that sometimes leads our patients to opt for the *passive* response. When people already have problems, whether physical or psychological, they are more prone to attribute new difficulties to themselves. Going back to the hot and stuffy room scenario this means that there is an option e) which is: "What's wrong with me that I feel so hot and stuffy?" Such an interpretation may lead the person to do something directed at self-control rather than environmental change (e.g. takes an aspirin, practises relaxation exercises, books an appointment with the GP). In a realistic appraisal of his situation, Peter may find that whilst it is good to learn new skills of self-control, some changes to the environment that triggers anger may be extremely important. Trying to sit quietly in his armchair reading his newspaper whilst the children are bouncing on the sofa and squabbling about television programmes sounds like a potential anger problem which can be directly managed by changing the environment (his or theirs) rather than immediately assuming that he has to sort himself out by exercising self-control.

Sometimes in our attempts to help our patients understand and cope better with their internal experiences we can fall into the trap of inadvertently encouraging this *passive* response to the external world. *Actively* responding to the demands of our surrounding rather than looking inwards for self change will still be the most healthy and effective form of response in very many circumstances. Many of the behavioural techniques used in a cognitive behavioural approach emphasise this interaction with the environment (e.g. Techniques: Activity monitoring, Purposeful planning, Stimulus control).

Remember that when an alarm bell goes off we are meant to be alarmed and not use it as an opportunity to practise relaxation exercises!

Practising and improving

The more Peter practises new methods for handling his children when they could be annoying him the more skilful he becomes and the more evidence he gains that change can be achieved. This gives a big boost to his belief in the methods, his feelings of personal control and his sense of effectiveness. Involving herself in domestic routines and going out and facing other people repeatedly, helps Margaret regain a normal lifestyle and relieve her boredom and depression. But pacing herself and finding the right words to fend off the well-meant but intrusive enquiries of other people both require practice because these are unfamiliar behaviours that need to become second-nature to her.

People also learn from their mistakes: so practice helps recovery from setbacks and with spotting potential pitfalls before people stumbled into them. We will look a little more at learning from errors in the next section; but when the real situation does not crop up very often or when making that "useful learning mistake" would cost one dear, then real-life practice needs to be beefed up by lots of "pre-real-life" rehearsal – just like actors need before putting on a play.

1) *Behavioural rehearsal* – Finding a way to simulate the situation may feel silly to begin with but it is a very powerful technique to help bring about the changes that may be wanted. For example: Peter wants to confront his children about their noisy squabbling, but he wants to avoid it turning into another of his angry rants. With somebody who knows this scenario and can "play" the part of the children Peter could practise different ways of saying things and try out different reactions from the children and how he might respond to these. In this way Peter can work out the best strategy and how best to react in a variety of circumstances.

2) *Imaginal rehearsal* – Some situations can be best rehearsed in imagination. Margaret can imagine being out in the local shopping precinct when a person she knows from her voluntary work appears and asks her how she is and what her plans for coming back to work might be. Imagining being in that precinct whilst practising her relaxation techniques and some stock answers to intrusive questions will help her build confidence that she knows what to do when a situation like that arises.

Rehearsal strategies are helpful for launching someone into practicing in the real situation. However, just as we cannot learn to swim by practising breast-stroke lying on the bedroom floor so we cannot acquire real confidence in managing difficult psychological situations by use of rehearsal strategies. The aim of practice should be the development of insight into whether or not one has the basic skills and the general principles of when and how to use them. Trying to anticipate every scene and script every conversation so that a response for every occasion has been developed is strictly for the stage and not helpful for real life where we discover that the other "players" do not play the scene as we saw it in our minds and never know their lines as we had written them in our heads.

Behavioural experiments

Having an enquiring, experimental approach can often be the quickest way of bringing about changes in what we think and what we do. We can use behavioural experiments to test our beliefs and assumption, trial problem solving and coping strategies and build a better understanding of the way one thing leads to another. This process of "experiential learning" can be summed up as: plan, experience, reflect on outcome and return to planning again (see Information sheet: Experiential learning circle).

There are several ways in which we extend our understanding and knowledge using behavioural experiments:

1) *Surveys* - Sometimes a "survey" of the opinions or actions chosen by others faced with similar situations can be helpful. In carrying out a survey those selected should be people whose opinion is particularly respected in this issue or who are generally considered to be a good role model. It will not be helpful to collect too many opinions or opinions from people whose views are not particularly valued or respected. Sometimes predicting the views of others and then putting that to the test by asking them is a helpful way of discovering just how good we are at interpreting situations or reading someone else's mind.

2) *Test runs* – Fear of making mistakes and avoiding failure at all costs can leave people very stuck and feeling incapable of taking any action at all. Finding a small "safe" experimental situation in which to try out an idea or new skills without provoking too much of this fear can be very useful. We can set up tests to check out an idea we have, too. To do a test properly, it will be necessary to be good at specifying what you are doing and either predicting or carefully observing what actually happens. The test run will have been wasted if it is not set up properly or you have no real understanding of the outcome. (See Techniques: Behavioural experiments – Setting them up)

3) *Trial and error* – Sometimes it's just not possible to work out the best way to deal with a situation in advance, in which case people have to fall back on their "best guess" and accept that "you win some and lose some" but either way they can "learn from my mistakes". For those situations where making a mistake will not have disastrous or irreversible consequences, this trial-and error is a great way to move situations forward quickly. We learn a great deal from our mistakes when we are prepared to acknowledge them and re-examine them constructively. Too often we are tempted to gloss over them or dwell on them destructively, but when we put them to good use they help us adapt and adjust very effectively provided we have the information to enable us to understand what has happened and why. Like a test-run, it is important to clearly observe what you have done and the results produced (See Techniques: Behavioural experiments – Setting them up).

Peter already knows his wife's opinion of how he should handle the boys better, but in the past he has been dismissive of her views as "too tolerant and lax". Now that he has decided that he has to change he will be more receptive to the possibility that she is making sensible suggestions if they are similar to the views of a few family and friends whom he sees as good parents with similar standards to his own. He and the physiotherapist discuss how he can sound them out informally without having to disclose much about his own issues if he prefers, although the physiotherapist suggests that some quite specific questions directed at addressing his difficulties may be even better.

They both agree that dealing with the pressures of Peter's work timetable will require a more "trial and error" approach. Discussion of assertiveness techniques and practising them with his wife may have prepared Peter to say "No" to some demands but maybe there are going to be difficulties putting that into practice or perhaps there will be other reasons why the pressures will prove impossible to resist. Until he has tried making the changes discussed, it will be impossible to accurately identify what other challenges need to be managed. Consequently, "having a go" without expecting it to work perfectly is a part of the plan.

Margaret has convinced herself that she will be very conspicuous when she goes out to the shops and will burst into tears and embarrass herself and others if someone asks how she is. A brief trip to the supermarket was arranged with her husband where she was simply to walk slowly through the shop and out again looking at other people to see if anyone stared at her. Her husband bought a loaf of bread and a celebratory bottle of wine at the fast-track till as planned in advance whilst she ambled back to the car still watching other people. Back at home they discussed the experience and agreed that neither of them had spotted anyone staring at her or avoiding her. One woman she vaguely knew had smiled and nodded from a little way off but otherwise they had not been approached by people. Margaret felt quite satisfied that she was not an object of curiosity after all, but as her planned response to enquiries about how she was feeling had not been put to the test they agreed that they needed to consider another experiment in which she was more likely to bump into a neighbour or someone she knew fairly well.

Confidence building (graded exposure)

When we lack self-confidence to do something, then telling ourselves to "just do it" runs into all the problems of a crisis in *motivation* mentioned above: intention often fails to turn into action. There can be a fear of letting ourselves down badly and suffering a frightening or humiliating experience: and not many of us want to let ourselves in for something like that! Usually the best strategy lies in starting with a less "risky" situation that helps to build confidence in performing this task. Few of us would benefit from driving round a bustling town centre on a first ever driving lesson. We do not typically learn to swim by being thrown in at the deep end. We usually learn, and build confidence as we learn, by starting with the small simpler tasks (often very hard for us to begin with – liking steering the car and floating in the swimming pool with floats) and steadily work up to the more challenging tasks as skilful application and confidence improve. Most goals that involve overcoming anxiety or lack of confidence will require this gradual exposure to more difficult tasks as the easier ones are achieved (see Technique: Graded activities).

Margaret has already begun to adopt this approach by visiting the supermarket very briefly and with her husband's support. If they had planned a full scale shopping expedition, she may have lost her nerve to do it and even if she went through with it she is unlikely to have felt encouraged by the experience because it would have been so long and arduous. Her short visit has helped her reduce her fear of these situations in much the same way as splashing about with water-wings in the shallow end of the swimming pool can help a child overcome fear of water.

This "step-ladder" approach to building confidence and skills is one of the most commonly used behavioural techniques used in a cognitive behavioural approach, but in order to ensure we do not miss any "rungs" in the ladder there should be careful consideration of all the factors that may make one situation more or less difficult than another. The presence of Margaret's husband, how busy the store is and how long they are staying in it are three factors that influence the level of difficulty for Margaret. In Margaret's case it was not important to consider the size of shop, time of day and whether or not the store is close to home; for another person these factors may have been important too when constructing the step-ladder.

Resisting avoidance and confronting fear

Avoiding feared situations seems like common sense. If we know that something is hazardous we normally consider avoiding exposure to it to be the responsible thing to do. Most of us do not walk straight up to dangerous animals, book holidays in war zones, take an evening stroll through lanes notorious for muggings or carelessly handle highly toxic materials. However, we are highly selective in the things we avoid. It would be rather different if we avoided contact with all animals *in case* they were dangerous, all foreign holidays *in case* we strayed into a war zone, all evening strolls *in case* we get mugged or touching any object *in case* it is toxic. We do not get into such extreme responses because we make some assessment of the risk and our ability to cope with it. Our day to day experiences allow us to build confidence in our judgement of risk and our coping skills. Regular exposure to pets, holiday travel, walking in the evening and handling objects provides us with the feedback we need to evaluate and adapt our judgement and skills.

It is much harder to have confidence in our judgement of hazard and our abililty to cope with foreign travel (for example) if we have no experience of it. If we never go out in the evenings, how are we to judge whether or not we are likely to be mugged? We read in the paper about people being mugged, tourists being kidnapped and killed, children being savaged by ferocious dogs. If we have no direct experience of these things, only know what we read or can imagine for ourselves and this information emphasises the hazards then our desire to avoid the situations is likely to increase because we will judge the risk as high and doubt our ability to cope. For most of us, most of the time, we have a sufficient degree of self-confidence, particularly our belief in our judgement and competence that lack of exposure to new and different situations will lead to caution rather than fear. For some, however, experience or current circumstances lead them to lack that confidence or exaggerate the degree of threat posed by certain situations. For anyone feeling that way avoidance is likely to seem the common sense strategy.

The problem is that avoidance is not a good idea because it tends to make the person more fearful. The lack of contact with the feared object increases its imagined threatening nature, and lack of experience in coping with it reduces belief in the ability to manage the fear. Margaret's lack of exposure to trips to the supermarket had contributed to an exaggeration in her own mind of the likelihood of aversive experiences (fatigue, conspicuousness and difficult conversations). If it had been possible for her to begin making these trips as soon as she was able, it is less likely that she would have developed these beliefs.

Avoidance behaviour not only exacerbates the fear of the challenging situation, but also extends the number of situations which are perceived as challenging. Margaret's fear of not coping with contact with other people has extended from public areas such as super-markets to include avoiding going into her own front garden and some self-consciousness about being spotted in the back garden too. Until this brief trip to the supermarket she had started to become restricted to the inside of the house. This type of sensitivity to a range of situations that could lead into the avoided one is a very common consequence of avoid-ance behaviour.

Confronting the challenge head on is not usually recommended because the ability to develop confidence in coping skills is impaired and motivation is likely to be low (see Confidence building above). Nevertheless, in using a cognitive behavioural approach some confronting of the fear is recognised as quite an essential ingredient too. Tolerating anxiety and allowing it to "wash over" you is not pleasant but is hugely effective for get-ting on with things. It is what we all do when we allow ourselves to go into scary situa-tions. Exams, public speaking, fairground rides, extreme sports and tense thrillers can all evoke anxiety which people put up with because they enjoy the achievement or the thrill. Those who employ avoidance behaviours may grow intolerant of any anxiety and indeed become fearful of anxiousness itself, as though it too was dangerous or a threat. When we help people to develop better coping skills for reducing anxiety, we can inadvertently teach them how to *avoid* anxiety and thus reinforce a belief that "I could not cope with being anxious" (See Problem: Panic attacks special note – safety behaviours). We could advise Margaret to practice breathing exercises and muscle relaxation in the car on the way to the supermarket. She might find that these exercises were helpful for keeping her calm in the store. She might come back from the trip completely relaxed and confident. However, she is likely to attribute quite a lot of that success to her systematic use of those exercises and judge being "anxiety-free" as a main criterion for success rather than the completion of the task without any of the anticipated catastrophes. This will reinforce her belief that she *should* be anxiety-free and *must* do her exercises every time she goes to the supermarket; in this way a *safety behaviour* ritual is established. Once the safety behav-iour is in place, anything that prevents it occurring is likely to cause renewed anxiety and the anxiety itself is more feared.

Understanding that anxiety is not dangerous and doing things despite the presence of anxiety and other feelings of discomfort is a more useful strategy for Margaret because in order to extend her range of activities and interests she is going to need to have exposure to situations in which some degree of anxiety is quite likely to be experienced. To avoid all anxiety will force her back into "safe" situations and dependent on "safety behaviours". Believing in her ability to tolerate and ameliorate anxiety without having to eliminate it will empower Margaret to approach challenges rather than avoid them.

Exercises

Before you proceed to the next chapter take time to do the exercises included at the end of this chapter. To use this book properly you need to complete all the recommended exercises.

Exercise 1

1. Select the types of change most likely to be beneficial where you have identified behavioural change as appropriate on the step-by-step records of the imaginary patients.

Exercise 2

1. Study the step-by-step plan developed for Norman in Chapter 10.

   a) Identify the steps and obstacles for which behavioural changes would seem appropriate
   b) Identify the type of behavioural change that seems most suitable

Exercise 3

1. Look at the formulation and step-by-step plan you developed for Geoffrey and identify the types of behavioural changes that could be beneficial for progressing steps and overcoming obstacles. Bear in mind:

   a) Geoffrey's desire and motivation to change and how this might affect the methods selected.
   b) His personal resources for being left to his own devices to deal with some steps and obstacles without additional assistance.

2. Review the steps and timetabling of action on obstacles in the light of the work identified for producing behavioural change.

3. Look through Part 3 of this book for material that may help in the achievement of these behavioural changes in the sections on Techniques, Information sheets and Record forms.

4. Identify and note down specific material that you recommend including those in Geoffrey's plan.

Recommended further reading:

Bennett-Levy, J., Butler, G., Fennell, M., Hackman, A., Mueller, M. and Westbrook, D. (2004) *Oxford Guide to Behavioural Experiments in Cognitive Therapy,* Oxford: Oxford University Press.
Cudney, M. R. and Hardy, R. E. (1991) *Self Defeating Behaviours.* New York: HarperCollins.

Chapter 14
Methods of Cognitive Change

In the previous chapter we have examined various ways in which we categorise and change behaviours; for many healthcare professionals some or all of these behavioural methods will already form part of usual practice even if they have not been categorised quite like that before. Most of us will also recognise these methods as part of our repertoire of strategies in daily life. Changing and adapting is a normal part of ordinary life and these are the ways in which we make behavioural adjustment (perhaps more informally and less systematically).

Studying and categorising the ways in which we adjust our thinking to bring about change or adapt to change that is thrust upon us is rather harder because it is not so readily observable in others and impossible to be truly objective about in ourselves. The cognitive behavioural model recognises the power of thought to influence behaviours, emotions and even physical reactions; some understanding of the strategies we commonly use to modify our thinking and applying this knowledge in a systematic way to facilitate constructive change is the most distinctive feature of the cognitive behavioural approach.

Attention, Analysis and Decision Making

But why do we need to involve ourselves with thoughts when they are so hard to observe and the strategies are therefore so "woolly"? Surely if we can bring about behaviour change and environment change then this will guarantee there are changes to the thinking too, as predicted by the Hot Cross Bun model. This would have been the position of behaviour therapists of the past and to some extent it is a reasonable argument; but every healthcare professional will have had the disappointing experience of the patient who, despite all the health improvements that have occurred, steadfastly holds to a gloomy and critical perspective or continues to do things in a way that repeats old problems. For a patient like that there has been no cognitive shift. The patient has not made the expected evaluation of the improvement, has failed to notice that improvement has happened or does not see a connection between the improvement and any of the actions taken to achieve it. By neglecting cognitive change, we leave to chance whether beneficial changes in behaviour, physical sensations and even emotions are viewed positively and managed constructively.

When we examine the possible explanations as to why the patient did not respond as we had expected we can see that there are different aspects of the cognitive processing that might be involved. The failure to make the expected evaluation suggests that the **analysis** made by the patient is not the same as the one we had supposed to be the most logical one to make; the failure to notice the benefit indicates that the patient's **attention focus** is on other things; and if the patient has a different understanding of the connections between one event and another then different **decision making** will follow. **Analysis, attention focus** and **decision making** influence each other and are important components of the **thought** process in the "Hot Cross Bun" model. They each play their part in influencing behaviour, emotion and physical reactions and in generating further thoughts. It will be in the methods we use to change these cognitive components that we are likely to find the techniques that we wish to apply systematically in our cognitive behavioural approach.

Barry is 60 years old and completed radiotherapy for prostrate cancer fifteen months ago. Treatment was effective and he appears to be physically very well. Everyone is optimistic that there is nothing more to worry about: everyone that is except Barry himself.

He remains very low in mood and takes a very negative stance about everything. He no longer enjoys socialising and has to be cajoled into meeting friends by his wife, Sheila. In the past Sheila was a golf-widow at weekends but Barry has not resumed playing golf and now does not see his old golfing friends at all. At work, Barry has never been quite the same since his treatment. He was always a supportive boss to his team and helpful colleague to fellow heads of department. Now he has become rather solitary, unapproachable and indifferent to the work; even conversations about retirement do not stir him to more enthusiasm. His family feel quite disappointed in how things have turned out because once the draining effects of the radiotherapy had worn off the consultant had assured them that Barry would be back to his old self. The consultant has made it quite clear that he can see no good reason for Barry to be lethargic still or to be so completely lacking in sex drive. He is also surprised at the frequency with which Barry continues to visit the toilet and suggests that Barry is perhaps over-sensitive about this.

If we consider this in terms of **analysis**, **attention focus** and **decision making,** the family and the consultant had expected that Barry would *analyse* his situation in terms of positive recovery, *focus* on resuming normal life and *decide* to take up his former activities. Instead, when carefully questioned, we will find that Barry has *analysed* his situation in terms of having embarked upon the downhill slide of old age, *focused* on persisting symptoms that confirm this view that he has now become an old man and *decided* to avoid doing anything that he sees as more appropriate to younger men or that might leave him vulnerable to having an accident with bladder control.

Before his prostate cancer was diagnosed, Barry already had a **belief** that cancer was an illness of old age: only old men get prostate cancer. Attitudes and beliefs can be as firmly established in our thinking as old habits can be in our behaviour. Like old habits they are also often quite resistant to alteration. People do not chop and change their opinions quickly and may take some time to be persuaded to think about a situation differently. Barry was more inclined to reassess his perception of himself and analyse this illness as an indication that he had become an old man, than he was to change his belief about the link between cancer and old age. A frequent need to visit the toilet, poor bladder control, fatigue, loss of sex drive and a general disinterest in things were all features of his negative view of old age and therefore he expected to continue to experience them and so has given lots of time and attention to reviewing their status as confirmatory **evidence** of his belief. Barry grew up in a household in which the needs of his frail grandfather had taken priority over other things to such an extent that he had come to feel very resentful of the old man and as an adult had always been rather impatient and intolerant of elderly people. Influenced by his boyhood experiences he had developed as one of his personal **standards** in life the idea that he must always avoid being a burden or hindrance to others. This guiding principle had helped him decide on several occasions to be supportive to others in the workplace when his own best interests would have been better served by putting himself forward. Now this same rule was influencing his decision not to slow down his old golfing chums, not to disappoint and upset his wife with feeble attempts at love making, and, in social situations, not to spoil the occasion for others through his constant need to run back and forth to the toilet.

This information about Barry identifies three important influences on thinking: **beliefs**, **evidence** and **standards**. You will repeatedly notice the presence of these three influences on **attention focus**, **analysis** and **decision making** as we start to build a set of strategies that may facilitate cognitive change.

Cognitive techniques for changing attention focus

Our ability to selectively attend to particular information enables us to make more sense of the world and our experiences, sifting the mass of information available and concentrating on those items of greatest relevance to us. We have the capacity to focus on one thing more than another thus being able to prioritise and emphasise information in a way we find most meaningful. That does not, of course, mean that we are selectively attending to the right things; we do not always focus in a way that is most helpful to us. At a roundabout a driver may nearly run into the back of another car because his attention has shifted to the roundabout traffic instead of that car in front; a pleasant conversation over dinner in a restaurant may be spoilt because it proves difficult to resist being distracted by the rather heated discussion at the next table. We may misjudge and get things out of perspective by attending too much to some things or by neglecting to attend enough to others.

Barry is giving considerable attention to whether or not he needs the toilet and by doing so thinks he needs to use it very frequently. He will have to shift his attention away from the state of his bladder rather more effectively if he is going to experience a reduction in this "need".

The techniques that encourage a change of thinking by shifting the focus of attention include:

1. Mental distraction
Trying to think about something completely different is a particularly valuable strategy when the patient is prone to becoming preoccupied with a particular line of thought that is unproductive or upsetting. Leaving the crossword puzzle and doing something entirely different can help to stop some fruitless problem-solving and enable the person to come at it afresh later. Changing the subject of conversation can help to stop someone brooding on an unhappy experience and lighten the mood again. The technique works well in the short term, breaking the chain of thought and producing a shift of attention that is sustained (see Techniques: Mental distraction). If the unhelpful thoughts intrude persistently then repeated efforts at mental distraction become less successful and tiring to maintain: analysis or decision making strategies (described later) are likely to be more useful with persistently intrusive thoughts.

2. Here-and-now focus

The more we feel in control of our lives the better we tend to feel about ourselves. That sense of personal control is determined by what we believe we are able to do to make a difference. Therefore the degree to which we focus attention on present time is very influential. Laura at 31 feels very low every time one of her friends has a baby. She had to have a hysterectomy two years ago and finds it very hard to come to terms with never being able to have a child of her own. What makes it especially hard for her to accept this situation is that she and her partner Jake put off having children so they could see more of the world. She reflects on those earlier times and experiences an overwhelming sense of helplessness because she cannot turn back the clock and do it differently.

Margaret is on regular check-ups since her breast cancer was successfully treated and she becomes very frightened, sick and sleepless for a whole week prior to her appointment with the consultant. She speculates about the possible (bad) results and how she will cope. She experiences anxiety and panic because she moves towards a future event which she cannot control. Critically reflecting on the past will often generate helplessness experiences such as Laura's, whilst anticipating future problems will instil fear and powerlessness. What we do, we do in the present, even if it is to compensate for the past or to prepare for the future. When our patients are depressed or anxious, it is very likely that a disproportionate amount of attention is being devoted to the past or the future and tasks that facilitate greater attention on the here-and-now will be beneficial. Nor should we ignore the possibility that Laura and Margaret can do much to change this simply by being more aware of how this shift of attention influences mood. For more information see Techniques: Attention strategies; Mindfulness; Problem solving; Purposeful planning and Information sheet: Serenity prayer.

3. Stimulus control

As time has gone on Janet has found that seeing her friends has become a rather depressing experience. She used to find them very good fun and she still always looks forward to their get-togethers but comes away feeling low. The problem is that they always want to ask about her MS and tell her about the encouraging news and helpful advice they have been reading about in magazines or hearing on the radio. Most of the time Janet tries to get on with normal life without dwelling too much on the MS or the problems it causes her. After spending time with her friends it becomes the only thing she can think about for the rest of that day. By controlling those things that shift her attention Janet may be able to reduce this adverse effect of seeing her friends. She could for example ask them not to discuss MS unless she specifically asks them to do so, or she could request that it only takes up the first ten minutes of their time together and then the subject is changed. Likewise Margaret will be helped in reducing her anticipatory anxiety about her next check-up if she does not have to see the appointment card pinned prominently to her noticeboard every time she walks into her kitchen. Barry will think less about his need to use the toilet by reducing his frequent checking of the availability of the nearest one. See Technique: Stimulus control for more information.

4. Vigilance modification

Dave has become preoccupied with what is happening inside his own body since well before his diagnosis of Crohn's Disease. He pays little attention to the general chit-chat of his girlfriend, Caroline, and devises his whole daily routines around managing his illness. He is reluctant to do anything that might require him to adapt his schedule or distract him from his physical state. He complains about how Crohn's now controls his life but does nothing to change that and takes no interest in the lives of his friends and family. He thinks that Caroline was completely unreasonable and uncaring when she accused him of being selfish a few days ago; but she has not apologised. A certain amount of time and attention is necessary for Dave to manage his disease reasonably effectively; however, the more time and attention he devotes to what is happening to himself, the less time and attention there remains available for other things. The more we attend to one thing the greater importance it assumes and the more sensitive we become to any differences. Dave's watchful attending to his internal environment at the expense of the external world increases the likelihood that he will be more aware of his discomfort and less aware of Caroline's loss of respect for him than he would be if he deliberately devoted more time to her needs and those of his friends (see Techniques: Attention strategies; Activity monitoring; Purposeful planning; Information sheet: Vicious cycle of anxious preoccupation and Record form: Achievements and pleasures). Janet had worked that out for herself and just needs the co-operation of her friends in maintaining that focus on the wider world. Barry is falling into the same trap as Dave. His continuous monitoring of the state of his bladder (hypervigilence) increases his awareness of the slightest change which in turn increases his belief that he needs to go to the toilet. Like Dave, Barry would benefit from giving more time and attention to what is going on around him, trusting his body to send the attention grabbing signals when necessary. Unlike Dave, Barry presents the added complication of excessive vigilance towards the outside world as well in his preoccupation with not being a nuisance to fellow golfers and friends. A little more attention to what is actually happening (i.e. no signs of impatience from golfers or embarrassment from friends), to the wishes of his wife (she gets pleasure from meeting up with their friends) and to his own needs (he feels back to normal when he and Sheila are more intimate) will enable him to maintain a better balance and keep a clearer perspective on how much prostate cancer has to change his life.

5. Challenging distorted selective attention (selective abstractions)

We have already mentioned that in order to sift through the vast amount of information in the world around us we selectively attend to some and, to varying degrees, ignore most of the rest. There are some things our minds are primed and ready to attend to such as hearing our names mentioned from amidst a babble of otherwise rather unclear conversation, or spotting a word we are looking for among all the words on a page of print. Both Margaret and Barry from our examples above have commented to friends that there seems to be a continuous stream of references to cancer in the newspapers and on television recently. It is, of course, a topic that is frequently considered news-worthy, sometimes because of discoveries and treatment developments, and sometimes because famous people are diagnosed with or die of cancer. Margaret and Barry are now mentally primed to attend to information about cancer and so have become more aware of these news items than before. Fortunately, this increased awareness of cancer information poses no real problem for either Margaret or Barry. But Margaret does have a problem with selective attention: she has been bored and depressed and this has provided plenty of opportunity for reflecting on the past. Margaret's low mood primes her attention just as a word search might do to select material from her reflections about the past that match her mood. She thinks about the sad times when her parents died, when her husband was out of work for several months, when her daughter was so ill during her first pregnancy and the troubles her son is having in his marriage and his job. This mental filtering of information reinforces her low mood and distorts her view of the world around her and of her own past to so great an extent that she becomes quite convinced that her whole life has been a catalogue of disasters. Whilst thinking like this she finds it hard to recall the many happy times she had whilst growing up and throughout her marriage, the joy of that first grandchild and relief when her daughter made a full recovery; she even manages to forget or overlook some facts about her son who has changed his job and sorted out the marital problems to the extent that as a couple they have been noticeably much happier for many months now. This type of mental filtering is one of the *mental traps* referred to in the next chapter. Putting in time and effort to examine objective evidence and refresh her memory of better times can enable Margaret to establish a more balanced perspective. Looking at family photo albums is often a good strategy since they are often full of snaps taken at happy times; reminiscing with a good friend can be a useful way of eliciting memories that seem to be blocked out by the low mood filter.

Cognitive techniques for changing analysis and interpretation

Just because we give time and attention to the relevant information does not guarantee that we put it to good use. Our analysis and interpretation of new information will be heavily influenced by the information we already have and the analysis we have made of that previous data. We are generally more inclined to analyse new information in a way that fits reasonably well with our existing ideas than to start afresh and completely rework our ideas to fit with the new information: we fit the brick to the wall not the wall to the brick. By and large we are quite resistant to a major overhaul of our existing beliefs and attitudes, especially those we have held for a long time and seem to have served us well.

Barry has seen plenty of evidence throughout his life to support his beliefs that getting old and ill is "bad news" and that caring for the elderly is burdensome to other people. The difficulties and demands of his grandfather have left a deep impression on him but both of his own parents died in their early 60s: his father from a heart attack and his mother following a short illness. Sheila's parents both died young, before he met her. He has not had cause to re-examine his beliefs and sees little reason to do so now. He is dismissive of reassurances from family and friends that "You've got a lot of life in you, yet!"

At its most straightforward, the role of the health care professional in facilitating change in the way the patient analyses and interprets information may involve providing encouragement to complete the analysis properly: to get the patient to think it through rather than analyse it as far as heightening awareness of possible problems or threats and then stop. Taking the change process a stage further, the health care professional may need to assist the patient to discover and examine alternative ways of analysing and interpreting the information in order to develop a new perspective. Finally, if it appears that there are specific blocks to a more helpful or useful way of thinking then the cognitive change process becomes focused on the specific obstacles to a constructive outlook and how they might be overcome. In clinical practice there is a great deal of overlap and interchange between these strategies of cognitive change and the techniques they employ. This overlap will be very apparent in the next chapter when we examine ways of challenging unhelpful thoughts in greater depth. For simplicity in this chapter we describe these strategies as three separate steps.

1. De-catastrophising
The tendency to think "It would be awful if X happened" is probably familiar to all of us. It is the problem-solving equivalent to the cliff-hanger ending to a TV drama episode: having reached a dramatic moment we are left in a state of high tension awaiting the next episode to find out how the crisis will be resolved. Unlike with the TV drama, however, we are not obliged to end our problem-solving at a moment of high drama; we can allow ourselves to continue to follow the thinking through to logical and realistic resolution straightaway. When we do not do this, it is usually because we are trying to avoid thinking about having to face the problem which we see as so awful. Unfortunately, having raised the spectre of this challenging situation or difficulty, it becomes harder to put it out of mind again (or the emotion it engenders).

Gillian is a 50-year-old divorcee who has rheumatoid arthritis. She has a well paid job working as the personal assistant to a senior executive of an events organising company. Her boss is a very dynamic and energetic woman who is constantly on the move and often expects Gillian to do a lot of running around for her. Gillian loves her job and admires her boss but she fears that she will not be able to maintain the pace in the future. Whenever she thinks of that she first feels very guilty and then very panicky. She lives alone and has a large mortgage to pay until she is 65; not being able to cope is "too terrible to contemplate" so she tries to block out any thought of that situation arising. The guilt feelings are because she thinks she ought to tell her employers about this diagnosis but avoids doing so because it might change the way she is treated at work.

Whilst it may not be pleasant for Gillian to think about the "worst case scenario" of her rheumatoid arthritis progressing and ending her career, nevertheless once this thought has occurred to her as a possibility she is more likely to benefit from thinking this scenario through than trying to push it from her mind. Similarly, Barry, having decided that he is now immersed in his most awful scenario (that of being old, sick and burdensome), may be helped by examining it more thoroughly rather than being resigned to how he believes it has fulfilled all his (worst case) expectations.

If, instead of stopping and staring at the problem in horror, we carry on to the "OK, so what is the likelihood and what would I do about it?" stage of the problem-solving process, then the following two thought patterns come into play.

a. Logical reasoning

Gillian can begin to examine her options for changing her job, retiring early, accelerating payment of her mortgage, buying a cheaper property and so on. Logically, there are a number of things she could also do to reduce difficulties in coping with disability. None of these things need to be decided on at the moment because her diagnosis is recent and her ability to work normally has not been impaired in any way. However, an awareness of possibilities, even if they are far less attractive than her present circumstances, can help remove the sense of being overwhelmed by catastrophe that has caused Gillian to panic. Socratic questioning can help the patient reason logically (see Technique: Socratic questioning)

b. Examining the evidence

Barry has made a lot of rather sweeping generalisations about aging and ill health throughout his life but does the evidence of his own eyes support these opinions? Of course he can think of examples that confirm his opinions, but are they the only examples he can think of and are they in the majority? What about the evidence supporting his own frailty? Is he really like his grandfather? Can he really not manage a round of golf? As to the burden he causes, does he have evidence of people showing impatience or depression because of his presence? What have other people actually said to him and about him?

Gillian, too, may be helped by examining the evidence concerning the probability of rapid progression of her rheumatoid arthritis. What has she been told? What developments would actually impair her work performance? What would be the changes in her condition that would trigger the need to consider changes to her work and lifestyle?

The Information sheet: Examining the evidence and the questions included in the **Developing alternatives to mental traps** section included in the next chapter may help with this work.

2. Cognitive restructuring

Taking a fresh look at the situation, re-examining our beliefs and understanding in order to acquire a new perspective that seems more useful for dealing with it, may require no more than just some new bits of information or educational insight into cause and effect relationships, misunderstandings, myths or erroneous assumptions. Acquiring this new perspective through information and awareness is referred to as "cognitive restructuring". Some of the fresh insight may emerge from logical reasoning and examination of evidence work already discussed. However, the Socratic method and formulation development are often the key tools and are used primarily to rework existing information in different ways to produce three "Re-"s.

a. Re-Attribution

In our endeavours to make sense of the world around us and between past and present experiences we make meaningful associations between things. Whilst these links may be largely appropriate the cause and effect relationships are not always what we assume them to be. Barry explains the cessation of the sexual relationship aspect of his marriage as due to a loss of sex drive he attributes to the treatment for his prostate cancer. His consultant is doubtful that this is the case in this instance. In view of what Barry has said about not wanting to disappoint Sheila the problem may not be one of sex drive at all but of fear of failure which then stops him from wanting to try to resume the sexual relationship. If it is a problem of sex drive the consultant suspects that it is more likely to be attributable to his low mood and general loss of interest in things. Re-attributing his sexual difficulties to either anxiety or depression will enable Barry to view this situation less fatalistically.

b. Re-appraisal

At times when there is a lot happening at once it can be hard to "see the wood for the trees" and we cannot identify what is most important to us and what deserves to be treated as a priority. Gillian does not have to match the dynamic and somewhat flighty style of her boss. She is actually valued in her job by her boss and others because she is an "anchor" and a steadying influence that ensures that there is a reliable communication flow to and from her boss and that work gets completed properly. Proper consideration of these facts enables Gillian to reassure herself that she is likely to be able to continue to work very effectively.

c. Re-conceptualisation

Sometimes new or neglected information enables us to completely rethink the situation so that the whole picture changes. Barry has conceptualised the unhappiness at home to his grandfather's old age and infirmity. He has built a framework for his relationships with other people based on the idea of not replicating this situation. When he reflected on this more carefully he recalled that his grandfather had always had a reputation for being domineering and self-centred: both his mother and grandmother had been rather frightened of him. It was his grandfather's personality not his age or health that made life so difficult with him around. Barry recognised that his sensitivity to the needs of others ensured that he was in no danger of becoming like his grandfather or causing his family to experience what he experienced as a child.

3. Cognitive awareness and constructive thinking

When a particular thought repeatedly influences the way in which a person analyses and interprets information, then the thought itself deserves closer scrutiny if it seems to stimulate negative emotional responses but without a constructive course of action to resolve them. Whilst it may be inevitable that Laura will continue to experience sadness and regret about not having been able to have children, it is not inevitable that she feels so self-critical about this, that distress is evoked every time one of her friend's gives birth or that meeting these offspring for the first time remains such an intensely uncomfortable event for her.

With the de-catastrophising and cognitive restructuring strategies already mentioned we can see how Barry and Gillian may quite effectively shift their thinking in order to analyse and interpret issues more constructively. However, both of them are acknowledging that certain beliefs and attitudes contribute to why the situation is difficult to manage. Laura is different because she is not recognising that her thinking plays a part in this process. She cannot see it as a case of analysis and interpretation but one of simple facts and raw emotion over which she can have no influence. In order to begin to think more constructively about her circumstances, Laura will need to acknowledge that thinking is already playing a major part in her responses and that this thinking process is modifiable. One of the Greek Stoic philosophers, Epictetus, said: "People are troubled not by events but by the meaning they give them" but for Laura and for many of us when we react strongly to "events" the experience seems rather different. It is as though the event brings a certain emotional impact as part of the event itself.

a. Awareness of automatic thoughts

A driving test may seem to have fear attached to it, but it will be the way the learner driver thinks about that driving test that generates the fear and not the test itself. If the learner can find a way of seeing the test as less of a threat (perhaps by belief in driving skills or less concern about failing) then the fear can be reduced. Death may seem to have the emotion of grief continuously attached to it when linked to someone close; but other emotions are stimulated when thinking about it include recalling the value of having known the person, the good manner of her or his death, the valuable lessons learned from the person's life that you will carry into the future etc. This frequent linkage between certain thoughts and emotions goes to the heart of the cognitive behavioural approach and takes us back to points raised in the earliest chapters of this book.

When the event provokes a fixed thought or seemingly evokes an emotional response without any thought attached then we are dealing with thinking that has similar properties to habitual behaviour: it is quickly triggered and is fairly inflexible. In cognitive therapy these are referred to as "automatic thoughts". The thought is so closely associated with the event and the emotion that it occurs very fast and does not develop properly. Automatic thoughts may be hard to recognise as thoughts at all and they are never questioned or reflected upon in the way that other thoughts are scrutinised. Because of this they are less likely to be modified by experience or new information. They go on having the same effect for as long as they remain automatic. The impact can be quite powerful when we enable the patient to become aware of the automatic thought and see the link between the event, this thought and the emotional response. Even if the person still favours a particular analysis and interpretation over others, being aware that it is *possible* to think about the event differently begins to change the relationship the person has with that event and the emotional response to it.

Laura will not suddenly stop getting worked up about meeting friends with young children just because she learns that she does not *have to react* that way. But the more aware she is of the thought that drives her to that emotional response, the more accessible it becomes for change; if she does not want to have that emotional response she becomes more likely to question the thought and to come up with alternative perspectives that help her cope better.

b. Identifying mental traps

Automatic thoughts are quickly aroused and quickly expressed. They are rather like slogans or attention grabbing newspaper headlines: the most powerful ones are short and punchy. "Dot Com Bubble Bursts" packed a lot of complicated information into a very short phrase. "Gotcha" and "Up yours, deLors" conveyed news and emotion even more concisely. A beautiful sunset may make us think "Life's just great" or "Nature is wonderful" whilst an earthquake report can lead us to think of how temporary life is and how cruel nature can be. Take a wrong turn and you might say "I always get lost". Say it enough times and you will begin to believe it; once you believe it you start to ask others to do the navigating and stop trying to improve your navigation skills. By that time the "I always get lost" thought has become a trap that you are caught in; because you believe it, you lose confidence, depend more on others and obstruct developing further learning.

The more Laura simplifies the history of her life prior to treatment to slogan-like comments like being just "wasted opportunities for having babies" the more dismissive she is of her past achievements and the more she is likely to blame herself for bad decision making. She will have used hindsight as a tool to simplify the issues and explain the unfortunate events as being her own fault.

In our quest for making sense of the world and being ready for its problems we are prone like Laura to fall into mental traps of

i. <u>oversimplification</u> of the information when, like Laura we over-generalise, label and stereotype, or think in dichotomies or all-or-none terms

ii. <u>speculation</u> about the missing information when we jump to conclusions by trying to read what is in someone else's mind or intentions, trying to predict what will happen in the future, or anticipate the worst logical outcome that might arise

iii. <u>biased</u> selection of information when we mentally filter the bits that fit our mood or point of view, select out contrary information such as discounting positive feedback that does not match negative self-appraisal and emphasising information in a way that personalises responsibility, culpability, mishap and coincidence

iv. <u>dogmatism,</u> whereby we adopt certain attitudes or principles that make thinking more rigid and inflexible such as when mood determines judgement and belief in a process of emotional reasoning, or when preoccupation with apportioning blame takes priority over problem resolution. The most common of the dogma mental traps is, however, the "should thinking" type which often amounts to a lengthy and harsh collection of informal rules which can tyrannise life, denying the person the right to choice and flexibility or producing guilt feelings for having not conformed.

Automatic thoughts will almost always belong in one of the mental trap categories and awareness of the trap helps in developing useful alternative ways of thinking. People are prone to repeatedly falling into the same traps so, as with automatic thoughts, heightened awareness of habitual mental traps can begin to change the relationship the person has with that kind of thinking. For a list and description of the twelve most commonly occurring mental traps see Information sheets: Mental traps; Mental traps – examples of how to get out of them. More will be said about these commonly occurring styles of thinking and when they qualify as problematic mental traps in the next chapter.

c. Challenging unhelpful thoughts

Awareness of automatic thoughts and the mental traps can enable the patient to metaphorically stand back and observe thinking in a way that is similar to evaluating behaviour. But, as with behaviour, knowing where one might be going wrong will often not be sufficient. Ideas for doing better also need to be developed. In the case of cognitions that means challenging the unhelpful aspects of current thinking and developing reasonable and realistic alternatives in which the patient can believe. When this is necessary it can form a major part of the cognitive behavioural intervention and for this reason it will be the subject of more thorough discussion in the next chapter.

Cognitive Techniques for Changing Decision Making

We can characterise the cognitive processing in terms of *attending* followed by *analysing and interpreting*, then culminating in *decision making*. This simplification of the process is useful here as we study the techniques that can be used to bring about changes in each of these cognitive processes but we should not forget that the "Hot Cross Bun" model is intended to serve as a constant reminder of the interplay with emotions, physical sensations and behaviour. This interplay will be colouring the *decision making* just as it has the *attending* and the *analysing*. Automatic thoughts are frequently associated with pronounced emotional reactions; and a tight feedback loop between thought and emotion which produces more emotive thoughts and yet more intense emotions is a common characteristic of these strong reactions. Prising this chain link open can be quite hard. The patient may be attending to the right information and analysing it in a constructive manner: resisting giving in to the automatic thoughts and the mental traps. But like the temptations of bad old habits, the "attractions" of the automatic thoughts and mental traps will still be there, contributing to an emotional context which can only be truly transformed if the decision-making process resists seduction. Barry is successfully attending to his social gathering rather than his bladder control and his sense of being viewed as a social outcast he now dismisses as merely a tendency to slip into the "mind-reading" mental trap; but he still has to brazen it out and stand there chatting if there is to be an emotional and behavioural shift that helps sustain the cognitive shift he is attempting to cultivate. If he decides to "pop to the loo anyway, just to be on the safe side" the whole exercise in cognitive change collapses: he will reduce the risk of "an accident" and give everyone "a bit of a break" from him and this "safety behaviour" will prevent him from gathering evidence that reinforces his new way of thinking. The next social gathering will be no less difficult cognitively than the last one. It would be a bit like attending one of those exasperating meetings where all the issues are aired very fully and everyone agrees that a certain course of action would be best but nowhere is it determined who will be responsible for doing it. At the next meeting nothing is different and the whole set of issues are discussed all over again.

Susan Jeffers (1987) succinctly captures the key to success in this decision-making component of the cognitive shift process in the title of her very helpful and extremely successful book "Feel the fear and do it anyway". Barry's potential for failure in this challenging situation despite apparent cognitive preparation highlights a distinction in the decision-making process that we cannot afford to neglect: the distinction between *intention* and *action*. His reasoned alternative thoughts are competing with unhelpful cognitions that are still a part of his thinking and bring with them uncomfortable emotional responses. It is a very common experience for people to determine to do something in a calm and logical manner only to lose their nerve at the last minute. We just have to reflect on all those broken New Year resolutions to lose weight, stop smoking, exercise more and drink less alcohol in order to understand something of the difficulties sometimes encountered in making the move from intention to action. As health care professionals we need to appreciate this distinction because it can intrude into every aspect of our involvement with our patients: from attending appointments on time to co-operating in treatment regimes.

So what are the means that can help consolidate changes in attention focus and analysis so that the patient effectively decides cognitive and behavioural changes that in turn will have emotional and probably physical and environmental change consequences?

1. Commitment

If Barry is determined that these are the best alternative cognitive strategies and is resolved to test them properly then he commits himself to a plan of action that enables him to conduct a fair test. To shift from intention to commitment to action he will need to be reasonably settled in his own mind on several points:

a. Acceptance

Barry needs to accept that he really has a problem, that it is a problem worth addressing and that this is the problem.

b. Belief

Barry has to believe that the tactics he plans to use to manage the problem are likely to work and that he has the ability to carry them out.

c. Weighing pros and cons

Barry wants to be sure that in doing this he will not pay too high a price (whether in financial terms, time, emotion, energy etc.) . This cost-benefit analysis will be part of a general evaluation of the advantages and disadvantages of making this commitment.

d. Considering the views of others

Barry will be reluctant to do anything that will incur the disapproval of people who matter to him, especially his wife. Consequently, he is unlikely to commit to a course of action of which Sheila would disapprove. Equally, he will be more determined to fulfil commitments he has made to her and his friends.

We can apply these same points to any one of our patients and the difficulties that might arise for them in making a shift from seeing merit in the advice we offer and putting it into practice. In this context you may like to consider Peter, the man with ankylosing spondylitis described in Chapter 12. These points on commitment issues serve to help his physiotherapist understand why effective self-care has broken down and what needs to be looked at with some care to re-establish a workable action plan.

In order to bring about change in decision-making, we need to influence the degree of commitment the patient develops to a new idea and not assume that the decision has been made once the idea has been developed.

2. Guides

Few of our decisions are made purely through logical reasoning based entirely on current information. As with our perceptions, our decision-making is influenced by past experience, personal values, moral standards, social norms, situational pressures and advice from others. These and other personal factors will guide decision-making and may offer opportunities for facilitating the change process.

Returning to Gillian's concerns about how rheumatoid arthritis will affect her future, she can use guides like these to help her to decide not to give a great deal of time to attempting to confront and problem-solve these issues.

a. Credible advice

Gillian has a great deal of respect for the consultant rheumatologist she has seen. The consultant offered the opinion that it was very unlikely that the RA was about to progress suddenly and dramatically and advised Gillian against hasty decisions regarding her future. Her experience of the consultant's skill and knowledge encourages Gillian to accept this advice as sound.

b. Rules of thumb

Gillian has an excellent reputation in her job for being quick-thinking and creative in a calm way. She focuses on the facts and priorities without becoming distracted and disconcerted by all the possibilities of what might happen when her boss is in "frenetic mode". She has small rules she applies to help her keep control and cope such as "Don't cross bridges before you come to them"; "Concentrate on what is most important right now – everything else can wait" and "When I leave this office, I leave the work here". She can apply these same rules to help stop problem-solving problems that have not yet occurred regarding her RA.

c. Assertive thinking

Handling other people assertively in order to look after the best interests of her boss has never been a problem for Gillian. Looking after her own needs and standing up for her right to do so, feels much harder to her and she may need to give time to learning to apply the same skills she uses on behalf of her employer for her own benefit. In particular she needs to be able to remind herself that she has a perfect right to choose when and what she tells her boss about her health; that she can admit to difficulties caused by symptoms without disclosing her medical history. She also has as much right to "off-days" and to adapt the way in which she works as anyone else, provided the work gets done and to a satisfactory standard.

d. Re-examined rules and standards

Gillian can remind herself that just because she admires her boss she does not have to be like her, nor does she have to keep up appearances with her nice looking but expensive-to-run sports car. The car, like her modern detached house, is a preference and not a standard that must be maintained at all costs. When she thinks about it, Gillian knows she could live perfectly happily in a more modest house if the neighbours and neighbourhood were to her liking.

3. Tolerance of uncertainty

What will follow once the decision is made? Suppose it doesn't work? What if it is the wrong decision? How are other people going to react? What if I don't like the result? Fear of the unknown and unknowable will at times put people off making a decision at all. Whilst we are able to determine the *probability* of occurrence for a particular consequence, it is very rare for us to be able to speak in terms of *certainty*. In the absence of certainty some people find it hard to make decisions and thus procrastinate.

Jake has become quite exasperated with Laura because, like her, he would like them to have children and now that she cannot he would like them to investigate the possibility of adopting. He sees this as a positive course of action which can help Laura to stop brooding on the past but she refuses to consider it because she asks "How can I know I will feel the right way about someone else's baby? I can't take the responsibility in case I get it wrong."

Some of the most distressing experiences of coping with uncertainty arise with patients with a terminal or progressive disorder. Living with not knowing how life is going to be changed by this disease over the next few weeks or months can heighten a sense of being out of control and unable to decide on anything. Being told "Who can be sure of anything, really? Any one of us could be run over by a bus tomorrow" will not be of much help because the patient, like the rest of us, has lived life up until now *deluded* by the belief that "Buses hit other people, not me". We get by very nicely by holding on to that delusion. The patient with the life threatening diagnosis no longer shares the delusion and is coping with the harsh reality from which, even as we mention our bus cliché, we remain safely cushioned.

So, when they are coping well, how do people cope with uncertainty? This could be the point at which another list of techniques is presented, but it is not because we manage our uncertainty by using the cognitive change strategies already discussed for attention focus and analysis. The "delusion" of immortality illustrates the manner in which we typically choose to focus on being alive rather than our certain knowledge of the fact that we will die because that is more helpful for dealing with the reality of day-to-day life. The terminal illness diagnosis encourages a shift of attention to the reality of the future but as this is generally unhelpful to us in our decision-making, we benefit from redirecting attention to the here and now.

Cognitive analysis strategies may also be relevant. For Laura the possibility of making a wrong decision paralyses her ability to make any decision at all, which of course means that, by default, the decision has been made for her not to adopt children. Using the cognitive restructuring techniques to recognise and reappraise the situation mindful of the fact that a decision is being made in any case, may help Laura recognise the value of playing a more active and constructive role in taking that decision. She will also be more encouraged to do this if there is some work done on de-catastrophising wrong decisions and studying how these can be well managed in the world of adoption.

Concluding remarks

In this chapter we have attempted to identify and categorise some of the most frequently used methods for bringing about changes in thinking. Much of the regular work of the health care professional involves providing new information and correcting misconceptions and sorting out misunderstandings. An acceptance of this educative role and the importance of good communication skills to perform it sensitively and effectively are hallmarks of the skilled caring professional. Using the cognitive behavioural approach, however, we ask that health care professional to go one step further and help the patient discover new and different ways of *processing* the information received. Our emphasis throughout is to encourage patients to develop their own alternative perspectives and avoid telling them how to think or that they are wrong to think in a particular way.

To complete our examination of facilitating cognitive change, we need to consider how we might modify the *content* of unhelpful thinking. Some quite specific thoughts are firmly held despite being harmful to the patient's best interests; some are justifiable knee-jerk responses to certain situations that have cropped up repeatedly; and some thoughts are part of an emotionally-charged package that seems appropriate even if the thoughts are unhelpful. In the next chapter we will look at specific thoughts like these more carefully and examined how we might assist patients to generate more helpful alternatives without making them feel that we consider them to be wrong-headed to have been thinking in this way.

Exercises

Before you proceed to the next chapter take time to do the exercises included at the end of this chapter. To use this book properly you need to complete all the recommended exercises.

Exercise 1

1. Look at Geoffrey's step-by-step plan and formulation and identify the types of cognitive change method from which he could benefit. As with the behavioural change methods, check out material in Part 3 of the book that may help facilitate this change.
2. Repeat this exercise with the imagined patients for whom you have developed some step-by-step plans.

Exercise 2

1. Review your own step-by-step plan to identify the types of behavioural and cognitive changes it may be useful to incorporate.

   a) Check Part 3 for material to assist this change process
   b) Adapt your record keeping to reflect changes in progress monitoring

c) Incorporate new strategies in the steps or plans for overcoming obstacles
d) Review your timetable of progressing steps in the light of work to be done overcoming obstacles.

2. Read all information sheets identified as potentially helpful.
3. Begin work on the first steps and priority obstacle tasks.

Exercise 3

1. Review volunteers step-by-step plans and record keeping and change in the light of any new information.
2. Identify types of behavioural and cognitive change you wish to recommend.
3. Discuss and agree which are to be incorporated in the plans and determine the details of the first steps to be taken.
4. Introduce any guidance or information material from Part 3 that is relevant at this stage including material related to identifying unhelpful thoughts.
5. Ask the volunteers to keep a record of negative and unhelpful thoughts that occur between now and the next session when you will discuss them in more detail. Also ask them to bring along their old CBT diary records too because these might be useful in this task.

Recommended further reading:

Burns, D. (1980) *Feeling Good* New York: Avon Books. A classic of the self-help genre.
Jeffers, S. (1987) *Feel the Fear and Do It Anyway* London: Random House. One of the most successful of all self-help books, this could have been recommended at the end of lots of chapters but perhaps fits just as well here as anywhere.
Neenan, M. and Dryden, W. (2004) *Cognitive Therapy: 100 Key Points and Techniques* London: Routledge.

Chapter 15
Challenging Unhelpful Thoughts

The most distinctive feature of the cognitive behavioural approach is the importance placed on changing unhelpful thoughts. The cognitive behavioural model focuses on studying the actions and reactions that are taking place in the present time; recent past and immediate future are also relevant to these considerations but the emphasis is on understanding the here and now. Capturing the flavour of the influential thoughts is pivotal to that understanding as already discussed in the previous chapter. If the content of those thoughts is unhelpful then our task is to assist the patient in recognising their unhelpfulness and developing suitable alternatives that seem to be more helpful. In this chapter we will look in more detail at how this is done. First of all, we should clarify what we mean by "unhelpful" thoughts.

James is a very successful racing driver. He travels the world winning prestigious events and earns lots of money for doing so. At this race event as he waits to get into his car he could think to himself:

"This is a big event which has attracted a big crowd and international media interest. All the world's best drivers are here and it is going to be an aggressive and tightly fought race. Under this pressure it would be easy to make reckless judgements, crash the car and die in a hideous inferno right there at the side of the track with the world watching it happen."

Alternatively he could think:

" I am a very successful and highly skilled racing driver with a brilliant record of making smart decisions in tough situations. From my trial runs earlier I know the track is in good shape; I know my car is performing well and I trust the team to keep it that way. Weather conditions are fine and I'm on peak form. Let's go out there and show the world what I can do."

Logically, both of these thoughts are perfectly reasonable. The first one rightly identifies the hazardousness of the situation and the increased risks associated with performance pressures. The second correctly identifies the experience and skill of James and his ability to cope well with these pressures. So neither alternative thought is wrong. However, one is probably more helpful to James than the other. The first thought encourages fear and doubt and the second encourages confidence and competitiveness. Consequently, for James, the second thought is most likely to help him compete and win; the first would probably finish his career.

The overused "half full – half empty glass" analogy delivers the message that there is more than one way to look at the same situation. However, in the cognitive behavioural approach we are not interested in the fact that the "half full" thought might be a *positive* way to look at the situation; we are interested in the alternative because it is a *helpful* or *useful* way to view it. To illustrate the difference let us just consider for a moment the possibility that you are the one who at the last minute has been obliged to stand in for James who has suddenly been taken ill. If we reconsider exactly those same two thoughts under these new circumstances then we find that whilst the second thought remains the *positive* one, there may be good reason to suppose that the first thought has now become more *helpful* or *useful*. Bearing in mind your lack of experience in high performance cars in competitive conditions and the pressures to succeed, you will be well advised to remember the penalties for taking risks. Whilst this *negative* thought may stop you from winning or perhaps even from taking part in the race at all, we can see that to think this way will be *helpful* if your priority is staying alive.

Back in the real world of clinical practice, let us consider another example of *helpful* or *unhelpful* thinking.

Adjustment to changed personal circumstances can prove very difficult to achieve when thoughts are rather rigidly held on to, especially if they reflect attitudes that have always been there and have never been challenged. This is particularly *unhelpful* when these thoughts lead to seemingly needless additional suffering or obstruction to progress. For example, many patients whose quality of life would benefit from effective pain management struggle on with quite high levels of pain and discomfort because they "don't like taking pills unless I really have to" or fear that "I will get too used to it and will not feel the benefits when it really matters."

After a cycle of chemotherapy, when she is feeling tired and unwell, Debbie, a divorcee with two teenage children could adjust her thinking to "I'm not up to doing much and they're quite capable of fending for themselves, so I'm staying in bed today" but if she is firmly attached to the belief that "Looking after them is my responsibility and they can't manage without me", she will try to struggle on and is very unlikely to ask for any help.

Adaptation may be problematic, too, if the thought processes are based on too little information or faulty information.

Six weeks ago, Bernie was discharged from hospital. He is the 70-year-old man with the chronic heart condition who we encountered in Chapter 4. At the time of his discharge the doctor he saw told him that she would get the dietician to call him in the next few days because she was still concerned about how underweight he was; but he has still heard nothing. He thinks to himself:

"They are very busy people and have to deal with much worse cases than me, so it's not surprising that they haven't got back to me yet." So he takes no action. Of course, he has no information to justify jumping to this conclusion and may have been helped to a more satisfactory outcome by thinking "It has gone on longer than a few days now, so maybe I had better contact the hospital again and find out what is happening."

When thoughts are rigid and ill-informed such as those above, they form a hindrance to constructive problem-solving and can prevent people from feeling and coping better. Thoughts like these serve to maintain things as they are already and because nothing else changes, the thoughts do not change either! So a self-perpetuating vicious circle is formed. In this book we refer to them as *mental traps*. The technical term for them in CBT is *cognitive distortions* but because "traps" more precisely describes the problems they frequently cause our patients, this is the term we use here.

Mental Traps

Descriptions of the most commonly occurring mental traps and examples of each one are provided in Information sheets: Mental traps and Examples of mental traps and how to get out of them. A quick perusal of the list is likely to produce recognition that we all have a tendency to make many if not all of these distortions in our thinking at different times. As you study the list you may even identify one or two that you use very frequently. However, you will probably also recognise that they generally do not cause you a problem. So if they are common occurrences that most of us are prone to, why would we see them as a problem for some people but not for others?

To answer this we return to the word "trap." Reflect for a moment on your own tendency to distort thinking in one of these ways and consider why it does not cause you to make bad decisions or leave you floundering. You may also be able to think of situations where this way of thinking has got you into trouble. By doing this you can probably see that whether a thinking distortion of this sort is a "trap" or not depends on whether it forms the whole or only a part of the thought process you go through. Much of the time people include cognitive distortions in the course of thinking through an issue; these thoughts form part of the discussion we have with ourselves but do not alone determine the outcome of our deliberations. However, if in our thinking we "lock on" to a cognitive distortion and it becomes the predominant thought about the issue and shapes the decisions we make and actions we take, then we have fallen into the *mental trap*.

In ordinary day-to-day reasoning we may be inclined at times to think in ways that distort the picture and are unhelpful to constructive action but we usually detect the errors and try to think of helpful alternatives. We engage in a dialogue aimed at problem solving and decision making. Largely we will have that dialogue privately, in our own heads. Sometimes we think out loud and share the process in discussions with other people. Often, when applying the cognitive behavioural approach, we are trying to help the patient use external dialogue to identify the errors and distortions that would otherwise remain undetected in the internal dialogue (or thinking).

Developing alternatives to the mental trap

Our patients do not need or want to be told how to think. Through the use of internal dialogue they adjust and adapt ideas, select and interpret information and make decisions just like other people. Also like anyone else, they can and do change ideas, opinions and perceptions all by themselves much of the time when persuaded that this is necessary. At times we need only to help them to the conclusion that this may be one of those occasions. But when we find that a patient has got stuck in a *mental trap* pattern of thinking, it is often necessary to offer some reminders and some coaching in the methods of "thinking it through" that may not yet have been applied this time.

Thinking is usually messier than conversation: it lacks all the grammar and syntax; it frequently jumps about from topic to topic; it trails off without arriving at conclusions; it goes back over the same points repeatedly; it mixes words with images; it includes memories, logical reasoning, associations, fantasies and fears. So, in order to get out of the mental trap, the patient may need to "tidy up" the process.

Looking for a more useful or helpful alternative way of thinking about the situation immediately gives a sense of direction and purpose to the thought process and reduces the tendency to just go round in vague circles. Finding suitable alternatives that are useful or helpful is another matter. It will not be sufficient that they are *positive*: after all, the positive "winning" attitude of racing driver James would not be helpful to most of us when sat in his car.

The process is illustrated in Figure 1.15.1 which includes a return to the two response sets described in Figures 1.2.2 and 1.2.3 whilst examining the situation of William once he had received his diagnosis of cancer.

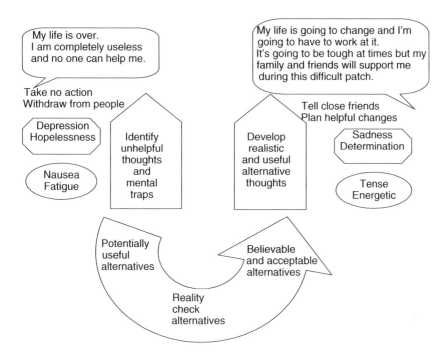

Figure 1.15.1 The process of cognitive change for William

Were it not for the mental trap that has been fallen into, the normal process that the patient would use to problem solve this dilemma would probably involve a certain amount of internal questioning and debate. Some of the internal debating themes that people use are summarised below, together with some typical self-questioning used in modifying thoughts. In the cognitive behavioural approach the health care professional encourages a more systematic use of these themes and turns some of it into an "external dialogue" either through discussion in interview or through written records of immediate thoughts and alternatives thought up by the patient. In summarising these themes, you will also notice that there is a lot of content that we could describe as "Socratic dialogue," reinforcing the point made in an earlier chapter that the Socratic method is an integral part of the cognitive behavioural intervention not just the assessment.

1. *Understanding*

How do I make sense of this information? How does this fit with what I already know? What caused that to happen? What difference did my actions make?

From birth people begin learning how to interpret the environment and how to effectively interact with it. Assimilating information, categorising it, identifying cause-and-effect relationships and learning from experiences occupies a great deal of thinking time throughout life.

2. *Usefulness*

Is this a helpful way of thinking and is it useful in solving the problem being considered? Is this information of any value to me? So what?

The practical benefits or problems of thinking in this way may influence the wish to scrutinise or change current thoughts and beliefs or to take on new ideas and information.

3. *Alternative approaches*

Is there any other way to look at this?

People like to sort problems out, so it is quite normal to keep looking at the same issue from lots of different angles until a helpful way of thinking about it has been found.

4. *Proportion or distortion*

Have I got this properly in perspective? Am I being reasonable and fair?

People like to believe that they are exercising good judgement and are not exaggerating, over-simplifying or being unreasonable.

5. *Consistency*

Does this contradict my normal standards and attitudes? Am I guilty of applying double standards here?

People like to believe that what they do and say to others matches their own general approach to life and the value systems they espouse. It is an important part of the person's sense of integrity that he or she is consistent in this. Therefore mental effort is exerted on rationalising and justifying any perceived inconsistencies. Sometimes where the contradiction is too great, a change of viewpoint will be made.

6. *Logical reasoning*

Does this follow from what went before? Is this a reasonable conclusion to draw or expectation to have? What is the sensible next step?

People often like to think of themselves as being reasonable. This involves the ability to think rationally, think things through, exercise common sense and come to a balanced judgement or decision. As with *Consistency,* rationalisation or changes to the views held will usually follow if illogical thinking is identified.

7. *Persuasion and influence*

Why do these other people have a different point of view from me? What are the advantages of changing my views to fit in with theirs?

Doubts and uncertainty about beliefs and knowledge will be important in motivating people to consider changes in their thinking. Often it will be social pressure or persuasive argument from a credible source that will begin to have this influence.

8. *Examining the evidence*

Do the facts justify this opinion? Do other like-minded people think this way?

The scientific approach: people will adopt this approach when faced with interpreting new information, evaluating its credibility and determining what attitude to take to it. Similarly, they will do this when they have reason to doubt previously held views.

9. *Belief and knowledge*

Do I believe that this is true or do I have information that means that I know that it is?

Believing something is true is not the same as knowing that it is. Belief and fact become confused when we do not personally have the information but trust others (such as experts) whom we believe to have this knowledge.

10. *Predicting outcome*
What could happen next? What's the most likely way this is going to end? What do those people really think about this? How do I know that I'm not going to enjoy myself?
Sometimes people act as though they can predict the future or as if they can read other people's minds. It is very tempting to fill in the gaps and to anticipate outcomes as part of the problem-solving thought processes. Sometimes a "calculated guess" can be made on the basis of expertise or previous experience, but it will still be necessary to leave room for doubt.

Practical difficulties when challenging mental traps

Having identified the unhelpful thoughts and the mental traps that obstruct progress there follows the debating and questioning strategies used in the "internal dialogue" as described above. There are a number of ways to assist this debate such as scrutinising supporting evidence, conducting behavioural experiments to test predictions and reality checking beliefs. The patient can generate suitable potentially useful alternative thoughts that can be similarly scrutinised, tested and checked. Equipped with a new way of thinking about the situation, the expectation is that there will now be a beneficial shift in behavioural and emotional responses. For various reasons this will not always prove to be the case.

1. *There is no alternative way of thinking about this*
There will be plenty of times when the health care professional will encounter this reaction from the patient because, just as the rest of us would, this person has wrestled with the troubling thought for some time already desperately seeking some crumb of comfort or new understanding. But there are always new and different perspectives to explore and amongst them the likelihood of something that will be of some help to the patient. Often the sticking point that seems to allow for only one perspective on the situation is one where emphasis is placed on the facts of the situation and an assumption that only one interpretation or conclusion can be drawn from those facts. "I've been told that it is terminal, so that's that. I'm going to die, so my life is over. There's nothing more to be said or done." Of course "that is <u>not</u> that" and life is not over until you are dead. The facts may be completely accurate, but there are inferences that are being drawn from those facts that move into the realms of modifiable perspectives. Helping the patient make that shift will need to be handled sensitively if the health care professional is to avoid being accused of trivialising important information but simply going along with the same conclusions will keep the patient in the mental trap.

2. *Offering alternative perspectives*
When the patient struggles to come up with alternative perspectives there is often a temptation to offer suggestions. Resisting that temptation is quite a skill in itself; asking questions that lean towards a particular alternative being offered in the patient's answer could help; or encouraging the patient to think about admired role-models who you think would adopt that option might lead to the desired outcome. Whatever method is used to generate alternative thoughts that might challenge the original unhelpful thought, those alternatives need to be thought up and thought through by the patient. We must try very hard to resist the temptation to step in and provide answers. When unhelpful thoughts are challenged by other people, including health care professionals, the effect is usually the opposite to the one intended. What happens to any of us when our ideas and beliefs are criticised or rejected by other people? We are rather inclined to defend our point of view and come

up with reasons to justify holding it. Quite often the most troublesome mental trap thoughts that the patient has will have been expressed openly and repeatedly to friends, family and professional care staff who, with the best of intentions, have offered alternatives and criticised the unhelpful thoughts in some detail. Unfortunately the effect of these discussions will be to give the patient opportunities to rehearse and repeat justifications that maintain the unhelpful thoughts, making them more resistant to change. The response of many patients who are going through this process of reinforcing their unhelpful thoughts is typified by the commonly heard phrase "Yes, that's all very well but … ." Since we never want to make these thoughts more resistant to change be ready to pull back and think again about how best to approach your task when you hear a "yes, but."

3. *Belief in realistic alternatives*

Recognising that a particular thought is unhelpful then coming up with an alternative can produce sudden and dramatic change. However, one of the frequent complaints that people make about these exercises in challenging unhelpful thoughts is that they can come up with what they are "supposed" to think but actually they admit that they still believe their old thoughts. There are two points to make regarding this:

a) There is no right and wrong way of thinking, so if the alternative that has been selected does not seem right then, just because some other people think that way, is not a reason why the patient has to believe it too. The guiding rule in this exercise of developing alternatives is: if it is not helpful then it is the wrong alternative for this person; so keep looking for one that really works.

b) Helpful alternatives rarely *feel* right to begin with. The initial unhelpful thoughts set up a negative frame of mind, so more thoughts of the same sort will fit most comfortably with this emotional framework (i.e. *feel* right). But if the alternative is reasonable and believable to the patient, then just by thinking it a process of doubting the old thought and moving to a different perspective begins to occur. This may take hours or even days the first few times this alternative is substituted. But when similar situations crop up time after time then the shift from the old to the new thought gets quicker. "There's no point in me getting up, the day will be empty and just drag" may be challenged by "I hate getting up when I feel so tired all the time, but when I get up early and get stuck into things I feel better about myself and the day brightens up and is full." If that new thought is followed by action and is proved true, then it will come quicker and be more persuasive with each succeeding day.

4. *"Positive thinking"*

People frequently run into problems with "positive thinking" as a way of challenging negative and unhelpful thoughts. The negatives are sometimes more realistic than these positives. A bad experience will still be a bad experience, regardless how much you try to say it was a good experience or "character building." Stating repeatedly that a negative experience is really a positive one will not produce some kind of self-induced brainwashing. On the other hand, recognising some good coming out of a bad experience can be a helpful perspective: "I've learnt from my mistake," "I've proved I can cope with a setback," "I've discovered some real friends through this." This type of shift in thinking from the very black to a shade of grey may represent a helpful change in thinking that can be achieved with some effort and lightens the emotional state without attempting to deny the bad experience.

5. *Rhetorical questions*

Often when people write down their unhelpful thoughts they write them in the form of a question: "Will I be able to cope?" "Is there any point in trying?" "Am I becoming a nuisance to my family?" Because these are questions they do not seem quite the same as the mental traps, they are not so definite, seem to be more reasonable thoughts and do not include unhelpful statements. But people leave these questions hanging; they do not answer them so the effect is much the same as the unhelpful statements: the unhelpful answer is taken for granted: "I won't be able to cope;" "There is no point in trying," "Yes, I am a nuisance to my family." When these negative "rhetorical" questions occur, encourage the patient to answer them or turn them into statements. It will then be much easier to come up with an idea of the mental trap that the person is falling into and the realistic, helpful alternative statement to work on developing.

6. *Writing thoughts down*

Writing these thoughts out on pieces of paper can be a bit tedious, sometimes embarrassing and often inconvenient. It is rarely possible to write them down precisely as events are happening. Nevertheless, writing is very important in escaping from the mental traps and greatly to be encouraged when using the cognitive behavioural approach. Putting thoughts down on paper helps with thinking it through slowly and carefully and also with committing new alternative thoughts to memory. By this method the person becomes more clearly aware of the old thought (so making it become less automatic) and builds a strong association with the new thought (so increasing the likelihood that it will pop into the mind when the unhelpful thought is triggered).

Talking it through out loud can work just as well if for some reason writing is not a practical method; the same steps are necessary: specifying the unhelpful thought, identifying the mental trap and then generating a reasonable and helpful alternative. It is harder to memorise a mental trap thought and its alternative when done this way but repetition helps.

Concluding remarks

It may seem a very insubstantial way of working to assist someone challenge unhelpful thoughts and generate reasonable alternatives that are both believable and helpful. The tangible proof of what has been done is very limited; but when this work is incorporated into an action plan with a clear goal, the benefits obtained from cognitive change can be very clearly demonstrated and produce beneficial repercussions well beyond the problem areas directly dealt with during these sessions. Handouts that give key information (such as Information sheets: Mental traps; Examples of mental traps; Examining evidence) together with accumulated records of the work done (using forms such as Record forms: Thought record; Event-emotion-thought analysis) provide the patient with a valuable set of resource materials to draw upon should reminders be required.

Exercises

Before you proceed to the next chapter take time to do the exercises included at the end of this chapter. To use this book properly you need to complete all the recommended exercises.

Exercise 1

1. Look at the CBT diary thoughts recorded by Norman and Geoffrey in the exercises at the end of Chapter 8.
   a) Identify which thoughts are unhelpful in these records.
   b) Specify which mental traps these thoughts fall into.
   c) Attempt to come up with alternative realistic thoughts that might work for Norman and Geoffrey.

Exercise 2

1. Go through your own CBT diary records to:

   a) Identify the unhelpful thoughts.
   b) Specify the mental traps.
   c) Think of useful and effective alternative ways of thinking about this.

2. Looking at this information

   a) Are you prone to falling into the same few traps?
   b) Do you repeatedly have the same unhelpful thought?
   c) Do you believe in the alternatives and find them more helpful?

Remember

   • Not all negative thoughts are unhelpful and not all positive thoughts benefit us.

Exercise 3

1. Review progress with the first steps for each volunteer

   a) Listen to self-report information
   b) Check record keeping information
   c) Use Socratic questioning to clarify and examine difficulties
   d) Determine whether to progress to further steps or re-work existing tasks

2. Discuss information on unhelpful thoughts

   a) Check through old CBT diary records for examples.
   b) Explain about mental traps and automatic thoughts
   c) Provide relevant information sheets
   d) Look at new record of unhelpful thoughts noted since last meeting
   e) Identify the mental traps
   f) Discuss ways of developing believable helpful alternatives
   g) Work together on developing some alternatives

3. Set new homework assignments

   a) Continue working on steps and overcoming obstacles
   b) Maintain current record keeping for monitoring progress
   c) Use a thought diary (Record forms: Thought record) to identify and challenge unhelpful thoughts.

Recommended further reading:

Freeman, A. and DeWolf, R. (1992) *The 10 Dumbest Mistakes Smart People Make and How to Avoid Them,* New York: HarperCollins. An in-depth discussion of the main mental traps.

McKay, M. and Fanning, P. (1992) *Self Esteem. Second Edition,* Oakland: New Harbinger Publications. Challenges unhelpful thoughts and behaviours that undermine self-esteem.

Chapter 16
Managing Emotions and Unpleasant Physical Sensations

In this chapter we consider the strategies we can employ to bring about change with emotions and in relation to physical experiences in life-changing illnesses. Whereas cognitive behavioural strategies directed towards thoughts and behaviours are typically focused on modifying those thoughts and behaviours, the cognitive behavioural approach to managing experiences of emotional and physical discomfort aim primarily at changing the nature of the patient's relationship to these experiences.

Managing emotions

Acute severe distress reactions are usually short-lived, have a quality that makes them seem understandable and feel "normal" (we can often think: "This is how I might react myself if that happened") and rarely do lasting harm. Strong negative emotions can be very disturbing to witness and it is always tempting to do or say what we can to comfort and calm the distressed person as quickly as possible. To stay with the emotion and allow the patient time to fully express the fears, rage and despair is very challenging and creates high levels of personal discomfort for staff and carers.

Hasty provision of advice, reassurance or calming medication, though seemingly kind, often gives an all too clear message to the patient that it is *not* OK to be upset or to upset others by expressing feelings openly. It is tempting for us as health care professionals to help the patient to "bundle away" these emotions and regard it as alleviating distress. Many of the patient's friends and family may also be reacting in this way. As a result the patient may only have rare opportunities to share intense feelings and to experience a satisfying sense of having really connected with someone else.

Different emotional responses will have their uses as appropriate (often beneficial) reactions in certain situations and at certain stages of illness. They are not simply either good or bad ways of coping although people sometimes believe that they are. What is important is that people are able to move flexibly through changing emotions and adopt ones which enable them to manage their adjustment to their illness constructively (see Information sheet: Emotional change – The "transition curve").

For example, brief periods of cognitive avoidance, or denial, can work well for William (whose treatment for his cancer is under review) after he has had tests and is awaiting the results. This emotional style allows him to "not think about it" and stay calm. Getting anxious would serve no purpose: it would not get the results faster, it would not help get treatment faster, and it lets him get on with life in the meantime, so it is a good option. However, a sense of mild anxiety and threat might help him remain alert to physical changes if his doctor had encouraged him to make contact immediately if certain developments occur.

In working to help people understand and manage their emotional reactions to their illness or disability, the focus of our work can be to help them:

1. Become more aware of the full range of the powerful emotions they experience.
2. Become more able to "own" and "allow" their emotional reactions to be there and not feel compelled to try and deny or change their feelings.
3. To value their emotional response as a part of themselves which helps them be in touch with their values and what is really important to them.
4. Work out when their most common emotional responses are helpful and when not.
5. Develop a sense of a greater degree of flexibility of emotional responses so that they feel they react to the feelings they have.
6. Use how they feel as part of how they make decisions about what to do and how to cope alongside other elements such as thinking things through and weighing "objective" evidence.

Bringing about change through increased emotional expression

Opportunities for emotional expression are often highly valued by patients and provide immense relief of suffering. Some patients are unable to go on to active problem solving and coping without having had an opportunity to ventilate their feelings.

Other people experience negative emotion but do not express them openly or directly, tending either to hide them behind smiles and other masks or acknowledging but firmly refusing to go into detail. If people do not want to express or share their feelings it is important to respect that choice while leaving the door open to allow them to share at a later stage if they wish.

Yet others may express feelings indirectly, perhaps by complaining a lot, 'forgetting' treatment tasks or becoming too busy to think about things. Sometimes there is a mismatch between what is said and what we actually believe the person is experiencing. The causes of this are usually simple and straightforward – not wanting to burden people, not expecting anyone to be concerned or care, and not expecting sharing emotions to be helpful, expecting oneself to "act one's age" or "not be a baby."

Very occasionally, the causes of emotional expression, or lack of it, are more complicated. They may perhaps relate to an unhappy or traumatic earlier emotional experience. There may be an underlying mental health problem such as clinical depression. Occasionally people use emotional expression as a way of manipulating the responses of others. Some forms of disease and types of medication cause disturbance in emotional expression. All these may be identified within the cognitive behavioural assessment and formulation.

The indications for encouraging us to focus on emotional expression with the patient will include:

1. Recent onset of emotional distress in setting of change in health status.
2. Marked fluctuations and unpredictable intrusions of emotional reactions.
3. Presence of strong appropriate emotions (sadness rather than depression, fear more than anxiety) and especially when the patient struggles to control them.

4. Rationality and logic are preventing acknowledgement of emotional content.
5. Exaggerated beliefs that expressing certain emotions is dangerous or inappropriate or the exact opposite: that allowing full emotional expression is absolutely essential.

If we are working with people on how they manage their emotions and encouraging them to continue to express these emotions, we need to be clear about our goals for doing this. These might include:

1. Helping the patient engage with emotions because it seems that expressing the emotions that are being ignored or suppressed might help the patient cope with events or access more support through relationships.
2. Clarifying and to properly take into account the emotional impact of certain problem situations which are hard to understand on the basis of logic alone and by doing so perhaps aid selection of appropriate treatment goals.
3. Establishing and maintaining the therapeutic alliance by acknowledging the patient's emotions and reinforcing the "right" to have them and express them.
4. Allowing the patient to step back and diffuse the situation by accepting these emotions as valid and an understandable reaction.
5. Using the emotional response as an element in goal setting and planning – as a clue to what important values are being challenged by the person's experience of the illness and how that may suggest a direction to pursue or to support decision taking that may feel impossible when there is simply consideration of the "facts."

We can encourage our patients to attend appropriately to their emotional experience as we work with them in session by:

1. Education: emotional reactions are normal and helpful.
2. Reducing activity. Being quiet and allowing silences allows you to attend to and notice how you feel.
3. Allowing emotions to emerge without reacting to them immediately – watching them unfold.
4. Encouraging attention to emotional experience by asking "What is it like for you?"
5. Keeping the focus on the "Here and Now" experience – bringing the person back when they move too quickly away to other aspects or experiences at other times.
6. Drawing attention to manner and postural expressions – how the patient holds him - or herself? What does the tone of voice tell us about how the person feels?
7. Using reflective comments "I sense you may be feeling," "It looks like you feel".
8. Encouraging the patient to use first person language ("I feel" rather than "It seems" often intensifies emotional awareness).
9. Challenging unhelpful thoughts about emotional expression (for example "It isn't natural to be positive all the time," "I don't think other people are being 'feeble' when they show emotion")

Further information on these methods is included in the Techniques section (see Attention strategies; Emotional expression; Psycho-education; Effective communication skills; Challenging unhelpful thoughts). Patients benefit from developing techniques for being in touch with uncomfortable emotions that can be used at a time of their choice. If they pay attention to emotions in this way, the feelings are less likely to be a problem in unexpected situations: emotions are less likely to suddenly well up and take them by surprise, intruding at inconvenient times.

Techniques that the patient can use outside of session that keep in touch with and pay appropriate attention to emotions include:

1. Allowing time to feel – taking a walk, or a long bath and just allowing themselves to be however the mood takes them
2. Talking to a friend who will just listen (not counsel, as counselling carries the risk of moving the person away from the feeling into looking for solutions before they are ready). Explaining and ventilating personal emotions and feeling understood can be very healing.
3. Meeting other people facing similar challenges can sometimes make people feel less alone and give a sense of being understood that no amount of talking to people who are not in the situation personally can ever bring.
4. Using emotionally expressive activities such as writing or creative artwork to develop a focus on particular emotional experiences (see Techniques: Emotional expression; Information sheet: Expressive writing).

    a. Dear Diary, un-posted letters, free-form writing enables someone to stop the mind whirling and give time to looking at the linkages between the troubling feelings in the same way that talking to a friend might do. The advantage is that this is something that can be done in complete confidence: it does not have to be shared for the effects to be beneficial.
    b. Posters, collages, painting, pottery.

5. Reminiscence activities (looking at photos and letters, visiting places, experiencing tastes and smells) that help you remember what is lost and what is good, allowing the experience of the mix of pleasant and unpleasant emotions to occur together.

Problems with expressing emotions

Whilst some people have problems allowing themselves to *experience* emotions, others have difficulties with *expressing* them. Three areas of emotional expression are often particularly challenging:

1. *Expressing anger*
Whilst suppressed anger is likely to lead to trouble later, finding an appropriate way of expressing it constructively can be difficult. Assertiveness reduces the risk of anger developing in the first place (see Technique: Assertiveness skills; Information sheets: Assertiveness model and Assertiveness techniques) and private emotional expression techniques such as writing the never-to-be-posted letter (see Information sheet: Expressive writing) can deal with the more destructive thoughts, but the physical sensations of the "fight response" may also need to be addressed through physical outlets (screaming into a pillow, or punching the pillow, or going for a very vigorous walk). Regulating the anger through these and other methods will often need to precede any attempt to problem-solve the triggering event.

2. *Handling denial*
Denial or some degree of avoidance of issues which evoke emotional responses may seem wrong or inappropriate but it is often adaptive and best left alone. For some people carrying on as normal enables them to maintain morale, motivation and quality of life, but they can only do this by minimising the amount of attention given to the illness, its future course and the impact on the family. Challenging this strategy needs to be carefully evaluated (see Technique: Denial – suggestions for questions to ask; Information sheet: Denial – assessing its pros and cons). See Problem: denial for a detailed description of its management.

3. *Coping with overwhelming emotions*

Some patients become very overwhelmed by intense emotions or prolonged emotional reactions and need to be taught techniques to enable them to feel more in control of the intensity and duration of their emotional experience. The indications for these cognitive behavioural interventions when emotional expression needs to be regulated rather than encouraged include:

a. Prolonged negative mood states – anxiety, depression, anger.
b. Extreme distress and agitation.
c. Ineffective coping or avoidance of things which really need to be faced.
d. Presence of emotions which discourage constructive action: guilt, self blame, severe hopelessness.
e. Destructive repercussions of emotional expression: unsuitable methods (for example, trashing the house), inappropriate timing (for example, crying in the supermarket queue), inappropriate disclosure (for example, over-burdening children).

The selection of specific techniques to try in these situations will depend on the formulation and goals you agree with the patient but will include the following items from the Techniques section: Mental distraction; Relaxation exercises; Attention strategies; Mindfulness. These are emotional regulation strategies and are to some extent "stop-gap" measures. Without a more inclusive plan and implementation of a range of cognitive behavioural strategies, the powerful emotion is likely to recur.

Targeting unpleasant physical sensations

Pain, discomfort, persistent irritations, nausea and fatigue are very common complaints for patients with life-changing illnesses. Physical sensations are usually more troublesome and overwhelming when emotions run high and are less so when the patient is relaxed. When people can manage stress and pressure effectively so that they feel calm pain and fatigue may be eased. However, the experience of prolonged ill health that has altered the daily pattern of life often challenges the ability of the patient to create this calm.

Some people allow their physical illness experiences to control their lifestyle. This tendency is learned through experience of mild illness in life and works well for normal, time limited illnesses like 'flu. These people feel entitled to drop certain standards they would normally maintain: for example, it might feel OK to be "a grumpy, rotten dad," ignoring the children's needs and staying in bed for a couple of weeks ("It won't do the family any harm; others can take the strain and I will soon make it up to them and be a really good dad when I am better").

Others try to cope in the same way they usually do, in the hope life does not have to change too much. They hold to the same plans and expect to push their way through the difficulties in order to "defeat" the illness.

As the months pass, both the "indulgent" and "defiant" types of strategy mentioned above tend to push people further away from their normal personal style and these experiences undermine how they feel about themselves. They feel worse, not better and sense a change of personality. This makes them feel more and more weighed down by the problems caused by the illness.

An example may help illustrate this point. Norman's blindness was getting worse fast. As a well paid and highly respected project manager, he had always expected to be able to keep working to allow his wife to stay home and support his children to complete their education in private schools. He had researched his condition, seen all the best people and tried all the latest treatments but none had really slowed the progress of his impairment. He suffered from severe headaches and fatigue which frequently compromised his work performance, his poor sight had prevented him from driving and this limited his ability to do site visits and presentations. He let all his hobbies and leisure activities lapse. His mind was constantly busy with schemes to keep the true extent of his difficulties from the family, his friends and employers. His GP recommended that he consider giving up work, so he stopped going to see her. His specialist nurse suggested various aids but he declined them all. He became short tempered and began to have rows with his wife and children. He was appalled when his wife began to talk about divorce. What more could he do? How could things have got to this stage?

In his private struggle to maintain his role in the family unchanged despite his deteriorating health, Norman had not reviewed what he really wanted to contribute in his relationship with his wife and as a father (and what exactly the family needed from him) as he continued to try to do what he always had done. Focusing on finding the medical solution to stem the progress of his blindness and manage his disability, Norman had hoped that each thing he tried would be "the answer." He had not considered changing his routines and commitments. He delayed letting the family know he could not cope. The cognitive behavioural interventions provided him with the support and encouragement he needed to focus on how much he valued that feeling of being able to make a difference to the lives of his wife and children. Then the cognitive behavioural approach helped him expand his ideas as to how a "non-breadwinner" could still "make a difference" and so go on being a good husband and father.

Norman's case presents a perfect opportunity to remind us of the message contained in **the serenity prayer**. This message has given support and guidance to many people facing physical pain and other adversities regardless of whether or not they believe in the power of prayer (see Information sheet: Serenity prayer).

Suffering is a normal and prevalent feature of life. Attempts to avoid or control it are sometimes quite useless and may escalate the problem because they distract attention away from what the person most values in life. We may not be able to control our physical pain but we can control our willingness to tolerate it. If the patient can tolerate and allow things that cannot be changed just to be there, it will free energy and attention to let the patient draw close to those things or people that are most valued and are found most rewarding and meaningful in life.

Lack of acceptance of the intrusiveness of pain or the limitations caused by fatigue may encourage the patient to adopt a "fighting approach" which heightens autonomic arousal and can lead to increased physical sensation awareness (including, unfortunately, signals of pain and fatigue). Techniques for increasing the patient's positive emotional reactions (pleasure in life, ability to enjoy things) may be useful.

The cognitive behavioural approach to pain and unpleasant physical sensations such as fatigue and nausea is in three stages:

1. *The patient is encouraged to turn attention toward the symptoms*, notice them and what makes them vary – for better or worse. The techniques include the practice of mindful meditation. Mindful meditation teaches people ways to constructively accept their limitations and tolerate the continuing presence of pain and discomfort rather than to waste their energy trying to ignore the symptoms (see Information sheets: Mindfulness attitudes; Mindfulness exercises; Mindfulness ideas).

2. *The patient is encouraged to review personal life values* and become really clear about the aspects of life which are most important and which the pain and other symptoms must not be allowed to distract the patient from pursuing. We ask the patient to notice how life is now compared to how he or she wanted and expected it to be. We ask the patient to look ahead and start to make difficult choices. Time, energy, activity compromises have to be considered as choices are made that take the patient back towards a sense of being in his or her own personality. These are tough choices to make. (see Techniques: Activity monitoring; Purposeful planning; Pacing; Information sheets: Pacing; Pacing examples; Change – bringing it about; Change – the desire for it; Coping with setbacks 1; Record forms: Pacing record form; Achievement and pleasure record form).

3. *The patient begins to actively plan* life and a personal schedule with a **commitment** to focus on and move towards highly valued aspects of what he or she wants to be like. At the same time, the patient does not ignore the challenging burden he or she carries, **accepting** that getting to be that desired personality and behaving accordingly will be accompanied by problems of pain, lethargy, nausea or other physical symptoms. Waiting for things to be better is not an option, life is going on now. A treatment plan that addresses these challenges may have a broad scope but will usually particularly require the techniques below (see Techniques section for underlined items):

i   Realistic pacing of tasks to minimise pain and fatigue.
ii   Sources of mental distraction and soothing sensory and mental stimulation used to provide support and respite at particularly difficult times.
iii   Activity schedules: trying new things and possibly things which gave pleasure in the past – in small doses (quitting whilst ahead and before fatigue and pain get too severe).
iv   Purposeful planning, and not waiting until "I feel like it" (because this will never happen): aiming for doing, not enjoying, at least in the first instance, to broaden the range of daily life experiences.
v   Challenging the unhelpful thoughts that perpetuate anxious preoccupation and self-critical non-acceptance of change. Specific physical sensations may act as the trigger event for strong emotional responses and unhelpful thoughts. For example a patient may interpret a new source of discomfort as highly significant (for example triggering fear that a cancer is spreading or a relapse of multiple sclerosis is underway); another may find that a patch of numbness is a reminder that the body is changed and then think of it as inferior, spoiled or defective. In these examples and situations like them, the therapeutic work concentrates on modifying these unhelpfully hasty interpretations.

To conclude we will consider the example of Nicola, an ex professional tennis player who has suffered from severe chronic pain and depression since a motor bike accident. She hates the way her body now looks out of condition in much the same way as she had always looked down on amateurs and considered their training efforts and fitness levels rather pitiful. She wants to be fitter and knows this would be good for her but somehow she cannot get started. Her goal, of going to the gym is clearly aligned with her sense of duty to keep herself fit, but to make progress with it she has to recognise and accept that the pain is going to be there: she cannot delay the start of her fitness programme until a medical solution can be found because the doctors have been saying there is nothing else to be done. Her shame about her appearance and how little she can do compared to former times similarly has to be carried with her: it is not going to magically disappear. Her disability makes her slow and she is under time pressure so she needs to make tough choices to set time aside for this activity. Nicola walked away from pain clinic help three times before she was ready to agree a treatment plan which would focus on making progress towards getting fitter whilst living with pain, but using a cognitive behavioural approach has helped her come to a point where she can see new and appropriate self-respecting goals that include managing ongoing pain and becoming fit.

Exercises

Before you proceed to the next chapter take time to do the exercises included at the end of this chapter. To use this book properly you need to complete all the recommended exercises.

Exercise 1

1. Review the step-by-step plans prepared for Norman and developed by you for Geoffrey in the light of the information included in this chapter on managing emotional and physical change.

   a) Do the plans in place to change behaviour and thought already address the issues sufficiently well?
   b) If not, what specific changes would be appropriate (refer to material in Part 3) and acceptable to them?

Exercise 2

1. Review your own plans with the contents of Chapter 16 in mind and similarly adapt the step-by-step record.

Exercise 3

1. Review each volunteer's progress

   a) Listen to self-report information
   b) Check record keeping information
   c) Use Socratic questioning to clarify and examine difficulties
   d) Determine whether to progress to further steps or re-work existing tasks.

2. Discuss information on challenging unhelpful thoughts

   a) Check thought record and review the mental traps and alternatives
   b) Discuss the merits of the alternatives in terms of being effective help
   c) Work together on improving some less helpful alternatives.

3. Review whether there is a need to modify plans to incorporate material on emotional change and physical reactions from Chapter 16.

4. Set new homework assignments

   a) Continue working on steps and overcoming obstacles with adjustments to the schedule in accordance with current progress and new material

b) Maintain current record keeping for monitoring progress

c) Continue to use the thought record form to challenge and alter unhelpful thoughts.

Recommended further reading:

Cole, F., Macdonald, H., Carus, C., and Howden-Leach, H. (2005) *Overcoming Chronic Pain*, London: Robinson. A recent volume in the "Overcoming" series all of which provide self-help guidance using a cognitive behavioural approach. See www.overcoming.co.uk for the full list of books.

Dahl, J. and Lundgren, T (2006) *Living Beyond Your Pain*, Oakland: New Harbinger Publications – uses an acceptance and commitment therapy variant of the cognitive behavioural approach in this self-help workbook.

Kabat-Zinn, J. (2006) *Mindfulness for Beginners*, Boulder: Sound True. A two CD audio guide to mindfulness by the master.

Chapter 17
Decision on a Course of Action: Part 2

In the first chapter about the decision-making process we considered the issues arising from the assessment and formulation processes including the level of information already available that might influence the amount of further detail that is required. The role of the health care professional was also identified as an important consideration in determining whether or not the identified work was appropriate to undertake or whether, with the agreement of the patient, referral to another specialist was desirable. The heavy demand for mental health services and the stigma sometimes attached to referral to these services were also mentioned as factors that may deter referral to those specialists together with their possible lack of knowledge of the special needs of patients with life-changing illness.

The fact that despite your own normal working practices you are reading this book and have decided to wrestle with the challenge of building skills in a cognitive behavioural approach is probably in part attributable to the difficulties you and your colleagues have had in attempting to access specialist mental health services for advice and support. Usually referral to the mental health team will require that the patient is assessed to be suffering from a fairly severe mental health problem such as a suicidal depression or psychotic episode. Services may be provided for more moderate mental illness such as acute anxiety and depression but often there is quite a long wait for the patient to be seen and where action is quite prompt it is likely to be for standardised treatment programmes and courses primarily focused on mental health care not life-changing illness.

None of this is intended to deter you from making an appropriate referral, but it is unlikely to be the simple solution or easy option that quickly addresses the identified problems; so in making your decisions as to how best to move forward you and the patient need to keep these considerations in mind.

Having decided to stay with your involvement with the cognitive behavioural approach beyond the formulation stage, the next decision point is with the goal setting.

Goal setting

An important feature of the structure of the cognitive behavioural approach is specification of objectives and being able to determine when they are achieved. For some patients, clarification of these objectives may prove quite a challenge either because they lack hope and purpose or because they find it harder to express the absence of problems in such constructive terms as "goals."

As with formulation, however, there may be no need to devote much time to the task of goal setting.

The goals may be implicit in the role of the health care professional. Many patients have a fairly clear idea as to why they are seeing a particular specialist and what they hope to achieve by seeing that person. Therefore in using cognitive behavioural methods the expectation would remain that their purpose was to facilitate achieving those same goals. Under these circumstances making explicit what the goals are, to ensure a mutual understanding, may be all that is needed.

Patients often determine quite definite goals before seeking help from health professionals and perhaps need no more than the SMART clarification to complete the goal setting exercise. Indeed, the more business-like of our patients may even have done that already and it just requires us to catch up!

Time is precious in these sessions and we do not want to spend a lot of it exploring an expansive range of possible alternative goals only to end up at the end of the exercise with a modest goal we could have identified and agreed on in the first few minutes. The need for a more lengthy exploration of possible goals developed through careful examination of the assessment and formulation will only be necessary for those whose lack of purpose and inability to think constructively around their problems are their primary psychological difficulties. Encourage the patient to consider alternative possibilities and dream of how things could be only with those whose goals seem problematic or who lack motivation or direction.

Clarification of goals will again give the health care professional cause to reflect on the appropriateness of undertaking this work. Firstly, it may seem that now the goal(s) have been identified, this work really goes well beyond the normal professional role or overlaps with the work of someone else within the team. Secondly, the goal may seem quite suitable but the timescale for its completion would exceed normal clinical practice arrangements. In either case an absence of alternative service provision may make it reasonable to consider taking exceptional action, but this probably means that further discussion with colleagues and service managers will need to occur before the health care professional can commit to her or his side of this contract with the patient.

Under circumstances such as these another possibility to consider is restructuring the goal in a way that defines the more limited involvement of the health care professional and identifies how the patient proceeds with the step-by-step action plan without that involvement. This might be through further self-help reading, attending classes, involving a friend or perhaps working on a well planned set of steps alone.

Interventions to bring about change

So often in health care we are programmed to act very quickly. Even if our course of action is to run a series of tests, there is still a sense of getting on with things and doing something about it. The patients quickly get the message that we are in charge and are taking over the problem: they can leave it to us to sort it out. One of the hardest adaptations for health care professionals shifting from their normal working practices to adopting a cognitive behavioural approach relates to this typical action bias. With this way of working the opposite is true. We cannot and do not take over responsibility for psychological problems: that remains with the patient. We do not run the tests: the patient collects data and we work out what is happening together. We do not take action on behalf of the patient:

we help the patient identify a course of action and help and advise the patient as she or he undertakes the action plan personally. It is not exactly a passive role that we take but it is not a controlling one either.

Therefore when the health care professional reaches the point of considering suitable cognitive behavioural interventions it will probably seem as if it has been a long journey to get to this point, but if assessment, formulation and goal setting have preceded this point in the decision-making process then we can be reasonably confident that we are undertaking the journey in the correct manner and are quite likely to be on the correct path. The only shortcuts lie with the ability of the patient to provide early information, insight and clear objectives that speed us through those preparatory stages.

Having reached this point the next challenge is to select useful interventions. Often the goal setting has already helped with this: logical steps between the start point and goal may point very clearly to specific actions or cognitive behavioural techniques that will facilitate progress. However, sometimes ideas about interventions are needed to develop the step-by-step process itself. Part 2 of this book should be able to assist at this juncture. Linked to each problem listed in this part of the book there are a set of suggested techniques to consider. It is not intended that this be an exhaustive list or that other methods should not be considered. However the suggestions may help you and the patient decide on things to include in the step-by step process action plan either as steps or as methods for dealing with obstacles. In the process of considering how a particular technique might be helpful, you may identify that another of the techniques included in the book would fit the bill better even though it was not listed for that particular problem. There is nothing wrong in selecting this alternative if both of you can see how it could be beneficial. Nor should you feel you must avoid techniques with which you are not familiar or pretend that you are more certain of them than you actually are. It is perfectly appropriate in the learning environment of a cognitive behavioural approach for you and the patient to study the technique information in the book together: it is after all the patient who is the "doer" in this approach.

A word of warning is required at this point. Not all the techniques of CBT have been included in this book nor all the detailed uses of the methods described here. As with the problems that have not been listed, exclusions are largely deliberate and have been made for good reasons. As responsible health care professionals we all hope to practise safely; this book provides training and insight into a cognitive behavioural approach but does not claim to train anyone to the level of being a fully-fledged cognitive behaviour therapist. Consequently, you are very strongly advised to be influenced and guided by the exclusions. In decision making phase 1 we advised that if the problem did not appear to be included in some guise in Part 2 of the book then assume that it is probably not a suitable problem for you to work on and seek advice. Similarly, if the technique you are considering is not in Part 3 Section 1 of this book then do not use it except under supervision from an experienced and qualified practitioner of that method.

With these considerations duly taken into account the decision making about which techniques to select comes back to the old chestnuts of role-appropriate involvement and collaborative endeavour. To summarise these points, the intervention should be appropriate to:

1. *Health care role with the patient*
The purpose of acquiring cognitive behavioural skills without pursuing CBT therapist training is to enhance skills within one's own area of expertise. In using these skills it is right for the health care professional to avoid working outside of those normal professional boundaries.

2. *Patient understanding of agreed goals for this working relationship*
The patient is quite likely to have expectations of the role of the health care professional, the methods of work used and the goals to be achieved. If cognitive behavioural methods are to be incorporated in this work then goals need to be clearly stated and understood, together with a rationale for why these methods may be relevant and helpful to work in this role.

3. *Patient's current health status*
Whilst it may be possible to identify a series of strategies which will address unhelpful thoughts and behaviours enabling the patient to move towards achieving agreed goals, these plans should always be sensitive to other limiting factors such as:

    a. likelihood of exacerbating pain or fatigue
    b. short life expectancy
    c. increased demands on key carers
    d. impact on financial resources.

4. *Time available with patient*
Having gained some understanding of the patient's needs and how to address them, it is important for the health care professional to limit any advice and strategy plans to what can be usefully and safely achieved within the limited time of contact that she or he has with the patient. Advice must not be rushed because the appointment time is too short, and actions should not be recommended that require follow-up if it is not possible to offer further appointments.

5. *Understanding of cognitive behavioural methods*
Health care professionals should not attempt to address psychological problems outside the themes covered in this book unless they have additional experience and expertise.

6. *Role relationships with other multi-disciplinary team members*
In applying a cognitive behavioural approach ensure that other health care professionals are not addressing similar problems using different methods or different problems with CBT methods. Careful consultation and co-ordination can avoid unnecessary overlap or conflicting advice, and also may help to enhance and reinforce effective change.

Using the Decision Tree

The guidance above aims to help determine when to act using a cognitive behavioural approach. The questions, methods of inquiry and answers mapped out in Figure 1.17.1 summarise the decision-making process. Where there remains doubt about the decision or where the recommendation is to seek further advice then review the patient's needs with an experienced colleague who also has cognitive behavioural knowledge or with a qualified cognitive-behaviour therapist.

Using Parts 2 and 3 of the book

With well-judged use of the resources in Part 2 of this book it should be possible to identify problems and tailor techniques (found in Part 3) to assist in overcoming them. Specific

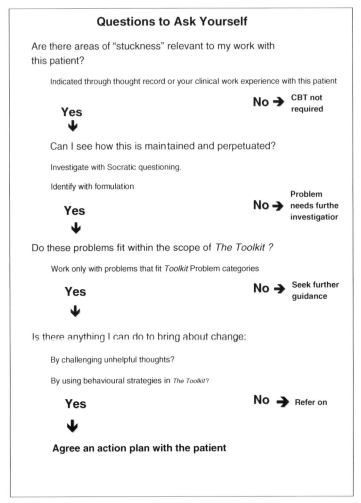

Questions to Ask Yourself

Are there areas of "stuckness" relevant to my work with this patient?

Indicated through thought record or your clinical work experience with this patient

Yes   **No →** CBT not required
↓

Can I see how this is maintained and perpetuated?

Investigate with Socratic questioning.

Identify with formulation

Yes   **No →** Problem needs furthe investigatior
↓

Do these problems fit within the scope of *The Toolkit* ?

Work only with problems that fit *Toolkit* Problem categories

Yes   **No →** Seek further guidance
↓

Is there anything I can do to bring about change:

By challenging unhelpful thoughts?

By using behavioural strategies in *The Toolkit*?

Yes   **No →** Refer on
↓

Agree an action plan with the patient

Figure 1.17.1 The decision tree questions.

comments in the Problems section draw attention to other factors which may contribute to the presence of the problem. These should be taken into account when making the assessment. Also in the Problems section there are further notes about the application of recommended techniques and tactics in relation to each specific problem. These should be read in conjunction with the more general instructions relating to the use of the techniques.

Resources in Section 3 can provide more information to facilitate patient and health care professional understanding, whilst Section 4 contains materials that may help in the assessment of problems and evaluation of progress. Materials from both these sections can be photocopied or downloaded from the website but may sometimes benefit from minor modifications to more precisely match the needs of the patient or the role of the health professional. In using record forms, it is common practice to start with general observation forms such as the CBT diary or Daily mood record and then switch to more specific ones to be used as part of therapy (such as Thought record form or Achievement and pleasure record) once goals and problems to tackle are more precisely identified.

Concluding remarks

Some of the material contained in Part 3 will be familiar to health care professionals who are faced with patients' psychological issues on a daily basis. The cognitive behavioural methods described in this book present a systematic approach to using and developing skills that many will recognise as having already emerged from common sense practice and clinical experience.

By bearing in mind the considerations mentioned in this chapter it should be possible to safely apply a cognitive behaviour approach to improve quality of life, adjustment to life-changing illnesses and psychological responsiveness to palliative care needs.

CBT may not be a panacea, but it offers a quick and effective way of approaching psychological challenges and as it continues to develop, offers promise of more help in the future.

There are no exercises related to this chapter. The "Final exercises" are included at the end of the next chapter.

Chapter 18

Applying a Cognitive Behavioural Approach to Clinical Practice

Before we consider how to progress the skill development, it might be helpful to have a better sense of the structure of a session using the cognitive behavioural approach and how a series of cognitive behavioural sessions might be sequenced. The hazard of including this information in the book is that it may seem a prescriptive template which ignores the individual circumstances of the patient and neglects the distinctive role of the health care professional who intends to incorporate *some* cognitive behavioural methods in sessions primarily structured around the usual work role. Treat it as a guide to typical cognitive behavioural practice that can be adapted to fit local circumstances; as much as possible the salient features will be incorporated into normal clinical practice.

Session Structure

A therapy session devoted to CBT will normally last between 45 minutes and an hour. These are typically on a one to two weekly frequency. There are a few specific types of specialist CBT work which lead to longer sessions or more frequent sessions, but for the non-specialist health care professional using a cognitive behavioural approach in normal work one might expect that no more than 20 to 30 minutes can be devoted to this work.

For a cognitive behaviour therapist the session sequence is likely to be:

1. *Progress report*
Check on how things have been in general for the patient since the last meeting. This does not include specific homework assignment tasks but the intention is to develop rapport and identify additional issues that may need to be considered. Normally this will be two or three minutes settling in time.

2. *Agenda review and session plan*
Following naturally from the update will be a check of the plan for this session, including any rethink necessary in the light of new developments or specific issues the patient wants to discuss. Again, this is likely to be a brief discussion.

3. *Homework feedback*
The assignment the patient was asked to undertake following the last session will often be the source of productive discussion and further use of cognitive behavioural methods, especially Socratic questioning. There will often be close links between the information emerging from this work and the topic planned for discussion in the session. The outcome of the assignment may also be a large determinant of the next homework assignment. If feedback about the assignment is not sought (and it can be tempting to skip it if time is tight) then valuable information may be lost and the patient's motivation to carry out further such assignments will be diminished.

4. *Session theme/topic*

Session topics vary according to the stage of cognitive behavioural intervention. Early topics are likely to be related to the approach itself such as development of the formulation and goal planning. Thereafter topics will be governed by patient needs and may include psycho-educational material such as understanding mental traps or learning to be more assertive.

5. *Homework setting*

Because a cognitive behavioural approach is intended to be a very practical form of psychological help based firmly in the realities of the patient's current situation, there is a need to carefully construct assignments that follow on from the session and enable the patient to quickly apply some of the new knowledge and insights or engage in "experiments" that will help develop learning and insight. So homework that is relevant to the work in the session should be a consideration for the health care professional throughout the duration of the session.

When the cognitive behavioural approach is embedded within other forms of health care intervention it may be appropriate to reduce the salient cognitive behavioural features to feedback, topic and assignment setting.

Sequence of cognitive behavioural approach sessions

For a patient with a mental health problem suitable for treatment by a skilled cognitive behaviour therapist a typical programme of CBT will be from 10 to 15 sessions. The series of activities included in this therapy programme will probably follow roughly the same sequence as the chapters of this book up to the point of implementing change. The speed at which progress is made through the process will vary according to assessment needs, complexity of problems and the requirements of the patient.

As with session structure, the sequence listed below is representative of typical practice but should not be treated as a template for all practice. Sometimes several items in the sequence will be completed within the same session, whilst on other occasions a single item may require more than one session to be examined thoroughly. Remember also that the sequence may be ordered differently; items may be omitted or re-visited as a result of new developments.

1. *Understand the patient's problem(s) as they see them and establish patient's goals in wanting help*

In using a cognitive behavioural approach, understanding the problem as the patient sees the problem (and in their own words) is the first step in the direction of providing effective help.

2. *Clarify patient's problems (assessment) in CBT terms (formulation)*

Developing a collaborative appreciation of the problem in cognitive behavioural terms that provide the patient with new insights and perspectives gives a message of hope that help is possible.

3. *Agree therapy goals, prioritise them and develop a treatment plan*

Goals give therapy a sense of purpose and direction. Also morale and motivation is often helped in any job that we undertake by knowing that there is a definite end-point for this work: both patient and therapist will benefit from knowing that the task is not open-ended. The treatment plan enables progress to be identified, makes disruption from the plan easier to recover from and improves our ability to understand when it needs to be changed.

4. *Implement plan*

Much of the implementation will be reflected in homework assignments and in-session topic discussions.

5. *Monitor effect of plan*

It helps to establish simple record keeping and assessment forms that are used as regular measures to judge progress and detect problems, as well as trawling for new information and insights.

6. *Modify plan, goals or formulation as indicated by progress evaluation*

The collaborative endeavour requires that difficulties with implementing the cognitive behavioural approach, even non-compliance problems, are treated as relevant information to be incorporated into our understanding of the problem and why it occurs. We need to ensure the patient tries to see difficulties in this constructive light, rather than as personal failure or wrong-doing. It is often in this management of setbacks that the collaborative nature of the relationship is truly tested because we have to be willing to share the responsibility for "failure."

7. *Prepare for continuing beyond therapy and preventing relapse*

Properly conducted, CBT is an opportunity for the patient to learn and become empowered to manage problems more effectively: sometimes by resolving them and sometimes by coping better. As therapy proceeds the role of the therapist as an agent of change diminishes and is taken over by the patient. Enabling the patient to fully appreciate this personal control and how to use it to best effect becomes the task for the therapist whilst moving from being coach to side-line observer.

8. *End therapy*

Constructive endings are an essential ingredient to successful therapy. Our memories of events are usually coloured by our recall of how things ended. This is just as true for therapy as for other events. Bringing therapy to an orderly and predictable end with a review of the successes and how setbacks were overcome enables the patient to be furnished with a memory that when accessed can point up a period of time when constructive action had made a real difference to life.

The health care professional for whom a cognitive behavioural approach represents a development whilst carrying out other work with the patient may find that the first three items of the list above are dealt with in a matter of a few minutes because the problems, their causes and goals for help have emerged from the current tasks being undertaken with the patient. Similarly, clearly specified goals may be achieved in a few steps and it may be that the second three items (implementing, monitoring and modifying plans) may constitute a few minutes work in two or three follow up sessions largely devoted to other issues. Ending the cognitive behavioural intervention may not coincide with the end of other aspects of the health care professional's role. If it extends beyond the normal role then that extension needs to be made clear as well as being sanctioned by professional managers. If the cognitive behavioural intervention is completed ahead of the conclusion of the regular work then the ending still needs to be handled as described above at the point when this cognitive behavioural work is finalised.

For some professional care staff working with people who have life-changing illness and palliative care needs, such as counsellors, social workers, occupational therapists and some specialist nurses, then it is quite likely that application of the cognitive behavioural approach will involve a substantial commitment of time and effort smaller but akin to the commitment of a cognitive behaviour therapist. For other professional carers, we have written this book in the expectation that you will "cherry pick" the material that offers the most help in performing your role in a way that enables it, in a few minutes here and there, to become part of your role. Nurses, doctors, physiotherapists, speech and language therapists, residential care workers, dieticians or one of the many other health care staff who seek to have a constructive relationship with patients who could benefit from their assistance, can invest small amounts of time in using cognitive behavioural methods to great benefit provided they have a reasonable understanding of the cognitive behavioural model and how to undertake a cognitive behavioural assessment and formulation.

What to do next

For those fortunate enough to be using this book as a basic text in an organised training programme or course, then the "Further learning plan" after the exercises for this last chapter of Part 1 may be replaced by a structured experiential learning process devised by your course and a quick overview of its contents may be a sufficient conclusion to this reading. If you are depending primarily on this book as a means for developing your skills in the application of a cognitive behavioural approach then you do need to plan some of the next steps in this learning process. The exercises at the end of this chapter provide the agenda for this development plan. As you move from practising on yourself to offering help to patients using this method, you will be well advised to be open and honest about inexperience and your own "voyage of discovery." For the patient who is uncomfortable with the idea that you are both learning together then the message will be clear that this is not someone for you to work with in this way, in which case you should seek alternative strategies or an experienced cognitive behavioural worker. For the many patients who will be comfortable helping you with your learning as you help them with their problems the bond of the collaborative endeavour will be especially powerful and rewarding to you both.

We wish you good luck with your professional development and much pleasure in this very satisfying work.

Exercises

Before concluding Part 1 follow the guidance on how to complete the exercises you have been doing throughout this book.

Final exercises

1. The agenda remains largely unchanged through the remaining sessions you have with each of your volunteers and for your own step-by-step plan:

   a) Review progress since last meeting
   b) Modify plans in the light of relevant new information
   c) Introduce new material and strategies when they become appropriate
   d) Set further between session assignments

2. Techniques applied are adapted to fit with the steps being taken and the obstacles to be overcome.
3. The goal remains firmly fixed and focused on.

4. A timetable of sessions is agreed for goal attainment and is also firmly fixed.
5. Changes to goal or timetable should be avoided unless there are exceptional reasons for doing so.
6. With your own plan you may find it helpful and motivating to now share your work with one of your volunteers.

Remember

■ Preparing for endings and endings need to be treated just as sensitively with friends and colleagues as they would be with patients.

Ten step further learning plan

1. Keep a log of the next 20 patients with whom you have to discuss emotional distress or psychological issues regardless as to whether or not you attempt to use a cognitive behavioural approach.

   a) The theme of the discussion
   b) Where it took place
   c) How long you allowed for it and how long it actually took
   d) Who else was present or in ear-shot
   e) At least one way in which you demonstrated each of the six **fundamental principles** of good communication
   f) At least one way in which you demonstrated each of the four **communication skill sets**
   g) Evaluate your use of the Socratic method in each of these interviews in terms of the two purposes (reframing and developing a way forward) and six features (naïve, curious minded, advice free, assuming nothing, non-judgemental and focused on constructive outcomes).

2. Study Part 2 of the book carefully so as to become familiar when a cognitive behavioural approach may be useful.
3. Begin to interview patients with a view to the possibility of using some cognitive behavioural interventions.
4. Start to routinely use measures to assess psychological discomfort and change (such as mood rating scales, HAD Scale, Distress Thermometer and so on).
5. Get used to asking patients to do small assignments between meetings.

   With these five steps achieved you are ready to move on to putting the cognitive behavioural approach to work, so the next five steps are associated with implementing the cognitive behavioural approach. Ideally do this in conjunction with another colleague at a similar stage of learning if this is possible.

6. Explain your "learner "status to at least the first ten patients you seek to help in this way and maintain that learner style whilst you work together collaboratively (being prepared to check the book and seek advice when feeling a bit stuck). Also allow extra time as a learner.
7. Review your notes after and before your meetings, re-read relevant book chapters, re-examine practice exercise materials you have used whilst reading this book and check through pertinent Part 2 problem information and Part 3 materials.

8. Write up your work using the Reflective practice diary forms included in the Record form section and downloadable from the website. For further information see Information sheet: Reflective practice diary guidance.
9. Select items from the further reading recommendations and broaden your perspective.
10. Find a skilled cognitive behavioural practitioner (preferably in your field of work) who will act as supervisor or guide to some of your work.

PART II

The Issues: Some Psychological Problems

How to use this part of the book

This list of twenty-four problems (twenty-five if you include safety behaviours as a problem) does not represent the full range of psychological problems encountered by people facing life-changing illness and their families. However, it does represent a range of problems for which the *Workbook* in Part 1 has provided you with training and the *Toolkit* in Part 3 offers practical advice.

Check the Glossary of everyday terms on the next page to check whether or not the identified problem for your patient is included in this list. Even if it is not there, you need to check whether the "Description" paragraph for these problems includes the problem you have in mind.

Each Problem section in Part 2 includes:

1. **Description** – which includes symptoms and features that relate to the problem for which help is being offered. The patient may benefit from advice offered on this page even if she or he does not have all these presenting characteristics.
2. **Possible contributing factors** – A list of potentially relevant context issues are mentioned here which may help to understand the problem and what maintains it. These may be important considerations whilst developing a formulation and in the planning of a treatment programme, including identification of obstacles to be overcome.
3. **Techniques and sample tactics** – Techniques from The Toolkit in Part 3 that are most likely to be of use with this problem are identified. Additional information is offered here as to how the specific technique may be tailored to the requirements of this particular problem. "Notes" included here also add extra advice about the application of the technique with reference to this problem. All additional information should only be used in conjunction with the detailed section for the use of this technique.

Glossary of everyday terms

Describing psychological difficulties included in Part 2

Problem term in Part 2		Alternative related descriptions/terms
Situations for patient to deal with	**Responses** shown by patient	
Adjustment difficulties		Struggling to come to terms; not got over it; labile mood
Altered body image		Conspicuousness; shame; self-conscious; embarrassed
	Anger	Irritability; frustration; argumentative; bad tempered; grumpy; resistant; obstructive; resentful;
	Avoidance	Social withdrawal; thought suppression; wary; phobic; reluctant
	Denial	Inappropriate affect; indifferent; not taking this seriously; reckless

Problem term in Part 2		Alternative related descriptions/terms
Fatigue		Exhaustion; tired all the time; flat; lethargic; hypersomnia
Fear of the future		Fretful; anxious; "what if..?"
	Inactivity	Bored; listless; drifting; under-stimulated
	Indecisiveness	Procrastination; hesitating; delaying; unable to choose
Intrusive/Distressing Thoughts		Preoccupied; agitated; obsessed; frightened; distracted; traumatic experience; overwhelming emotions
	Lack of motivation	No drive; lack of purpose
Loss of pleasure		Inability to enjoy things
	Low mood	Hopelessness; no drive; despair; despondency
Low self-esteem		Self-critical; self-blame; worthlessness
	Negative outlook	Gloomy; pessimistic; without hope; purposeless
Pain		Physical discomfort; symptom flare up
	Panic attacks	Anxiety attacks; feeling out of control; feel like fainting; can't breathe; gets hot and sweaty
Physical tension		Can't relax; fidgety; restless; jumpy; nervy; does things very fast; under pressure
Poor concentration		Can't remember things; clumsy; can't think straight; vague; does not complete things; careless; "I'm stupid"
Problem solving difficulties		Difficulties overwhelm; problem situations unresolved; floundering; repeating old errors; poor judgement; lacks confidence
	Safety behaviours	Protective strategies; anxiety avoidance; fear of fear
Setbacks		Disease recurrence; treatment failure; social or psychological let-downs
Sleep difficulties		Insomnia; restless; over-stimulated; over-active
	Unassertiveness	Timid; passive; manipulative; overdoes things; feels put-upon; can't say "no"
	Worrying	Anxious thoughts; edgy mood; reassurance seeking; procrastinating; indecisive; checking; feels responsible

Problem

Adjustment difficulties

Description

Emotionally labile; mood unpredictable; reactions inconsistent and not typical of normal self; preoccupation with own thoughts; limited concentration and receptiveness to others; little interest in external events; hypervigilant to key phrases and experiences; disturbed sleep; frequent and lengthy discussion of events related to the adjustment difficulties and their significance.

Possible contributing factors

Still very recent; change process is continuing and outcome remains uncertain; encouragement from others to expect other outcomes; non-acceptance of others; pressures from others to take certain actions; this event is latest of a series of adverse life events.

Techniques and sample tactics

1. Basic counselling skills

a) Allow plenty of time for the telling of the whole story and advise the patient how much time has been set aside for this.

b) Encourage a description of events to include emotional and interpersonal information together with personal interpretation of the meaning of this change.

Note:
The presence of other people will affect the information given and the way it is talked about, so some time alone with the person is necessary to get a full picture of the personal reaction. It may also be important to interview a close family member in order to establish whether the picture presented is as seen and experienced by others. Discrepancies need to be openly acknowledged if adjustment difficulties are to be tackled.

2. Psycho-education

a) Normalise the confusing emotional experience by explaining the adjustment process (Information sheet: Change: the Transition Curve).

b) Identify typical unhelpful thoughts associated with the change process and useful alternatives, relating these to the Transition Curve.

c) If this is the latest of a sequence of adverse events then explore links and helplessness feelings (Problems: Low mood; Lack of motivation; Techniques: Socratic questioning; Behavioural experiments).

Notes:

a) Ongoing change produces a rather different reaction than the single change event response but this is largely in the prolongation of the adjustment process and mood variability, rather than in the actual sequence of this process.

b) Repeated adverse events may be helpfully represented by a redrawing of the Transition Curve to illustrate a flattening at the bottom of the curve with only a small upturn towards Acceptance before the next Change Event. Again, the normality of this experience may be of some assistance to the patient and other carers.

3. Emotional expression

Identify a suitable method for channelling these emotions to assist adjustment and adaptation (such as Information sheet: Expressive writing).

Notes:
   a) Advise the patient to express emotions freely in this controlled way but avoid alarming or distressing close family, being mindful that they too may be having adjustment difficulties as a result of this event.
   b) It may be that different methods of expression will be required for each of the changing emotional states experienced.

4. Attention strategies

   a) Adjustment to change requires time to think about the realities of the new situation but this will be helped by being mixed with here-and-now focused tasks.
   b) The urge to do something may be used to block a realistic acceptance of change and this will delay the adjustment process (see 2. Note a) above) therefore problem-solving should be delayed until adjustment is underway unless fast action is required.
   c) Distraction and Mindfulness can help shift that orientation to action (see Techniques: Mental distraction; Mindfulness; Information sheets: The Serenity prayer; Mindfulness attitudes)

5. Challenging unhelpful thoughts

   a) Personalisation and blaming mental traps are likely to be associated with the **Anger** phase of the adjustment process. Thoughts about this being unfair, "why me?" and reasons to blame self or others may be strongly expressed. It may be a while before the person wants to engage in a Socratic questioning exercise to examine these statements and begin to generate some helpful alternatives around acceptance, randomness of these misfortunes and the value of constructive action.
   b) Fortune telling thoughts about the possible implications of this change will probably cause fear and will be associated with the **Anxious** phase of the adjustment. Reassuring information may be of use in challenging these thoughts but repeated reassurance will be part of a worry cycle (see Problem: Worry) and not helpful. Refocusing on here-and-now priorities and self reminders not to speculate are more effective most of the time.
   c) Catastrophising thoughts are associated with the **Despondency** phase of the adjustment and are frequently partially suppressed by the patient. De-catastrophising these thoughts may involve a more realistic appraisal of probabilities. These probabilities may relate to the occurrence of the worst possible outcome or of certain consequences following from that. Examining the evidence and how to deal with the worst case tends to modify the catastrophic thought, normalising it into a problem-solving or acceptance situation. This type of constructive appraisal of worst case scenarios seems to play an important role in arriving at acceptance in the change process.

Notes:
People who have had prior warning of the likelihood of the change event may not experience a pronounced Despondency phase. It seems that for some, advanced warning has an inoculation effect.

Problem

Altered body image

Description

Changes in body appearance that occur suddenly (perhaps as a result of surgery or injury) or quite quickly (perhaps as a result of disease progression or results of treatment); hair loss; weight loss; weight gain; body scarring; amputation; disfigurement; loss of mobility (requiring use of crutches or wheelchair); surgical changes (such as breast reconstruction or stomas).

Possible contributing factors

Pre-existing body image or self-esteem problems; degree of public exposure experienced in normal daily life (such as working at home vs. being a classroom teacher); appearance may be considered important for work (such as sales rep or air stewardess); difficulties in close relationships; sexual difficulties; adjustment to limitations caused by changes (especially mobility but also things such as speech loss with laryngectomy or management of a colostomy).

Techniques and sample tactics

1. **Graded activities**
   a) Identify a series of situations causing increasing degrees of anxiety or self-consciousness.
   b) Practice each step until it gets comfortable, going from least to most difficult.
   c) It may help to have moral support from the presence of someone close in the early stages, moving to being less dependent on them as confidence builds.
   d) "Ambassadors" can also be helpful – friends who speak on your behalf (see Information sheet: Sharing and mixing with other people)
   e) Debriefing after a social encounter may be necessary because it will be hard to make an objective evaluation of how it went.

Notes:
Simple criteria for success such as how long the patient stayed or how many people they spoke to may be necessary to help get some sense of achievement in these graded exposure social encounters. They are so hard to evaluate at a subjective level because of the amount of stress experienced and the potential for unhelpful thoughts about what others are thinking and distorted subsequent recall of events. Debriefing will involve active use of cognitive challenges.

2. **Emotional expression**
   a) "Off-load" – Have specific times to express low feelings and fears to a close and trustworthy person would need to be a listening ear only, not trying to explain or reassure.
   b) Expressive writing:
      i) Put thoughts and descriptions of images on paper as soon as practicable.
      ii) Write for as long as the ideas and imagery remain strong.
      iii) Keep the written material safe and confidential.
   c) Allow time to grieve for the losses – remembering, looking at old photos and letting the sadness about these changes be felt and let out.

Notes:
Putting on a brave face can be very helpful but there is a need to ensure that in preventing the perfectly natural negative emotions from becoming overwhelming, they are not being completely stifled.

3. Behavioural rehearsal
a) Recall of any past situations with relevant lessons as to what might help.
b) Practice coping skills that may be useful (e.g. slow breathing, relaxed postures).
c) Rehearse with a friend dealing with challenging situations (see Information sheets: Sharing and mixing with other people and The reactions of other people).
d) Rehearse body image accounts – plan a series of stock replies to the questions from others and for when you need assistance, so that it feels effortless quick, non-intrusive and emotionless.
e) Focus on broad coping strategy only – details of what to do if… can lead to other problems (See Problem: Fear of the future).
f) Have a complete break from thinking about it for a little while before dealing with it.

Notes:
Behavioural rehearsals can be very good for confidence building provided there is not an expectation of achieving perfection of performance. Improvisation as and when needed remains the coping strategies approach.

4. Assertiveness skills
a) Understand the general concept and principles of the Assertiveness model (see Information sheet: Assertiveness model).
b) Asserting that "I have a right to: be the way I am; look the way I do; preserve my privacy and dignity; not to be judged by others." These are among the assertive attitudes that can help preserve self-respect (see Information sheet: Assertiveness rights).
c) Being sensitive to the same rights for others in exercising assertiveness increases the likelihood of constructive communication and a positive outcome.
d) Positive presentation can be a useful assertive strategy: the flamboyant hat or scarf may draw attention in an acceptable way for someone who has lost hair; a jokey or outgoing style asking about how other people are coping may help reassert a sense of equality.

Notes:
Being pleasant but firm with people will often be necessary when there are visual indications of being unwell or disabled. Accepting that this will always be the case and responding accordingly reduces the likelihood of building frustration or repeatedly demeaning oneself.

5. Challenging unhelpful thoughts
a) "Everyone is looking at me and thinking that I look like a freak" is the sort of over-generalised thinking that can be triggered simply by catching someone's gaze.
b) Because of the personal sensitivity even *not* being looked at can trigger negative personalisation thoughts such as "I look so awful everybody is trying to avoid having to see me."
c) Compliments and encouragement are discounted as "people are just trying to be nice, but they don't really mean it."
d) Harshly self-critical labels such as "I look ugly," "I'm just a fat blob" or "I'm not a man any more" will all undermine confidence and can be challenged as over-simplifications and harsh double standards that most would not judge others by.
e) "I cannot mix with other people because it would be awful if I was to have an accident with my colostomy bag" assumes catastrophic consequences which when fully explored are unlikely to be worse than rather unpleasant and a bit embarrassing.

f) "I can't face meeting other people" is just as restrictive and is a rather black and white style of unhelpful thought. Probably certain people have already been met or would at least be easier than others. Challenging this thought will be helped by behavioural experiments involving the graded exposure methods mentioned above.

Notes:

When self-deprecating thoughts are openly expressed, other people will often try to offer reassurance or positive alternatives. The unfortunate effect is to enable the person to respond with even more negative remarks, thus getting to practice them more. Examining the evidence, carrying out small behavioural experiments and surveys, and exploring the "so what?" alternatives may be methods that will be more useful.

Problem

Anger

Description

Becomes impatient and intolerant; shifts from disappointment to criticism and blaming when setbacks occur; sensitive and resistant to any attempts by others to take control or influence decision making. Displays this disapproval or resistance by using verbal and physical aggression. Rejection of others and social withdrawal (including sulking).

Possible contributing factors

Overloaded with commitments and task; attempting to reassert control when feeling panicky or frightened; struggling to adjust to change; overwhelmed by fatigue or low mood; adverse response to alcohol consumption (sometimes quite small quantities); defensive response in situation perceived as threatening or attacking; attacking response to someone perceived to be behaving in an unfair manner; cognitive impairment to ability to comprehend or reason; psychotic interference with ability to comprehend or reason.

Techniques and sample tactics

1. **Assertiveness skills**
   a) Study the assertiveness rights with the rights of others to think and behave differently in mind (see Information sheet: Assertiveness rights).
   b) Re-examine conflict situations and identify desirable constructive outcomes and how assertiveness skills could have helped achieve them (see Information sheet: Assertiveness model).
   c) Record all incidents of anger and irritability and attempt to apply assertive strategies to achieve constructive outcomes (Record form: Assertiveness).
   d) Encourage the patient to constructively and respectfully address issues which may be a source of later annoyance as soon as is reasonable, ensuring that information is communicated well (see Techniques: Effective communication skills and Respectfulness skills)

Notes:
Angry people do not always want a constructive outcome in which case the assertiveness model is useful for demonstrating that anger and aggression begets more anger and aggression. Emotional expression strategies may be helpful in order to avoid this perpetuation of anger.

2. **Attention strategies**
   a) Focus on the task in hand reduces risk of being overwhelmed.
   b) Focus on practicalities of resolving problem situation rather than why it occurred.
   c) Encourage awareness of the impact of anger displays on the other people.

Notes:
Most people do not want to be considered frightening or intimidating, so encouraging awareness of this effect by surveying reactions from others can be very helpful; but it needs to be done as a well structured behavioural experiment (Technique: Behavioural experiments)

3. Emotional expression

a) Angry people need to give vent to their feelings in some way and wherever possible we need to be able to give them the opportunity to do so safely. Shouting and swearing may be socially offensive and sometimes intimidating but if we can tolerate it calmly when we are not being personally threatened then it is likely to burn out and leave the person more able to co-operate constructively with us.

b) Do not challenge angry behaviour whilst the person is still angry or defend the position of those to whom the anger is directed because this will increase the likelihood of drawing the anger towards yourself and enflaming it.

c) Physical exercise can be a good way to burn off the extra adrenalin charge induced by anger. A vigorous walk or a workout in the gym can do this.

d) Putting all the emotions on paper in the form of a never-to-be-sent letter allows the person to be unreasonable and unpleasant safely, usually by writing until exhausted and drained.

Notes:

a) Unacceptable behaviour is a legitimate area for discussion with the patient and can be examined in detail including heightening awareness of its effect on you, but this should be kept for a time of calmness when the issues can be explored safely and constructively.

b) Writing on the computer can easily be turned into an email and sent just as a letter can be put in an envelope and sent. As well as getting the patient to agree not to send it, also encourage him or her to handwrite this material on scraps of paper with no heed to spelling or handwriting. This will help the flow of emotional expression and further reduce the temptation to send it in its current form.

4. Problem solving

a) If an effective shift of focus to problem solving can be achieved then the use of this technique becomes effective.

b) The problem-solving task will need to be carefully defined and be achievable independent of the co-operation of others who may have been or could become the target for anger.

c) Task orientated activity will provide a channel for constructive use of energy generated by anger. It also provides time-out from the annoyance and a chance to calm down. Therefore the problem solving task does not have to go to the very heart of the difficulty that provoked the anger in order to be effective.

Notes:

Do not obstruct a return to the anger or blaming style of thinking. However, do not continue the problem solving task either. Encourage the patient to consider these as alternative responses and to choose between them, not try to do both simultaneously.

5. Stimulus control

a) For current anger, get the angry person away from any source of provocation if at all possible.

b) Typically, people remain in close proximity to the source of annoyance for too long, reducing their ability to calm down and think rationally. Recording incidents as they occur will highlight this and other relevant triggers and maintainers of the anger (Record forms: CBT diary; Event-action-outcome).

c) Physical exercise and problem solving tasks may help reduce contact with provocative stimuli.

6. Relaxation exercise

a) If the person is angry and irritable because of tension then there may be benefit from using soothing exercises before anger is induced. The exercises are unlikely to prove effective once anger has erupted.

b) Similarly, relaxation may enable the person to rest between tasks or soothe intrusive pain, in which case the risk of feeling overwhelmed may be reduced.

7. **Challenging unhelpful thoughts**

a) Mind-reading unhelpful thoughts that might provoke anger include being "looked down on," "pitied," "pushed around," deliberately ignored and "not cared about." Confrontations usually result in social rejection that is used as evidence to reinforce these beliefs. Gathering data that challenges these beliefs requires follow-up from the patient without having caused upset to others. Working out how to achieve this may require very careful consideration.

b) "Should" thoughts are often a source of anger and annoyance either when the person feels under obligation to do something ("It's not fair, I've got to go and weed my mother's garden for her") or when the person believes others are failing to fulfil their obligations and responsibilities ("Nobody else living in this road bothers to clear up the litter. They are so selfish").

c) The "should" way of thinking also leads people into setting themselves up to be angry. This happens when the person expects something to be a certain way because it "should" be that way, even though experience contradicts this expectation: "I don't know what's happening to this country these days. It should only take me half an hour to get here at this time of day."

d) As with rules, so with boundaries: many people get angry because of thinking in very black-and-white terms. It is either right or it is wrong, good or bad. Consequently, when there are setbacks and disappointments they are viewed as complete let-downs and failures.

Problem

Avoidance

Description

Fearful of specific situations perceived to be threatening in some way and therefore not to be encountered; frightened of own emotional and behavioural reactions so needing to keep away from situations which might trigger these reactions; evading tasks for fear of failure or public ridicule; blocking conversations or avoiding contacts which might induce distressing thoughts and images.

Possible contributing factors

Traumatic past experiences; reluctance to expose actual lack of knowledge or skills; critical family or friends who will not cope supportively with emotionality; fear that not thinking positively will induce physical health deterioration or depression.

Techniques and sample tactics

1. Graded activities
   a) Identify a series of situations causing increasing degrees of fear.
   b) Practice each step until it gets comfortable, going from least to most fearful.
   c) This can be done with distressing thoughts as well as places and tasks.

Notes:
Before working out a list of steps, it is important to have identified a specific goal which is of value and desired by the person.

2. Relaxation exercises
   a) Muscle relaxation tapes or CDs (and see Information sheet: Muscle relaxation exercise).
   b) Use techniques learnt whilst in situations on graded activities programme.

Notes:
Relaxation techniques can become "safety behaviours" (see Special note in Problem: Panic attacks) and should be phased out as a routine preparatory activity as familiarity and confidence develop. Encourage growing tolerance of anxiety symptoms.

3. Challenging unhelpful thoughts
   a) The evidence supporting catastrophic thoughts of danger, humiliation or overwhelming emotional states needs to be examined and realistic alternatives based on past experience and some behavioural experiments can be generated.
   b) All-or-none thinking often encourages people into believing that they must "just get on and do it" and then fail to even start. Allowing the possibility of building confidence in small steps, doing it less than perfectly, be like a learner who gets better with practice: these are the types of alternative thinking that can help.

Notes:
Linking graded exposure tasks to thought records is often a good way to identify the unhelpful thoughts, carry out small behavioural experiments and collect the evidence.

Special note

"Thought suppression" is a problem often associated with cognitive avoidance. The person tries to control their thinking, but in trying not to think specific thoughts and images they make the problem worse: they get more frequent and unexpected intrusions of these thoughts, becoming more distressed by them in the process of trying harder to stop them. See Problem: Intrusive/distressing thoughts for more information on dealing with these.

Problem

Denial

Type of denial	Definition	Suggested courses of action Read in conjunction with Notes: ABCD Steps
Positive (Constructive) Avoidance	Fully aware of diagnosis but does not enquire or discuss further. Getting on with life, refusing to dwell on things over which he/she can do nothing useful whilst co-operating in treatment, making realistic plans etc. May also be a partial or selective state varying over time or with people.	• Discuss issues raised in assessment in pragmatic way – not referring to illness • Problem solving approach (see for example Techniques: Goal Setting; Graded Activities; Pacing; etc)
Fearful avoidance	Becomes quickly agitated and distressed if health issues are raised. Hides from situations where issues might be raised – visits, tv programmes etc. Sometimes linked to a "**Compulsive Positiveness**" in which negative thoughts are viewed as a health hazard. Treatment compliance may be haphazard.	• Muscle and Mental Relaxation skills • Mental Distraction activities • **Step B** needs slow, careful handling to avoid disengagement • Challenging unhelpful thoughts See Techniques and Tactics under Panic Attacks, Avoidance, Fear of the Future
Refusal to accept (believe)	Minimises symptoms, challenges diagnosis and expertise, generates alternative explanations, seeks further opinions and goes along with treatment reluctantly.	• Discuss issues raised in assessment in pragmatic way – side-step disagreements, emphasise areas of concurrence • **Step C** will be area for care re threats to engagement • Strategies for encouraging acceptance

Total denial	A "dissociative" state. Blanks out all memory of the diagnosis and creates own, maybe bizarre, explanations for what is happening. Sees no need for treatment.	• Make this a team approach • Strategies for engagement will dominate throughout • Acknowledgement of assessed disadvantages will take time • Work carefully through the ABCD steps, giving plenty of time to each • Look for clues to gaining passive acquiescence and so help you avoid challenging denial directly
Public denial	Privately acknowledges diagnosis but sees it as shaming and does not admit to it. Alternatively, fears the intrusion of others into personal affairs and so admits to it to a very select few.	• Strategies for engagement • Problem solving approach to overcoming assessed disadvantages (as in Positive Avoidance above)
Ignorance or confusion	Overwhelmed by the information and failed to understand what was really said (because of technical terms, euphemisms etc) and so has not grasped the seriousness of the situation. Alternatively, disease site, medication or another disorder prevents effective assimilation of the information.	• Assessment of pre-morbid comprehension • Enlist family support • Lots of checking back on understanding whilst going through ABCD steps

Special notes

1. Although a difficult and time demanding problem to deal with, the very nature of denial issues leads to the exclusion of specialist help such as offered by counsellors, clinical psychologists or psychiatrists. It usually falls to those providing normal care to have to assess and address these issues – hence the level of detail provided in this *Toolkit*.
2. Challenge denial only if it appears really necessary (see Information sheet: Advantages and disadvantages of denial)
3. Engagement is more important than achieving change (see Technique: Strategies for engaging the patient)
4. Follow the steps below in proceeding work with denial or cognitive avoidance:

ABCD steps in handling denial or avoidance

A. Assessing and deciding to act:

1. Assess costs and benefits as you engage with the patient (see Record form: Denial – assessing its costs and benefits)
2. Identify if any steps need to be tackled with extra time and attention (see Record form: Action plan for denial)

B. Helping with acknowledged distress

1. Gentle questioning searching for non-coping difficulties (see Technique: Denial – suggestions for questions to ask).
2. Introducing simple (safe) facts.
3. Careful observation of reactions and understanding.
4. Explanation for why it may help to know more (see Information sheet: Advantages and disadvantages of denial).

C. Increasing awareness and learning to cope with that

1. Gentle questioning of what is known and accepted.
2. Suggestions for coping with that knowledge.
3. Checking back on coping.
4. Summarising what is known so far.
5. Encouraging extra recall of details and offer more information.

D. Increasing acceptance and becoming more open

1. Gentle questioning on attitude to treatment and compliance – no challenges.
2. Encourage acceptance where value of treatment is not accepted (see Technique: Denial – strategies for encouraging acceptance).
3. Gentle questioning on communication and relationships with family and friends.
4. Identify discrepancies in patient–family reports.
5. Encourage acceptance where relationship problems identified as due to denial.

General considerations

- Trust must come first.
- Only challenge denial if you really need to and only in the ABCD step as above.
- Allow retreats into denial – progress may be uneven.
- Expect anger, frustration, guilt and depression.
- Work through these steps over several visits even if there is some urgency.
- Watch for tiredness or growing anxiety in the patient and for impatience and frustration in yourself – being trusted is more important than getting it done.
- It may be useful to have a close family member present but they must agree to remain silent and only offer comfort.
- Don't be afraid to ask for extra help and psychological expertise.

Problem

Fatigue

Description

Tiredness that saps the will to do things; problematic when persists beyond periods of rest; especially frustrating when experienced as energy suddenly draining away; increased irritability and distress as exhaustion sets in.

Possible contributing factors

Excessive workload; poor sleep pattern; symptom of physical ill health; reaction to radio-therapy or chemotherapy; side-effect of medication; symptom of clinical depression.

Techniques and sample tactics

1. Pacing

a) Slow down in movements: walk and do things more slowly.
b) One thing at a time, and time for one thing.
c) Pause between tasks to relax and rest.
d) Set a baseline just achievable on bad days.
e) Stick to this baseline until easily achieved on bad days
f) Activity level can be gradually increased as stamina increases.
g) Manage energy slumps by reducing activity levels on worse days to regain control (see Technique: Pacing and Record form: Pacing).

Notes:
"Bad days" can be confused with "I don't feel like it" days and the distinction between **physical sensation** feelings and **emotion** feelings becomes important here. Challenging the emotional reasoning will be more appropriate if it is an emotion bad day. On the basis of their past experiences, people can often make a distinction between "good tired" (when they feel satisfied with what they have achieved) and "bad tired" (when they feel wrecked by the effort regardless of achievement). Successful pacing aims to achieve "good tiredness" every time.

2. Purposeful planning

a) Plan and prioritise daily activity to take into account the limiting effect of fatigue (see Record form: Activity schedule).
b) Identify clear and realistic goals to work on (see Information sheet: Goal setting and the Step-by-step approach).
c) Encourage modifying high standards to reduce unnecessary demands.
d) Plan ahead and spread tasks to avoid overdoing things where possible.
e) Achieve a balance between achievement and enjoyment (see Record forms: Achievement, Pleasure and Your Ideas for Goals).

Notes:
Pacing can only work effectively if there is sensible planning and adaptation of personal expectations (and those of other people). "Catching up" on a good day after a series of bad ones may be very tempting but will

lead to further exhaustion and educating the patient about this may be an essential first step in making effective changes.

3. Challenging unhelpful thoughts

a) "I'm too tired to even try" may be an obstacle to getting started and is the sort of emotional reasoning that is best challenged by an experimental attitude that is around the idea that "you don't know what you can do until you try; after all, if it is too much for me I can always stop again."

b) At the other extreme, fatigue will be made worse when the person ignores the signals from the body and keeps going because "I must not be weak and give in to this." This falls into the twin mental traps of labelling oneself ("weak") and fixed rules ("should"). "I'll do what I can whilst being sensible and taking care of myself" represents the more helpful alternative.

c) "I have so little energy that I never do anything anymore" is probably an overgeneralisation which can be challenged by examining the evidence of daily life (including using Daily activity schedules), but it may be true in which case identifying purposeful activities that match current levels of stamina may be quite an appropriate way of introducing change.

d) Mental filtering is another mental trap that can occur in these circumstances, when the person is quite unable to recall the fact that they do not feel this way all of the time. Careful examination of recent past events will help in developing an alternative way of thinking about those past events.

Notes:
See under Pacing above.

Problem

Fear of the future

Description

Anxious anticipation of a range of possible problem situations; speculative thinking about outcomes and results; reluctant to make decisions at the present; finds it difficult to concentrate on current activities; finds it hard to settle to one thing; finds it hard to go off to sleep or go back to sleep when awakened; becomes irritated and quickly overwhelmed when new ideas and possibilities are introduced.

Possible contributing factors

High level of uncertainty or instability in present circumstances; bad experiences in the past caused by lack of vigilance or planning; bad past experiences expected to recur; speculative discussion engaged in my others; planning and future commitment pressed for by others.

Techniques and sample tactics

1. Purposeful planning

Convert apprehensions into constructive actions – realistic holiday planning, "affairs in order," personal history writing, photo labelling etc (see Information sheet: Goal setting and the Step-by-step approach and Record form: Goal planning: Step-by-step record form).

Notes:
"If there is nothing to be done about it now, then there is no point in dwelling on it at this time." This is the general *rule of thumb* that is being encouraged with this action planning approach and not the idea that "I've always got to be constructively employed." It can easily slip into a pressure to be doing something unless this is watched out for.

2. Distraction

a) Verbal distractions: conversation or talking radio.
b) Discourage unnecessary planning/speculation by others

Notes:
a. Whilst pleasant distractions will often work for a while, too much emphasis on "I've got to distract myself or else…" will lead into attempts at thought suppression (See Problem: Intrusive/distressing thoughts).
b. Stopping others from stirring up speculative anxious thoughts may require some examination of personal assertiveness skills, especially if the other person is off-loading their own worries by doing this.

3. Mental relaxation

a) Relaxation tapes and CDs with visual imagery exercises.
b) Mindfulness meditation exercises such as focusing on the rhythm of breathing – counting the in-breaths up to 100.

Notes:
Mindfulness exercises will not be effective as simple mental distractions and so will only work once the principle of staying in the here-and-now is accepted as appropriate. See Techniques: Mindfulness for more information.

4. Attention strategies

   a) Resist future-gazing.
   b) Create demanding tasks on which to concentrate.

Notes:

Because speculating about the future and trying to solve problems that might occur are demanding mental activities, it is often possible for people to just stop themselves from doing it so much just by telling themselves not to do it and not making time for it. Firstly, however, there is the need to be persuasive that this is not reckless and irresponsible. Some behavioural experiments in "non-planning" and review of past evidence of coping when unprepared should be of help with this.

5. Challenge unhelpful thoughts

"Crossing bridges before we've come to them" and speculating about what might happen next are aspects of the fortune telling mental trap and lead into anxious thinking about the future. The intention is to be prepared for the unknown but by generating a set of possible problems the effect is quite the opposite: creating, instead, a sense of being beset by daunting tasks and insurmountable difficulties.

Notes:

Examine the evidence for having correctly anticipated problems in the past; also the value-gain of having thought about them before hand for improving coping. Thought records linked to the behavioural experiments mentioned in 5 above will also probably be quite fruitful.

Problem

Inactivity

Description

Complains of loss of drive; lacks energy and can't be bothered; may be reluctant to get up; sits and watches TV all day; intends to do things but never gets round to them; catnaps a lot; feels a lack of purpose; seems aimless.

Possible contributing factors

Loss of role; low mood; poor sleep pattern; illness or treatment induced fatigue; lack of plans; unused to having so few demands to react to; always been inactive and dependent; nothing interesting or rewarding to do; fear of doing harm; blocked by carers from doing things.

Techniques and sample tactics

1. Psycho-education
The adverse link between health, low mood and low activity levels needs to be explained.

Notes:
  a) It is important that in encouraging increased activity that you are satisfied that it really is in the patient's best interests and that what is communicated conveys this rather than a moral judgement about indolence.
  b) Resistance to changing this pattern of inactivity may indicate a need for anti-depressant medication or referral to specialist mental health professionals.

2. Graded activities

  a. Monitor daily activity (see Record form: Activity schedule) to establish baselines for good and bad days.
  b. Identify past normal activities not included.
  c. Establish new schedule of activities (see below).
  d. Introduce identifiable daily achievements and pleasures into the activities (see Record form: Achievement and pleasure record form).
  e. Plan a series of events which steadily increase physical demand and personal involvement into the daily schedule.

Notes:
The record keeping needs to be done to gain accurate information rather than vague impressions (often excessively negative) and to help the patient develop a constructive approach.

3. Purposeful planning

  a) Reduce things to be decided by working to a timetable: create a simple plan for the chores that needs little further thought and only gets changed when absolutely necessary.
  b) Restructure it as necessary to ensure consistency of effort day-to-day (see Techniques: Pacing).

Notes:
Flexibility with the timetable will need to be minimal at the beginning although some spare time for other things can be built in to it. Once established more flexibility for competing demands will be desirable, but not for "not feeling like it today" reactions.

4. Activity monitoring

a) Commit self openly to specific undertakings.
b) Report back to someone (who will give positive feedback) on time use and achievements.
c) Commit to small tasks for other people.

Notes:
Whilst this work can be undertaken by the therapist there is more scope for frequent and prompt encouraging feedback if a family member or friend is involved. The other person needs to properly understand their role, however, and not be tempted to exceed it by setting tasks or pushing the patient to do more.

5. Challenging unhelpful thoughts

a) Fortune telling: "There's no point in trying, I won't cope." A range of similar negative expectations may be used to justify maintaining inertia and can often be challenged by Socratic questioning around the examination of how the patient thinks about him or herself having done nothing, compared with self-regard having made an effort.
b) Emotional reasoning: "I'm feeling tired, so I can't do anything but rest." The psycho-educational work may help in challenging this line of thinking.
c) "Should" thoughts about being a good patient and doing as one is told by over-anxious carers may stop the patient from achieving things.

Notes:
Sensitivity to the pacing needs and genuine low points in energy, make these mental traps difficult to evaluate at times. Flexibility of attitude is to be encouraged rather than a rigid approach. The emphasis is on enhancing personal satisfaction and a sense of purpose.

Problem

Indecisiveness

Description

Finds it hard to prioritise; becomes frustrated and agitated with making small decisions; seeks lots of reassurance and guidance from others; gets muddled and flustered; is rather disorganised and worries about this; complains of lying awake trying to work out what to do.

Possible contributing factors

Loss of traditional routines; disruptive events and people; high levels of uncertainty regarding health or other important issues (especially in the immediate future); fear of failure; obsessional tendencies; lack of confidence; very critical people around; long-standing chaotic lifestyle.

Techniques and sample tactics

1. Purposeful planning

Reduce things to be decided by working to timetable – create a simple plan for the chores that needs little further thought and only gets changed when absolutely necessary.

Notes:
Routines are good for reducing the need to think about things too much but flexibility is also important. Rules are made to be broken: they are a guide to provide structure not a straightjacket.

2. Weighing pros and cons

For difficult or delayed decisions use the systematic method described in Technique: Weighing pros and cons.

Notes:
a) If there are realistic choices to be considered then the pros and cons method will be useful but be wary of it being used on small issues as a delaying tactic.
b) The opinions and ideas of others may go into the weighing but it is important that the "weight" is entirely the value relevant to the person who has the decision to make.

3. Challenging unhelpful thoughts

De-catastrophising by asking "What is the worst that can happen if you make the wrong decision."

Notes:
An exaggerated fear of disaster can paralyse people into states of indecision. Examining the realities of the consequences when things go wrong including the positive learning experience can be very helpful in regaining perspective. Don't use this method if the person is likely to come up with a catastrophe that is overwhelming and unchallengeable.

4. Assertiveness skills

a) Understand the general concept and principles of the Assertiveness model (see Information sheet: Assertiveness model).

b) Asserting that "I have a right to:do it my way; have my own opinion; make my own mistakes; be guided by my feelings." These are among the assertive attitudes that enable people to make judgements and take decisions that are their own.

c) Being sensitive to the same rights for others in exercising assertiveness increases the likelihood of constructive communication and a positive outcome.

Notes:

a) You may need to explore the assertiveness ideas in some detail (see Assertiveness rights handout), but it may be that a few simple statements of an alternative point of view may be enough to set the person thinking.

b) Be aware of the possibility of an abusive partner or carer who could react with violence or some other form of punishment if assertiveness methods are used.

Problem

Intrusive/distressing thoughts

Description

Thoughts go round and round in the head which are full of worry; problems that might occur are preoccupying thinking so that it's hard to concentrate on other things; images occur that produce intense emotional reactions as if currently living through the event; memories of past events are gone over looking for the ways in which present circumstances could have been avoided or prevented; thoughts and images anticipating future events and "what it will be like when…" take over when there is nothing specific to concentrate on.

Possible contributing factors

Traumatic experiences may be relived through flashbacks when triggered by associations; trying to plan and be prepared may induce speculation about the future; other people may encourage a lot of "preparatory" thinking in order to be properly responsible; trying not to think about these things may induce a degree of intensification of these thoughts; clinical depression can cause an increase in morbid preoccupation with thoughts of death and dying; obsessive-compulsive disorder can increase the tendency to think of the most frightening, disgusting or upsetting ideas and images that the person can imagine.

Techniques and sample tactics

1. Mental distraction

   a) Verbal distractions: conversation or talking radio.
   b) Discourage unnecessary planning/speculation by others.

Notes:
Distraction can be helpful to give periods of pleasant relief but as stated in the Notes in Problem: Fear of the future, thought suppression or exhaustion through over-activity can result from excessive use of this technique in the absence of other methods for persistent thoughts.

2. Relaxation exercises

   a) Mental relaxation tapes and CDs with visual imagery exercises (see also Information sheet: Mental relaxation exercise).
   b) Mindfulness meditation exercises such as focusing on the rhythm of breathing – counting the in-breaths up to 100 (see Technique: Mindfulness and Information Sheet: Mindfulness exercises).

Notes:
As well as offering another distraction with relaxation images, it is also possible to develop a greater acceptance of unanswerable questions or worries that cannot be "dealt with" through the use of mindfulness meditation. Allowing thoughts and images to just be there without trying to interpret them or solve the issues linked to them may seem a difficult undertaking but it can be very effective at preventing thought suppression and stopping the distress related to the thoughts.

3. Emotional expression

a) Expressive writing:

    i) Put thoughts and descriptions of images on paper as soon as practicable.

    ii) Write for as long as the ideas and imagery remain strong.

    iii) Keep the written material safe and confidential.

b) Alternatively speak to trustworthy friend as soon as possible, providing a similar outpouring of thoughts and feelings; but this person would need to be a listening ear only, not trying to explain, reassure or curb the flow of thoughts.

Notes:
Expressive writing needs to be an exercise in which confidentiality is fully assured. To be completely effective the person needs to feel that their words will not be judged or interpreted by anyone else: that they are writing exclusively for themselves. It is not necessary to write in sentences or to avoid repetitions. Sometimes the expressiveness will also involve drawing. The person can share these notes if that feels important to them but they should not be encouraged to do so unless there is good reason to do so.

4. Attention strategies

    a) Resist future gazing.

    b) Create demanding tasks on which to concentrate in the present.

    c) Resist blaming by attempting to re-write history (if only this or that hadn't happened then it would have been different, if only I had known then what I know now).

Notes:
Not giving time to the efforts of predicting the future or explaining the past will help to minimise these activities once the person is persuaded of their lack of value and can resist similar from other people.

5. Challenging unhelpful thoughts

    a) Any thoughts that attempt to control or change the past are going to be unhelpful since this cannot be achieved. Helpful thoughts about the past are ones which enable us to learn for future occasions.

    b) Similarly, thoughts that speculate about future tasks or experiences can only be of value to the extent that they help in deciding what to do right now: beyond that, in the absence of time-travel, they can only create an out-of-control feeling which is very unpleasant.

    c) Often the most persistent intrusive thoughts relate to unanswerable questions such as "what will it be like when I die?", "what's it all been for?" or "what have I done to deserve this?" These "meaning of life" questions can produce prolonged periods of pre-occupation in which thoughts seem to go round and round in the head. Recognising their un-answerability and challenging the value of spending time on them will be a useful task.

    d) "Should" thoughts often occur when the person is distressed by their own thoughts and images ("I mustn't think like that") and this in turn encourages attempts at thought suppression, which will intensify the frequency and distress of the thoughts. It therefore needs to be discouraged and challenges to the thoughts need to focus on their justification not their distress-causing ability.

Notes:
Challenging thoughts and developing alternative ways of thinking are not the same as thought suppression but there may be an expectation that having "thought it through," the old thoughts should not persist and must be blocked. These intrusive thoughts and worries will continue to recur and will need to be challenged each and every time that they do: the process will, with practice, become quicker but the need for it will remain.

Problem

Lack of motivation

Description

Sees no point in doing things; feels that tasks lack purpose or value; lacks enthusiasm to follow up interests; thinks about things but takes no action; complains of lack of drive; feels detached from things that are going on; wanting to feel less tired, more energetic; self-critical of "can't be bothered attitude."

Possible contributing factors

Clinical depression; lack of roles and structure; diminished roles and responsibilities – at work and in the family; repeated failure in tasks attempted; fatigue induced by treatments or illness; passive response style established during illness or as part of a passive-aggressive reaction.

Techniques and sample tactics

1. **Purposeful planning**
   Reduce things to be decided by working to timetable – create a simple plan for the chores that needs little further thought and only gets changed when absolutely necessary.

Notes:
The passive patient (especially the passive-aggressive one) may be resistant to all the above techniques and tactics. The temptation is to be encouraging and supportive, generating lots of ideas to help rouse him or her from this state. The effect tends to be the opposite: therapist enthusiasm reinforces beliefs in inadequate drive and therapist energy is seen as pressurising. The aim needs to be to shift the patient out of the passive mode. Whilst conveying interest and desire to help, it is often better to match therapist effort to patient effort: displaying disappointment not problem solving when obstacles occur.

2. **Activity monitoring**

   a) Commit self openly to specific undertakings.
   b) Report back to someone (who will give positive feedback) on time use and achievements.
   c) Commit to small tasks for other people.
   d) Set daily goal of recording one event that gave pleasure and one that is an achievement –however small.

Notes:
   a) Scheduling activities and committing to tasks whilst difficult for all with poor motivation, will be strongly resisted by those who are resolute in their passivity.
   b) It can be very beneficial to morale to get into the habit of recognising positive events and of making positive evaluations. Keeping a record of pleasures and achievements can facilitate this and emphasize the value of seeking these things out as worthwhile daily objectives.

3. Graded activities

a) Start with tasks that are familiar, interesting, simple and short.
b) Break all tasks into manageable chunks (see Information sheet: Goal setting and the Step-by-step approach).
c) Increase difficulty and length with success.

Notes:
People often need a lot of guidance on breaking tasks into smaller chunks and working through them step by step. What may seem obvious to an outsider is harder to spot in one's own activities.

4. Challenging unhelpful thoughts

a) Emotional reasoning thoughts of the "I don't feel I can do it, so that means I can't do it" type will need to be identified and challenged.
b) "I always do it wrong" or "I can never do things properly anymore" fall into the mental traps of over-generalisation and mental filtering and an examination of the evidence of the accuracy of these statements may be fertile ground for generating alternative thoughts.
c) When positive feedback and encouragement is dismissed as "kind of you, but I used to be much better than that," then the person has fallen into the mental trap of discounting positives and may need to spend time recalling and recording positive feedback to counterbalance this distorted self-evaluation.
d) People will use "Should" thinking as simple shorthand for their own priorities but when it gets used to identify guilt rather than importance, it doesn't motivate any more. Identifying the importance and challenging the guilt are important parts of the challenge to this mental trap.

Notes:
The poorly motivated, passive and inactive individuals have plenty of time to think – and they usually do. A lot of negative thoughts are generated and the task of recording them can be yet another overwhelming one which may need reducing to smaller chunks as per graded activities (3. above). In fact, recurrent themes in these thoughts probably mean that a sample will serve to provide what is needed for developing a small set of alternatives that can be applied in many situations.

Problem

Loss of pleasure or ability to enjoy things

Description

Life feels dull and rather flat; there seems little point in making the effort; opts out of social situations; feels a dampener on the enjoyment of others; gets depressed about being depressed; does not pursue former interests and hobbies.

Possible contributing factors

Clinical depression; sedating or anti-depressant medication; non-acceptance of current health status; unrealistic expectations of future improvement (so life "on hold"); passive-aggressive punishment of loved ones.

Techniques and sample tactics

1. Purposeful planning

a) Do things that gave pleasure in past and try new ones – do not pressure to *enjoy* now – *doing* it is enough.
b) Book ahead: plan the time for the pleasurable activity rather than "wait and see how I feel" to reduce the effect of emotional reasoning unhelpful thoughts.
c) Novelty and challenge may surprise and stimulate.
d) Ignoring fatigue will spoil enjoyment – work within realistic limits and, if it is enjoyable, stop while it's still fun.
e) "Enjoying myself" should not be set as a goal – in normal life it is an emotional product of pursuing or attaining goals.

Notes:
a) It's hard to have an upbeat mood if you do not experience some positive events, but "not feeling like it" can lead people to deny themselves the opportunity of such events. "Do it anyway and see how it goes" is the approach here. A record of what has been done (regardless of pleasure experienced) will give feedback and encouragement. Challenging emotional reasoning thoughts may also be necessary.
b) Shifting the focus away from "pleasure" to "interest" or "being memorable" can help reduce the excessive emphasis that is placed on the role of enjoyment.
c) "I don't feel like it" may not be a good way of determining whether or not to pursue an activity (see 1. above) but fatigue and discomfort should not be ignored either. Getting the balance right will often involve having a go but being prepared to bow out early if the fatigue or pain are pronounced.

2. Challenging unhelpful thoughts

a) Feelings do not conform to rules and expectations so 'Should' statements about enjoying oneself or feeling pleased and happy can be seen as unhelpful and alternative ways of thinking encouraged.

b) Jumping to conclusions about what is going on or going to happen are features of the fortune telling mental trap. Recognise this type of unhelpful assumption and identify alternative ways of thinking – especially not trying to predict the future possibility of finding something pleasurable.

c) Is emotional reasoning stopping the opportunity for pleasure being taken?

d) Is emotional reasoning blocking the chance for pleasure to be experienced?

Notes:

The problem with "pleasure" and "enjoyment" is that we can deprive ourselves of it through a self-fulfilling prophesy. In fact, the more consciously aware someone is of the "pleasure" issue, the less likely they are to experience it (because the awareness encourages emotional detachment). So, not only does "I'm not going to enjoy this" cause detachment but so does "I'm expecting to really enjoy this." Typically people "hope to enjoy it" beforehand and afterwards reflect that they "found it enjoyable" but usually "just get on with it" at the time.

Problem

Low mood

Description

Gets little or no pleasure from things; feels down most of the time; takes little or no interest in things; sees no point in doing things; lacks a sense of purpose; feels tired most of the time.

Possible contributing factors

Grieving the loss of roles and future opportunities caused by illness; preoccupation with own thoughts; belief that "I am to blame;" rejection/avoidance by friends; self-critical of lack of "usefulness;" lack of understanding by others; reduced mobility.

Techniques and sample tactics

1. Attention strategies

a) Engage in tasks that demand attention (preferably for short periods of time to begin with) – puzzles, games and quizzes, reading, phone calls or a hobby.

b) Give attention to the needs of other people: find out how they are and what has been going on in their lives, look for ways of helping someone else out (advice, listening time or practical assistance).

Notes:
This needs to be an *active* process. If outside events are thrust on the person he or she remains passively engaged and distraction may be achieved but not a shift of mind-set towards seeking things out. The task setting should be left to the patient, but ask for a record to be kept of what has been achieved for you to see.

2. Purposeful planning

a) Identify worthwhile goals for the near future.

b) Do things that gave pleasure in past and try new ones – do not pressure to enjoy now – doing it is enough.

Notes:
a) Identify specific, realistic goals that can be achieved in a reasonably short time scale and are not too dependent on health status. This can be helpful in challenging uselessness thoughts but be alert to counter-productive self-critical thoughts.

b) It's hard to have an upbeat mood if you do not experience some positive events, but "not feeling like it" can lead people to deny themselves the opportunity of such events. "Do it anyway and see how it goes" is the approach here. A record of what has been done (regardless of pleasure experienced) will give feedback and encouragement. Challenging emotional reasoning thoughts may also be necessary.

3. Emotional expression

a) "Off-load" – Have specific times to express low feelings and frustration.

b) Meet similar people – "Not the only one" opportunities to share.

Notes:
  a) It is important to be allowed to feel low and frustrated, and not to have to be "positive" all the time. That is an important message to get across to patient and carers alike. Setting aside specific time to do this helps to make it "legitimate" and to reduce its intrusion at other times.
  b) Spending time in the company of others sharing similar life experiences seems to be uplifting for very many people, but there will be some for whom socialising will create other challenges and these should be identified and tackled as well if the benefits of socialising are not to be lost. Some people have a lifetime history of being very private and their wish not to be publicly "exposed" should be respected.

4. Challenge unhelpful thoughts

  a) Look at the self-critical thoughts and check out if double standards are applying.
  b) Examine the "uselessness" ideas and explore if they might be too black and white.
  c) Is emotional reasoning stopping the opportunity for pleasure being taken.

Notes:
In challenging unhelpful thoughts, it will important to take a few minutes to explain something of the CBT model (and especially the role of vicious circles in emotional reasoning) before using these techniques.

Problem

Low self-esteem

Description

Poor opinion of self and abilities; harshly self-critical; devalues personal contribution; often lacks self-confidence; sees others as superior as people even if not in terms of skills etc; usually sees others as more lovable and likeable.

Possible contributing factors

Recent problems and difficulties undermining plans and confidence; recent social problems such as falling out with close friend; unwanted break-up of marriage or close relationship, especially if a third party involved; harshly critical partner or parents.

Techniques and sample tactics

1. Assertiveness skills

a) The lack of self worth is often linked to a set of double standards that lead the person to deny the same rights to make mistakes, have off-days etc that he or she will allow to others. Adopting the assertiveness rights may provide useful guidance.

b) Applying the Assertiveness model to interactions with others may also provide a more "objective" measure of successful social interaction than the felt sense of failure engendered by the low self-esteem.

Notes:

Anxiety may increase whilst putting this into practice and the reactions of any who may have exploited the person's low self-esteem will need careful consideration.

2. Attention strategies

a) The highly self-critical nature of someone with low self-esteem leads to excessive attention being given to personal failures and "character defects." Tasks requiring a focus on successes and strengths help shift the attention. Record form: Achievements and pleasures may be of use.

b) Shifting the focus from self to others may also be helpful. For example behavioural experiments can be designed to observe the mixture of success and failure, strength and weakness in other people.

3. Graded activities

a) Precisely defined SMART goals increase the likelihood of "objective" success being acknowledged.

b) Creating a sense of achievement by working through a confidence building programme of activities is likely to enhance self-esteem.

Notes:

A step-by-step programme is also likely to encounter setbacks, so the person needs to be well primed to handle these cognitively for this technique to work.

4. Purposeful planning

a) A constructive plan of action enables the person with low self-esteem to feel that he or she is doing something about the problem. This helps enhance a sense of self-effectiveness.

b) Tasks to include in this plan would need to be ones which the person agrees to be worthwhile and would enhance a sense of self-worth.

5. Challenging unhelpful thoughts

a) Automatic labelling thoughts including many self-deprecatory messages about being weak, stupid, useless etc often occur with high frequency for people with low self-esteem. We need to help the person become more aware of them and when they occur, and challenge them through recognition of the double standards being applied to other people.

b) The blaming mental trap also plays a role and thoughts to be explored and challenged include beliefs that when things go wrong "it was probably my fault."

c) Personalising of responsibility for the unhappiness and misfortunes of other people also reinforces the low self-esteem and needs to be examined closely.

d) "Shoulds" provide the harsh and unrelenting standards and rules which the person with low self-esteem is likely to use as the basis of much of the self-criticism. Once again, as with the other unhelpful and critical thoughts mentioned here, these need to be teased out and scrutinised, challenged with regard to double standards and tested with carefully constructed behavioural experiments.

e) Discounting positives is yet another mental trap that plays a key role in sustaining low self-esteem. If someone does not believe or downplays every piece of positive feedback and encouragement then it is not easy to build a positive self-image. The effect of this particular mental trap is of significance to everything else in the list of techniques for managing low self-esteem. To acknowledge success and progress with any other strategy the person has to be able to effectively challenge the tendency to discount positive information.

Problem

Negative outlook

Description

Expects the worst to happen; resists taking any "risks," resists close family taking chances; depressed by the news; avoids having to make decisions; seeks lots of reassurance (but rarely fully believes it); expresses feelings of hopelessness and helplessness; questions the point and purpose of things; doubts the motives and sincerity of others; views positive attitudes and enthusiasm as naïve and silly; obstructs attempts at change.

Possible contributing factors

Clinical depression; past traumatic experiences; passive-aggressive response to help; belief and acceptance of the imminence of death.

Techniques and sample tactics

1. Purposeful planning

a) Reduce things to be decided by working to timetable – create a simple plan for the chores that needs little further thought and only gets changed when absolutely necessary.
b) Do things that gave pleasure in past and try new ones – do not pressure to *enjoy* now – doing it is enough.
c) Identify worthwhile goals for the near future perhaps of benefit to others if not any identified for oneself.

Notes:
a) The intention is to reduce passivity without necessarily expecting an increased awareness of the possibility of enjoyment or achievement to be gained.
b) These plans need to be flexible enough to allow for variations in health and if ambitious in scope or time frame, should be broken down into a series of smaller "chunks" each with its own identifiable goal.

2. Attention strategies

a) Resist future-gazing unless it has a useful function in the present moment.
b) Work on skilful tasks which demand concentration on the present.

Notes:
Involvement in present time events reduces scope for being the "detached observer" which is often an important element of the passive-aggressive style of thinking. Resisting later evaluation of these activities will also be necessary.

3. Challenging unhelpful thoughts

a) "Nothing I do is going to make any difference" is an over-generalisation thought linked to saving one's life which whilst true for that situation perhaps will certainly not be true with reference to the quality of the life remaining or one's effect on others.

b) "There's no point because I'm going to die" is rather too black-and-white in style since it is a justification for inaction people can use all their lives but normally do not.

c) "Everything always goes wrong for me" is a thought that falls into the mental filtering trap of ignoring all the past evidence of better times and the personalisation trap (with "for me") suggesting a harsh God or force of nature deliberately targeting the person for special punishment.

d) "She's just saying that to make me feel better" thoughts discount the positive effects any reassurance or good news that has been offered.

e) "Why me?", "What's the point?", "What next?", "How do they think that's going to help?" are all examples of the rhetorical questions which *imply* the negative outlook without actually stating it. These benefit from conversion to statements before being challenged: "I'm being punished" (personalisation mental trap), "There is no point" (black-and-white thinking mental trap), "More bad things are going to happen" (catastrophic thinking mental trap), "They can do nothing to help me" (fortune telling mental trap).

Notes:

It is easy to fall into the trap of supplying the alternative thoughts and letting the rhetorical questions slip by unchallenged. Someone with a very negative outlook will produce very many of these negative cognitions and will find them easy to generate. If change is to be achieved then the patient must be working at spotting and changing every one of the rhetorical questions and must always do the leg-work in supplying alternatives. When alternatives are supplied by others (as they often are by family members in day-to-day conversations) the person with the negative outlook is given opportunities to practice and develop even more unhelpful thoughts.

Problem

Pain

Description

Physical sensations of discomfort; sometimes dull and persistent, other times sharp and intermittent; can be experienced as hot or cold; can be associated with fatigue, difficulty sleeping, memory and concentration problems, irritability and loss of ability to perform ordinary daily activities.

Possible contributing factors

Loss of fitness, stamina and flexibility so that ordinary daily activities result in increased pain: often patients fall into the trap of then overdoing it on better days. Depression, anxiety about pain, lack of distraction, stress and lack of sleep all heighten the negative experience of pain.

Techniques and sample tactics

1. Pacing

a) Set a baseline achievable on bad days.
b) Stick to this baseline until they have better control over their pain.
c) Activity level can be gradually increased as stamina for particular activities increases.
d) Manage acute flare ups by reducing activity levels on worse days to regain control over the pain (see Technique: Pacing).

Notes:
"Bad days" can be confused with "I don't feel like it" days and the distinction between physical sensation feelings and emotion feelings becomes important here. Challenging the emotional reasoning will be more appropriate if it is an emotion bad day.

2. Purposeful planning

a) Plan and prioritise daily activity to take into account the limiting effect of pain.
b) Identify clear and realistic goals to work on (see Information sheet: Goal setting and the Step-by-step approach).
c) Encourage modifying high standards to reduce unnecessary demands.
d) Plan ahead and spread tasks to avoid overdoing things where possible.
e) Achieve a balance between achievement and enjoyment.

Notes:
Family and friends may heavily influence activity scheduling so it may be essential to offer them some guidance on realistic maximums and minimums as well, together with encouraging the patient to be assertive with other people.

3. Relaxation exercises

a) Mental relaxation tapes and CDs with visual imagery exercises (see also Information sheet: Mental relaxation exercise).
b) Mindfulness meditation exercises such as focusing on the rhythm of breathing – counting the in-breaths up to 100 (see Technique: Mindfulness and Information sheet: Mindfulness exercises).
c) Warm baths (see Technique: Relaxation exercises).
d) Massage.

Notes:
a) The aim is to relax *into* the pain rather than to try to mask it or drive it away: achieving relaxed acceptance and tolerance.
b) Muscle relaxation tapes and CDs are sometimes not suitable because the exercises often involve tensing and relaxing muscle groups and this may do more harm than good unless very carefully managed.

4. Mental distraction

a) Focus on external events and reduce the focus on somatic sensations.
b) Verbal distractions: conversation or talking radio.
c) Discourage unnecessary describing of symptoms or speculation of what is wrong to others.

Notes:
Talking about things can be a great emotional release, but it can also be a constant reminder of troubles. Recalling past experiences may help the patient become aware of when talking is helpful and when distraction works better.

5. Challenging unhelpful thoughts

a) Watch out for catastrophic assumptions about the future e.g. "If it hurts this much now what will it be like in two months."
b) Self-critical labelling may occur: "I'm being weak and pathetic, other people put up with a lot worse than this." This may lead to the pain being poorly managed and medication not being used when appropriate.
c) "I must not give in to this pain" is the sort of "Should" statement which may lead people to again fail to use medication appropriately and to engage in activities that exacerbate pain and other symptoms.

Notes:
Poor use of medication and inappropriate exercise are most likely due to unhelpful cognitions that need to be examined. However, there is plenty of scope for misunderstanding and misconceptions in this complicated area, so repeated education on what to do and why should not be overlooked. Expectations, myths and prejudices of family and friends may also need to be taken into account in the educational exercises.

6. Assertiveness skills

a) Asking for help without shame or aggression.
b) Accessing support and setting limits on daily activity may require the co-operation of others which may in turn require clear communication and persistence (see Information sheet: Assertiveness model).

Notes:
Practicing asking in a friendly, dignified and unapologetic way in front of the mirror or with a very good friend is a good way to improve this important skill (see Technique: Behavioural rehearsal).

7. Ergonomics
   a) Rearrange the environment to make daily chores easier to manage
   b) Make use of aids and equipment (this can sometimes require graded exposure techniques and challenging unhelpful thoughts to overcome shame and awkwardness such as the use of a wheelchair).

Notes:
The convenience and comfort of other people may be a factor limiting the adaptation of the environment, so their co-operation may need to be sought.

Additional references:

Cole, F., Macdonald, H., Carus, C. and Howden-Leach, H. (2005) *Overcoming Chronic Pain*, London: Robinson.
Dahl, J. and Lundgren, T. (2006) *Living Beyond Your Pain*, Oakland: New Harbinger Publications.

Problem

Panic attacks

Description

Feelings of being about to go out of control; experiences of intense anxiety and impending catastrophe; strong physical reactions including racing heart and difficulties breathing; general sense of being overwhelmed and powerless; feelings of having to fight to avoid going mad.

Possible contributing factors

Any form of breathing difficulty; any problem inducing palpitations or arrhythmias; a current overwhelming event; past experience of actual loss of control (such as traumatic accident events); a history of panic disorder or phobic anxiety disorder (especially agoraphobia); recent introduction of SSRI anti-depressant.

Techniques and sample tactics

1. Relaxation exercises

Muscle relaxation tapes and CDs (see also Information sheet: Muscle relaxation exercise).

Notes:
Relaxation can be threatening to someone who is anxious to be in control all of the time. The idea of "letting go" can be enough to produce an out-of-control panic reaction. If this happens then the relaxation exercises should be used in small sections, relaxing a few muscles at a time perhaps at regular intervals throughout the day. There will be no benefit to be gained from "toughing it out"; it will only make the panic feelings get worse.

2. Breathing control

a) Learn to relax the abdomen.
b) Breathe gently from the diaphragm – no upper chest movement, slightly expanding the abdomen as you breathe in (see Information sheet: Relaxed breathing exercise).
c) Practice relaxing abdomen and then two to three diaphragmatic breaths every hour or so until it becomes easy and natural (usually after about ten days)

Notes:
Being able to relax the abdomen is important with the breathing exercises. Without this ability the person may be inclined to swallow air and hyperventilate in the attempt to breathe from the diaphragm. Discourage prolonged use of the method: a few such breaths once an hour or so is quite sufficient in normal daily life. Only in highly stressful (panic inducing) situations would it be appropriate to make more use of this technique.. See also Special note about "Safety behaviours" below.

3. Pacing

a) Explain the central role of breathing pattern in inducing a panic attack.

b) Learn to walk, talk and do things slower and also perhaps to take rests as part of a process to minimise creating this disrupted pattern. But see "Safety behaviours" in Special note below.

Notes:
Rushing to get things done will help to induce hyperventilation and this can often be the direct cause of a panic attack especially when the person was already anxious. Trying to "escape" from the current situation will similarly induce these feelings. Taking things more slowly is therefore a logical coping strategy but runs counter to the fight-flight feelings which will be hard to resist.

4. Psycho-education

a) Understand causes and effects of hyperventilating.

b) Understand that panic does not cause death: poor breathing regulation will not induce asphyxia, panic attacks do not lead to madness and their affect on the body is like a short burst of vigorous exercise and will not cause heart attacks.

c) Recognise the role of "safety behaviours" in perpetuating panic attacks and the fear of their recurrence.

Notes:
a. An understanding of the panic process and why the coping strategies do work is an important part of reinstating a sense of personal control. It is often worth investing a lot of time in doing this thoroughly.

b. It may also be useful to get the person to deliberately hyperventilate to demonstrate the link with the cluster of symptoms that have been experienced.

c. Deliberately induced hyperventilation is also valuable in showing the effectiveness of the re-breathing with a paper bag method and the value of diaphragmatic breathing.

5. Challenging unhelpful thoughts

a) Catastrophic thoughts of perpetual panic inducing death or madness lead to belief that such awful experiences must be avoided at all costs and a range of safety strategies are put in place to reduce this risk. Challenging the death or madness thoughts with more realistic alternatives based on the actual unpleasant experience will be necessary if the safety behaviours are to be dropped.

b) "I won't be able to cope" is an anticipatory thought which generates anxiety about the possibility of experiencing a panic attack. Jumping to conclusions of this sort is a part of the fortune telling mental trap for people to fall into once they have had a panic attack, even if they never have another one. Challenging these thoughts needs to involve examining the assumption that without "coping" it won't stop or it can't be survived, together with a review of the evidence from past experience of both coping and non-coping.

Notes:
a. Challenging unhelpful thoughts will be of little value in the immediate build up or midst of a panic attack. These challenges are of most value in advance of situations to minimise anticipatory anxiety and reduce the temptation to resort to safety behaviours.

b. Thought records may also be useful in reviewing coping with an event once it has passed because safety behaviour thinking could still influence the evaluation of "success" to be in terms of being anxiety-free, thus leading to a negative perception of a valuable goal-attaining achievement.

Special note

Safety behaviours

1. This term refers to those things done in order to attempt to remain free of anxiety or attempt to prevent challenging situations arising.
2. Any form of safety behaviour serves to reinforce the problem because it aims to keep the person "safe" from anxiety, thus supporting the unhelpful belief that "If I become anxious then terrible things will happen."
3. Tolerating the unpleasant anxiety feelings and proving that even more terrible things do not happen is a key part of the shift away from anxious thinking; so safety behaviours need to be gradually removed once their unhelpfulness has been thoroughly explained.
4. The most obvious safety behaviours are avoidance strategies: the person stays away from any situation where there is a risk of problems occurring.
5. The other very obvious one is the need "to take my pill before I do that." In this way, as with many safety behaviours, a psychological dependency is created.
6. Only facing these situations when accompanied by a trusted companion is a common safety behaviour tactic.
7. Less obvious but just as "safety" minded is insistence on always being in control and vigilant. Examples of this would be: insisting on being the car-driver, planning out every detail of an activity or knowing exactly where other people are.
8. Coping skills developed in therapy can also fall into the trap of becoming safety behaviours: having to do certain coping methods in order to avoid getting into difficulties. Relaxation exercises, breathing correctly, challenging anxious thoughts are all examples of these methods that become "essential" in the person's approach.

Problem

Physical tension

Description

Restlessness and fidgety behaviour; feeling stiff and achy; wobbly legs, trembling and unsteady; sweaty and hot; butterflies in the stomach, bloated and windy; nausea and diarrhoea; complains that noises are too loud and lights too bright; clumsy; impatient; rushes things; speaks quickly.

Possible contributing factors

Pain; physical ill health triggers associated anxiety reactions; sensitisation to bodily reactions; hypervigilance due to fear of illness recurrence; over-tired; controlled anger; under pressure from others; a history of hyperactivity.

Techniques and sample tactics

1. **Relaxation exercises**

   a) Muscle relaxation tapes and CDs (and also see Information sheet: Muscle relaxation exercise).
   b) Warm baths (see Technique: Relaxation exercises).
   c) Massage.
   d) Sensory relaxation methods such as using
      i)   aromatherapy oils and pleasurable smells
      ii) soft lighting
      iii) soothing music and sounds
      iv) gentle touching or stroking
      v)   slow rocking or swaying actions

   Notes:
   a) If physical tension is directly linked to pain and illness symptoms then sensory relaxation and mental imagery relaxation will be important, but muscular relaxation (*differential* type especially) may be useful too because "bracing oneself" against pain can make it worse. The use muscular relaxation exercises should always be carefully evaluated in relation to the physical problems of the patient. Make sure you are familiar with both the exercises and the health problems.
   b) Sometimes people seek an absence of any sensory experience, thinking this to be the most relaxing state of all. It usually doesn't work out that way because of the minor intrusions (such as small distant noises) that mar the effect and cause further frustration and tension. Therefore pleasant sensory experiences usually work better and can serve to mask the other intrusions too.

2. **Pacing**

   a) Slowing down in movements: walking and talking more slowly.
   b) One thing at a time and time for one thing.
   c) Pause between tasks to apply relaxation skills.

Notes:

Heightening awareness of pacing doesn't always produce instant results because of the deeply ingrained habits. But encouragement to persist with trying to change can often produce sufficient modification to make a difference and improves the likelihood of becoming aware of messages from the body about fatigue and the need to rest.

3. Psycho-education

a) Explain the adverse effects of a stressful lifestyle (see Information sheets: Effects of stress and Stress response).

b) Examine sources of pressure and ways to re-prioritise use of time to reduce this pressure (see Record form: Activity schedule).

c) Encourage an attitude change towards sources of pressure (see Technique: Mindfulness).

Notes:

a) Physical tension will often be linked to sources of anxiety and fear rather than lifestyle issues in which case it is these that need to be addressed in the psycho-education (see Problems: Fear of the future, Anxious thoughts and moods, and Avoidance).

b) Being very busy and under great pressure can be part of a set of beliefs and behaviours about being valued or important in which case it will be necessary to challenge these unhelpful thoughts (see Technique: Challenging unhelpful thoughts).

4. Challenging unhelpful thoughts

a) "Should" thinking: "I've got far too much to do to worry about how it's making me feel." The sense of personal responsibility and duty will often discourage compliance with strategies which are fully recognised to be helpful, but are seen as "self-indulgent" in comparison to the performance pressure the person places on her or himself.

b) Emotional reasoning: "I may be tense but I'm full of energy, so I'll use it on catching up." This way of thinking encourages a peaks-and-troughs variability in the patient's physical well-being and forms the basis of problems with pacing.

Notes:

These thoughts will be important to address if compliance with other strategies is to be achieved. But the thoughts themselves are not "wrong" and do reflect important values that have been influential throughout the person's life, so a careful examination of them needs to draw out a distinction between taking care of oneself (and one's health) and self-indulgence or pampering.

Problem

Poor concentration

Description

Inability to sustain mental effort on demanding task; mind wanders onto other issues; problems recalling what has been done; gets muddled and flustered; feels overwhelmed by tasks seen as requiring sustained attention; has difficulty retaining new information or recalling details when under pressure.

Possible contributing factors

Neurological cognitive impairments; fatigue; anxiety (especially self-consciousness and fear of failure); clinical depression; medication or alcohol impeding cognitive functioning; distracting environments; boring or very difficult tasks; pre-occupation with other thoughts; highly critical other people.

Techniques and sample tactics

1. Graded activities

a) Start with tasks that are familiar, simple and short.
b) Break all tasks into manageable chunks.
c) Increase difficulty and length with success.

Notes:
Setting sights very low is important to build an atmosphere of success and reduce the self-conscious performance evaluation. The more interesting and pleasurable the task the more rewarding the effort. If reading books is one of the troubling issues then re-reading an old favourite in small steps may be a good place to start.

2. Challenging unhelpful thoughts

a) It is an over-generalisation to say that it is not possible to concentrate on anything, so identify those things that get the longest periods of attention and what makes them easier to concentrate on. Can practical lessons be learnt from them?
b) All-or-none (or black-and-white) thinking sometimes leads to a "no point in bothering at all" attitude because concentration and memory are not as good as they used to be. Adapting to change and achieving the goal by whatever means necessary will be a more helpful attitude to develop.
c) "Should" statements and self-critical comments about not concentrating "properly" will be a distraction from the task in hand – further reducing concentration. Focus on "doing, not how you are doing" is a useful reminder.

Notes:
Anxious thoughts about losing one's mind and becoming demented are frequently triggered by concentration and memory problems and often contribute to an exacerbation of these problems and avoidance of testing situations which might validate these fears.

3. Stimulus control

a) Minimise distractions..
b) Don't distract self with self-critical and apologetic comments
c) Keep to one task at a time.
d) Use memory aids.
e) Take short breaks.

Notes:
Making changes that might enhance concentration is not "giving in" to the problem. Concentration and memory are improved by favourable conditions, not by willpower.

Problem

Problem solving difficulties

Description

Apprehension about personal coping skills; speculation about reactions of others; anxiety about mishandling or misjudging the situation; doubts about making correct decisions; fear about being wrong; dread of confrontation; worries about displeasing or upsetting others; concern about personal emotional control; difficulty in deciding between alternatives.

Possible contributing factors

A history of not successfully addressing this situation; lack of support from others; high risk situations; lack of experience of similar situations; misunderstanding about the nature of the situation; a history of poor emotional control; intimidated by others involved; lack of belief in the proposed course of action.

Techniques and sample tactics

1. Problem solving

a) Identify main issues of concern to you (**start point**).
b) Identify your desired positive outcome (**goal**).
c) Plan what steps need to be taken to go from start point to goal (see Information sheet: Goal setting and the Step-by-step approach and Record form: Goal planning – Step-by-step record).
d) Identify the possible obstacles and methods for overcoming them.
e) Focus on broad strategy only – too many details of what to say or do will lead to other problems (See Problem: Fear of the future for more details).

Notes:
In deciding to take action, it is probable that a constructive rather than destructive outcome is wanted. It is therefore important in planning steps intended to move towards this that proper account is taken of the obstacles and pitfalls which could lead to a destructive outcome. If they are too great and a destructive outcome seems very likely, there may need to be a re-evaluation of the whole plan (see Weighing pros and cons).

2. Behavioural rehearsal

a) Recall of similar situations in the past and lessons learnt re what helps.
b) Practice coping skills that may be useful (e.g. slow breathing, relaxed postures).
c) Focus on broad coping strategy only – details of what to do if . . . can lead to other problems (See Problem: Fear of the future).
d) Have a complete break from thinking about it for a little while before dealing with it.

Notes:
Practising in front of the mirror or rehearsing a situation with a friend can be very helpful for establishing a confidence in a new behavioural pattern and reduce the likelihood of falling back into "bad old ways" when the situation occurs. But the downside of preparation like this is that it can feed anticipatory anxiety; so strict limits need to be placed on when and how much to do.

3 Weighing pros and cons

a) Seek the opinions/advice of one or two people whose views you will respect in this matter (not necessarily people closest to you).
b) Identify the disadvantages of confronting the problem and compare them to the disadvantages of *not* confronting it.
c) For the bigger decisions that do need careful thinking about use the more systematic method described in Technique: Weighing the pros and cons for deciding between courses of action or even deciding to do nothing.

Notes:
Procrastination can be overcome by using these methods, but they can also be used to facilitate further procrastination! Strict limits on the number of advisors sought and documentation of the weighing of pros and cons should reduce this risk; but it may be that the person is genuinely reluctant to take responsibility for making the decision and may even hope that someone else or other events will remove the burden. Beware that pitfall.

4. Challenging unhelpful thoughts

a) De-Catastrophising: asking "What is the worst that can happen if you make the wrong decision." As people hesitate, problems can magnify in the mind.
b) "Shoulds" often enter thinking and steer towards undesired decisions as though there is no real choice to be made. Challenging the justification of the "should," "must" or "have to" can be very helpful.

Notes:
In challenging unhelpful thoughts it is important not to fall in to the opposite trap of minimising problems: possible consequences need to be realistically faced. Similarly the person whose thinking is ruled by "shoulds" will be susceptible to adopting another set of "shoulds" from therapy unless this hazard is carefully avoided.

5. Assertiveness skills

a) Understand the general concept and principles of the Assertiveness model (see Information sheet: Assertiveness).
b) Asserting that "I have a right to: do it my way; have my own opinion; make my own mistakes; be guided by my feelings." These are among the assertive attitudes that enable people to make judgements and take decisions that are their own.
c) Being sensitive to the same rights for others in exercising assertiveness increases the likelihood of constructive communication and a positive outcome.

Notes:
Assertiveness is an option not an obligation. Rationally and constructively it often appears the most sensible or attractive option, but that does not make it necessarily the right option for this person on this occasion: it remains a *choice.*

Problem

Setbacks

Description

Mix of reactions to things not going according to plan including: demoralised; crushed; hopelessness; despondency; resentment and frustration; feeling let down; expectations are *not* met; hopes are disappointed; sense of being betrayed by people or fate; preoccupied with apportioning blame for this situation.

Possible contributing factors

Unrealistic goals; high expectations; lack of support with planned goals; poor appreciation of health advice provided; poor appreciation of probability and ratio data in health outcomes; false reassurance and hope provided; side-effects or difficulties minimised by health advisers.

Techniques and sample tactics

1. Psycho-education

a) Use Socratic questioning to ascertain prior understanding and knowledge.
b) Correct any health advice misunderstandings.
c) Work through coping with setbacks information using the relevant information sheets (Information sheets: Coping with setbacks: 1 Physical health setbacks; 2 Mental attitude setbacks).

Notes:
The Information sheets should be used as the basis for discussion and only given to the patient to take away if you both agree that the information is pertinent.

2. Problem solving

a) Re-evaluate the situation in terms of possibilities for constructive action and constructive acceptance (Information sheets: Change – The desire for it; Change – Bringing it about; The Serenity prayer).
b) Identify appropriate new goals for constructive action (Information sheets: SMART guidelines; Goal setting and The step-by-step approach).
c) Use methods that enhance tolerance of temporary setbacks (Information sheets: Antidotes to bad days; Relaxation; Technique: Mental distraction).
d) Identify changes to adapt constructively to problems arising from setbacks which represent permanent change for the worse (Techniques: Attention strategies; Behavioural experiments; Behavioural rehearsal; Mindfulness; Stimulus control).

Notes:
The negative mind set often induced by setbacks can make people quite resistant to problem-solving initially. Allow time for emotional expression and resolution of unhelpful thoughts (with or without professional assistance) before introducing problem solving for setbacks. Stimulus control may need to be considered when toleration of the setback is impeded by repeated reminders that can be minimised.

3. Emotional expression

a) Encourage discussion of the setback experience and its implications for the person (Techniques: Basic counselling skills; Listening skills; Socratic questioning).

b) Help the person understand the strong emotional reactions produced by setbacks (Information sheet: Change – the transition curve).

c) Identify a suitable method for further channelling of these emotions to assist adjustment and adaptation (such as Information sheet: Expressive writing).

Notes:

Ensure that a time limit is set for a), that this time will be free from interruptions and that the patient knows of these boundaries.

4. Challenging unhelpful thoughts

a) Self-critical thoughts may be quite justified if the person has made an error of judgement or acted carelessly and thus caused the setback. Minimising this fact will not be helpful. Helpful thoughts will acknowledge the personal responsibility for the mistake and emphasise the lessons learnt together with the problem solving or coping strategy. Potential mental traps will be Blaming – "If I had stuck to the treatment, I won't be in this mess"; Labelling – "I am such a complete fool"; Personalising – "These things always happen to me – I never get a lucky break".

b) Demoralising thoughts are linked to predictions such as "I will never be able to cope with this" and over-generalisations such as "Everything I try fails. It's all hopeless".

Notes:

The unhelpful thoughts may be part of a transient adjustment state and will only need to be looked at in detail if they persist and obstruct a constructive response.

Problem

Sleep difficulties

Description

Long periods of wakefulness without any desire to go to bed and sleep; problems of becoming more wakeful when trying to go off to sleep; waking intermittently throughout the night; waking early in the morning and not going back to sleep; waking frightened, possibly following bad dreams; sleeping excessively and waking tired; sleeping excessively during the day.

Possible contributing factors

Clinical depression; anti-depressant medication; anxiety; pain; pain management strategies, medications and postures; bowel and bladder problems; breathing difficulties; reduced daytime activity levels; bedtime and bedroom changes; external disturbances.

Techniques and sample tactics

1. Stimulus control

 a) Reduce activity two hours before bedtime.
 b) Don't plan tomorrow in bed.
 c) Create quiet, relaxed atmosphere.
 d) Don't stay trapped in bed – this will heighten anxiety.
 e) Avoid large alcoholic "nightcaps".

Notes:
There may be a range of night-time routines that contribute to increasing mental and physical alertness by bedtime and whilst modification will be helpful, it should not be at the cost of creating an unhelpful thought such as the performance expectation of making things "just right for getting a good night's sleep".

2. Challenging unhelpful thoughts

 a) Don't "try" to go to sleep. Pressure to perform through this type of self-instruction induces wakefulness. Passive acceptance is the mind-set to be encouraged through restful thoughts.
 b) Broken sleep will not be desired but nor is it a catastrophe. A restful night with short periods of sleep will be sufficient for the body's needs even if it leaves the person feeling mentally tired through parts of the day.

Note:
Reducing both the expectation of and the belief in the need for "a good night's sleep" is quite important. Recall of past experiences of successfully managing without much sleep can be useful, together with recognition that the body's needs reduce as we age (especially through childhood into adulthood, but going on into older ages too) and even more so as we reduce our activity levels and shorten our active day.

3. Mental distraction

Verbal distractions will help if the mind has shifted into worry or planning modes: reading, story tapes or talking radio may be useful.

Notes:

For the person who is having a bad night with a busy mind then mental distraction activities for 30 minutes before attempting sleep again may be helpful. If the intrusive thoughts return then refer to Problem: Intrusive thoughts.

4. Relaxation exercises

a) Mental relaxation with visual imagery exercises using ideas from Information sheet: Mental relaxation exercise).
b) Focus on gentle rhythm of breathing – counting the in-breaths up to 100.
c) Muscle relaxation tapes and CDs, warm baths and massage prior to bedtime may contribute to "winding down".

Notes:

a) Relaxation tapes and CDs are probably not good to use in bed, but they can be of value before going to bed or after having got up during a bad night. The breathing exercise is best practised during the day before trying it in bed and the person should be careful not to try to control the breathing which would spoil the whole purpose and its effect.
b) Muscle relaxation is probably important for the tense and restless person who has not had a quiet and settled lead up to bedtime. Again the exercises should be done before going to bed and it is important to be aware that baths and massage make some people more alert as well as relaxing them.

Problem

Unassertiveness

Description

Reluctance to openly and directly express personal opinions or wishes; tendency to complain to family, friends and others without involving those most directly affected or most likely to be able to help; anxious about being a nuisance to others; fearful of hurting the feelings of other people; frightened of being rejected or attacked for disagreeing.

Possible contributing factors

Previous experience of unpleasant consequences from speaking up; loss of confidence in ability to sustain logical thinking (perhaps because of memory or concentration difficulties); restrained by family and friends ("You mustn't say that"); aphasia and verbal expressiveness problems; history of poor self-esteem; perceived high dependency on the good will and cooperation of specific individuals (such as a surgeon); lack of knowledge of rights and entitlement.

Techniques and sample tactics

1. Psycho-education

a) Explain rights and entitlement.
b) Explain about informed consent and choices.
c) Identify appropriate advocacy and support services (such as CAB).

Notes:
Providing information can empower the patient, but information overload will have the opposite effect. Also, the unassertive person may be frightened off by too much talk of "rights", fearing that he or she is now being expected to enter a battle with someone.

2. Assertiveness skills

a) Understand the general concept and principles of the Assertiveness model (see Information sheet: Assertiveness).
b) Asserting that "I have a right to: do it my way; have my own opinion; make my own mistakes; be guided by my feelings". These are among the assertive attitudes that enable people to make judgements and take decisions that are their own.
c) Being sensitive to the same rights for others in exercising assertiveness increases the likelihood of constructive communication and a positive outcome.

Notes:
There are a number of good self-help books on assertiveness which may interest some patients, but often it is the specific situation that strips them of their usual assertive skills and a more general knowledge of assertiveness is not required. The non-assertive influence of other people may also be significant and should be checked out (especially partners who are themselves embarrassed by or fearful of discord or conflict).

3. Challenging unhelpful thoughts

a) Catastrophic thoughts of being refused treatment may cause someone to avoid expressing criticism or even asking for more information.

b) Jumping to the conclusion that the other person will be "far too busy to listen to me" will also produce reticence and needs to be challenged.

c) Labelling oneself as "not important" may be another reason for not speaking up. This is especially likely when the person is in awe of the skills and knowledge of the professional help providers. Another label of being "weak" or "useless" can often inhibit someone asking for the help they need.

d) From childhood people are instructed in being a "good patient" and this involves cooperating with care givers, complying with instructions, not being too demanding and appreciating gratefully the help that is offered. This transforms into a set of "Should" or "must" thoughts which will often provide the rules that determine what people can or cannot say or do when ill or seeing a doctor.

e) Taking personal responsibility for the happiness of others can also limit the willingness to be assertive."I will make this nurse unhappy, if I tell her I don't like the way she did that" would be an example of this; as would "My husband will be extremely embarrassed if I ask my doctor to explain that to me again in less technical language."

f) Previous bad experience of challenging or questioning may lead to the over-generalisation thought that this will always produce conflict and bad outcomes. Behavioural experiments with using assertiveness skills may be necessary to change this attitude.

Notes:
Self-reliance and self-sufficiency principles may cause resistance to being more open and honest about personal needs. It can be helpful to acknowledge these and to encourage the patient to hang on to them as desired standards whilst examining the unhelpfulness of some of the "old" thoughts linked to them and finding "new" alternatives that fit better with present circumstances.

Problem

Worrying

Description

Has frightening images and ideas; worries about things all the time; doesn't feel in control of the situation and therefore feels personally out of control; speculates about possible problems that could occur; thinks about future events and the problems that could arise; plans a long way in advance and in great detail; worries about being late or letting people down; expects things to go wrong and frets about it; lies awake at night with thoughts buzzing; checks things very carefully to avoid making mistakes.

Possible contributing factors

Big events coming up; is used to being very busy and carrying a lot of responsibility but now under-occupied; lack of emotional, economic, environmental or physical security; obsessionality; fear of failure and embarrassment; hostile or critical home environment; established habit of long term planning; lifelong worrier.

Techniques and sample tactics

1. Mental distraction

Verbal distractions: conversation or talking radio.

Notes:
People who worry can also worry about worrying, so they try too hard with this and all the other "anxiety prevention" techniques. The message needs to be that "it's ok to worry and be anxious but that it can be helpful to do things to help reduce it".

2. Relaxation exercises

a) Mental relaxation tapes and CDs with visual imagery exercises (see Information sheet: Mental relaxation exercises).
b) Focus on gentle rhythm of breathing – counting the in-breaths up to 100.

Notes:
There are a range of soothing tapes and CDs on the market, but unless the exercises encourage active use of mental processes (like imagery) then it will be possible to listen and worry at the same time! That is why music often does not help in these situations unless listened to by a musician or music expert.

3. Attention strategies

a) Resist future-gazing unless it has a useful function in the present moment.
b) Work on skilful tasks which demanding concentration on the present (e.g. cooking, driving, writing).

Notes:

People often feel that it essential to "be prepared" and feel irresponsible if they are not thinking and planning ahead, so it may take some persuasion and small behavioural experiments to prove that this is a reasonable attitude change to adopt.

4. Challenging unhelpful thoughts

a) Self-reassurance: remind self of past experiences, advice and coping strategies that have been helpful in similar situations.

b) Jumping to conclusions about what is going on or going to happen is part of the fortune telling mental trap. Recognise this type of unhelpful assumption and identify alternative ways of thinking – especially not trying to predict the future.

c) Catastrophising about the future or even refusing to think about it because it's "all too awful" can cause a great deal of distress. De-catastrophising involves looking realistically at the likely outcomes and also examining in detail how one would cope with the "worst case scenario".

Notes:

Reassurance can sound hollow and artificial if it is not based firmly on fact, so if it isn't really believed then it is important to examine why it isn't and search for more confirming evidence to reinforce the belief. Alternatively reject the reassurance altogether and seek out more helpful ways of thinking about the situation. Remember that the unhelpful thoughts will only be effectively challenged if the patient is generating the alternatives – not you.

PART III

The Toolkit: CBT Methods in Practice

Section 1
TECHNIQUES

Technique

Activity monitoring

Purpose

Raise awareness in the patient and others with regard to what the patient is doing so that a feedback loop is created. This loop serves to provide psychological and social pressure for change and psychological and social reinforcement for its attainment.

Method

1. Identify potential areas for personal change and agree which to target.
2. Establish a baseline of current performance using an appropriate monitoring procedure (Record forms: Activity schedule, Achievement and pleasures record form, Event-action-outcome record form are good examples).
3. Agree objectives for the week and record results on the appropriate form.
4. Daily objectives should be set one day ahead and feedback to a partner or friend of results provides the ideal mechanism, although you or another health professional could perhaps fulfil that role.
5. Feedback from the other person should not extend beyond expressing pleasure and congratulations for successes and disappointment for failures.
6. New daily objectives should not be greater than the previous day's and there should be no attempt at "catch-up" on failures from previous days.
7. Increases in performance demands should only occur on a weekly basis following consistent success and be agreed in session not at home.

Additional notes

1. People who need this type of activity monitoring often have unrealistic expectations and place inappropriate demands on themselves, so it becomes quite important that the objective setting is strictly regulated and over-performance is given negative feedback.
2. The other people involved need to be clearly aware of their role and the limits to comment and advice that is placed on them. Similarly, they need to respect the regulation of objectives and resist encouraging over-performance or alternative objectives.
3. Careful checking of the record sheets is important at each meeting. If they are overlooked or squeezed out because of other issues this may adversely affect the persistence of the patient with this task.

Techniques

Assertiveness skills

Purpose

Enable the person to have the choice to deal with issues in an open, honest and direct manner if they so wish to do so.

Method

1. Explain the difference between assertiveness , aggression and unassertiveness (see Information sheet: Assertiveness model).
2. Identify problem situations: It is rare for someone to be unassertive or aggressive all the time, so it is important to establish which situations are more easily handled than others (and why).
3. Examine the attitudes and beliefs that inhibit the use of an assertive style (perhaps using Record form: CBT diary for some data collection).
4. Discuss assertive attitudes and how they fit with the patient's own values and standards (use Information sheet: Assertiveness rights).
5. Rehearse applying assertive attitudes and assertiveness techniques (see Information sheet. Assertiveness techniques).
6. Identify suitable situations in which to put assertiveness into practise, starting with simpler and innocuous situations, only moving to more complicated and important ones once some confidence has developed. Use Record form: Assertiveness record form to keep notes of these situations.

Additional notes

1. Fear of punitive reactions from other people often inhibits assertiveness. It is important to establish the real risk and consequences of such reactions before pursuing the development of assertive behaviours.
2. If the assertiveness principles and "rights" conflict with the standards and values of the patient then this should be respectfully acknowledged and this approach should not be pursued further.
3. Sometimes the patient needs to consult with someone who shares similar standards and values (such as a priest or close friend) before committing to adopting an assertive approach.
4. Adult education classes are regularly provided on assertiveness training and are a very effective way for people to learn and practise these skills.
5. Assertiveness at work courses tend to be too superficial and narrow in their focus to be of much general value and should not be taken as having given more than a general introduction to the basic principles.
6. There is a large number of books available on the subject, of which these are some of the best:
   - *Your Perfect Right* by Alberti and Emmons (2001) ISBN: 1-886230-36-6
   - *Assert Yourself* by Lindenfield (1986) ISBN: 0-00-712345-0
   - *A Woman In Your Own Right* by Dickson (1982) ISBN: 0-7043-3420-8

   As with assertiveness at work courses to with work-related books: there are a number of them on the market but they do not address the issues in the best way for application in personal life.

Technique

Assessing psychological distress

Purpose

1. Evaluate the current degree of psychological problems experienced by the patient in order to help determine whether or not the health care professional can offer sufficient support or whether the need for more specialist mental health service providers is indicated.
2. Evaluate change in psychological status over time, often linked to measuring progress with a programme of psychological treatment.

Methods

1. Activity schedule – particularly with 5 point ratings for pleasure or achievement attached to tasks.
   a) Few entries alert to the presence of apathy, lethargy and low stimulation suggestive of depression or a depression generating environment.
   b) Normal range of entries but low pleasure and achievement scores may be indicative of depression and this should be investigated further.
   c) High number of entries suggests the likelihood of stress and possibly anxiety.
   Record form: Activity schedule is suitable for Purpose 2 and useful re Purpose 1.
2. Daily mood record – usually used for monitoring daily changes in levels of depression, but can be adapted to mean "distress", "fatigue", "irritability" or any other "mood" state you agree on with the patient. Ratings 4–6 are usually agreed with the patient to be their "usual range in normal times" scores.
   Record form: Daily mood record is suitable for Purpose 2; persistent extremely adverse scores ("depressed" low scores, "distressed" high scores) may indicate the need for specialist mental health advice.
3. Thought record – normally a therapy tool but the number and frequency of unhelpful and negative thoughts can be a useful measure of depression and anxiety.
4. Distress thermometer – a suitable tool for Purpose 2 but designed for Purpose 1 and used in the USA with cancer patients. Current research will help determine its Purpose 1 usefulness in the UK with this patient group. It can be downloaded from www.nccn.org
5. Hospital anxiety and depression scale – designed as a quick questionnaire measure of the presence of these clinical conditions particularly in patients with physical health problems, this highly researched and well respected tool can be downloaded from numerous websites such as http://dop.hawaii.edu or purchased from www.nfer-nelson.co.uk. It is a suitable tool for Purposes 1 and 2.
6. PHQ9 – a 9 item questionnaire specifically about depression this tool is increasingly used in primary care to determine clinical action. It can be found at www.depression-primarycare.org where there are also instructions on how to interpret scores for Purpose 1 decisions.

Technique

Attention strategies

Purpose

Shift focus of attention to reduce exacerbating distress or improve constructive thinking.

Method

1. Reducing hypervigilance:
   a. Explain the effect of overly watchful behaviour in increasing concern or the experience of physical discomfort (see Technique: Psycho-education and Information sheet: Vicious cycle of anxious preoccupation).
   b. Demonstrate the effect of focusing undivided attention on a small part of the body (where there is no known discomfort), showing how heightened attending creates an awareness of sensations, even creating feelings of discomfort.
   c. Use mental relaxation and distraction techniques (see Techniques: Mental relaxation and Mental distraction).
2. Reducing anticipatory anxiety:
   a. Explain the role of unhelpful thoughts about the future (especially fortune telling and catastrophising) in generating anxiety (see Information sheet: Mental traps and technique: Challenging unhelpful thoughts).
   b. Demonstrate the benefits of present moment focus of attention by using a mindfulness exercise (see Information sheet: Mindfulness exercises).
   c. Encourage attention focus on the here-and-now and reducing to a minimum any planning for and speculation about the future. Identify which planning is helpful and which is unnecessary.
3. Reducing self-consciousness and intense self-awareness:
   a. Explain the distorting effect of attending more to internal states of mind and emotion than to external events and information.
   b. Encourage involvement in demanding activities that require attention on the external environment not the inner state (see Information sheet: Mental distraction).
   c. Ask the patient to "people watch" by placing him or herself in a public area and carefully observe the behaviour and appearance of other people for periods of time on a regular basis: looking whilst getting used to being seen.
   d. Encourage the patient to take an interest in the well-being and activities of others, asking questions about them and offering help to them.

Additional notes

1. The shift of attention from one thing to another is usually surprisingly easy, but when people are worried, ashamed or in discomfort then often they continue to attend to these things as if by doing so they should be able to resolve them. Therefore not attending to them may seem a very strange suggestion even though they can achieve the right results.

2. Planning ahead is a classic problem for some, who like to know precisely what they will be doing this time next week. But in striving for certainty, these people encounter the possibility of obstacles which become problems to try to solve (even though the problems have not actually happened).

3. Planning my shopping list for tomorrow is useful because I can work out what I need and will then go and get it. Planning what to pack for my holiday in 4 months is not useful because I have no intention of packing it now and may have different things I want to pack in 3 months' time.

Techniques

Basic counselling skills

Purpose

Develop a trusting, non-judgemental opportunity for the patient to identify and explore issues and feelings of particular relevance whilst facilitating emotional expression and personal goal development.

Method:

- Engage through general conversation – perhaps making some typical friendly observations as one might to a neighbour or new friend.
- Explore with questions – using "open" questions that introduce a topic area in such a way as to leave the patient free to say as much or as little as they wish.
- Allow silences – pausing a while after the patient has spoken, allows him or her to added further comment after thought or to steer the conversation to another topic if desired.
- Reflect what is said – by paraphrasing and summarising what the patient has told you, giving some sense of the impression given by these remarks. This enables the patient to feel listened to and understood and provides an important opportunity to correct misunderstanding or wrong impressions.
- Show empathy – through remarks and listening skills. Allow free expression of emotion and facilitate this by appropriately matched responses of your own.
- Seek to understand – by asking questions and checking back on anything that seems vague, ambiguous or difficult to comprehend. Never try to work it out for yourself or assume you know what was really meant; always ask.
- Identify goals – by encouraging the patient to consider what it is they wish to gain from this session, correcting unrealistic expectations and otherwise endeavouring to help in attaining those objectives.
- Accept problem solving limitations – by resisting the temptation to jump in with ideas for solutions to problems which the patient has chosen to share with you. The counselling is the patient's opportunity to think out loud and express feelings.

Additional notes

1. Advice giving and problem solving are important activities but are not part of this counselling process and can undermine it.
2. Reflecting impressions should avoid becoming judgemental and should not become interpretation (where you attempt to draw connections and explain processes).

Technique

Behavioural change methods: a summary

Purpose

To modify existing behavioural response patterns in order to produce better outcomes.

Methods

The following is a key-word reminder of the methods described in Chapter 13 and sometimes elsewhere in the Techniques section.

1. Deciding to change.
2. Breaking old habits – stopping.
    a) *Consciousness-raising*
    b) *"Cold turkey"*
    c) *Interference strategies*
    d) *Reward schemes*
3. Making new habits – committing.
    a) *Positive self talk*
    b) *Thinking about the benefits*
    c) *"Chunking"*
4. Learning new skills.
5. Changing the environment.
6. Practising and improving.
    a) *Behavioural rehearsal*
    b) *Imaginal rehearsal*
7. Behavioural experiments.
    a) *Surveys*
    b) *Test runs*
    c) *Trial and error*
8. Confidence building (graded exposure).
9. Resisting avoidance and confronting fear.

Technique

Behavioural experiments

Purpose

Test formulations, thoughts (old and new), behavioural skills and response outcomes. Use the results of experiments to modify treatment plans, beliefs and behaviour patterns.

Method

1. Identify specific purpose for using a behavioural experiment, especially the questions you expect it to answer.
2. Develop an experiment that will answer those questions in a way that is acceptable to and clearly understood by the patient.
3. Specify ways of collecting data during the experiment.
4. Set boundaries to the experiment in terms of its duration, commitment of patient and what to do if problems arise with the experiment (e.g. plans are disrupted, patient is too distressed).
5. Review the data when the experiment is completed and discuss the implications. Identify further experiments needed if more questions are raised or data does not produce useful conclusions for the patient.

Additional notes

1. Some experiments will require the patient to take direct action and others to seek out information. Either way there is some risk of distress or other threats which need proper evaluation prior to commitment to the experiment.
2. Ensure that experiments that include the possibility of performance failure are set up in such a way as to be able to constructively utilise "failure" data. Also ensure that the patient can tolerate this type of learning experience.
3. The experiments are part of the experiential learning process and the Information sheet: Experiential learning cycle will usually be appropriate in these tasks and sets out the basics of the procedure to be followed.
4. Bennett-Levy et al. (2004) describes in detail a very thorough preparatory checklist for conducting behavioural experiments together with an enormous collection of experiments for a host of common mental health problems.

Bennett-Levy, J., Butler, G., Fennell, M., Hackman, A., Mueller, M. and Westbrook, D. (2004) *Oxford Guide to Behavioural Experiments in Cognitive Therapy*, Oxford: Oxford University Press.

Techniques

Behavioural rehearsal

Purpose

Establish a new pattern of behaving, including practising better coping skills. Practise makes the learning more effective and enhances confidence.

Method

1. With the patient develop a new strategy which may deal with the situation differently and more effectively than the old one.
2. Together attempt to predict some of the effects or consequences it will produce (including the less desirable ones).
3. Plan how the new strategy will cope with each of these scenarios and how the patient will respond to the undesired outcomes.
4. If the strategy involves dealing differently with particular social interactions:
   a) Try it out, probably with you playing the patient first whilst they role play others in the situation. Reverse roles when both of you are satisfied with how the strategy works in various scenarios.
   b) Ask the patient to practise with a friend or in front of the mirror.
5. If the strategy involves applying specific coping techniques (such as breathing exercises):
   a) Practise the strategy in session.
   b) Ask the patient to practise at home on a very regular basis (usually at least once a day).
   c) Where a new strategy is intended to replace an old "automatic" habit (such as diaphragmatic breathing replacing rapid, shallow breathing) then it will be necessary to "over-learn" the strategy by practising many times each day.
6. Ask the patient to keep a record of situations where the new strategy has been applied and evaluate its effectiveness need for modification (see Record form: Event-action-outcome).

Technique

Believable alternative thoughts

Purpose

Thoughts that are not credible to the thinker are not going to produce change. Therefore, alternative thoughts that are both helpful and believable are needed for constructive change to occur.

Method

1. Check the alternative thoughts offered in the thought record and ask how much the patient believes each alternative on a scale of 0–100%.
2. For new thoughts that are strongly believed (with ratings above 85%) then rehearsal of the new thought may be sufficient to enable it to be an effective influence in the future.
3. For new thoughts with a 50–85% rating then discuss ways in which credibility might be enhanced (by further behavioural experiments, surveys, opinions of respected other people, and so on).
4. For new thoughts with a rating of less than 50% and for those which do not respond to attempts at enhancement follow these steps:

   a. Identify the unhelpful or negative thought that is produced alongside this new but not very credible alternative thought.
   b. Check into which type of mental trap this unhelpful thought falls.
   c. Develop an alternative to this new automatic thought.
   d. Rate the belief in this new alternative.
   e. Once again, if its believability is relatively low then identify the further automatic thought that undermines its credibility and challenge this thought too.
   f. Repeat the process until a highly credible alternative is produced.

   See Record form: Believable alternatives

Additional notes

1. The second layer unhelpful thought can be characterised by "That's all very well to say, but…" at which point a negative thought that underpinned the previous unhelpful thought emerges.
2. This may seem like an endless process but it is very likely that new unhelpful thoughts will be effectively challenged by the second or third layer.
3. If the "Yes, but . . ." process seems to be repetitive then there is likely to be a circular argument being created because of an assumed link between things which is not being challenged or investigated. For example, someone might say "I wouldn't be able to do that because nobody in my family ever listens to me." Alternatives that explore the art of getting through to family members and challenging the over-generalisation about their deafness may overlook the fact that the link between persuading them and taking action may be irrelevant or the wrong way round – maybe their agreement is irrelevant or maybe they take more notice when something actually happens.

Technique

Breathing control

Purpose

Prevent hyperventilation and feelings of anxiety, panic and loss of control induced by self-induced laboured breathing or rapid and shallow breathing.

Method

1. Establish that breathing difficulties are not caused by physical disorder.
2. Explain the effects of rapid-shallow breathing on the body (see Information sheet: Stress response).
3. Explain and demonstrate the diaphragmatic breathing method (see Information sheet: Relaxed breathing exercise).
4. Encourage the patient to briefly induce these symptoms by deliberately breathing in a rapid-shallow way.
5. Guide the patient in using diaphragmatic breathing to remove the symptoms again.
6. Explain that neither rapid-shallow breathing nor the induced symptoms are dangerous.
7. Explain about hyperventilation and re-breathing with a paper bag.
8. Ask the patient to practise muscle relaxation exercises daily with special emphasis on abdominal relaxation (because of the restrictive effect abdominal tension has on diaphragmatic breathing). See Techniques: Relaxation and Information sheet: Muscle relaxation exercise.
9. Ask the patient to practise diaphragmatic breathing for 2–3 breaths every hour throughout the day (see Techniques: Behavioural rehearsal and Information sheet: Relaxed breathing exercise).

Additional notes

1. The deliberate over-breathing exercise should only be undertaken if the patient fully understands the rationale and has confidence in your judgement (see Techniques: Psycho-education).
2. Over-monitoring of breathing can produce a laboured and over-controlled style of "deep breathing" (that is, upper chest breathing) and air swallowing which is just as likely to induce symptoms as a state of anxiety. Learning to breathe easily from the diaphragm but not to monitor it can be a hard (and seemingly contradictory) message to get across.
3. Patients may struggle at first to get to grips with diaphragmatic breathing. Encourage them to focus on abdominal relaxation rather than the breathing per se.

Techniques

Challenging unhelpful thoughts

Purpose

Develop a different perspective and attitude that is more helpful to achieving change, including emotional benefit.

Method

1. Identify the association between certain events and certain thoughts (see Record forms: CBT diary).
2. Identify "automatic" thoughts – those where the patient believes the event triggers feeling without any thought (often gaps in the "Thought" column in the CBT diary).
3. Identify thoughts that create and maintain negative emotions, obstruct beneficial change and prevent constructive learning from experiences (see Information sheet: Mental traps).
4. Examine any evidence that supports these thoughts and the ways in which belief in them is sustained (see Information sheet: Examining the evidence).
5. Explore alternative ways of thinking about these same events that could be more helpful, identifying how these alternatives could impact on personal perspective, feelings and behaviour.
6. Try applying these alternative thoughts when those same events occur in order to discover whether they are effective and believable.
7. Repeat testing alternatives to refine and improve them and enhance belief.
8. Rehearse "new" thoughts that are beneficial and believed in, so that old ways of thinking do not re-establish themselves out of habit.

Additional notes

1. People commonly confuse positive affirmations and "thinking positively" with this method. The aim here is to achieve a realistic and constructive perspective not an "upbeat" outlook.
2. Self-reassurance and even thoughts like "I shouldn't think so negatively" can sometimes get used as alternatives, but these are themselves unhelpful thoughts and may need to be challenged.
3. Thoughts are nebulous things, so a written record using a form such as the Event-emotion-thought analysis form is important to success in using this method.
4. Belief in the new thought may take time to develop; there is rarely an overnight change.

Examples

A range of techniques are used in helping to examine and challenge unhelpful thoughts. See Techniques: Cognitive change methods: a summary for further information.

Technique

Cognitive change methods: a summary

Purpose

To enable the person to develop an alternative perception of a situation or respond to it in a different manner

Method

The following is a key-word reminder of the methods described in Chapter 14 and sometimes elsewhere in the Techniques section.

Cognitive techniques for changing attention focus

1. Mental distraction.
2. Here-and-now focus.
3. Stimulus control.
4. Vigilance modification.
5. Challenging distorted selective attention (selective abstractions).

Cognitive techniques for changing analysis and interpretation

1. De-catastrophising.
   a. Logical reasoning
   b. Examining the evidence

2. Cognitive restructuring.
   a. Re-attribution
   b. Re-appraisal
   c. Re-conceptualisation

3. Cognitive awareness and constructive thinking.
   a. Awareness of automatic thoughts
   b. Identifying mental traps
      i. oversimplification
      ii. speculation
      iii. biased selection
      iv. dogmatism
   c. Challenging unhelpful thoughts

Cognitive techniques for changing decision making

1. Commitment.
   a. Acceptance
   b. Belief
   c. Weighing pros and cons

2. Guides.
   a. Credible advice
   b. Rules of thumb
   c. Assertive thinking
   d. Re-examined rules and standards

3. Tolerance of uncertainty.

Techniques

Denial: strategies for encouraging acceptance

Purpose

If, on balance, denial is considered a major obstacle then the following steps are suggested for helping a change of attitude towards greater acceptance.

Method

Starting from the position that the patient denies that anything is wrong:

- Examine the facts together
  1. What other view has been expressed? [*for example, explore the idea that there is a serious/terminal illness*].
  2. What evidence has supported this other view? [*encourage the patient to voice this view*].
  3. If this other view were right, what thoughts would that lead you to have? ["*however awful or unlikely and even though you don't believe this view*"].

- Examine the negative thoughts in 3. above
  1. Get them all fully stated, help amplify them if necessary [*Explore the myths, exaggerations and distortions slowly and carefully*].
  2. Write them all down for further consideration [*accept them as reasonable*].
  3. Examine and discuss each of them in turn and check out the supporting evidence for those ideas and fears [*looking for a more realistic perspective as you go along.But don't be too positive, don't over-reassure and don't do all the work!*].

- Identify alternative approach
  1. If this other view were right, what actions and plans would you do differently? [or *"how would you advise someone else in this situation?"*].
  2. Would there be problems in making these changes?
  3. How might these problems be overcome?

- Re-assess current belief and plan
  1. Do you still believe nothing's wrong?
  2. Would there be advantages in making changes in your approach?

Additional notes

1. Plenty of time and patience will be needed, so do not begin unless you can proceed at the right pace for the patient.
2. If you do not have the time or temperament to do this or if your relationship with the patient is not strong enough then identify a colleague who will work better with the patient on this task.

Techniques

Denial: strategies for engaging the patient

Purpose

Establish a constructive and trusting relationship which becomes available to give support and advice as and when the patient requires it.

Method

1. Choosing the right person – gentle, watchful approach.
2. Taking time – a little and often.
3. Collaboration – finding a recognised need to work on.
4. Self disclosure – making openness safe.
5. Respectfulness – recognising the right to deny/avoid.
6. Telling anecdotes – relating relevant and irrelevant case histories.

Additional notes

1. The limitations in role may be frustrating but can be seen as an investment in the future.
2. Self disclosures should be relatively light as with a fairly good friend, but without any sense of confiding.
3. Irrelevant case histories can be useful for creating the right tone without creating pressure. They may also sometimes provoke a response from the patient highlighting the difference.
4. Care should always be taken to ensure that anecdotes do not identify people or make the patient fear breech of confidence or reveal a judgemental attitude.

Techniques

Denial: strategies for reducing distressing thoughts

Purpose

Enable the patient to think about and discuss issues and concerns without feeling emotionally overwhelmed and out of control.
Eliminate the need to use cognitive avoidance as a method for trying to cope.

Method

1. **Emotional expression** – setting aside limited time to allow "unpleasant" thoughts, think the worst and then get busy again. Perhaps use a diary as a way to express these thoughts and feelings (See Techniques: Emotional expression and Expressive writing).
2. **Desensitisation** – repeated exposure in short bursts to avoided thoughts or words whilst physically relaxing. Also, allowing others to talk briefly about avoided issues whilst relaxing (see Techniques: Graded activities).
3. **Cognitive restructuring** (especially de-catastrophising) – examining the really awful possible implications and the myths and hidden fears, then putting them in context with the reality, getting information to challenge the misconceptions and re-examining the daily priorities and the influence of dying on decision-making (for all of us).

Additional notes:

None of these methods should be used to challenge denial without clear agreement and trust from the patient. Engagement with the patient is more important than trying to force change.

Technique

Denial: suggestions for questions to ask

Purpose

Explore whether or not the patient is finding that the denial coping strategy is causing problems, whilst avoiding confronting the denial process directly.

Method

1. Embed questions about denial within a more general interview that feels comfortable and safe to the patient.
2. Clarify that it is denial not lack of information that is the difficulty.
3. Raise questions about areas of emotional difficulty or sensitivity which may indicate that the denial strategy produces distress or breaks down.
4. Raise questions which explore any interference with normal life or treatment produced by the denial strategy.

Additional notes

1. Usually this type of interview is best done without others present – especially if they are likely to speak for the patient or press for the information that the patient is trying to avoid.
2. Ensure that questions do not confront or attempt to breech the denial strategy.

Examples

♦ **Coping difficulties: Is denial no longer working protectively?**
♦ Are you having odd dreams or nightmares?
♦ Do you get sudden, unexplained feelings of anxiety or panic?
♦ Do you become irritable or angry for no obvious reason?
♦ Do you avoid certain people or places or avoid reading or hearing certain things?
♦ Do you feel very alone, separate from or different from other people, maybe even your own family?

♦ **Struggling with knowledge: Is fearful avoidance causing emotional problems?**
 ♦ What do you know about your illness?
 ♦ What do you remember other people telling you about it?
 ♦ How do you feel when you think about that?
 ♦ What do you do to cope with those feelings?

♦ **Treatment compliance: Will it be obstructed by the patient's denial response?**
 ♦ Would you like to know more about treatment options?
 ♦ To what extent do you want to be involved in the decisions about your medical treatment?
 ♦ Do you need more time to think about the treatment options before a decision is made?
 ♦ Do you have any particular worries about the treatment we've been discussing?
 ♦ Do you want to know any more about why this treatment has been recommended?

Techniques

Effective communication skills

Purpose

Convey to others information, opinions, questions, suggestions and ideas in a manner that is clear and understandable to the recipient.

Method

- Allow enough time – to be confident of explaining fully and responding to questions and other comments. It is important to remember that the recipient may take longer to assimilate new information (especially if it is complicated or emotionally demanding) than it will take you to say it.
- Get attention – because without it you cannot communicate and expect the information to be fully or correctly assimilated. Do not assume that because you are ready to communicate the other person is ready to listen.
- Make one point – at a time. If there are several pieces of information to impart, then the other person will helped in taking it all in if it is dealt with one item at a time (perhaps after laying out a mini-agenda of topics to cover at the beginning of the conversation). Resist moving to the next topic until satisfied that the current one is fully covered. Recognise before the other person begins to suffer information overload that it is time to stop.
- Be prompt and simple – getting quickly to the main point helps understanding. Further elaboration and explanation may be useful but usually makes more sense to the recipient after the main point has been made.
- Don't rush – by talking fairly slowly and allowing pauses. Give opportunities for the other person to interrupt and pick up on non-verbal signals that indicate that they are not understanding or no longer paying full attention (see Information sheet: Listening skills).
- Speak clearly – by not mumbling, ensuring the person can hear you, not gabbling and taking care that your accent is understandable to that person. Just because others understand us and hear us clearly is not enough reason to assume that this person can do so, too.
- Avoid jargon – means not just the technical stuff (such as medical terms), but also pet abbreviations and everyday business-speak. You may not be able to entirely avoid it or even spot it happening but you can give the other person encouragement to point it out when you do.
- Encourage questions – as part of the communication process. Without questions and comments the communication is one-way and there is no feedback on how effective it has been.
- Resist tangents – involves the same issues as in "Make one point" above and has the added danger that it may confuse both of you as to the main points to be made.
- Respect disagreement and emotion – because they do not indicate a communication failure but a difference of perspective to which the recipient is entitled. In communicating effectively it is not a good idea to try to control the outcome because that may encourage you to manipulate or even distort the information you wish to convey.

Techniques

Emotional expression

Purpose

Give an opportunity to release emotions safely, identify them, understand them more fully and (especially with negative emotions) reducing their intensity by giving vent to them.

Method

1. Ascertain that the patient wants change in this emotional experience.
2. Examine the nature, intensity and current expression of the emotion.
3. Establish its "rationality" for the patient: events (including memories) repeatedly trigger the same emotional reaction and helpful thoughts and behaviours (although in other ways effective) do not significantly change this.
4. Identify an activity medium by which the emotion can be safely released (physical exercise, screaming into a pillow, writing, painting, playing music).
5. Set a regular (usually daily) schedule for deliberately giving time to memories and events that will trigger the emotional response in such a way that the emotional expression methods can be used.
6. Set a limit to the time for this emotional exposure so that an end time and follow-up distraction or relaxation can be determined. Often about 30 minutes will be more than sufficient.
7. Follow-up activities need to be intellectually distracting but emotionally undemanding.
8. If the emotion intrudes at times other than those scheduled, then prompt use of the usual emotional expression method is desirable. If this is not practical then an alternative coping strategy needs to be prepared for use at such times and until the normal method for emotional expression can be safely employed.

Additional notes

1. Do not assume that the patient wants ease from the emotional distress. Sometimes people want to feel these intense experiences and hold on to them.
2. Grieving for loss, feeling terror at the recall of traumatic experiences or being angry whilst being treated badly are all examples of strong emotions which will persist whilst the person is constructively addressing their problems.
3. Reading or listening to music are not personally expressive and act as soothing distractions rather than sources of emotional expression.
4. Often the opportunity afforded to "off-load" without being judged is quite sufficient and further active interventions are not needed (see Technique: Basic counselling skills).
5. Meeting people who have had similar experiences can, for some be an extremely valuable opportunity to share and learn whilst getting the additional benefit of not feeling the only one in this position.

Examples:

See Technique: Expressive writing for a detailed examination of a particularly effective method.

Technique

Expressive writing

Purpose

Expressive writing can supplement brief CBT – allowing extra reflective opportunity between sessions or beyond the end of therapy.

Method

There are various methods and the choice is often largely patient preference. Actual writing is not required – for patients who cannot hand write, typing or audio tape may be a better option.

1. Keeping a daily free text journal or diary is popular with many patients.
2. Keeping a structured diary – recording reflections on certain kinds or themes of events or experiences can be helpful as an adjunct to therapy.
3. Writing stories – creating metaphorical tales – helps some patients.
4. The most researched technique is as follows:

Encourage the patient to pick a topic such as a recent traumatic experience, a difficult decision, a problem in a relationship which is troubling them deeply and suggest the patient find a time and somewhere where he/she will not be disturbed and **write for 15–20 minutes** on this subject. They should try to write about:

a. What happened.
b. What led up to it.
c. What has happened since.
d. Include all their innermost thoughts and feelings about it.
e. Write about how it connects with other times and events and themes in their life.

It does not matter if they repeat themselves. Spelling, grammar and correct use of English are not important. But they need to keep writing all the time if possible and not keep stopping to read and correct what they have put. It may help to tackle the same subject in the same way two or three days running. Reading and/or sharing what has been written is optional. The patient should expect the process to be quite an emotional one because the topic they pick is one they are struggling with. Sometimes people find they cry for much of the time they are writing. Others feel quite intense anger or anxiety as they write. This is evidence they are dealing with important material and they should not be put off by it. Encourage them to allow enough time (15 to 20 minutes) at the end of the session to reflect and collect themselves before trying to get on with their normal day-to-day life.

Additional notes

People for whom English is not the first language, may wish to experiment with writing in their native language which is often more powerful

Technique

Graded activities

Purpose

Provide a means of building confidence or stamina.

Method

1. Develop an agreed goal to aim for.
2. Identify what can be achieved now.
3. Plan a series of steps between current situation and goal that take into account the confidence or stamina issues (see Information sheets: Goal setting: The step-by-step approach and Examples of goal setting; and Record form: Goal planning: step-by-step record).
4. Encourage strict adherence to the step-by-step plan, only moving on to next step once previous step is <u>repeatedly</u> achieved in comfort.

Additional notes

1. Where stamina or pain is a limiting factor you may need to consider the Pacing Technique section before proceeding.
2. Make sure that the goal is realistically achievable and is specific enough to be recognised when it is achieved.
3. Be prepared to add in extra steps if the current steps turn out to be too ambitious.
4. If the goal needs to be modified, only allow it to be more modest, do not let it become harder – it's better to achieve success and then move on to setting new goals, rather than move the goal posts!

Techniques

Listening skills

Purpose

Provide signals that reassure the speaker that you are giving your full attention, understand what is being said and wish the speaker to continue.

Method:

- Eye contact – by looking directly at the speaker or (less usually) perhaps staring at some other point. Looking away from the speaker and especially allowing one's gaze to wander over a wide area are frequently taken as signals of a loss of interest in the conversation.
- Posture – interest and involvement, together with respect and empathy can all be conveyed through the orientation of the body, the distance of the one person from the other and the relative positioning (on equal height chairs, one standing whilst one sits etc.). Attentive listening can be communicated by sitting reasonably close, with body directed towards the other patient and leaning slightly forward.
- Head nods – with slight movements of the head the listener communicates understanding and agreement (with nods) and empathy with distress and concurrence with negatives (with head shakes).
- Facial expression – our pleasure, disapproval, understanding, confusion, annoyance and joy are easily communicated in our face, so the speaker will seek out these or other messages from our expression and is likely to interpret a blank expression as indifference or inattention.
- Vocal signals – we communicate interest, understanding and agreement through small vocal signals such as "uh-uh" and sometimes words like "yes" or "really." With these we are not contributing to the conversation or interrupting the flow, but instead, encouraging the speaker to continue.
- Stillness – movement will suggest to the speaker that the listener is in a hurry to get away and does not have the time or inclination to listen. Indeed it is a l way of beginning to curtail a conversation that many of us use in normal daily life. Fidgeting and gestures will be distracting for the speaker and communicate impatience or inattention.
- Checking back – summarising, clarifying points or simply echoing what has been said sends a signal to the speaker that he or she has been attended to and understood. Even if there is apparent lack of understanding, the checking back assures the speaker of interest and concern.

Additional notes

1. A special listening style will come across as insincere, so whilst adopting the listening skills as above, it is important that your manner continues to accord with what the patient will have already observed.
2. Mannerisms, head nods and vocal signals can all be distracting and off-putting, so moderation is recommended.
3. Similarly, excessive stillness can seem like inhibition or fear, so a degree of natural ease is required.
4. Self-conscious application of listening skills will probably mean that you are not actually concentrating and truly listening! If you are not confident about your ability to convey a listening manner, then practise it with friends and colleagues, so that it is less self-conscious by the time you really need to use it.

Technique

Mental distraction

Purpose

Produce an effective shift of attention away from a cycle of unhelpful thoughts and memories or persistent emotional or physical distress

Method

1. Identify events and activities which are effective in drawing the patient's attention, making it difficult or impossible for her or him to sustain concentration on other things.
2. Ask the patient to introduce one of these distracters whenever the sources of distress occur and do not pass quickly.
3. Clarify that the object of the exercise is not to suppress the thoughts or feelings, but simply to prevent them dominating the patient's attention.
4. If attention begins to drift back to the source of distress, then the introduction of other distracters may be effective but other techniques may be more appropriate than persistence with mental distraction.

Additional notes

1. Mental distraction is not the same as mental relaxation and often involves becoming busier rather than quieter. Consequently, tiredness may be a limiting factor in the use of this method.
2. Distraction is intended to disrupt a specific pattern when it is expected that from that point forward the patient will then settle into a different pattern of thought or emotion. If the unwanted pattern quickly returns (such as focusing on the pain) then other techniques may be more appropriate (such as Information sheet: Mindfulness exercises or Techniques: Emotional expression).
3. Mental distraction should never be used to totally avoid or suppress unwanted thoughts or feelings. Attempts to block thoughts and emotions in this way often increases their intensity and frequency of occurrence.

Examples

1. Typical methods include intellectually demanding tasks, conversation, absorbing reading or listening to talking radio. These things will disrupt the "thought dialogue" in the patient's head. TV works less well unless it is very absorbing because it is possible to gain visual information from the set whilst thinking verbally about something else.
2. Similarly, if the thoughts or memories are primarily visual, then a visually changing and demanding scene is likely to be more intrusive and disruptive to the distressing pattern than will be conversation or other verbal inputs.
3. Music tends to work only for musicians or musical connoisseurs unless people are prepared to focus attention on music that is not congruent with their mood.

Technique

Mindfulness

Purpose

In mindfulness training we are not trying to change belief in thoughts, just to introduce the idea of <u>thought watching</u>. Many patients find it highly liberating to see that their thoughts are just thoughts – not "me" or "reality." When we are able to remember that thoughts are just <u>events in the mind</u> – we can turn <u>towards</u> the difficult thoughts and feelings with curiosity, rather than expend energy trying to avoid or defend ourselves from awareness of them. In turn this can make it easier to manage difficult situations in life and frightening experiences in a calmer, clearer sighted way. Mindful meditation can also help to reduce the tendency to ruminate on what cannot be resolved.

Method

1. 8–10 x 2 hour weekly sessions and daily homework of up to 10–60 minutes.
2. Usually done in groups of 12+.
3. Formal practise of mindful meditations in group followed by discussion of what is experienced and later for homework daily. The meditations require participants to perform the activities focusing with curiosity on the experience.
   a. mindful eating
   b. body scan
   c. mindful stretching/yoga
   d. mindful walking
   e. mindfulness of breath/body/hearing/thinking/choiceless awareness
   f. informal practise
      i. mindfulness of everyday activities
      ii. mindfulness of pleasant/unpleasant events
      iii. mindfulness of breathing – "anchor" – "breathing with"
   g. thoughts aren't facts exercises

Additional notes

1. Mindfulness training is not part of this CBT programme and it is recommended that you undertake further training yourself before using the methods with patients.[1]
2. Tape and CD sets of the meditations commonly used in mindfulness training are available to buy Their use on a standalone basis has not been evaluated but some patients have reported benefits.[2]

Example

See Information sheet: Mindfulness exercises for simple introductory exercises to try.

---

[1] UK based training is available from the North Wales Centre for Mindfulness Research and Practice on site or as a distance learning package – http://www.bangor/mindfulness.

[2] Jon Kabat Zinn CDs and Tapes available from http://www.mindfulnesstapes.com.

Technique

Pacing

Purpose

Reduce the risk of self-induced fatigue or pain through careful self-management including awareness of signals from the body.

Method

1. Outline the role of pacing in minimising symptoms of pain and fatigue (see Technique: Psycho-education).
2. Ask the patient to keep a record of activities and evaluate each day as "Good" or "Bad" in terms of fatigue or pain (or both if relevant). The patient can use a slightly adapted activity schedule for this (see Record form: Activity schedule).
3. Based on information from the activity schedule that justifies concern about pacing, explain in greater detail the need for careful self-management and the types of self-regulation to employ. Provide the patient with Information sheets: Pacing and pacing examples.
4. Identify activities which appear to contribute most to the generating of these symptoms.
5. Set time limits for each of these activities based on estimating how much could be done on a bad day without adverse effects (see Record form: Pacing record form).
6. Monitor the number of good days achieved with the strict time limits observed. Record form: Goal setting: Step-by-step can be used for this work with the start point indicated by time limit for bad days and current number of good days per week. Goal will be 6–7 good days + a realistic estimate of maximum time limit.
7. As good days increase, so it is possible to step up time limits on the identified activities (by 5–10% each step).

Additional notes

1. Many patients find it very difficult to understand or comply with pacing requirements despite grasping the basic principles. It may take several attempts and detailed scrutiny of what went wrong before success is achieved.
2. Record forms may have to be specially adapted or invented to meet the specific requirements of individual patients.
3. It is easy to confuse resting, relaxation and changing activity. Whilst in some instances physical exertion or mental concentration induces fatigue and resting is therefore required, in other instances the tension and stress of the activity means that relaxation is the beneficial course of action. However, there will be other occasions where changing from mental to physical activity, or from sitting to standing, or from working with others to working alone will provide the pacing changes that are required. Careful initial assessment needs to distinguish the issues and the pacing strategies.

Examples

See Information sheet: Pacing examples

Technique

Problem solving

Purpose

To resolve an issue that is causing difficulties when it is within the power of the person to achieve that resolution. Normally this is appropriate where the problem is likely to persist unless resolved and the benefits of solving it outweigh the costs of doing so. The health care professional is aiming to help the patient learn how to determine when to commit to problem solving and how to work through the process in a systematic and adaptive manner.

Method

1. Ask the patient to describe the precise nature of the problem and its consequences.
2. Help the patient decide what outcome is desired (Information sheet: SMART guidelines).
3. Help the patient review and identify the factors causing and maintaining the problem that will need to be sorted out (see Technique: Socratic questioning).
4. Encourage the patient to explore options for strategies for dealing with this problem including logical alternatives and advice from experts or friends with relevant experiences.
5. Ask the patient to examine the advantages and disadvantages of each possible strategy.
6. Help the patient to develop a plan for a systematic approach (Information sheet: Goal setting and the step-by-step approach may be relevant).
7. Get the patient to set boundary limits related to the advantages versus disadvantages of the strategy chosen (such as time limits, cost and assumed level of difficulty of the challenge).
8. In taking the first steps towards resolving the problem advise the patient to be aware of the need to adapt plans as new and feedback information become available (see Information sheet: Experiential learning cycle).
9. As progress is made towards resolving the problem, ask the patient to repeatedly reassess to ensure boundary limits are not crossed.
10. If progress is not made or boundary limits are exceeded then recommend that the patient return to step 4.

Additional notes

1. The temptation can be very strong to problem-solve situations on behalf of the patient, but this will foster dependency and do nothing to enhance the patient's confidence or self-esteem.
2. Sometimes the patient has become stuck because there is more than one problem that is being tackled. People do at times lump problems together and seek a single solution to them all. Often the only single solution is then the fantasy one such as winning the lottery or the miracle cure. The patient may need help with "chunking" problems into smaller separate ones.

Technique

Psycho-education

Purpose

Provide information about psychological processes and physiological responses that assist the patient gain a greater sense of personal control over what is happening to them and enables them to understand the rationale behind the use of psychological methods.

Method

1. Allow the patient plenty of time to fully explain all the issues and concerns including perceived links and associations between events and responses. Do not offer explanations or correct mis-understandings or misinterpretations. See Technique: Listening skills.
2. Ask relevant and insightful questions which further clarify your understanding of the issues to be discussed and provide the patient with reassurance of knowledge in this field.
3. Provide a clear explanation of the processes and rationale for how to bring about beneficial change following the guidance in Techniques: Effective communication skills.
4. Use diagrams and handouts to illustrate and reinforce the information.
5. Encourage the patient to ask questions and take notes.
6. Reassure the patient that it is alright to go back over the information.
7. Offer to go over it all again at the next meeting.
8. Stop before the patient becomes confused by information overload.
9. Check back about the patient's assimilation of the information at follow-up meetings and before attempting to put it into practise.

Additional notes

1. Psycho-education is usually an early feature of psychological interventions, but if introduced too soon, it may lead the patient to doubt you have a full understanding of the problems.
2. Handouts (such as many of the Information sheets in this *Toolkit*) and self-help books can offer a wealth of support information, but it is important to take the patient through this material rather than simply pass it to them to read later. There needs to be opportunities for elaborating how these rather more generalised statements specifically apply in this particular instance. Without that, the patient may fail to grasp the full relevance and value of the information.
3. Whilst a session devoted to psycho-education may take on the form of a lesson more than a treatment consultation, it is important that the relationship between you and the patient remains responsive to the personal needs of the patient rather than sticking to a lesson plan.

Examples

See

1. Techniques: Assertiveness skills and related Information sheets for a typical example of help which includes a high level of psycho-education.
2. Problem: Panic attacks is a good example of a difficulty involving various treatment methods the effectiveness of which depends heavily on the psycho-educational rationale and explanation about safety behaviours.

The Mental Health Handbook by T. Powell (ISBN 0-86388-107-6) is a valuable source of further information sheets that are suitable for photocopying.

Technique

Purposeful planning

Purpose

Provide structure, system and direction for activities and help motivate and simplify decision making.

Method

1. Realistic expectations and goal setting
   a. Identify worthwhile possible goals (see Information sheet: SMART guidelines and Record form: Your ideas for goals).
   b. Work out the steps that need to be taken towards achieving each goal and obstacles to be overcome (see Information sheets: Goal setting: the step-by-step approach and examples of goal setting; and Record form: Goal planning: step-by-step record).
   c. Keep a record of progress towards goals and adapt goals (and steps) if circumstances change.
2. Scheduling activities
   a. Structured day/week
      i. Identify "working day" and "working week" so as to determine "free time" (perhaps use Record form: Activity schedule).
      ii. Specify days and times for particular routine tasks and other times for the non-routine work.
      iii. Preserve "free time" for relaxing and doing pleasurable activities.
   b. Achievements and pleasures
      i. See Technique: Activity monitoring.
      ii. Create awareness of activities that provide a sense of achievement or pleasure using Record form: Achievements and pleasures.
      iii. Introduce new daily achievements or pleasures if record form indicates too few.
      iv. Refer to realistic expectations and goal setting if there is difficulty identifying any valued achievements or pleasures.
3. New things to do
   a. Identify novel and potentially interesting activities (Information sheet: SMART guidelines and Record form: Your ideas for goals may assist with this).
   b. Resist unhelpful thoughts about trying to predict enjoyableness. See Techniques: Challenging unhelpful thoughts and Congitive change methods: a summary if necessary.
   c. Experiment with new activities and evaluate each afterwards (use Record form: Event-action-outcome if there are a number of such activities to be evaluated).

Additional notes

1. Success encourages success, whilst failure demotivates. It is important that any purposeful planning has a high probability of at least some success. Many of those requiring these techniques will be prone to setting unrealistic expectations and plans which then fail: hence the problems currently being dealt with.

2. Record keeping helps establish structure to thinking and so to the plan or schedule, so encourage its usage.
3. When planning a structured day, the patient needs to feel that this is of personal benefit rather than a moral a duty.

Technique

Relaxation exercises

Purpose

Provide an enhanced sense of personal control and calm.

Method

1. Muscle relaxation:
   a. "Progressive relaxation" – based on Jacobson's exercises
      i. Lie on comfortable floor or other firm surface in low light.
      ii. Close eyes.
      iii. Working round the body, tense and then relax muscles. Tensing heightens awareness of the muscles and enables the subsequent resting period to contribute to the relaxation sensation (see Information sheet: Muscle relaxation exercise for more details).
   b. "Differential relaxation"
      i. Sit in chair and relax the whole body.
      ii. Once relaxed begin to look around whilst maintaining physical relaxation throughout the body.
      iii. Get up and move around and carry out various small actions recognising the tension in the parts of the body involved but maintaining relaxation elsewhere.

2. Mental relaxation
   a. Images that produce feelings of wellbeing
      i. Sit comfortably or lie down, usually with eyes closed and few distractions.
      ii. Use a planned image or taped guided image to introduce a pleasant scene to be observed and studied in detail.
      iii. Imagining walking through the scene may enable it to last longer than if the image is of lying still on a grassy river bank or similar.
   b. Images that produce distraction from worry
      i. Sitting comfortably or lying down, usually with eyes closed.
      ii. Imagine walking through a familiar environment (such as a room of the house or the garden) and try to picture all the objects there.
      iii. Alternatively imagine studying an object in great detail (see Information sheet: Mental relaxation exercise) or a simple set of colours and shapes which are hard to visualise and hold in the mind.

3. Sensory relaxation
   a. Relaxing music
   b. Sound effect tapes and CDs (sometimes with exercises as above) such as whale sounds or bird song

   c. Massage

   d. Pet stroking

   e. Scented candles and some aromatherapy oils

   f. Hot baths and saunas

Additional notes

1. Some people become anxious about letting go and so paradoxically become panicky whilst doing relaxation exercises. Psycho-education about potential benefits (see Information sheet: Effects of stress) and the issues about loss of control will need to be dealt with before they can benefit from relaxation.

2. Good imagery control is necessary with mental relaxation exercises and they are not recommended for anyone who may experience intrusive distressing thoughts (such as being attacked whilst lying on the beach).

Techniques:

Respectfulness skills

- **Address the person in their preferred way**

  Do not assume you know how the person wishes to be referred to – always ask. If their name is hard to pronounce, take time for the person to teach you properly. If you are being asked to refer to them by their first name then reciprocate but accept their right not to do so because sometimes the person will prefer it that way. When talking about the person to others stick to formal styles of address and if the person is present include them in the conversation with eye contact and checking back, giving them opportunities to speak up and ask questions.

- **Accept differences of outlook and feeling**

  Resist making critical or humorous observations that emphasise your different perspective. Do not allow personal opinions expressed by the other person to encourage you into expressing your own views, although you may wish to point out that your non-committal responses do not necessarily imply agreement with theirs.

- **Avoid being judgemental**

  Approval or disapproval of other people is rarely appropriate outside our close circle of family and friends. Even in matters of health care and compliance with treatment it is important to respect their rights to choose to do things differently from what is recommended. Professional concern needs to be clearly distinguishable from any personal disapproval. In the event of the person detecting signs of personal disapproval then there should be a sincere re-emphasis of their right to make their own choices. In health care, if it is genuinely difficult to resist being judgemental then it is important to seek to be relieved of involvement in the patient's care.

- **Avoid becoming defensive**

  Critical comments and questions about the service you or others may be providing need to be listened to sympathetically with an emphasis on seeing things from that person's perspective. If necessary, guidance on how to make a formal complaint should be offered. Frequently, the person is primarily concerned with expressing her or his feelings and being listened to and does not seek an explanation. It is important to clear up misunderstandings but do not offer any other explanation unless it is wanted even if you feel the perception is unfair.

- **Focus on solutions, not blame**

  The response needs to be one of offering guidance and encouragement together with understanding of the personal perspective and circumstances of the other person. Carelessness, errors of judgement and lifestyle issues are among the number of avoidable causes of mishaps (including causing health problems or setbacks in treatment) so focus on avoiding them, not allotting blame.

- **Make allowance for distress**

  Difficult, demanding, even disruptive, behaviour will often result from the fear, depression, frustration and discomfort caused by the illness or the sense of impotence in being able to do something about it. Whilst it is important to effectively manage unreasonable behaviour assertively, this should be done with clear communication of an awareness of these issues.

- **Never raise your voice**

  A raised voice is indicative of an aggressive stance and should never be used whilst in a professional role even in response to aggressive behaviour or raised voice from the patient or carer. Even with a person who is hard of hearing it can be perceived as aggressive if the volume is misjudged so it is important to be guided by the person and use facial expressions to convey a milder manner.

Technique

Socratic questioning

Purpose

Guide discovery through asking ("naïve") questions in order to understand the patient's point of view and help discover alternatives.

Reframe the issues by teasing out:
  – false assumptions
  – inconsistencies of beliefs
  – contradictory views
  – double standards
  – faulty conclusions

Develop a way forward by clarifying:
  – alternative perspectives
  – choices
  – means by which to make choices

Method

Ask questions that:
1. *Naïve* – Are simple and informal.
2. *Assume nothing* – Enable you and the patient to:
   a. understand more fully what is being talked about
   b. identify what is not understood.
3. *Non-judgemental* – Examine inferences being drawn by the patient from specific events.
4. *Advice free* – Enable you and the patient to distinguish between fact, belief and opinion.
5. *Curious* – Explore the possibility of alternative perspectives.
6. *Focused* – Encourage identification of the most helpful perspective.

Additional notes

1. Padesky* defines a number of characteristics of good Socratic questions:
   a) the patient has the knowledge to answer;
   b) the patient's attention is drawn to information relevant to the issues;
   c) thinking moves from the concrete to the abstract;
   d) the patient is helped to re-evaluate previous conclusions and develop new ideas;
   e) the patient learns to be able to use this questioning technique for him or herself.
2. Do not ask leading questions; do not plan where the questioning is intended to lead. The best guided discovery is a genuine collaborative effort between two people who do not know where the questions and answers will eventually lead.
3. Naïve questions mean that it is ok to be puzzled. Curiosity and effort to understand are part of the guided discovery process for both participants.

See Information sheet: Socratic questioning examples for further ideas.

• Padesky C A " *Socratic questioning: changing minds or guided discovery*?" www.padesky.com

Technique

Stimulus control

Purpose

Provide an environment in which disruptive and counter-productive influences are kept to a minimum.

Method

1. Determine what it is that the patient wishes to achieve.
2. Clarify precisely what happens to obstruct the achievement of the desired goal.
3. Identify those events that block or interfere with achieving the desired goal.
4. Look for ways of removing those events or reducing their interference effect. Also examine alternative ways of achieving the desired goal.
5. Keep a record of actions taken and results (Record form: Event-action-outcome).
6. Modify strategies based on effectiveness in controlling the adverse events.

Additional notes

1. Often the "events" are simple practical concerns such as noise levels, sources of physical discomfort, interruptions, excessive caffeine consumption etc. Although aware of them the patient will have decided that he or she "should not" allow these things to be a source of disruption and therefore failed to take effective action.
2. Recognising the adverse effects on sleep and concentration of over-stimulating environments may require some psycho-education (see Techniques: Psycho-education) and relaxation training (see Information sheets: Muscle relaxation and Mental relaxation).
3. Effective use of pain-killers would also count as a stimulus control technique.

Technique

Weighing the pros and cons

Purpose

Facilitate decision making.

Method

1. Establish all the realistically achievable choices.
2. Eliminate any that will not be chosen regardless of evaluation (not acceptable, disliked, conflicts with personal values and so on).
3. List on paper all the possible advantages and disadvantages for each choice.
4. Do the same exercise as in 3. For the "do nothing" (that is, make no choice) option.
5. Devise a rating scale of importance.
6. Assign a rating score to each item in the lists.
7. Add up the scores in each column (advantages and disadvantages columns) for each choice.
8. If there is more than one choice where the advantages score is greater than the disadvantages score then the one with the highest advantage over disadvantage difference-score is the strongest choice.

Additional notes

1. This may be a task the person prefers to do alone or with which to involve others but the intention is to be imaginative and creative, so people with fixed ideas will not be helpful.
2. The brainstorming of all advantages and disadvantages should also be imaginative and creative and can involve the same other people or different ones.
3. Scorings are usually on a 0–3 or 0–5 scale and based on rating the importance of this item to the decision maker. Sometimes rational advantages or disadvantages are actually of no importance to that person, so although the item gets listed, it ends up with a 0 rating. No one other than the decision maker should give importance ratings.
4. If the outcome doesn't feel right, the person may wish to re-examine the advantages and disadvantages to see if anything has been missed or evaluated wrongly. Ultimately, the choice is with the decision maker who can still choose any option that she or he prefers.

Examples

1. See Problem: Denial and Record forms: Denial – assessing its costs and benefits and Denial – examples of pros and cons assessment for a detailed description of using this technique in a specific situation.
2. See Information sheets: Desire for change and bring about change for points to consider whilst brainstorming alternatives.

Section 2
INFORMATION SHEETS

Information sheet

Antidotes to bad days

Accepting that bad days happen and planning for them can be very constructive:

1. Know what helps and what hinders – maximise the helpful and eliminate hindrances wherever possible.
2. Prepare things that will distract and pamper you on a bad day – perhaps keep some things as special treats only available on bad days.
3. Plan good things to look forward to on your next good day (but remember the Pacing advice not to use good days to compensate for bad ones).
4. Remind yourself that bad days don't last for ever and remember previous good days after bad ones.
5. Warn people about bad days and advise how best they can behave on those days.

Tell people when today is a bad day and be prepared to remind them if they seem to forget. You can use a visual chart they can all see (like a weather barometer) if you'd rather not have to keep talking about it.

Information sheet

The Assertiveness Model

Say "Yes" to anything   Controlling
"Martyr"   Emotional blackmailer
Whingeing   Bully

Unassertive   **Assertive**   **Aggressive**
Secretive   *Open & honest*   *Opinionated*

Key Features of Assertive Behaviour

Open about my feelings and opinions
Honest and self -respecting
Direct and firm
Tactful and encouraging
Respectful of the person
Respectful of the position (status)
Sensitive to effect on other people
Content of the message fits intent
Style of the message fits intent

Saying No assertively can vary
from the pleasant/approving style:
For example "I don't like to disappoint you but on this occasion I'm going to say No"
to the disapproving/annoyed style:
For example "I am feeling cross that you do not seem to be respecting my wishes in this situation and, whilst it will be a pity for us to fall out over it, my position remains unchanged

---

Assertiveness Principles

1. Respect your own needs and feelings *and at the same time:*
2. Be sensitive to the needs and feelings of others.
3. State your own position honestly and openly.
4. Encourage the other person to be similarly open and honest.
5. Listen carefully to what is said.
6. Stick to one issue at a time.
7. Calmly and constructively discuss areas of misunderstanding/discomfort.
8. Seek a positive solution that respects and takes account of other options.
9. Accept that solutions are not always possible.
10. Prompt action is usually easier and almost always better.

Information sheet

Assertiveness rights

1. I have the right to state my own needs and set my own priorities as a person independent of any roles that I may assume in my life.
2. I have the right to be treated with respect as an intelligent, capable and equal human being.
3. I have the right to express my own feelings.
4. I have the right to express my opinions and values.
5. I have the right to say "yes" and "no" for myself.
6. I have the right to make mistakes.
7. I have the right to change my mind.
8. I have the right to say I don't understand.
9. I have the right to ask for what I want.
10. I have the right to decline responsibility for other people's problems.
11. I have the right to deal with others without being dependent on them for approval.
12. I have the right to privacy.
13. I have the right to succeed.
14. I have the right to be illogical.

Other people have these same rights and, like me, have the right to expect these rights to be respected.

Including ideas from books by Ann Dickson, Gael Lindenfield and Beverley Hare

Information sheet

Assertiveness techniques

There are a number of methods that can help with assertiveness. The most important are to be focused on a single issue and on a constructive outcome. In achieving a satisfactory outcome it will be necessary to avoid being defensive and backing down when you do not believe that it is the right thing to do.

The methods listed below can help in maintaining an assertive approach.

Technique	Strategy	Effect
Broken Record	By calm repetition - saying what you want over and over again - helps you be persistent without having to rehearse arguments or angry feelings beforehand to deal with persistence in others.	Allows you to feel comfortable in ignoring manipulative verbal side traps, argumentative baiting, irrelevant logic, and helps you stick to your point.
Workable Compromise	It is practical, whenever you feel that your self respect is not in question, to offer a workable compromise to the other person. You can always bargain goals unless the compromise affects your personal feelings of self respect. If the end goal involves a matter of your self worth, however, there can be no compromise.	Allows you to feel reasonable and flexible without feeling that you are losing or being manipulated.
Free Information	The recognition of someone's body language in everyday conversation indicates what is of interest or importance to that person.	Allows you to feel less shy in entering into conversation while at the same time prompting the other person to talk more easily about themselves.
Self-disclosure	The acceptance and initiation of discussion of both the positive and negative aspects of your personality, behaviour, lifestyle etc. to enhance social communication and reduce manipulation.	Allows you comfortably to disclose aspects of yourself and your life that previously caused feelings of ignorance, secretiveness, anxiety or guilt, and fears of gossip.
Fogging	Acceptance of manipulative criticism by calmly acknowledging to your critic the probability that there may be some truth in what he/she says, yet allows you to remain your own judge of what you do.	Allows you to receive criticism comfortably without becoming anxious or defensive, while giving no reward to those using manipulative criticism.

Negative Assertion	Acceptance of your errors and faults (without having to apologise) by strongly and sympathetically agreeing with hostile or constructive criticism of your negative qualities.	Allows you to look more comfortably at negatives in your own behaviour or personality without feeling defensive and anxious, or resorting to denial of real error, while at the same time reducing your critic's anger or hostility. Allows you time to think of effective responses and solutions as needed.
Negative Inquiry	Active prompting of criticism in order to use the information (if helpful) or exhaust it (if manipulative) while prompting your critic to be more assertive and less dependent on manipulative ploys.	Allows you more comfortably to seek out criticism about yourself in close relationships while prompting the other person to express honest negative feelings and improve communication.

Remember that assertiveness is an OPTION that you need to feel free to choose. It is not necessarily always the RIGHT thing to do, but it is always important to feel that it was a CHOICE you could take if you wanted to do so.

Information sheet:

Bad old habits: avoiding relapsing into them

> **Keep practicing** – Looking back at the handout "Methods of Behaviour Change" from session 3 provides a number of reminders of the techniques used to stop old ways and establish new ones. Knowing which ones worked for you and keeping them going will be the most effective way of avoiding drifting back to how things used to be.

> **Don't take short cuts** – Setbacks are especially likely to occur when someone is doing really well and start to believe that they've "cracked it." If you forget what you've learnt (about yourself, what works or new skills) then old habits are almost certainly going to come back. Stick to the methods that work and don't assume you don't need them any more.

> **Never assume you can't slip back** – Deeply ingrained habits may lie dormant for many years and still come back to mess you about, so you need to be aware of the things that may trigger them:

>   – What are the temptations? – Look out for those things which may make the old ways particularly attractive and seductive. Typically fatigue will make doing nothing seem very appealing, and a celebration may make that "just this once" cigarette or drink seem ok.

>   – What are the pressures? – Sometimes when you change habits you may be surprised to find that other people have been a big influence in maintaining the bad old ones. You discover this when you feel under pressure to change back. Sometimes husbands become critical and suspicious when their wives go on a diet, whilst wives complain about being given no private space when their husbands stop watching Sky Sport all weekend. Cutting back on shopping sprees or gambling will often produce sarcastic comments from old shopping-spree or gambling partners.

> **Mental traps need time and attention** – For those who have developed skills in dealing with the hazards of mental traps, there is a common misconception that they "should" be able to do all this cognitive therapy stuff at the time and in their heads. It's simply not true. If you are especially prone to falling into these traps then it is very important to work the thoughts through properly and that means using pen and paper. The most damaging of these thoughts last for hours or days, so a bit of delay in performing this written task will not do a great deal of harm. The sooner the better, but not at the expense of doing it properly. Quickly doing it in your head is exactly what caused the problem in the first place – quick thoughts lead to quick answers lead to mental traps.

> **Write a letter to yourself** – The frame of mind you are in on a good day makes it hard to imagine what it is like for you on a bad day AND vice versa. It can be a great help on a bad day to be able to access the "good day" frame of mind. One way of doing this is to write yourself a letter from your more positive mind-set perspective in which you refer to all the things that you know you brood on in your more negative mind-set, identifying the more helpful ways of looking at them, and putting them in the context of all the other important things in your life that you know get overlooked when you are in that negative mind-set.

> **Expect change (including slip-ups)** – Nothing stays the same. You have lived with uncertainty and change all your life. Expect that to continue and to include successes and failures, and changes for the better and the worse.

Information sheet

Change: bringing it about

<u>The motivation equation:</u>

Relevance to me

+

Importance in my life

+

Benefits to be gained

+

Self-belief

>

(is greater than)
Obstacles to doing it

1. Wanting to achieve a goal, even strongly wanting to, and doing something about achieving it are by no means the same thing.
2. Our determination and commitment is increased when we expect our goal to have direct impact and importance on our own lives.
3. The greater the benefits to be gained, the more determined we are likely to be to achieve this goal.
4. To shift from good intentions to doing something about it also requires that we have belief in our ability to follow through. This self-belief is not just about skills: it includes our belief in our sticking power, our ability to apply ourselves methodically, our track record in challenging setbacks and other personality qualities we see in ourselves as relevant to attaining this particular goal.
5. The difficulties that stand in the way of achieving our goal will sap some of that energy for action, sometimes counteracting the benefits and perhaps undermining the self-belief. Other events may even change the relevance or importance of this goal.

Information sheet

Change: the desire for it

<u>The change equation:</u>

Dissatisfaction with status quo
+
A vision of how things could be
+
Knowledge about first practical steps
>
(is greater than)

Cost of the change
(in money, emotions, energy, friendships etc)

1. We are most interested in achieving new goals when we want something different from how things are at present, we have a fairly clear idea of what we want to achieve and a belief in its achievability.
2. In addition our interest is fuelled when we feel we have the ability to set about starting this process and some sense of where to start.
3. All of this enthusiasm for action has to be set against the price we will have to pay. There may be a financial cost involved in achieving our goals but the greater cost may be in other ways – the physical effort, the disruption to valued routines, the conflict with other people, the fear of failure etc.
4. If the price is too high then we will put up with things as they are – at least until our dissatisfaction increases or until our vision for how we want things to be intensifies.

Information sheet

Change: the transition curve

The work of many social scientists and practitioners of psychological therapies have observed that people who are faced with sudden changes to life go though a series of powerful emotional reactions as they accept and adjust to the reality of those changes and begin the process of adapting to them. This diagram provides a simplified illustration of that adjustment process as it will occur for most people whether about losing a job, facing an unexpectedly huge bill, bereavement or the onset of a life-changing illness.

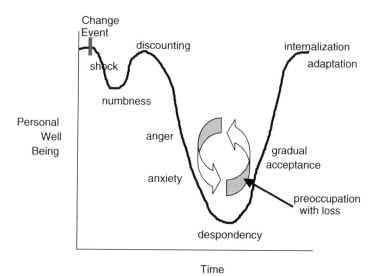

This diagram is adapted from Jones S. (1995) *Coping with Change at Work*, London: HarperCollins. She based it on information from Hopson, Scally and Stafford (1992) *Transitions: the Challenge of Change*. Management Books (2000).

The process described in the diagram is closely allied to the 5 stages described in her classic text by Kubler-Ross, E. (1969) *On Death and Dying* London: Tavistock/Routledge Publications.

Information sheet

Coping with setbacks 1

Physical health setbacks

- **Open, honest emotional expression**

  - <u>To people who are close</u> – Feelings of sadness, anger and fear are going to be quite natural at such times and the constructive approach is to express them openly if you can.

  - <u>Through expressive writing</u> – Sometimes openness is not possible or is not enough. If it's still churning around (especially in the middle of the night when everyone else is asleep) then pouring all those thoughts and feelings onto the page is a good method for achieving expressive release. For some, drawing it or talking it out loud to a tape recorder or the cat can do much the same thing.

- **Resist thought dominance**

  - <u>Remember the other important things</u> – Whilst working on the CBT programme physical ill health has been part of your life, but you have still got on and done other, important, self-rewarding and satisfying things. Get a clear sense of that and come back to this workbook and its contents as a reminder at any time when physical health or any other issue starts to monopolise your thoughts and feelings. You may even like to write yourself a special message to keep in this workbook for such occasions reminding yourself that there's more to you and your worth than your physical health.

  - <u>Mindfulness exercise</u> – At times of emotional turmoil and apprehension these exercises are the best way of achieving a little oasis of inner peace and calm. It's not running away, just giving you a chance to breathe and settle yourself before continuing.

  - <u>Here-and-now focus</u> – Remember the CBT approach is always to place the major focus of attention on the reality of the present moment and being fully aware of it. The more you are in the present time the more you are in a place where you have some control.

- **Adapt plans**

  - <u>Accept the new reality</u> – Changing circumstances need to be recognised and worked with constructively in the CBT approach. Adjusting to the changes can be an emotional rollercoaster as you go through the transition process. The mindfulness exercises and honest emotional expression can be very helpful with this process.

  - <u>Review and adjust goals and steps</u> – Recognising the new reality may come quicker than accepting it. Using this recognition to modify goals and rework positive steps can help to ensure that it is constructive acceptance that is worked on, not denial or hopeless acceptance.

Information sheet

Coping with setbacks 2

Mental attitude setbacks

• **Setbacks are normal**

  – <u>Be kind to yourself</u> – "You can't get it wrong if you don't try" is the do-nothing philosophy that we have been resisting with this programme. So if you suffer a setback, it has to mean you've been doing something! Give yourself credit for that at least. You are not expected to achieve 100% success, and if you have expected that of yourself then you've fallen into one of the biggest mental traps; look out for it and avoid it.

  – <u>Treat setbacks as learning experiences</u> – Look back through your workbook handouts at the behaviour change methods discussed in session 3 and you will find Trial and error and Confidence building discussed. In both of these important methods our setbacks can be seen to an essential part of the learning process.

  – <u>Identify triggers/pitfalls</u> – Study and understand your setbacks because they will tell you important things about what to do differently next time.

  – <u>"What do I need to do to avoid them in the future?"</u> – Learning from them and making changes as a result does not mean you should then be setback-free. There will be more unless you "play safe." The advice would be: Don't go out of your way to avoid them, but do learn not to unnecessarily repeat them.

• **Resist mental traps**

  – <u>Some mental trap avoidance reminders:</u>

  – A setback does not make me "a failure" – *Labelling*
  – A setback does not make it pointless trying – *Black & white thinking*
  – A setback doesn't mean it's always going to be like this – *Fortune telling*

• **Adapt plans**

  If you are using the Goal setting: step-by-step method:

  – <u>Work with the new information</u> – If you're learning from setbacks then you see the relevance of the information to your goals and steps.

  – <u>Review and adjust goals and add more steps</u> – If you're using the information constructively then setbacks mean that there are changes being made to your positive steps and possibly your goals.

Information sheet

Denial: advantages and disadvantages

Advantages of denial:

Self protective qualities:

Allows gradual adaptation to bad news, preventing being overwhelmed.
Can facilitate coping and communication in terminal stages.

Maintaining hope qualities:

Enables people to keep planning and daydreaming for the future.
Helps with "looking on the bright side."

Resilience qualities:

Tolerance/minimising of pain and discomfort and its implications.
Reduces anxiety about hospital appointments and treatments.

Disadvantages of denial

Neglectful qualities:

Encourages failure to react to symptoms constructively.
Leads to failure to put personal affairs in order.
Causes damaging errors of judgement in planning.

Obstructive qualities:

Reduces compliance with treatment and reporting of changes.
Blocks important family communication and emotional expression.
Blocks important professional advice and support.

Information sheet

Experiential learning cycle

Kolb's model of the experiential learning process is illustrated in the diagram below. In using a cognitive behavioural approach it is a very relevant model to describe the work we are doing to bring about beneficial changes. We learn from our experiences by **attending** to those experiences, **analysing** and **interpreting** them, then **deciding** on a suitable response. This response then provides us with a new experience to attend to and we begin the process again.

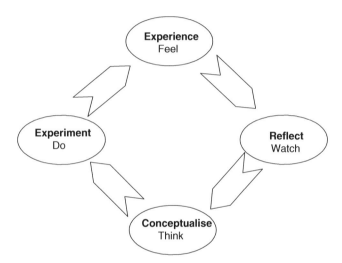

This experiential learning process is going on all the time but is at its most intense when we are analysing an experience differently from before and/or deciding to try a new response in order to discover what changes that produces in our experiences.

Adapted from Kolb, D. A. (1984) *Experiential Learning: Experience as the Source of Learning and Development*, New Jersey: Prentice-Hall (0 13 295261 0)

Information sheet

Goal setting and the step-by-step approach

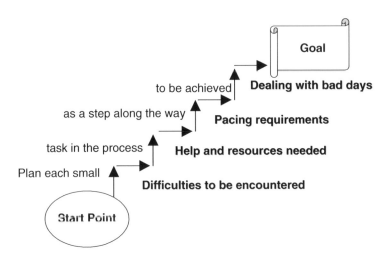

The Step By Step Approach

1. Describe the situation as it is now
2. Describe how you want it to be when you've achieved your goal
3. Identify the things that will have to change to get to the goal
4. Arrange a sequence of mini goals or steps to make those changes
5. Design a plan for each of those steps
6. With each of the steps plans should take these things into account:

➢ **Difficulties to be encountered**

There may be a range of practical problems that get in the way. There may be skills or knowledge required that you do not have. There may be people who object or obstruct your plans.

➢ **Help and resources needed**

Awareness of the things and people you need to make this work must not be ignored or taken for granted. Any successful project requires planning and preparation of necessary equipment and manpower.

➢ **Pacing requirements**

Knowing your own limits reduces the risk of failure.

i. Fitness and stamina may be important considerations. Exertion must be balanced with sufficient rest otherwise exhaustion sets in, which takes longer to recover from and at worst produces despair and depression. So learning about how to pace yourself is an important skill.

ii. Similarly there may be financial implications of your plans which need to be taken into account and progress may need to be paced to fit what can be afforded.

iii. Confidence is the other area where pacing should be considered. As we build confidence in doing something we need to take time to enjoy the satisfaction of reducing our apprehension and doubt before moving on to the next challenge. Success needs to be savoured to make it more solid.

➢ Dealing with bad days

However carefully you plan you are likely to have setbacks. Being flexible and adaptable will be the key to success in handling bad days.

i. Some setbacks will be due to changes in your health and stamina. It is important to ensure that plans take this into account and the very best plans will often include some tasks that can be done on those bad days. Never let plans dictate what you must do regardless how you feel, but equally don't let feelings dictate what you do: there's a balance to be struck and learning where that is can be quite an important task in its own right.

ii. Other setbacks will arise because things do not go according to plan. There is bound to be some frustration and low mood caused by this, but it's all part of the learning process and some of the cognitive therapy techniques come in very useful at these times to dig you out of the mental traps.

Information sheet

Goal setting: examples

Example A: Step ladder

With "ladder" steps, each step builds on the achievement of the last, for example increasing confidence or skill or stamina.

1. What do I want to achieve? What is my overall goal?

"I would like to be able to walk more."

2. How can I break this down so that I can make it more achievable?

"I would like to walk for 30 minutes twice a week."

3. What can I do now on good days or bad days?

"I can walk for about 10 minutes."

4. What could be the first step or mini goal towards my main goal?

"To walk for 10 minutes twice a week to gain some confidence."

5. What could be the next step?

"To walk for 15 minutes twice a week, maybe for two weeks."

6. What else could I do as steps towards my goal?

"If this is ok I could go up to 20 minutes twice a week. If not. I may need to put in a rest break or take a bit longer before I increase the time again."

7. How long will it take to reach my overall goal?

"It doesn't matter"

Example B: Stepping stones

With "stepping stones" we plot a path through the flow of problems and around the obstacles that get in the way of achieving our goal. Each stepping stone represents a practical next step in a logical sequence of putting things in place.

1. What do I want to achieve? What is my overall goal?

"I would like to be able to visit my sister in Edinburgh."

2. How can I break this down so that I can make it more achievable?

"I will need to have a plan to deal with all the different obstacles."

3. What can I do now on good days or bad days?

"I can travel for about an hour before needing a bathroom and a rest."

4. What could be the first step or mini goal towards my main goal?

"To get my husband's support for this project and deal with his concerns."

5. What could be the next step?

"To talk to my sister about the practical arrangements for staying in Edinburgh."

6. What else could I do as steps towards my goal?

"If this is ok I could look into travel arrangements that cope with my "bad day" needs. If not. I may have to look into who else can support me on this trip or where else I can stay in Edinburgh."

7. How long will it take to reach my overall goal?

"It doesn't really matter! But I will agree a target date with my sister because that will be of help to her"

Information sheet

Goal setting questions

The phases of the goal setting process

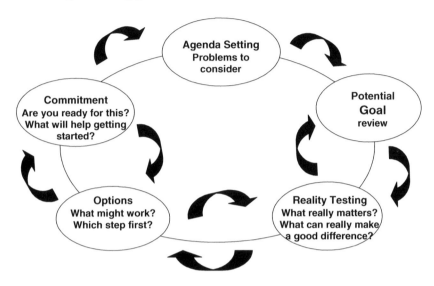

Questions for helping generate goals

- What would you like to achieve?
- What would need to have happened for you to walk away feeling this time was well spent?
- What would you like to be different when we finish this work?
- What would you like to happen that is not happening now?
- What would you like not to happen that's happening now?
- How realistic is that outcome?
- Can we do that in the time we have available with these sessions?
- Will that be of real value to you?

Questions for reality testing goals

- What changes have you tried so far?
- What happened when you tried them?
- What would happen differently if you made this change?
- Do you know of any situations when that has happened?
- How do you feel when you imagine making this change?
- What obstacles to progress do we need to consider?
- What else do we need to consider?
- Who else will be affected if you make this change?
- How do they see the present situation?
- How are they likely to react to the change?
- What other consequences (good and bad) might follow from this change?

Questions for exploring options for steps

- What could you do to change the situation?
- What alternatives are there to that approach?
- What possibilities for action do you see?
- What have you tried in similar situations in the past
- What have you seen others do in similar situations?
- Who might be of help to you in this situation?
- Who else should you involve or consult before you act?
- Would you like suggestions from me?
- Which options do you like/value most?
- What are the benefits and pitfalls of these options?
- Rate from 1–10 your interest level practicality of these options.
- Would you like to choose an option to act on?
- How difficult would it be for you to do this?
- Which would be the easiest step for you to take first?
- Is it easy enough, or do you think you would like to make it a little easier to be sure of doing it?

Questions to check on commitment

- Will the achievement of this goal really make a difference to you?
- Will the achievement of this step really help towards achieving your goal?
- What are you feeling ready to tackle at the present time?
- Which of the next few steps seem frightening or impossible?
- Does the thought of them put you off making a start?
- What do we need to change to make these do-able?
- When will you take this next step?
- What might get in the way?
- What support do you need?
- Will you enlist that support?
- Will it be better to fail to make this step at all or to do it and for it to go wrong?

Information sheet

Mental traps

We tend to fall into certain habits in our thinking. We take short cuts, make assumptions and apply rules that simplify the thinking process and speed it along. Unfortunately, by doing this we can easily fall into certain mental traps – unhelpful thoughts that block us, undermine our confidence and lower our mood, increase our anxiety or make us angry.

There is no such thing as a right or wrong way to think but it is wise to be able to see the way in which our thinking is affecting the decisions we are making and the way we are feeling. If we are stuck in an unhelpful way of thinking then knowing what type of trap it is can help us in looking for a way out of it.

"Black and white" thinking

Looking at things in terms of absolutes. Everything is an extreme - completely good or bad, issues are cut and dried with no room for middle ground.

Fortune telling

Always trying to think ahead and second guess what the future could hold, anticipating problems and trying to solve them but then thinking of more problems. Never taking things as they come and always trying to prepare for every eventuality.

Emotional reasoning

Assuming that *feeling* and *being* are the same. Feeling guilty means you are guilty (therefore "bad"). Feeling embarrassed means you are being an embarrassment to others. Feeling unconfident means you are not capable.

Over-generalisation

Taking a particular event or experience and turning it into a general rule. Assuming that because one person does or thinks something everybody else does or thinks the same. Expecting that because something happens one time it will always happen like that in the future.

Mind reading

Reading between the lines and analysing what other people are "really" thinking or feeling. Never taking people as they are or remarks, emotions and behaviour at face value. Questioning people's motives and intentions and speculating about what they will do next.

"Should" statements

Leading life by a set of fixed rules in which there are no choices. Assuming that we *must* do what others expect from us, and assuming that others have strong expectations without checking it out with them. Assuming that "I want..." and "I think..." statements are selfish and wrong.

Mental filtering

Hearing or seeing only those things that fit in with expectations - ignoring anything that doesn't. Selectively remembering the bad things that happen whilst "forgetting" the better ones. Noticing and taking to heart criticisms and insults whilst not hearing or recalling any praise and compliments.

Blaming

Taking the blame whenever things go wrong or focusing on mistakes you have made in the past and how life would have been different if you had done things another way. Also reflecting on errors and bad decisions of others. Also dwells on the problems caused, and the lack of justice or fairness in the world.

Personalising

Assuming that others see you as responsible for mistakes as soon as they happen. Even bad events not connected directly to you can "feel somehow my fault". Believing that your presence has a bad effect on things. Also believing that somehow "fate", "luck" or some other forces of Nature are directed at you or are influenced by you

Discounting positives

A bit like mental filtering because, although the "good news" is heard or remembered, it's rejected as not really meant or "the exception that proves the rule". Praise or compliments get denied as insincere or "because you feel sorry for me". Successes and happy times are brought low by beliefs that they will be "paid for" with bad times yet to come.

Catastrophising

Making a bad situation seem worse than it already feels. Turning the mole hill into a mountain. Exaggerating the effects of the event and anticipating things getting even worse. Often happens in advance of the event and leads to backing out "just in case". MINIMISING will often at the same time, playing down the good effects and possible future benefits.

Labelling

Attaching judgmental labels to yourself and your behaviour. Worries are labelled "silly" or "stupid" or even "pathetic", mistakes are labelled "foolish" or "idiotic", general personal difficulties are described as signs of being "useless", "hopeless" or "a failure".

Information sheet

Mental traps: examining the evidence

Once you have begun to identify the thinking traps you may be failing into, the next step is to evaluate your thoughts and look for more helpful alternatives.

To challenge negative thinking, it is helpful to list all of the alternative ways of looking at a situation or experience you have interpreted negatively. It will be useful to write this down. It may help to ask yourself the following questions:

- **Is this a useful way to think about this?**

How are my thoughts affecting my feelings? Is this a helpful way of thinking about the situation? We like to sort problems out, so it is quite normal to keep looking at the same issue from lots of different angles until we find a way of thinking about it that is of use to us.

- **How would I advise a friend who said this?**

Am I guilty of applying double standards here?

We are often much harder on ourselves than we would be to someone else in our situation.

- **Does the evidence stand up?**

Would this stand up as evidence in a court of law?

If you had to face questioning from a barrister, would the jury believe that your interpretation was actually factual?

- **Is this belief or fact?**

Am I confusing a thought with a fact?

Believing something is true does not mean it is. Try and stick with the bare facts rather than drawing conclusions prematurely.

- **Am I trying to predict the future?**

Am I jumping to conclusions?

Sometimes we act as though we can predict the future or as if we can read other people's minds, For example just because something has failed before doesn't mean it will automatically fail again.

- **Is this one of those "wind-up" questions?**

Am I asking questions which have no answers?

Having regrets about the past is unproductive. Questions such as "Why did this have to happen to me?" only make you feel demoralised.

Information sheet

Mental traps: examples of how to get out of them

Negative (unhelpful) thought	Mental trap	Realistic (helpful) alternative view
He's not said "Good morning" and smiled at me so he must be about to tell me bad news.....	*Mind reading*	He is probably pre-occupied with other things. I'll assume it's nothing to do with me.
.... about something very bad that is going to happen to me.	*Fortune telling*	I am not clairvoyant and don't have a brilliant track record of predicting the future, so I won't try to guess what he's going to say.
This operation is not going to work; there will be no future for me. I will never get to see my children grow and I will die in great pain.	*Catastrophising*	It won't help to dwell on it now, but if the worst came to the worst, I'd find a way to cope like I've done before but this is not the time for me to need to think about it.
When I think back over my life I can only remember a catalogue of illness and disappointments.	*Mental filtering*	Depression makes it hard to remember the good things that have happened but I know that I have had good times and there are things around which can help me recall them.
I'm a useless parent who can't do any of the normal things for my children.	*Labelling*	I am a perfectly normal parent, because it is so difficult for any of us to know what to do for the best - sometimes we get it right and sometimes we don't. Labelling myself upsets me and condemns me unfairly.
My whole life has been one big disaster area – this setback just proves that there is nothing I can do to help myself.	*Over-generalisation*	My life has been a mix of good and bad, much like everyone else's. I'm certainly having a very bad time now but I can still do things to make life a little better for myself.

I must have done something really bad to cause me to be punished with this disease.	*Personalising*	I have met other people with the same illness as me and I don't believe they have deserved to get it as punishment for misdeeds. I can also think of wicked people who have died comfortably in very old age.
The consultant is so busy, it would be wrong for me to take up more of her time explaining why she is going to give me this treatment.	*Should statements*	It is her responsibility to organise her time and it is ok for me to ask for information when I need it. She can always say "not now" if this is not convenient.
I feel too tired and ill to be bothered, so there's no point in trying to do anything.	*Emotional reasoning*	Even though I don't feel like it, it will do me good to be active and might help my mood if I do something that is useful or interesting. I don't have to enjoy it for it to be worthwhile.
I must stay cheerful and positive or I will let my family down.	*Black and white thinking*	My family won't fall apart just because I have a down day. We all have our ups and downs. It's just part of normal life.
There is a 7% chance of recurrence over the next five years so it's quite likely to come back.	*Discounting the positives*	I must not count on staying well, but there is good reason to be optimistic when more than 9 out of 10 people stay well for that long.
I should have listened to my family and got rid of the motorbike then I would never have had that accident and have to suffer this pain	*Blaming*	What's happened is past, the important thing now is to get fit again and find ways to manage this pain better

Information sheet

Mindfulness attitudes

Knowing what you are doing while you are doing it – When you pay more attention to what you are doing, it changes your relationship to things; you see more, taste more, etc. and so this influences our experience of things and the decisions we make about them. In tasting more, for example, we may be aware of wanting to eat less.

Simplifying life – By giving greater emphasis to the experience of the present moment, there is less attention given to the past and future and the complexity of anticipation, reflection, critical judgement and regret produced by these attention shifts. Heightened awareness of the moment enhances acceptance and reduces needless struggle.

Fully experiencing the moment – Mindfulness meditation involves "letting your experiences unfold from moment to moment and accepting them *as they are*. It does not involve rejecting your thoughts nor trying to clamp down on them or suppress them, nor trying to control anything at all other than the focus and direction of your attention" (p.23).

Allowing – "Mindfulness does not involve trying to get anywhere or feel anything special. Rather it involves allowing yourself to be where you are, to become more familiar with your own actual experience moment by moment" (p.23).

Non-judging – Almost everything we observe is labelled and categorised. Our minds are involved in a constant stream of judgements. Step back from judging and simply observe.

Trust in yourself – Greater awareness of the moment enables greater ability to listen to oneself and the body and to trust that awareness.

Not striving – Doing less in order to be being more! By allowing the experiences to be what they are, being fully aware of them moment by moment without judging them or controlling them, we can *achieve* mindfulness.

Accepting – Acceptance does not mean you have to like things as they are or even that you have to adopt a passive attitude. It does mean that you need to have a willingness to see things as they are at this moment and that this needs to be independent of any judgements, associations or expectations with which your perception could be distorted.

Letting go – There are certain thoughts and feelings that our minds hold on to, some good and some bad. These thoughts and feelings are familiar and they are powerful. Letting go of them can feel wrong or even dangerous, but they can cloud our view of the present moment and our awareness of our being. By detaching from these thoughts and feelings we can experience the present moment as it is.

Based on the ideas of Jon Kabat-Zinn (1990) *Full Catastrophe Living*, New York: Dell Publishing.

Information sheet

Mindfulness exercises

- **The mindfulness breathing exercise:**

Although extremely similar to the relaxed breathing exercise, the purpose is somewhat different. With relaxed breathing the aim is to alleviate or prevent symptoms of anxiety. With the mindfulness exercise the aim is to focus on the relaxed breathing itself so as to clear the mind of other thoughts and be fully aware of the present moment.

1. Assume a comfortable posture lying on your back or sitting. If you are sitting, keep the spine straight and let your shoulders drop.
2. Close your eyes if it feels comfortable.
3. Bring your attention to your abdomen, feeling it rise or expand gently on the in-breath and fall or recede on the out-breath.
4. Keep the focus on your breathing, "being with" each in-breath for its full duration and with each out-breath for its full duration, as if you were riding the waves of your own breathing.
5. Every time you notice that your mind has wandered off the breath, notice what it was that took you away and then gently bring your attention back to your abdomen and the feeling of the breath coming in and out.
6. If your mind wanders away from the breath a thousand times, then your "job" is simply to bring it back to the breath every time, no matter what it becomes preoccupied with.
7. Practice this exercise for ten minutes at a convenient time every day, whether you feel like it or not, for one week and see how it feels to incorporate a disciplined meditation practise into your life. Be aware of how it feels to spend some time each day just being with your breath without having to do anything.

- **The mindfulness food exercise:**

The aim is similarly to be fully aware of the present moment including of the objects and experiences contained within it, bringing to full consciousness some which may otherwise pass unnoticed. The effect of that increased awareness of the smallest and simplest things is often quite dramatic.

1. Bring attention to seeing the raisin, observing it carefully as if you have never seen one before.
2. Feel its texture between your fingers and notice its colours and surfaces.
3. Be aware of any thoughts you might be having about raisins or food in general. Note any thoughts and feelings of liking or disliking raisins if they come up.
4. Then smell it for a while.
5. And finally, with awareness, bring it to your lips, being aware of the arm moving the hand to position it correctly and of salivating as the mind and body anticipate eating.
6. Take it into your mouth and chew it slowly, experiencing the actual taste of one raisin.
7. When you feel ready to swallow, watch the impulse to swallow as it comes up, so that even that is experienced consciously.
8. Imagine, or "sense," that now your body is one raisin heavier.

Both exercises are taken from
J. Kabat-Zinn's book *Full Catastrophe Living* (1990). ISBN: 0-385-30312-2

Information sheet

Pacing

This handout explains how you can do everyday activities at home, at work and in your hobbies or social life without making fatigue or pain worse.

Good days and bad days

Often people with fatigue and pain problems do more when they feel better, trying to 'catch up", and very often overdoing it. You may recognise that when this happens, the fatigue or pain is made worse and the same evening or following day you can do very little. In this situation the fatigue or pain is in control of your life.

Pacing

Pacing means keeping to the same amount of activity each day whether you are having a good day or a bad day.

You can do this by basing what you do on a plan and not on how you feel.

If you can successfully pace activities, you will find that over time your stamina will improve. Your body will adapt and adjust and you will not have to keep taking time out for rests. Because you will have more stamina you will be able to do more without getting more fatigue or pain. Whilst pacing may be frustrating at first because you just want to get on and finish the task you will find that pacing actually puts you back in control of your life: you can plan more reliably and don't have to be controlled by fatigue or pain.

Time limits

The first part of the plan is to work out what your limits are in some basic activities. This will help you to keep your activities the same on both good and bad days. The time limits will be different for everyone.

Most activities involve either sitting, standing or walking and concentrating.

1. Think about how long you could do each of these activities on a bad day and then write these times down. Then think about how long you could do them on a good day and write these times down.
2. Set your own time limits for each of the activities beginning with your bad day time or a time limit which falls between the two.

This means that you would sit, stand and walk using these time limits, changing your position for about two minutes at the end of each time limit if the limiting factor is pain or lying down and resting for that length of time if the limiting factor is fatigue.

To begin with you are pacing everyday activities using your "bad day" times. This means that you are not going to make your pain or fatigue any worse because you can manage these activities on your bad days. The greatest difficulty for you will be not doing too much on your "good days."

To begin with it is a good idea to limit the amount of time spent doing one activity:
If the whole house needed to be hoovered or the back and front lawn both needed to be mowed, then it would be sensible to do a total of only 20 or 30 minutes a day (including change of position or rest periods). This is because your body needs time to adapt to doing more.

Information sheet

Pacing examples

Set your own time limits for each of the activities beginning with your bad day time or a time limit which falls between the two. For instance:

	Bad day	Good day	Time limit
Sitting	5 minutes	20 minutes	5-10 minutes sitting
Standing	1 minute	5 minutes	1-2 minutes standing
Walking	2 minutes	10 minutes	2-5 minutes walking 10-15 minutes concentration *but*
Concentrating	10 minutes	30 minutes	*further limited by relevant sitting, standing, walking limits*

- Every time you did the hoovering or mowed the lawn you would be using a walking position. Sot after three minutes you would stop and sit down for two minutes before starting again.
- If you did the ironing or washing up you would stand for only two minutes before resting again.
- If you were watching television you would sit for five minutes and then stand or have a walk around for two minutes before sitting down again. After ten minutes you would stop watching the TV altogether for a few minutes (this is where adverts can be useful!).

Remember

➢ Good pacing means keeping to your time limits whether you feel good or bad.
➢ This means not overdoing it on a good day or doing very little on a bad day, but doing a steady amount of activity every day.
➢ In time as you improve your stamina you will be able to increase these time limits and be able to do more without making your fatigue or pain worse.
➢ You want to be in control of the fatigue or pain and if you wait until it is bad before you stop you will have overdone it and lost that control.
➢ Resist the "just five more minutes" temptation – you may tidy up this task but you'll do less tomorrow as a result, so it's not worth it.

- Know your limits and plan
- Little and often is best
- Quit while you're ahead

Information sheet

The reactions of other people

It is often a shock to discover the varied reactions of other people to life threatening illness and changes in appearance brought about by illness, accident or treatment. Often people just do not know how to behave and they may need help in working it out. Sometimes their solution is to avoid meeting at all, which can feel a very upsetting rejection.

Whilst it is not your responsibility to sort out these difficulties for other people, it may be in everyone's best interest (including your own) to give some help since you will be the expert on what you do or do not like and what you do and do not want to talk about.

Three "A"s to deal with social discomfort:

- Acknowledge the problem – if you try to pretend it 's not happening it won't go away
- Assess the difficulty
  - Avoidance
  - Focusing
  - Rationalising
- Assert yourself – treat yourself with respect (including your right to privacy)

The chart below may be of use in helping you identify the reactions of others, why they are reacting that way and what you can do in response.

Reaction of other person	Possible origins of this reaction	Possible responses you can make
Avoidance The other person avoids: a. looking at you or that part of the body that has been changed h. talking about the affected part of the body or the process leading up to that change c. getting physically close or making contact with that part of the body	1. Friend fears they will hurt your feelings/depress you *or* 2. Friend fears they will not be able to control their own emotions/reactions if they look or the subject is raised in conversation *or* 3. Friend does not understand enough about the nature of the problem and fears possible infection.	Establish why the friend is using this strategy. If 1. then a pact of openness can help: "I will warn you when I get fed up with the subject". If 2. then ascertain readiness of other person to receive more information, look and touch. Recall own experience of getting used to change. If 3. then explain and reassure.

Focusing The other person stares or otherwise concentrates attention on the subject	Friend may be searching for a practical way to help or may be trying to overcome their distress at change in your appearance.	Decide whether this makes you feel uncomfortable. Advise other of your feelings and perhaps agree a full briefing to "clear the air" as in 2. above.
Rationalising The other person makes the subject an academic or dispassionate topic devoid of feelings. devoid of feelings	Friend may be struggling to cope with their own feelings, or be eager to help you gain control (however superficial this is). "Emotional distancing" is like avoidance above.	Confront the issue. Use: a. a direct approach – "How does this make you feel?" b. an indirect approach – "Can I tell you about how I'm feeling about this?"

Adapted from: Price, B. (2000) Body image: perceptions of the patient with lymphoedema. *Proceedings of 1999 Conference of British Lymphology Society.*

Information sheet

Reflective practice diary guidance

As part of learning how to use a cognitive behavioural approach you are strongly advised to use a structured reflective practice diary in order to fulfil the experiential learning cycle (see Information sheet: Experiential learning cycle). Completing this diary material as you work with the patient can help you with your own confidence building and problem solving.

1. Diary sheets are available in Record form: Reflective practice diary.
2. These record forms can also be downloaded from the website.
3. Three types of diary forms are provided for
   a) Problems
   b) Techniques
   c) Information sheets and Record forms
4. Each form consists of two pages.
5. Complete these forms carefully for every piece of work you do using the material in this book for at least the first ten patients.
6. Under each heading you will see some points you are asked to consider whilst completing your entry.

You may also find it helpful to continue to keep a CBT diary of your own during the first few weeks of working in this way or perhaps use one of the other record forms (especially Record form: Event-emotion-thought analysis form) for this purpose. This material can help you to recognise the unhelpful thoughts that interfere with your cognitive behavioural practice development. Identifying and challenging these thoughts will further assist skill development.

Information sheet

Relaxation: mental exercise

A busy mind is hard to quiet down. Simple imagery and meditation exercises can be very effective ways of clearing out the clutter of worry thoughts, nagging doubts, speculation about the future and mental problem solving activities.

Imagery exercise

1. Think of a small perfectly round orange.
2. Imagine you are studying it closely.
3. Think of the surface of the orange – the mix of smooth and bumpy sensations on your finger tips.
4. Sniff the mild orangey smell from its surface.
5. Now imagine picking it up and feeling its slight weight in the palm of your hand.
6. Imagine placing your other hand over the top of it and then rolling it back and forth between the two hands, feeling its surface and weight as you do so.
7. Think of what it feels like as you dig your thumb into the surface of the orange – the sensation around your thumb nail.
8. Feel the squirt of orange juice as your thumb digs into the peel and pulls it back.
9. Sniff the strong smell of orange that is now released.
10. Continue to peel the orange, study the inside of the peel and its soft texture.
11. If you don't like oranges you can stop with studying its unpeeled surface texture.
12. If you do like oranges then move on to imagine breaking off a segment, putting it to your lips, feeling it, biting it, tasting it, chewing it and swallowing it.

Other exercises can be invented like this such as
- Lying on a warm soft beach and listening to the sea

or
- Sitting on a grassy bank under a shady tree and watching the butterflies and hearing the birds.

Information sheet

Relaxation: muscle exercise

After a tough day of heavy demands that leave you with a lot of physical tension, then a muscle relaxation exercise can be very helpful

Relaxation exercise

1. Sit with your feet flat on the ground.
2. Tightly clench your hands and your shoulders raised towards your ears.
3. Hold that position to a count of 10.
4. Relax and feel all the tension drain from your shoulders, arms and hands.
5. Let your arms hang heavy and loose and enjoy that warm, relaxed glow – for another count of 10.
6. Repeat the clenched hands and raised shoulders for another count of 10.
7. Then relax everything and count to 10 again.
8. Now pull your tummy muscles in very tight and hold yourself in like that for a count of 10.
9. Relax and let your middle expand against your belt.
10. Feel your body and your breathing relax.
11. Sit quietly for a moment feeling the muscles in your shoulders, arms and abdomen completely relaxed and loose.

Hot baths are another good way of relieving muscle tension.

Information sheet

Relaxed breathing exercise

When we are getting tense and frustrated we tend to breathe in a rapid, shallow fashion which matches that mood. Learning to breathe in a gentle, calm and deep manner produces a soothing effect.

- With this exercise, try not to breathe from the upper chest.
- As you breathe in allow your abdomen to expand gently against your belt whilst the upper chest remains still.
- As you breathe out, let the belt area loosen, again without moving the upper chest.
- Using this method the breathing should be quiet and gentle with no huffing and puffing effort.

The breathing exercise

1. Close your eyes.
2. Drop your shoulders.
3. Relax your abdomen (tummy muscles).
4. Gently breathe in and out.
5. Concentrate all your attention on your in-breath.
6. Feel the lungs gently expand as you breath in.
7. Feel the body relax as you breathe out.
8. Breathe slowly and gently.
9. Think only about the slow rhythm of breathing.
10. Count each in-breath.
11. When you reach fifty open your eyes.
12. Sit quietly for a few more moments.

Information sheet

The Serenity Prayer

This prayer has a history that may go back to soldiers of the fourteenth century or just back to Dr Niebuhr in 1932! Either way, it got taken up by Alcoholics Anonymous and has wide application in our modern life strivings. Its basic message (with or without God) represents a corner stone of constructive acceptance and helps to focus the "do-something" drive:

God grant me
Serenity to accept the things I cannot change
Courage to change the things I can
And wisdom to know the difference

It goes on:

Living one day at a time
Enjoying one moment at a time
Accepting hardship as the pathway to peace.

These last three lines represent something of the challenge of the methods described in the "Mindfulness" handout.

A fun "pagan" variation which sounds rather good runs like this:

Gods and goddesses grant me

The power of Water, to accept with ease and grace what I cannot change
The power of Fire, for the energy and courage to change the things I can
The power of Air, for the ability to know the difference
The power of Earth, for the strength to continue my path.

Information sheet

Sharing and mixing with other people

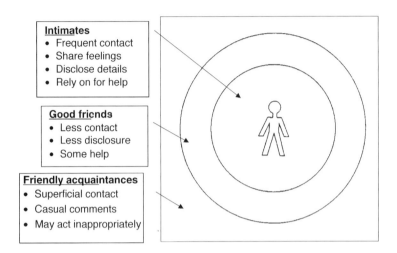

Intimates
- Frequent contact
- Share feelings
- Disclose details
- Rely on for help

Good friends
- Less contact
- Less disclosure
- Some help

Friendly acquaintances
- Superficial contact
- Casual comments
- May act inappropriately

This diagram illustrates a plan of action for getting back into the swing of mixing with other people after a period "out of circulation" due to illness.

The stress of meeting so many people who are looking at you and asking lots of questions can be overwhelming and put you off doing it at all. So it can help to have a plan of action for how you will respond to different people and perhaps even who you wish to meet first.

It may be helpful to use the chart above and identify a spot for each of the people you know and are likely to meet in the next few weeks.

"Ambassadors" can be a good idea for cutting down on the amount of going over the same old things that you have to do. You ask some of your closest family and friends to act as ambassadors for you by telling other people on your behalf, and perhaps giving guidance on what you do and don't want to talk about. This can reduce the pressure on you and put other people more at ease in your company.

Adapted from: Price, B. (1999) Altered body image. *Nursing Times: NT Monograph*

Information sheet

SMART guidelines

Ideally your goals should follow the SMART guidelines. This means that your goals should be **S**pecific, **M**easurable, **A**chievable, **R**elevant and **T**imely.

Specific

Think of what it is you want to accomplish; how will you know when you have achieved it? What will have noticeably changed? Break large goals into a series of smaller ones that can be accomplished more quickly and be a source of encouragement. It is often easier to be specific with the somewhat smaller goals than the big ones.

Measurable

There should be some means of determining whether or when you've achieved a goal. "Getting in better shape" is not a good goal because it is too vague and it's difficult to know when you have achieved it. A better goal might be something like doing 20 minutes of physical exercise each day: you will know whether or not you are succeeding in achieving that goal!

Achievable

Choose goals that are potentially attainable. Even though you might like to return to a previous demanding job or sporting activity, this may not be realistic if you have significant physical limitations as a result of your ill health. So your goals may have to be more modest than you would like ideally. Alternatively, you may prefer to set more challenging goals that accept these limitations and focus on completely different things that are more achievable.

Relevant

You will find it much easier to motivate yourself to work on goals which you see as very relevant to things that matter to you. "Going through the motions" with goals that don't seem of value can be very dispiriting, so try to make sure the goals have usefulness in your life.

Timely

For many goals any time is a good time to be getting on and doing them, but there are some where it is important to ask "Is this the right time to be doing this?" It may be that you already have too much else to do, or that something else needs doing first before you can achieve this goal; perhaps you require the cooperation of other people who are not available at present. All sorts of reasons may lead you to decide that another time will be better. But beware of using "time" as an excuse: if it is not timely, then identify when will be and what else needs to happen first.

Information sheet

Socratic questioning: examples

Some useful questions:

- What do you mean when you say X?
- What is the evidence that X is true?

- What might be the worst that could happen?
- And if that happened, what then?
- What leads you to think that might happen?

- Can you think of anyone else who copes well with difficult situations?
- How do you think they would deal with this challenge?

- How does thinking that make you feel?
- Is there another way of thinking about it that might make you feel differently?

- Is there any other way of seeing the situation?
- What do you think you could change to make things better for you?

- Is there something else you could say to yourself that might be more helpful?
- What might you tell a friend to do in this situation?

A simplified example of a Socratic dialogue

Patient:	How long have I got to live?
Therapist:	What have you been told?
Pt:	My consultant says it's impossible to predict.
Th:	Don't you believe your consultant?
Pt:	I think she is just trying to avoid upsetting me.
Th:	If she said you'd be dead in 6 weeks, would that upset you?
Pt:	Yes, of course it would, but I can't bear this uncertainty.
Th:	Would you be less upset if she said you would live for a year?
Pt:	Probably. I could do more with my life if I live that long.
Th:	Amongst those things you would do, are there things you want to do even if your life is shorter than that?
Pt:	Yes, I can think of some.
Th:	If we prioritise these and see what you could do about them, would that help you cope better with this uncertainty?
Pt:	Perhaps. But supposing I don't have time to do them all.
Th:	Do you always achieve everything you set out to do?
Pt:	No, that's true, I don't.

Information sheet

Stress: the effect it has

on:

Emotional state
Nervousness
Edginess
Anxiety (phobias, panics)
Depression (apathy and fatigue)
Sadness
Lowered self-esteem,
Guilt and shame
Moodiness
Loneliness

Mental activity
Difficulty in concentrating
Difficulty in making decisions
Frequent forgetfulness
Increased sensitivity to criticism
Negative self-critical thoughts
Distorted ideas
More rigid attitudes

Health
Coronary heart disease
High blood pressure
Strokes
Stomach upsets, indigestion and nausea
Diarrhoea
Migraines and headaches
Worsens asthma and hay fever
Skin rashes
Period problems and worsens PMT

Physical reactions
Increased heart rate
Rapid, shallow breathing
Muscle tension (aches, pains, spasms)
Fidgeting and restlessness
Hot most of the time (blushes easily, sweats quite a lot)
Cold hands and feet
Numbness and tingling sensations
Increased blood glucose levels
Dilation of pupils (lights seem brighter)
Frequent urination
Increased blood and urine catecholamine and corticosteroids

Behaviour habits
Impulsive and impatient
Excessive eating or loss of appetite
Excessive drinking
Heavier smoking
Accident prone and clumsy
Disorganised or over-organised
Disturbed sleep – insomnia, early wakening, or excessive sleeping
Rushing – walking and talking fast

Work
Absenteeism
Poor industrial relations
High labour turnover rates
High accident rate
Poor productivity
Low job satisfaction

Information sheet

The stress response

Stress is not the same as Anxiety

Stress occurs when pressure exceeds ability to cope.

Hans Seyle described the stages of the stress response, showing the changes that occur, their usefulness in adjusting to demands, and the problems that occur when the demand continues for too long.

<u>Stages of the stress response</u>

Alarm
Mobilising the resources to cope
■ Heart rate, breathing and blood pressure increase
■ Pupils dilate, hearing sharpens, reactions speed up
■ Alertness increases, thinking focuses, appetite drops

Resistance
Effectively coping
■ Alert
■ Quick, energetic
■ Determined, enthusiastic
■ Attentive, precise
■ Systematic, automatic

Exhaustion
Sapping resources for coping
■ Hot, sweaty, palpitations, headaches
■ Tense, slower, aching muscles
■ Poor concentration, distracted
■ Irritable, flustered, low morale
■ Tired, careless, disorganised

Information sheet

A vicious cycle model of anxious avoidance

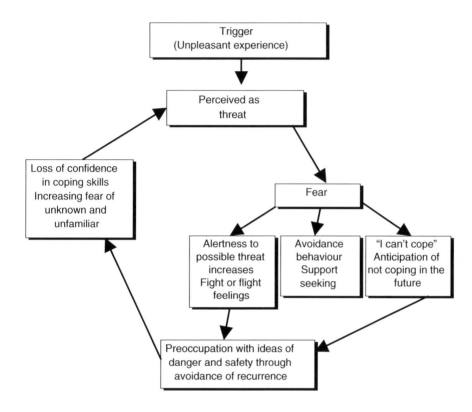

Information sheet

A vicious cycle model of anxious preoccupation

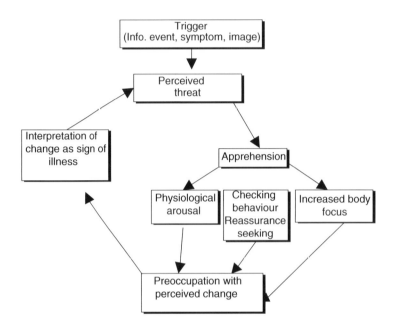

Information sheet

A vicious cycle model of hopelessness-helplessness

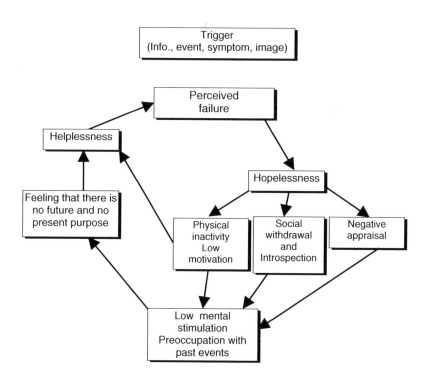

Section 3
RECORD FORMS

Record form:

Event-emotion-thought analysis form

STEP ONE:

Describe the upsetting event

STEP TWO:

Record your emotional reactions and rate the strength of each (1–100). Use words like "sad", "angry", "lonely", "guilty", "anxious", "low", "gloomy", "worried", "frightened", "irritated".

Emotion	Rating

Emotion	Rating

Emotion	Rating

STEP THREE:

Record your thoughts, spot any mental traps and identify suitable alternative thoughts.

Actual Thought	Mental Trap	Alternative Thought

Actual Thought	Mental Trap	Alternative Thought

Actual Thought	Mental Trap	Alternative Thought

Actual Thought	Mental Trap	Alternative Thought

Adapted from Burns, D. (1989) *The Feeling Good Handbook*, Harmondsworth: Penguin Books.

Record form

Example of event-emotion-thought analysis form

STEP ONE:

Describe the upsetting event

> I went to a leaving-party for someone I work with. It was difficult to mix with people and I got hot and nervous. I left after 45 minutes when no one was looking. I went home feeling that it was a waste of time me trying to improve myself, I'm never going to change.

STEP TWO:

Record your emotional reactions and rate the strength of each (1–100). Use words like "sad", "angry", "lonely", "guilty", "anxious", "low", "gloomy", "worried", "frightened", "irritated".

Emotion	Rating
Anxious	80

Emotion	Rating
Annoyed	60

Emotion	Rating
Low	90

STEP THREE:

Record your thoughts, spot any mental traps and identify suitable alternative thought

Actual Thought	Mental Trap	Alternative Thought
Everybody else is having a really good time. Other people here just don't have anxiety problems like mine.	Black and white thinking Mind reading	Some people here really enjoy parties and get on very well together, but others are a bit quieter, less jolly. I can't really know how people feel. We all put on a bit of an act sometimes.

Actual Thought	Mental Trap	Alternative Thought
I don't have anything interesting or amusing to say to people. I'm a really boring person.	"Shoulds" Labelling	The important thing is to be here to say goodbye. There is no rule that says we have to be entertaining – just friendly will do. Branding myself "boring" won't help

Actual Thought	Mental Trap	Alternative Thought
I will never over-come these prob-lems in dealing with other people. I've always failed to cope with every social situation I've ever been in.	Fortune Telling Mental filtering	I'm working hard at understanding these problems and why they affect me. I am learning new methods for coping too. I can't know yet what will happen in the future. There have been some ok social events.

Actual Thought	Mental Trap	Alternative Thought
If I don't get better at dealing with peo-ple then I will spend the rest of my life alone and miserable.	Catastrophising	Just because I lack confidence in social situations does not mean that people dis-like me and reject me. I get on fine with those who get to know me. There are lots of shy and quiet people in the world and most of them are not lonely or unhappy.

Adapted from Burns, D. (1989) *The Feeling Good Handbook*, Harmondsworth: Penguin Books

Record form

Believable alternatives

STEP ONE:

Describe the upsetting event

STEP TWO:

Record your emotional reaction and rate the strength of this emotion (1–100). Use words like "sad", "angry", "lonely", "guilty", "anxious", "low", "gloomy", "worried", "frightened", "irritated"

Emotion	Rating

STEP THREE:

Record your thought; identify the mental trap and a suitable alternative thought. Then follow the route to the "believable" alternative.

Actual Thought	Mental Trap	Alternative Thought

Yes But...

Actual Thought	Mental Trap	Alternative Thought

Yes But...

Actual Thought	Mental Trap	Alternative Thought

Yes But...

Actual Thought	Mental Trap	Alternative Thought

Adapted from Burns, D. (1989) *The Feeling Good Handbook*, Harmondsworth: Penguin Books.

Record form

Thought record

Date	**Unhelpful Thought** (Worrying/Downer/Angry/ Self-critical)	**Mental Trap**	**Realistic Alternative View**
E.g.	When I do things like this I always get them wrong……….. ……..and then it will be obvious that I'm completely unable to be helped.	Overgeneralising Catastrophising	Not every form that I've ever filled in has been wrong. If I make mistakes we can use them to help me learn

Record form

Pacing record form

Task	Maximum Time		Paced
	Bad Day	Good Day	Time limit

* Set your paced time limit at or just above your bad day time maximum and only increase it as the bad day time maximum improves.

Record form

Denial: assessing its costs and benefits

The role and value of denial needs to be carefully weighed in the balance when trying to decide whether or not to challenge it. Itemise each advantage and disadvantage of doing nothing and for patient, family and treatment. Then give a value for each item from the patient's perspective.

To:	Pros **Advantages of denial** Specify Benefits + 0–3 rating	Cons **Disadvantages of denial** Specify Costs + 0–3 ratings
Patient *Points:* *0 = not important to patient* *3 = very important to patient*		
Family *Points:* *0 = not important to patient* *3 = very important to patient*		
Treatment *Points:* *0 = not important to patient* *3 = very important to patient*		
Do nothing *Points:* *0 = not important to patient* *3 = very important to patient*		
What does the cost/ benefit analysis favour?	**Leave Alone**	**Encourage Change**

Add up the points

➤ **Highlight the specific issues in pros and cons list which will need greatest time and attention**

Record form

Denial: example of pros and cons assessment

Mapping out the likely effects as in the example below, may help the decision-making process (ratings in italics). Careful questioning of the patient and family should enable you to gain enough information to complete a form in this way.

To:	Pros Advantages of denial Benefits	Cons Disadvantages of denial Costs
Patient	Normal daily life *1* Stick with current plans *2* Mood normal *2*	Intolerance of health discussions *2* Disturbed dreams *3* Sudden irritability *0*
Family	Normal daily routines *1* Plans unchanged *3* Priorities unchanged *0* No expressed distress *1*	Restricted communication *3* Hidden feelings *3* Uncertainty or confusion *0* Tense atmosphere *1*
Treatment	Minimum demands on staff time *1* High tolerance of discomfort *0* Positive outlook *3* Active life *3*	Poor reporting of symptom changes *3* Poor compliance *1* Overdoes things *3* Family need lots of support and advice *3*
Do nothing	Maintain positive atmosphere for patient *3*	Reduce longevity *0* Poor symptom control *2* Fail to plan realistically *1*

What does cost/benefit analysis favour?	Leave Alone 20	Encourage Change 25

Other questions to ask yourself:

Collusion or confrontation – who will benefit: patient or staff?

Are there ways of addressing the disadvantages while avoiding challenging the denial?

Record form

Action plan for denial

Name:_____   Date _____

Step	Aim	Action Plan
A	**Assessing and deciding to act**	1. Type of denial * 2. Pros and cons for action ** 3. Issues of greatest demand ** 4. Identify issues re family **
B	**Helping with admitted distress**	
C	**Increasing aware-ness and coping with it**	
D	**Increasing accept-ance and openness**	

*   See Information sheet: Denial differentiated
** Using information from Record form: Denial – assessing its costs and benefits

Record form

Goal

Start Point

Goal planning: step-by-step action plan

Record form

Your ideas for goals

It is helpful to keep balancing achievement with pleasure in mind when identifying potential goals for yourself. Give some thought to goals you could set yourself under the following categories.

Exercise
1)
2)
3)

Work (housework/voluntary/paid)
1)
2)
3)

Social activities
1)
2)
3)

Leisure activities
1)
2)
3)

Creative activities
1)
2)
3)

Other (e.g. use pain medication more effectively)
1)
2)
3)

CBT diary

Date	Event	Thoughts	Emotions	Physical sensations	Behaviour

Achievements and pleasures record form

Week 1	Monday	Tuesday	Wednesday	Thursday	Friday	Saturday	Sunday
Achievement							
Pleasure							

Week 2	Monday	Tuesday	Wednesday	Thursday	Friday	Saturday	Sunday
Achievement							
Pleasure							

Week 3	Monday	Tuesday	Wednesday	Thursday	Friday	Saturday	Sunday
Achievement							
Pleasure							

Week 4	Monday	Tuesday	Wednesday	Thursday	Friday	Saturday	Sunday
Achievement							
Pleasure							

Daily record of mood

Date		V. Low				So-so			V. Good		Comments about the day					
	Mon	1	2	3	4	5	6	7	8	9						
	Tues	1	2	3	4	5	6	7	8	9						
	Wed	1	2	3	4	5	6	7	8	9						
	Thurs	1	2	3	4	5	6	7	8	9						
	Fri	1	2	3	4	5	6	7	8	9						
	Sat	1	2	3	4	5	6	7	8	9						
	Sun	1	2	3	4	5	6	7	8	9						
	Mon	1	2	3	4	5	6	7	8	9						
	Tues	1	2	3	4	5	6	7	8	9						
	Wed	1	2	3	4	5	6	7	8	9						
	Thurs	1	2	3	4	5	6	7	8	9						
	Fri	1	2	3	4	5	6	7	8	9						
	Sat	1	2	3	4	5	6	7	8	9						
	Sun	1	2	3	4	5	6	7	8	9						

Activity schedule

Start Date:

Wake to 9 am	Monday	Tuesday	Wednesday	Thursday	Friday	Saturday	Sunday
9 – 10							
10 – 11							
11 – 12							
12 – 1pm							
1 – 2							
2 – 3							
3 – 4							
4 – 5							
5 – 6							
6 – 7							
7 – 8							
8 – 9							
9 – Bed							
Through night							

Assertiveness record form

Date	Situation/activity challenging your rights	Assertiveness right number (1–14)	Action taken	Outcome and ideas for Future occasions

Managing low points

Date	Situation/activity making self-esteem lower	Your thoughts and behaviour at the time	Alternative thoughts and behaviour that might have been helpful

Event-action-outcome record form

Date	Event	Action taken	Outcome and ideas for future occasions

Vicious Cycle Format

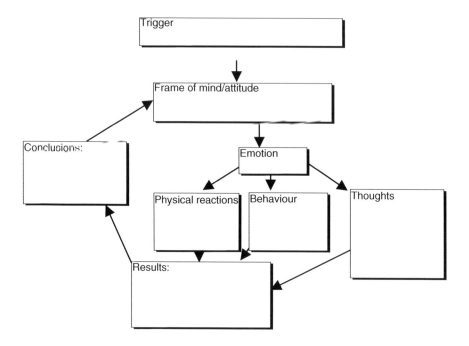

Reflective practice diary

Problem:

Line 4

Specify need or problem Consider: Identifying Hot Cross Bun and triggers; Identifying incapacitating effects
How was this need/problem detected? Consider: Observation; Learning from the patient; Use of open question enquiry; Discovery through behavioural experiments; 3rd party reporting
How was need/problem assessed? Consider: Socratic questioning & guided discovery; assessment tools; record forms;
What techniques were used to deal with this need/problem? Consider: Techniques used in accordance with Toolkit recommendations; Clear rationale in evidence for use of methods other than those recommended in *Toolkit*.

Reflective practice diary

Problem:

Line 4

What was the outcome?
Consider: Evaluating outcome in terms of agreed goals; Evaluating outcome in terms of SMART criteria; Awareness of patient's evaluation of outcome
What did you learn from this experience?
Consider: New ideas for assessment/treatment; Growing understanding of therapy *process*; Consolidation of CBT theory; New insights into nature of this type of problem; Insights into the patient experience; Insights into skill, knowledge, limitations and role

Other comments:

Reflective practice diary

Technique:

Line 4

What was the need/problem to which this technique was applied?
Consider: Use of this technique on this occasion conforms to *Problem* recommendations

---

What was the reason for selecting this technique?
Consider: A clear rationale is given for the use of this technique; This rationale conforms to a CBT approach

---

How was its suitability explained to the patient?
Consider: Collaborative approach; Guided discovery; Clarity of aims; Linkage to treatment goals

---

Describe the details of how this technique was applied and why it was done in this way. Include details of materials used including record forms and information sheets.
Consider: Systematic approach; Consideration of *Workbook* Notes for this problem; Sensitivity to potential obstacles in planning; Realistic, achievable steps; Appropriate use of educational and self-help materials.

Reflective practice diary

Technique:

Line 4

Were there later changes to its application? If so, why were they made?
Consider: Adaptations to plans in the light of setbacks and new information/developments

How was its effectiveness assessed?
Consider: Pre-post comparison; Effective use of behaviour and self report; Mood ratings; 3rd party reports

What was the outcome?
Consider: Evaluating in terms of agreed goals; Evaluating to SMART criteria; Improved functioning and coping; Generalised learning and new skills; Subsidiary benefits; Awareness of patient's evaluation of outcome; Assessing usefulness of the technique

What did you learn from this experience?
Consider: New ideas for assessment and treatment; Growing understanding of therapy *process*; Consolidation of CBT theory; New insights into the use of this technique; Insights into the patient experience.

Other comments:

Reflective practice diary

Information sheet / Record form:

Line 4

Provide title and page number if from the _Toolkit_. **Provide description if designed by you or summary and source if from elsewhere.**
What was the need/problem and technique with which this was used? Consider: Use of this record form/info sheets on this occasion conforms to _Toolkit_ recommendations; Other reasons why its use appears relevant on this occasion
What was the reason for selecting this form or information? Consider: A clear rationale is given for the use of this form/info sheet; Rationale fits CBT model
How was it explained to the patient? Consider: Collaborative approach; Clarity of aims.

Reflective practice diary

Information sheet/Record form:

Line 4

What were the benefits gained by using this material? Consider: Linkage to treatment goals; Linkage to treatment steps; Linkage to formulation; Evaluation of comprehensibility to the patient; Evaluation of its usefulness	
Were there problems with its use? If so, how were these dealt with? Consider: Seeking expert advice; Seeking peer supervision; Collaborative approach; Flexibility/creativity in application; Sensitivity to usage problems; Using other resources	
What did you learn from this experience? Consider: New ideas for assessment/education; Growing understanding of use of therapy *tools*; Consolidation of CBT theory; New insights into the use of this material; Insights into the patient experience	

Other comments:

References

American Thoracic Society (1999) Pulmonary rehabilitation. The official statement of the American Thoracic Society. *American Journal of Respiratory and Critical Care Medicine,* 159, 1666–1682.

Anderson, R.J., Freedland, K.E., Clouse, R.E. and Lustman, P.J. (2001) The prevalence of comorbid depression in adults with diabetes. A meta-analysis. *Diabetes Care,* 24, 1069–1078.

Beck, A.T. (1976) *Cognitive Therapy and the Emotional Disorders.* New York: International Universities Press.

Beck, A.T.; Rush, A.J; Shaw, B.F. and Emery, G. (1979) *Cognitive Therapy of Depression.* New York: Guilford Press.

Beck, A.T., Steer, R.A. and Brown, G.K. (1996) *Manual for the Beck Depression Inventory II.* The Psychological Corporation, San Antonia.

Bennett, P. and Carroll, D. (1994) Cognitive-behavioural interventions in cardiac rehabilitation. *Journal of Psychosomatic Research,* 38, 169–182.

Blake, R.L., Vandiver, T.A., Braun, S., Bertuso, D. and Straub, V. (1990) A randomised controlled evaluation of psychosocial interventions in adults with chronic lung disease, *Family Medicine,* 22, 365–370.

Blumenthal, J.A. and Emery, C.F. (1988) Rehabilitation of patients following myocardial infarction. *Journal of Consulting and Clinical Psychology,* 56, 374–381.

Bruggimann, L. and Annoni, J.M. (2004) Management of anxiety disorders in neurological disease. *Schweizer Archiv fur Neurologie und Psychiatrie,* 155 (Dec), 407–413.

Carney, R.M., Freedland, K.E., Stein, P.K., Skala, J.N., Hoffman, P. and Jaffe, A.S. (2000) Change in heart rate and heart rate variability during treatment for depression in patients with coronary heart disease. *Psychosomatic Medicine,* 62, 639–647.

Cole, K. and Vaughan, F.L. (2005) The feasibility of using cognitive behaviour therapy for depression associated with Parkinson's disease: A literature review. *Parkinsonism and Related Disorders,* 11, 269–276.

Coyne, J.C., Stefanek, M. and Palmer, S.C. (2007) Psychotherapy and survival in cancer: the conflict between hope and evidence. *Psychological Bulletin,* 133(3), 367–394.

Crews, W.D. and Harrison, D.W. (1995) The neuropsychology of depression and its implications for cognitive therapy. *Neuropsychological Review,* 4, 81–123.

Cunningham, A.J., Lockwood, G.A. and Cunningham, J.A. (1991) A relationship between self-efficacy and quality of life in cancer patients. *Patient Education and Counseling,* 17, 71–78.

Cunningham, A.J., Lockwood, G.A. and Edmonds, C.V. (1993) Which cancer patients benefit from a brief, group, coping skills programme? *International Journal of Psychiatry in Medicine,* 23, 313–398.

Cunningham, A.J. and Toccom, E.K. (1989) A randomised trial of group psychoeducational therapy for cancer patients. *Patient Education and Counseling,* 14, 101–114.

Cupples, M.E. and Dempster, M. (2001) Improving quality of life for patients with angina pectoris – A team approach to disease management. *Disease Management & Health Outcomes,* 9 (9), 373–481.

de Godoy, D.V. and de Godoy, R.F. (2003) A randomised controlled trial of the effect of psychotherapy on anxiety and depression in chronic obstructive pulmonary disease. *Archives of Physical Medicine and Rehabilitation,* 84, 1154–1157.

DCCT Research Group (1993) The effects of intensive treatment of diabetes on the development and progression of long-term complications in insulin-dependent diabetes mellitus. *New England Journal of Medicine*, 329, 977–986.

Department of Health (2001) *Treatment Choice in Psychological Therapies and Counselling: Evidence based clinical practice guidelines.* London: Department of Health.

Dreisig, H., Beckmann, J.M., Wermuth, L., Skovlund, S. and Bech, P. (1999) Psychological effects of structured cognitive therapy in young patients with Parkinson's disease: a pilot study. *Nordic Journal of Psychiatry*, 53(3), 217–212.

Dobkin, D.R., Allen, L.A. and Menza, M. (2006) A cognitive behavioural treatment package for depression in Parkinson's disease. *Psychosomatics: Journal of Consultation Liaison Psychiatry*, 47(3), 259–263.

Dobkin, D.R., Allen, A. and Menza, M. (2007) Cognitive-behavioural therapy for depression in Parkinson's disease: A pilot study. *Movement disorders*, ISSN 0885-3185.

Edelman, S., Bell, D.R. and Kidman, A.D. (1999a) A group cognitive behaviour therapy programme with metastatic breast cancer patients. *Psycho-Oncology*, 8, 295–305.

Edelman, S., Lemon, J., Bell, D.R. et al. (1999b) Effects of group CBT on the survival time of patients with metastatic breast cancer. *Psycho-Oncology*, 8, 474–481.

Edgar, L., Rosenberger, Z. and Nowlis, D. (1992) Coping with cancer during the first year after diagnosis. Assessment and intervention. *Cancer*, 69, 817–828.

Eiser, N., West, C., Evans, S., Jeffers, A. and Quirk, F. (1997) Effect of psychotherapy in moderately severe COPD. A pilot study. *European Respiratory Journal*, 10, 1581–1584.

Ellgring, H., Seiler, S., Perleth, B. et al. (1993) Psychosocial aspects of Parkinson's disease. *Neurology*, 43 (suppl 6), 41–44.

Emery, C.F., Schein, R.L., Hauck, E.R. and MacIntyre, N.R. (1998) Psychological and cognitive outcomes of a randomized trial of exercise among patients with chronic obstructive pulmonary disease. *Health Psychology*, 17, 232–240.

Fawzy, F.I., Fawzy, N.W. and Hyun, C.S. et al. (1993) Malignant melanoma: effects of an early structured psychiatric intervention, coping and affective state on recurrence and survival 6 years later. *Archives of General Psychiatry*, 50, 681–689.

Fawzy, F.I., Kemeny, M E., Fawzy, N.W., et al. (1990) A structured psychiatric intervention for cancer patients: Changes over time in methods of coping and affective disturbance. *Archives of General Psychiatry*, 47, 720–725.

Feeney, F., Egan, S. and Gasson, N. (2005) Treatment of depression and anxiety in Parkinson's disease: A pilot study using group cognitive behavioural therapy. *Clinical Psychologist*, 9(1), 31–38.

Fonargy, P. and Moran, G.S. (1990) Studies on the efficacy of child psychoanalysis. *Journal of Consulting and Clinical Psychology*, 58, 684–695.

Fosbury, J.A., Bosley, C.M., Ryle, A., Sonksen, P.H. and Judd, S.L. (1997) A trial of cognitive analytic therapy in poorly controlled Type 1 patients. *Diabetes Care*, 20, 959–964.

Frasure-Smith, N., Lesperance, F. and Talajic, M. (1995) Depression and 18-month prognosis after myocardial infarction. *Circulation*, 91, 999–1005.

Friedman, M., Thoreson, C., Gill, J., Powell, L., Ulmer, D., et al. (1984) Alteration of type A behaviour and reduction in cardiac recurrences in post-myocardial-infarction patients. *American Heart Journal*, 108, 237–248.

Gift, A.G., Moore, T. and Soeken, K. (1992) Relaxation to reduce dyspnoea and anxiety in COPD patients. *Nursing Research*, 41, 242–246.

Gonder-Frederick, L.A., Cox, D.J., Clarke, W. and Julian, D. (2000) Blood glucose awareness training. In Snoek, F.J, and Skinner, T.C. (eds.) *Psychology in Diabetes Care.* Chichester: Wiley & Sons, 2000: 169–206.

Greer, S., Moorey, S., Baruch, J.D.R. et al. (1992) Adjuvant psychological therapy for patients with cancer: a prospective randomised trial. *British Medical Journal*, 304, 675–680.

Guthrie, D.W., Sargent, L., Speelman, D. and Parks, L. (1990) Effects of parental relaxation training on glycosolated haemoglobin of children with diabetes. *Patient Education and Counseling*, 16, 247–253.

Hains, A.A., Davies, W.H., Parton, E. and Silverman, A.H. (2001) A cognitive behavioural intervention for distressed adolescents with Type1 diabetes. *Journal of Pediatric Psychology*, 6, 409–416.

Hatch, A., Coombs, J. and Sowden, M. (2005) Can four key psychosocial risk factors for chronic pain and disability be modified by a pain management programme? A follow up study. Poster presented at the International Association of Pain (IASP) World Conference, Sydney, Australia.

Hawton, K.; Salkovskis, P.M.; Kirk, J. and Clark, D.M. (1989) *Cognitive Behaviour Therapy For Psychiatric Problems: A Practical Guide,* Oxford: Oxford University Press.

Henry, J.L., Wilson, P.H., Bruce, D.G. and Rawlings, P.J. (1997) Cognitive-behavioural intervention for patients with non-insulin dependent diabetes mellitus. *Psychology, Health & Medicine*, 2, 109–118.

Johnston, D.W. (1992) The management of stress in the prevention of coronary heart disease. In *International Review of Health Psychology* (Edited by Maes, S., Leventhal, H. and Johnston, M.) Chichester: Wiley.

Kenardy, J., Mensch, M., Bowen, K. and Dalton, M. (2000) Disordered eating in non-insulin diabetes mellitus. *International Journal of Behavioural Medicine, 7*: A48.

Kubzansky, L.D. and Kawachi, I. (2000) Going to the heart of the matter: do negative emotions cause coronary heart disease? *Journal of Psychosomatic Research*, 48, 323–337.

Kunik, M.E., Braun, U., Stanley, M.A., Wristers, K. et al. (2001) One session cognitive behavioural therapy for elderly patients with chronic obstructive pulmonary disease. *Psychological Medicine,* 31(4), 717–723.

Lewin, R.J.P. (1999) Improving quality of life in patients with angina. *Heart,* 82, 654–655.

Linn, M.W., Linn, B.S., and Harris, R. (1982) Effects of counselling for late stage cancer patients. *Cancer*, 49, 1048–1055.

Linden, W. (2000) Psychological treatments in cardiac rehabilitation: a review of rationales and outcomes. *Journal of Psychosomatic Research*, 48, 443–454.

Linton, S.J. and Hallden, K. (1998) Can we screen for problematic back pain? A screening questionnaire for predicting outcome in acute and subacute back pain. *Clinical Journal of Pain*, 14, 209–215.

Lustman, P.J., Griffith, L.S., Freedland, K.E., Kissel, S.S. and Clouse, R.E. (1998) Cognitive behaviour therapy for depression in Type 2 diabetes mellitus. A randomized controlled trial. *Annals of Internal Medicine*, 129, 613–621.

Mayou, R.A., Bryant, B.M., Sanders, D., Bass, C., Climes, I. and Forfar, C. (1997) A controlled trial of cognitive behavioural therapy for non-cardiac chest pain. *Psychological Medicine*, 27, 1021–1031.

McCracken, L.M. and Eccleston, C. (2005) Coping or acceptance: what to do about chronic pain? *Pain,* 105, 197–204.

McCracken, L.M. and Turk, D.C. (2002) Behavioral and cognitive-behavioral treatment for chronic pain. outcome, predictors of outcome, and treatment process. *Spine,* 27(22), 2564–2573.

Mohr, D.C., Boudewyn, A.C. Goodkin, D.E. et al. (2001) Comparative outcomes for individual cognitive-behavioural therapy, supportive-expressive group psychotherapy, and sertraline for the treatment of depression in multiple sclerosis. *Journal of Consulting and Clinical Psychology,* 69, 942–949.

359

Mohr, D.C., Classen, C. and Barrera, Jr. (2004) The relationship between social support, depression and treatment for depression in people with multiple sclerosis. *Psychological Medicine*, 34, 533–541.

Mohr, D.C. and Goodkin, D.E. (1999) Treatment of depression in multiple sclerosis. *Clinical Psychology: Science and Practice*, 6, 1–9.

Mohr, D.C., Hart, S. and Goldberg, A. (2003). Effects of treatment for depression on fatigue in multiple sclerosis. *Psychosomatic Medicine*, 65, 542–547.

Montgomery, E.B. Jr., Lieberman, A. and Singh, G. et al. (1994) Patient education and health promotion can be effective in Parkinson's disease: a randomised controlled trial. Propath Advisory Board. *American Journal of Medicine*, 97, 429–435.

Morley, S., Eccleston, C. and Williams, A. (1999) Systematic review of randomized controlled trials of cognitive behaviour therapy and behaviour therapy for chronic pain in adults, excluding headache. *Pain*, 80, 1–13.

Moorey, S. and Greer, S. (2002). *Cognitive Behaviour Therapy for People with Cancer*. New York: Oxford University Press.

Moorey, S., Greer, S., Bliss, J., et al. (1998) A comparison of adjuvant psychological therapy and supportive counselling in patients with cancer. *Psycho-Oncology*, 7, 218–228.

Moorey, S., Greer, S. and Watson, M., et al. (1994) Adjuvant psychological therapy for patients with cancer: outcome at one year. *Psycho-Oncology*, 3, 39–46.

Moynihan, C., Bliss, J.M., Davidson, J. et al. (1998) Evaluation of adjuvant psychological therapy in patients with testicular cancer: a randomised trial. *British Medical Journal*. 316, 429–435.

National Comprehensive Cancer Network and American Cancer Society (2005) *Distress Treatment Guidelines for Patients. www.nccn.org*

Olmsted, M.P., Rodin, G.M., Rydall, A.C., Lawson, M.L. and Daneman, D. (1997) Effect of psycho-oeducation on disordered eating attitudes and behaviours in young women with IDDM. *Diabetes*, 46, 88A.

Ost, L.G., Hellstrom, K. and Kaver, A. (1992) One versus five sessions of exposure in the treatment of injection phobia. *Behaviour Therapy*, 23, 263–282.

Ostelo, R.W.J.G., van Tulder, M.W., Vlaeyens, J.W.S., Linton, S.J., Morley, S.J. and Assendelft, W.J.J. (2005) Behavioural treatment for chronic low-back pain. *Cochrane Database of Systematic Reviews*, Issue 1. Art No: CD002014. DOI: 10.1002/ 14651858. CD002014.pub2.

Padesky, C.A. and Mooney, K.A. (1990) Clinical tip: Presenting the cognitive model to clients. *International Cognitive Therapy Newsletter*, 6, 13–14 also available at www.padesky.com

Petticrew, M., Bell, R. and Hunter, D. (2002) Influence of psychological coping on survival and recurrence in people with cancer: Systematic review. *British Medical Journal*, 3257(372), 1066–1069.

Piette, J.D. (2005) Use of a walking program for veterans with diabetes and depression. *Psychiatric Services*, 56 (Mar), 355.

Price, B. (1999) Altered body image. *Nursing Times: NT Monograph*.

Price, B. (2000) Body image: perceptions of the patient with lymphoedema. *Proceedings of 1999 Conference of British Lymphology Society*.

Ratner, H., Gross, L., Casas, J. and Castells, S. (1990) A hypnotherapeutic approach to the improvement of compliance in adolescent diabetics. *American Journal of Clinical Hypnosis*, 32, 154–159.

Richardson, J.L., Shelton, D.R., Krailo, M. et al. (1990) The effect of compliance with treatment on survival among patients with hematologic malignancies. *Journal of Clinical Oncology*, 8, 356–364.

360

Roberts, A.H., Kewman, D.G. Mercier, L. and Hovell, M. (1993) The power of non-specific effects in healing: implications for psychosocial and biological treatments. *Clinical Psychology Review*, 13, 375–391.

Roelofs, J., Boissevain, M.D., Peters, M.L., de Jong, J.R. and Vlaeyen, J.W.S. (2002) Psychological treatments for chronic low back pain: past, present and beyond. *Pain Reviews*, 9, 29–40.

Rose, C., Wallace, L., Dickson, R., Ayres, J., Lehman, R., Searle, Y. and Burge, P.S. (2002) The most effective psychologically-based treatments to reduce anxiety and panic in patients with chronic obstructive pulmonary disease (COPD): Systematic review. *Patient Education and Counseling*, 47, 311–318.

Rossy, L.A. Buckelew, S.P., Dorr, N., Hagglund, K.J., Thayer, J.F. et al. (1999) A meta-analysis of fibromyalgia treatment interventions. *Annals of Behavioural Medicine*, 21, 180–191.

Rubin, R.R. and Peyrot, M. (1992) Psychosocial problems and interventions. A review of the literature. *Diabetes Care*, 15, 1640–1657.

Rydan, O., Nevander, L., Johnsson, P., Hansson, K., Kronvall, P., Sjoblad, S. et al. (1994) Family therapy in poorly-controlled juvenile IDDM: effects on diabetic control, self-evaluation and behavioural symptoms. *Acta Paediatrica*, 83, 285–291.

Sassi-Dambron, D.E., Eakin, E.G., Ries, A.L., and Kaplan, R.M. (1995) Treatment of dyspnoea in COPD. A controlled clinical trial of dyspnoea management strategies, *Chest*, 724–729.

Scheidt, S. (2000) The current status of heart-mind relationships. *Journal of Psychosomatic Research*, 48, 317–320.

Schwartz, C.E. (1999) Teaching coping skills enhances quality of life more than peer support: results of a randomized trial with multiple sclerosis patients. *Health Psychology*, 18(3), 211–220.

Sebregts, E.H.W.J. (2000) Risk factor modification through nonpharmacological interventions in patients with coronary heart disease. *Journal of Psychosomatic Research*, 48, 425–441.

Siegert, R.J. and Abernethy, D.A. (2005) Depression in multiple sclerosis: a review. *Journal of Neurology, Neurosurgery and Psychiatry*, 76, 469–475.

Skinner, T.C., Channon, S., Howells, L. and McEvilly (2000) Diabetes during adolescence. In Snoek, F.J. and Skinner, T.C. (eds.) *Psychology in Diabetes Care*. Chichester: Wiley & Sons, 25–59.

Snoek, F.J. and Skinner, T.C. (2002) Psychological counselling in problematic diabetes: does it help? *Diabetic Medicine*, 19, 265–273.

Snoek, F.J., van der Ven, N.C.W., Lubach, C.H.C., Chatrou, M., Ader, H.J., Heine, R.J. et al. (2001) Effects of a cognitive behavioural group training (CBGT) in adult patients with poorly controlled insulin-dependent (Type 1) diabetes: a pilot study. *Patient Education and Counselling*, 45, 143–148.

Sowden, M., Hatch, A., Gray, S. and Coombs, J. (2006) Can four key psychosocial risk factors for chronic pain and disability be modified by a pain management programme? A pilot study. *Physiotherapy*, 92, 43–49.

Spiegel, D., Bloom, J.R., Kraemer. H.C. et al. (1989) Effect of psychosocial treatment on survival of patients with metastatic breast cancer. *Lancet*, ii, 888–891.

Spiess, K., Sachs, G., Pietschmann, P. and Prager, R.S. (1995) Program to reduce onset distress in unselected type1 diabetic patients: effects on psychological variables and metabolic control. *European Journal of Endocrinology*, 132, 580–586.

Stanley, M.A., Veazey, C., Hopko, D., Diefenbach, G. and Kunik, M.E. (2005) Anxiety and depression in chronic obstructive pulmonary disease: a new intervention and case report. *Cognitive and Behavioral Practice*, 12, 424–436.

Tesar, N., Baumhackl, U., Kopp, M. and Gunther, V. (2003) Effects of psychological group therapy in patients with multiple sclerosis. *Acta Neurologica Scandinavica*, 107, 394–399.

Thieme, K., Flor, H. and Turk, D.C. (2006) Psychological pain treatment in fibromyalgia syndrome: efficacy of operant behavioural and cognitive behavioural treatments. *Arthritis Research and Therapy,* 8 (4).

Thomas, P.W., Thomas, S., Hillier, C., Galvin, K. and Baker, R. (2006) Psychological intervention for multiple sclerosis. *Cochrane database of systematic reviews,* ISSN: 1469-493X.

UK Prospective Diabetes Study Group (1998) Intensive blood glucose control with sulfonylureas or insulin compared with conventional treatment and risk of complications with type 2 diabetes (UKPDS 33). *Lancet,* 352, 854–865.

Viinamaeki, H. and Niskannen, L. (1991) Psychotherapy in patients with poorly controlled type 1 (insulin-dependent) diabetes. *Psychotherapy & Psychosomatics*, 56, 24–29.

Watson, P. and Kendall, N. (2000) Assessing psychosocial yellow flags. In L. Gifford (eds.) *Topical Issues in Pain 2: Biopsychosocial Assessment and Management,* Falmouth: CNS Press Ltd, pp. 111–129.

White, C. (2001) *Cognitive Behaviour Therapy for Chronic Medical Problems. A Guide to Assessment and Treatment in Practice.* John Wiley & Sons, Ltd.

Wysocki, T., Harris, M.A., Greco, P., Bubb, J., Danda, C.E., Harvey, L.M., et al. (2000) Randomized controlled trial of behavior therapy for families of adolescents with insulin-dependent diabetes mellitus. *Journal of Pediatric Psychology,* 25, 23–33.

Wysocki, T., Greco, P., Harris, M.A., Bubb, J. and White, N.H. (2001) Behavior therapy for families of adolescents with diabetes: maintenance of treatment effects. *Diabetes Care,* 24, 441 446.

Wysocki, T., Harris, M.A., Greco, P., Harvey, L.M., McDonell, K., Danda, C.E. et al. (1997) Social validity of support groups and behavior therapy interventions for families of adolescents with insulin-dependent diabetes mellitus. *Journal of Pediatric Psychology*, 22, 635–650.

Zettler, A., Duran, G., Waadt, S., Herschbach, P. and Strian, F. (1995) Coping with fear of long-term complications in diabetes mellitus. *Psychotherapy & Psychosomatics,* 64, 178–184.

Zigmond, A.S. and Snaith, R.P. (1983) The Hospital Anxiety & Depression Scale. *Acta Psychiatrica Scandanavica*, 67, 361–370.

Index

Index

Printed and bound by CPI Group (UK) Ltd, Croydon, CR0 4YY